Ajax Patterns and Best Practices

Christian Gross

Apress®

Ajax Patterns and Best Practices

Copyright © 2006 by Christian Gross

ISBN-13 (pbk): 978-1-59059-616-6

ISBN-10 (pbk): 1-59059-616-1

Printed and bound in the United States of America 9 8 7 6 5 4 3 2 1

Lead Editor: Jonathan Hassell
Technical Reviewer: Paul Tyma
Editorial Board: Steve Anglin, Dan Appleman, Ewan Buckingham, Gary Cornell, Jason Gilmore, Jonathan Hassell, James Huddleston, Chris Mills, Matthew Moodie, Dominic Shakeshaft, Jim Sumser, Matt Wade
Project Manager: Beth Christmas
Copy Edit Manager: Nicole LeClerc
Copy Editor: Sharon Wilkey
Assistant Production Director: Kari Brooks-Copony
Production Editor: Ellie Fountain
Compositor: Susan Glinert
Proofreader: Elizabeth Berry
Indexer: Broccoli Information Management
Artist: Kinetic Publishing Services, LLC
Cover Designer: Kurt Krames
Manufacturing Director: Tom Debolski

Distributed to the book trade worldwide by Springer-Verlag New York, Inc., 233 Spring Street, 6th Floor, New York, NY 10013. Phone 1-800-SPRINGER, fax 201-348-4505, e-mail orders-ny@springer-sbm.com, or visit http://www.springeronline.com.

For information on translations, please contact Apress directly at 2560 Ninth Street, Suite 219, Berkeley, CA 94710. Phone 510-549-5930, fax 510-549-5939, e-mail info@apress.com, or visit http://www.apress.com.

The information in this book is distributed on an "as is" basis, without warranty. Although every precaution has been taken in the preparation of this work, neither the author(s) nor Apress shall have any liability to any person or entity with respect to any loss or damage caused or alleged to be caused directly or indirectly by the information contained in this work.

The source code for this book is available to readers at http://www.apress.com in the Source Code section.

38721242
12547324
53087351
21687294

Contents at a Glance

Contents

■CHAPTER 3 Content Chunking Pattern 53

■CHAPTER 4 Cache Controller Pattern 79

About the Author

CHRISTIAN GROSS is a consultant/trainer/mentor with vast experience in the Internet paradigm. He has worked on software development and other solutions for many corporations, including Altova, Daimler-Benz, Microsoft, and NatWest. Gross has written multiple books, including *Applied Software Engineering Using Apache Jakarta Commons, Open Source for Windows Administrators, A Programmer's Introduction to Windows DNA,* and *Foundations of Object-Oriented Programming Using .NET 2.0 Patterns.* He has been a regular speaker at many conferences, including Software Development, JAX, and BASTA, and has been track chair at many conferences as well.

About the Technical Reviewer

■PAUL TYMA is president of Outscheme, Inc., a software consultancy based in Silicon Valley. He received his Ph.D. in Computer Engineering from Syracuse University with a research focus in dynamic language performance. Paul is a frequent industry writer, including lead author of the book *Java Primer Plus,* the "VM Roadtest" Java VM column in *Java Pro* magazine, and various articles in *Dr. Dobb's Journal* and *Communications of the ACM.*

Acknowledgments

Let me express my undying gratitude to the good folks at ActiveState, both for being so incredibly cool and for ActiveState Komodo, truly a killer IDE for dynamic languages. If you're developing with Perl, Python, PHP, Tcl, or Ruby, Komodo makes life simpler.

Komodo is the award-winning, professional IDE for dynamic languages, providing a powerful work space for editing, debugging, and testing applications. Komodo offers advanced support for Perl, PHP, Python, Ruby, and Tcl, and runs on Linux, Mac OS X, Solaris, and Windows.

Introduction

You probably picked up this book because of the buzzwords *Ajax, REST,* and *patterns.* You will probably read this introduction and skim through the pages. But I want to stop you from skimming through the pages, at least for a moment. I want you to read this introduction and then decide whether you want to buy the book.

Here are the things you need to know about Ajax:

- Ajax is an acronym, and the ramifications of the acronym are immense.

- Ajax is not just about a fat client, JavaScript, XML, or asynchronous behavior, but about developing the next generation of web applications.

- We are at the beginning of building the next generation of web applications.

You are still reading, and that means I still have your interest, which is a good thing. So now let me tell you what this book is about:

- Using Ajax is the act of creating a web application that implies using REST, that implies using HTTP, and that implies using the Internet. The patterns of this book illustrate how JavaScript can be used to control the XMLHttpRequest object to make XMLHttpRequest calls that process XML or HTML.

- This book for the server side focuses on using Java and C# .NET. The patterns can be used with Python or Ruby on Rails. I focus on Java and C# because at the time of this writing I feel that most developers are using them. In the next edition of this book, I want to extend the materials to include Python and Ruby on Rails examples, because I happen to be an avid Python programmer.

- The patterns in this book can be used in other contexts, such as Flex (Flash Ajax). For example, the Permutations pattern can be used to generate Flex content.

Good, you're still reading and haven't closed the book. That means you are still interested and probably willing to spend a few more moments. Here is what I suggest: finish reading the Introduction because it includes a road map of the patterns. Skim Chapter 1 to get an idea of what Ajax does and is. Then skim the patterns and focus on reading the "Motivation" and "Architecture" sections. And if after that you are still interested, please buy this book because the remaining sections fill in the details of what the patterns are trying to achieve. If you would like to experiment with the patterns, I suggest you surf to the site http://www.devspace.com/ajaxpatterns, which will either have the live patterns or redirect you to where the live patterns are.

What's My Vision of Ajax?

Philosophizing about the vision of Ajax raises the question of what Ajax really is. Some say Ajax is a client-side–only technology. Some say it is an extension of a server framework. Yet others say, "Heck, it's new technology blah and now technology bleh can be ignored." However, ignoring REST is like saying if it's a liquid, it can be drunk by humans. Sure, humans can drink anything that is a liquid, but the bigger question is, will you survive? Sometimes you will, and sometimes you won't! Drinking without questioning is playing Russian roulette. The same can be said of writing Ajax that ignores REST, ignores XML, ignores JSON, and ignores JavaScript. Ajax is Ajax because of these new technologies that can be combined in new and interesting ways.

My vision of Ajax goes beyond the technologies and represents a new way of building applications. In the early days when building web applications, the server was responsible for generating the content, navigating the content, and controlling the content. The web application became a technology that depended on the sophistication of the server framework to determine whether the application would be interactive. Ajax breaks those bonds!

Ajax breaks those bonds because it decouples the client from the server. An Ajax application still needs a server, but an Ajax application can decide when, where, and how that content will be delivered. A web application that relies on the server is a tightly coupled web application that can exist only while the server exists. Any content required by the client is controlled by the server. With Ajax, content can be focused because pieces of content can be assembled, as illustrated by the Content Chunking pattern.

Where I become very concerned with respect to Ajax is when individuals like to sell a server framework that relies on said framework to implement Ajax. If Ajax is about decoupling the client from the server, why must a server framework be used to implement Ajax? The logic simply does not make any sense. I can understand the argument that a framework has extensions to enable Ajax-like architectural designs. But I cannot accept the argument that a sever framework is necessary to make an Ajax application happen.

The focus of this book is the advantages of Ajax using specific patterns that, among other techniques, extensively use de-coupling to create architectures that can be maintained and extended. I personally believe that productivity is a good thing, but in specific situations what may be more important is the ability to figure out what you did and why you did it.

Book and Pattern Road Map

The book is pattern based, with the exception of Chapters 1 and 2. Following is the road map for those first two chapters:

- **Chapter 1**: This chapter is used as an introduction to the book and the topic of Ajax. The focus of the chapter is to provide the context of Ajax and to compare an Ajax application to other methodologies (for example, traditional client-server).

- **Chapter 2**: This chapter introduces the XMLHttpRequest object. When you are writing Ajax applications, the XMLHttpRequest object is a core technology used to communicate with an HTTP server. Best practices when using the XMLHttpRequest object are also illustrated.

Chapter 3 and thereafter present patterns. A hierarchy of the patterns is illustrated in Figure 1.

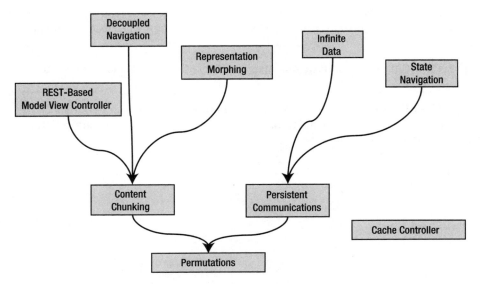

Figure 1. *Hierarchy of patterns explained in the book*

The road map for the patterns of Figure 1 is as follows:

- **Chapter 3—Content Chunking pattern**: Makes it possible to incrementally build an HTML page, allowing the logic of an individual HTML page to be distributed, and allowing the user to decide the time and logic of the content that is loaded.

- **Chapter 4—Cache Controller pattern**: Provides the caller a mechanism to temporarily store resources in a consistent manner, resulting in an improved application experience for the caller.

- **Chapter 5—Permutations pattern**: Used by the server to separate the resource (URL) from the representation (for example, HTML or XML). This separation makes it possible for an end user to focus on the resource and not have to worry about the content. For example, if a client's bank account is at the URL http://mydomain.com/accounts/user, the same URL can be used regardless of device (phone, PC, and so on).

- **Chapter 6—Decoupled Navigation pattern**: Defines a methodology indicating how code and navigation on the client side can be decoupled into smaller modular chunks, making the client-side content simpler to create, update, and maintain.

- **Chapter 7—Representation Morphing pattern**: Combines the state with a given representation, and provides a mechanism whereby the representation can morph from one representation to another without losing state.

- **Chapter 8—Persistent Communications pattern**: Provides a mechanism whereby a server and a client can communicate on a continuing basis, allowing the server to send data to the client, and vice versa, without prior knowledge.

- **Chapter 9—State Navigation pattern**: Provides an infrastructure in which HTML content can be navigated, and the state is preserved when navigating from one piece of content to another.

- **Chapter 10—Infinite Data pattern**: Manages and displays data that is seemingly infinite, in a timely manner.

- **Chapter 11—REST-Based Model View Controller pattern**: Accesses content that is external to the web application and transforms the content so that it appears as if the web application generated it.

CHAPTER 1

■■■

Introduction to Ajax

Asynchronous JavaScript and XML (Ajax)[1] is both something old and something new—old because already existing technologies are used, but new because it combines these existing technologies into techniques that very few considered previously. Simply put, because of Ajax a new generation of applications and ideas are bubbling on the developer scene.

A very brief definition of Ajax is as follows:

Ajax is a technology that complements Web 2.0 and the integration of many web services at once.

This brief definition poses more questions than it answers, as now you are likely wondering what Web 2.0 is and what the integration of many web services are.

Web 2.0 can be thought of as the Internet economy.[2] Think about something as typical as an encyclopedia, and you will start to think about salespeople who carry extremely heavy books and knock on doors. In a Web 2.0 context, an encyclopedia means Wikipedia (http://www.wikipedia.org). The Wikipedia project is an open effort by humanity to record itself. Whereas for a traditional encyclopedia a set of writers and editors write about certain topics, Wikipedia is created by people who write about what they know. Get enough people together and you get an encyclopedia that is on the Internet. What is thought-provoking about the Wikipedia project is that anybody can edit it, and therefore it usually contains more current and unusual information than a traditional encyclopedia. In some instances Wikipedia's self-correcting capabilities have proven to be problematic, but considering the scale and depth of the project, those instances have been exceptions.

The second part of Ajax is the integration of many web services at once. Ajax allows a higher level of interactivity in a HyperText Markup Language (HTML) page than was possible without Ajax technologies. The result is that an Ajax application changes from a web application to a web service manipulation technology. In a traditional web application, navigating content meant changing HTML pages. With Ajax, navigating content means navigating web services that could be generating HTML content, or Extensible Markup Language (XML) content, or other content.

---

1. http://en.wikipedia.org/wiki/AJAX
2. http://www.oreillynet.com/pub/a/oreilly/tim/news/2005/09/30/what-is-web-20.html

Pictures Are Worth a Thousand Words

The definition explains Ajax, but you are probably still wondering what Ajax does. There is a saying that a picture is worth a thousand words, and the following images and their associated explanations illustrate best what Ajax does. Map.search.ch was one of the first major Ajax applications, and it illustrates the elegance of what an Ajax application can be.

In a nutshell, Map.search.ch is used to find restaurants, houses, parking spots, and more throughout Switzerland. When you surf to the website http://map.search.ch, you will see something similar to Figure 1-1.

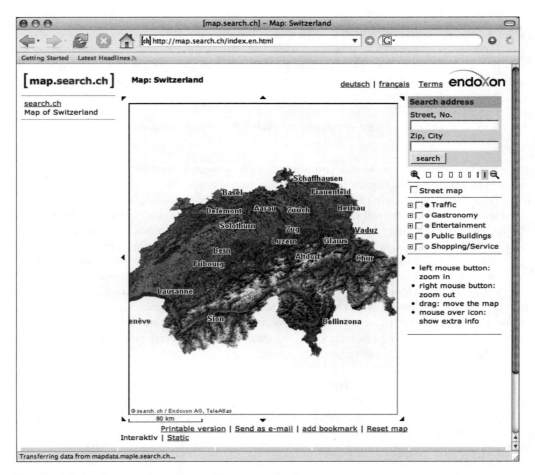

Figure 1-1. *Initial screen shot of* http://map.search.ch

The initial web page seems very similar to those of most web applications, but the difference becomes apparent when you input an address to search for. Let's search for my old address: Muelistrasse 3, 8143 Stallikon, which is illustrated in Figure 1-2. You enter the address in the two text boxes in the upper-right corner and then click the Suchen (Search) button. Figure 1-3 illustrates where to put the address details (or those who don't speak German can reference Figure 1-1, which is in English).

Figure 1-2. *Searching for my old address in Switzerland*

The page changes, and in the map portal a red circle appears along with some smaller colored-in circles and some satellite images of houses. The red circle highlights the house I lived in, and the other smaller circles represent landmarks. The picture generated by Map.search.ch is an aerial view overlaid with a semitransparent street map. The combination is a map that makes it possible to explain where something is in relation to something else. For example, in Figure 1-2 you can see that the house I lived in has a red roof, and to the left seems to be some type of grey complex. The grey complex is a specialty meat company.

The multilayer map is not Ajax specific because traditional web applications could have done the same thing. What is Ajax specific is the map's capability to dynamically reconstruct itself as you drag the mouse over a part of the map. As you click and hold the mouse button and drag across the map, Ajax retrieves map pieces from the server. In a traditional web application, you would have clicked buttons to the left, right, top, and bottom of the map to change your view of it.

The advantage of the multilayer approach is the user's ability to easily explain directions. Usually we say, "Turn left, and on the right is a gas station." It is easy to understand that there is a gas station on the right, but how far down the street? Is it on the corner? Is it one or two houses down the street? However, with Map.search.ch I can say, "Turn right, and see on the map the meat company? Well, there is a parking lot, too, right on the map." The person who is receiving the explanation can mentally coordinate their driving to what they expect to see. Using this approach, when they see a gas station on the right, they will know precisely where on the right.

The problem of explaining directions is that one person knows the area, and the other does not. The person who knows the area will highlight things that he remembers and considers important—or worse, will explain according to things as he thinks they are. The person who does not know the area will focus on irrelevant things when driving through and hope to find the landmarks explained. With the overlaid map illustrating the color of houses, orientation of fields, and so on, each person has a common base to explain and understand the directions.

Let's focus on some other aspects of Map.search.ch. Notice the little blue circle to the northeast of my old house. That little circle represents a bus stop. If you hover your mouse over the circle, a dialog box appears, telling you the bus stop details and starting and ending points of the route, as illustrated in Figure 1-3.

Figure 1-3. *Investigation of the bus stop near my old address in Switzerland*

With the information in the dialog box, you know the details of the busses, trains, or trams that pass by. The dynamically appearing dialog box is Ajax specific because the information within it is dynamically retrieved after you hover over the bus stop circle. In the dialog box the word "Sellenbueren" is highlighted, indicating that there is more information. If you click the link, a web page similar to Figure 1-4 is generated.

Figure 1-4. *Web page used to find a public transportation connection from my old address*

The web page in Figure 1-4 is a link to the SBB, which is the Swiss train service, but the page also includes bus stops. From this page you could plan your travel to another destination based on some date.

Note The shifting of focus from one HTML page to another HTML page is not Ajax specific, as that is possible without Ajax. What is interesting, though, is that a user will consider the entire process of finding a connection that clearly involves two websites, as one application. There is a cooperation between the two websites so that the user has a good experience. This shifting of focus is an example of the Internet economy.

For the sake of exploration, let's go back to the web page illustrated in Figure 1-3 and hover over the other circle, which displays a dialog box containing information about the restaurant and is similar to Figure 1-5.

Figure 1-5. *Restaurant details near my old address*

Based on the restaurant details illustrated in Figure 1-5, you could phone and ask for a reservation, menu, or hours of operation. This is another example of Web 2.0, as information is retrieved dynamically from a server without requiring the user to look up the information in a telephone book. With Ajax information is assembled in a multidimensional fashion, that is, the combination of a map with telephone information.

The functionality that was illustrated goes beyond restaurants and public transportation. It includes public parking garages, government buildings, and whatever is of interest to the user of the website application.

Another Ajax Example

Another Ajax application that has received plenty of attention is Google Maps, which is illustrated in Figure 1-6.

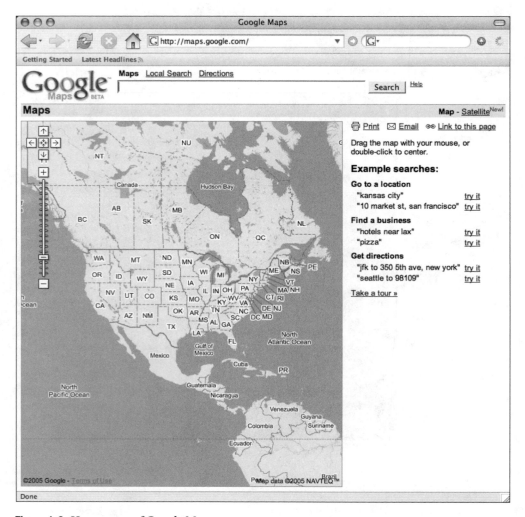

Figure 1-6. *Home page of Google Maps*

The home page http://maps.google.com is a view of North America. Like map.search.ch, the web application is multidimensional and combines a search with geographic information. Take the example where I am driving in to Montreal and want to know where a Starbucks coffee shop is. In the text box I type in **Starbucks Montreal**. The results are displayed in Figure 1-7.

Figure 1-7. *The various Starbucks in Montreal*

The search results are presented by combining the addresses of the search results with a map. My search was "Starbucks Montreal," and some Starbucks were found, which is good. However, also found was a Souvlaki Restaurant, and oddly, National Car and Truck Rental. What we are witnessing is an imperfect search due to imperfect data. In a perfect world, search strings are perfectly and concisely formulated on a perfectly organized database. However, with ever-growing databases that have ever-growing data, searches are not perfect because of time constraints, data organization, and scope.

A creative multidimensional Ajax application is the site http://www.housingmaps.com. Housingmaps is an appropriate example because it is an early example of a Web 2.0 application. The purpose of Housingmaps is to allow a user to search for housing rentals. The rentals are based on data from Craigslist, and the maps are provided by Google. If I search for an apartment rental in Montreal, the resulting output is illustrated in Figure 1-8.

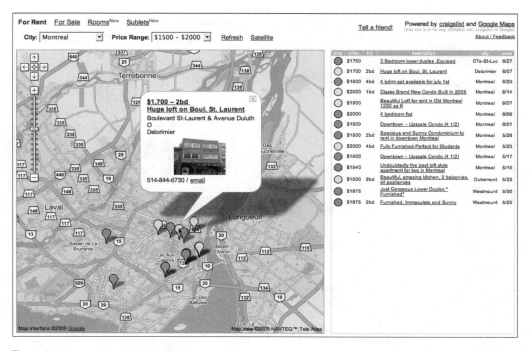

Figure 1-8. *Apartment rentals in Montreal*

The generated results are perfect. As most Montreal people know, when they ask for Montreal, they mean Montreal the island, and Figure 1-8 includes only the island. Additionally, by clicking on one of the found rentals, a balloon appears that gives more details on the rental and if possible some images. The user can easily click on each found location and quickly decide whether it is of interest to them.

Ajax Architecture Basics

You have a quick definition and some examples that illustrate the basic ideas behind an Ajax application. The next step is to illustrate an Ajax architecture. See Figure 1-9.

In Figure 1-9 there is a browser. The browser has two pieces of content: Content 1 and Content 2. Each piece of content is fetched from a different server. Content 2 is fetched from a server that also has two pieces of content, which are also retrieved from separate servers. From an architectural point of view, Ajax implements the Pipes and Filters pattern.[3]

---

3. John Vlissides et al., *Pattern Languages of Program Design 2* (Boston, MA: Addison-Wesley Professional, 1996), p. 430.

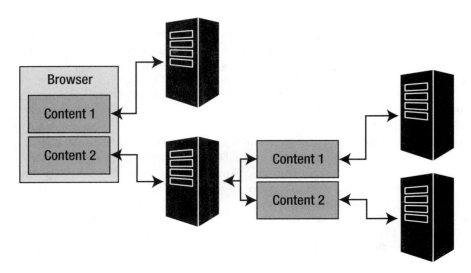

Figure 1-9. *Ajax architecture*

The data is fetched from the server by using a Representational State Transfer (REST)[4] architecture style. The essence of REST is to create a simpler web services architecture by using HyperText Transfer Protocol (HTTP). REST is used solely for the transfer of data, and in particular is used extensively with Ajax applications. The overall idea is to generate content and to have that content filtered and processed. The filtered and processed content serves as an information basis, where another process acts as a client that filters and processes the information. The filtered and processed information acts as an information basis for another client. Content is fluid and constantly modified.

In Figure 1-9, the browser seems to be an end point where the data is not filtered or processed any further. However, that is very far from the truth. In an Ajax infrastructure, the data is always in a state of flux. A script can be used to retrieve HTML content that is saved to a file. Another script processes the saved HTML content that could serve as content for a web service. Putting it simply, when writing an Ajax application the data is never final and always in a state of flux.

It's About the Data

At the time of this writing, many people were working furiously on getting toolkits ready to make it possible to write Ajax applications. In fact, it has been mentioned that Ajax was already invented long before it became popular.[5] Although I agree that Ajax has been around a long time, the question is why is Ajax popular now? Mainly because Ajax involves the manipulation of data streams. We have an Internet economy and Ajax makes that economy work better.

Let's focus on Google and Map.search.ch. What do both of these sites sell? They don't sell software; they sell data! Map.search.ch sells information about Swiss addresses. Google sells information about basically everything on this planet. The strength of Google is not in the software that it sells or offers, but in the ability to manage and present the data.

4. http://en.wikipedia.org/wiki/REST
5. http://radio.weblogs.com/0001011/2005/06/28.html#a10498

When you create your own Ajax application, think of the data that you are managing. Think of how that data can be sliced, diced, and made presentable to the end consumer. Getting the data in the right form is half of the battle. The other half is the presentation. Ajax applications operate from the client side and download data streams that can be manipulated or executed. Many will believe that this means people are ready to use the thin client and to always use applications from the network. However, Ajax does not mean the network is the computer. In fact, going back to the original Ajax fundamental concept, it means that a user uses Ajax and REST to get at the data they are interested in and will use that data locally. For example, say I am going to buy a book. I search Amazon.com and Barnes & Noble.com. Because neither Amazon.com nor Barnes & Noble compare the prices, I need to download the search results and manipulate them locally. In other words, I need to manipulate the search results to get the information I want. What Ajax and REST promote is the people's ability to slice and dice data in a format that is best suited to their requirements.

One last point about the data. Throughout this book, XML or HTML content that is XML compliant will be used. Many people might think that XML has its problems and have proposed protocols that are better. Frankly, I think that is plain wrong. The strength of XML is not its ability to encode data in a verbose format. The strength of XML is its ability to be understood by any platform, its ability to be parsed, sliced, and diced by a wide array of tools. To rebuild as sophisticated an infrastructure as XML is virtually impossible because it would be a gargantuan task. Therefore, when writing your own Ajax and REST applications, stick to XML. Having written on the strengths of XML, there are specific situations where other formats such as JavaScript Object Notation (JSON) would work well.

It's About the Navigation

Ajax applications have the ability to quickly sift through large amounts of data in a very short period of time in a very reasonable fashion. Contrast this to previous times when people would hire experts, or buy expert magazines that already sifted through the data for the client. Now we have applications to do this automatically because applications have this expert knowledge built in.[6] An example is the Amazon.com Diamond Search,[7] shown in Figure 1-10.

Using the diamond search, a client can select from a series of parameters such as price, quality, and cut to find an appropriate diamond. Typically, comparing these details would have required surfing different sites and performing different queries. Amazon.com, on the other hand, created an easy-to-use program that uses graphical sliders to query and find the diamonds that are of interest.

It could be argued that the Amazon.com Diamond Search site could have been reproduced without the fancy graphics or any Ajax technology. Fair enough, that is true, but remember that Ajax is not only about technology. Ajax is also about the Internet economy, and the diamond search utility is an example of creating a dynamic, fun-to-use site. The more time people spend at the site, the more likely they are to buy. You could argue that the Amazon.com Diamond Search makes it unnecessary to seek the advice of a professional.

---

6. Amazon has introduced Mechanical Turk, which does specific tasks for users, at http://www.mturk. com/mturk/welcome
7. http://www.amazon.com/gp/search/finder/103-8737513-3625466?productGroupID=loose%5fdiamonds

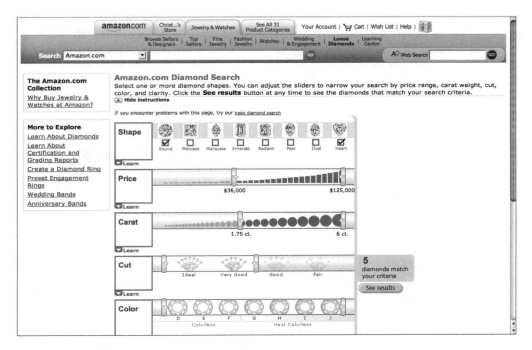

Figure 1-10. *Amazon.com Diamond Search*

To further illustrate the fundamental change of web applications, I will talk about my recent car buying experience. To choose a car, I used the power of the Internet and some specific information sources that rated and compared cars. I used Google to search the car makers for personal experiences and detailed information. Having whittled down my choices to three car makers, I decided to hit the road and visit some dealers. What happened shocked me. All the car dealers rebuffed me because they could not do their half-hour shtick on why I should buy from them. I peppered them with questions that surprised them. It was disappointing, and I was saddened. My wife said, "You know, for the car you like, is there another dealer?" In fact, there was, and it turned out to be the region's biggest and central dealership. At this dealership, an older gentleman approached us and I again peppered him with questions. His answer was, "Ah, you did research. Which car do you want to take for a drive?" He did not go into a long spiel but let us control the process, and of course we bought the car.

The moral of the story is that the experts on the Internet might be familiar with only certain parameters, but because websites allow these parameters to be compared in an easy-to-use interface, users are more informed. Informed people expect those human experts that they are seeking to have knowledge that goes deeper than their basic parametric comparisons. In other words, car salespeople need to assume that they will have informed clients and therefore must provide some added value to interest a client in purchasing a vehicle.

It is more important when building an Ajax application to understand the data being presented and then to design the user interface fitted to the data. In traditional development, it is the other way around. The data is fit to the software because software designers are good at designing software but bad at designing user interfaces.[8] I could be controversial and state that Ajax applications have stormed in because the applications are built by mature web designers who know more about user-interface design than software design. I do not mean to belittle the web designers; in fact I mean to illustrate that because of them we have these cool applications. If there is one downside to Ajax, it's that you need to be a user-interface designer who is an expert in the domain being presented. Software development is moving from a horizontal approach (general-purpose software) to a vertical approach (domain-specific software).

Comparing Ajax to Other Application Types

There you have it, the description of the Ajax application. The remaining question is how an Ajax application compares to applications using other technologies and methodologies.

To fully understand the ramifications of Ajax, let's put on our software architect's hat and reengineer Map.search.ch in the context of other architectural models.

Rich-Client Local Installation

In the traditional software model, you download an application, install it, and then execute it. Converting Map.search.ch into a traditional piece of software would require writing a client. The client would have to be written in a platform-neutral language such as Sun Microsystems' Java, or a Microsoft .NET language, or the open source Python (if I missed your programming language, for example Ruby, please do not consider it an insult. I just mentioned the languages that I regularly code in). If the client were written in a language such as C++, then it would need to be recompiled for each platform.

Choosing a programming language often is not the difficult part because languages exist on all platforms. The difficult part is how to code the graphical user interface (GUI). Often the problem is deciding whether to code using a GUI toolkit that takes advantage of the platform and therefore is specific to the platform—or to use a GUI toolkit that might not be as specific to the platform and might not be able to use all the tricks of the platform, but therefore is cross-platform. The decision the developer makes has significant ramifications.

A large percentage of applications are coded by using C++ and the Microsoft Windows GUI toolkit. This means that these GUI applications will most likely execute only on Microsoft Windows. Another choice for Map.search.ch could have been Java. Then the application could execute on multiple platforms, but the Java runtime would need to be installed on each of the platforms. Choose C++ and Windows, and you have one set of problems. Choose Java and multiple operating systems, and you have another set of problems. Sadly, there is no single best solution because each solution has its problems.

The last consideration is the data that is used to power the Map.search.ch application. The problem is that there would be a large amount of data. The only possible solution is to distribute the application with a single or multiple DVDs. The client would either install all the DVDs to the local hard disk or reference the DVDs from the computer's DVD drive while doing the DVD shuffle. The DVD shuffle is when the program constantly asks you to switch DVDs for one piece of information, causing much frustration as you are constantly opening and closing the DVD drive.

---

8. Alan Cooper, *About Face: The Essentials of User Interface Design* (New York, NY: John Wiley & Sons, 1995), p. 21.

This architecture has the following problems:

- Writing a multiplatform client has its challenges and requires extra resources in terms of time and money to be invested.

- The data has to be available locally, which can be a challenge for larger applications. Switzerland has more than 7 million inhabitants. Imagine the size of the data for a country such as the United States, which has nearly 300 million inhabitants.

- There are associated production costs that are not negligible; DVDs have to be mastered, boxes printed, and materials assembled.

- Updating the DVD data is a tedious process that requires an online connection or the purchase of another DVD data set. There is always a time lag between assembling the data and letting the consumer use the data.

- Updates of the client software require a new distribution of the software. Clients without an Internet connection cannot have their software updated dynamically.

- To use the software on multiple machines on a local area network, the software has to be installed on the multiple machines. It is not straightforward to share the data or to have the software automatically installed on multiple machines.

- Integration between Map.search.ch and the public transportation system is not possible unless Map.search.ch integrates the logic.

Overall, the rich-client local installation is not suited for the type of application that Ajax solves. The rich-client local installation application has too many issues regarding logistics and overhead. Granted, some of the issues are solved with money, which is earned by selling the software, but the application is still time lagged.

In general, the rich-client local installation application is threatened by the Ajax solution because you could create a local edition of an Ajax application by installing the HTTP server locally. The local edition would still have the problems associated with distributing the DVD data. But the big advantage is that the locally installed Ajax application can be installed on a local area network and accessed by multiple clients without having the client installed on multiple computers.

Rich-Client Web Services

The rich-client web services application is similar to the rich-client local installation application, except the data is not distributed via DVDs. A rich-client web services application uses web services, which are Internet-based method calls using XML as the protocol. In the formal specification sense, web services are based on Simple Object Access Protocol (SOAP). Like the rich-client local installation, the rich client has to be installed locally on each machine. The data that the rich client accesses is somewhere else on the Internet.

This architecture has the following problems:

- As outlined in the Rich Client Local Installation scenario, writing a multiplatform client has its challenges and requires extra resources in terms of time and money to be invested.

- The client can be downloaded from a central site, but the client still needs to be installed locally for each machine. This makes updating the software more complicated.

- Web services that are implemented by using SOAP can either be simple or very complicated, depending on the requirements.

- Rogue third parties may end up using your data without your explicit permission.

- Integration between Map.search.ch and the public transportation system is not possible unless Map.search.ch integrates the logic.

A web service has become a commonly used rubber stamp for making Internet-based method calls using XML. In many cases, web services are associated with SOAP. There is no specific problem with SOAP, or with Web Services Description Language (WSDL), except that the "simple" is being taken out of the technology. Web services using SOAP have a large number of other specifications associated with them, and those specifications are useful for enterprise-to-enterprise communications.

Plain-Vanilla Web Application

The plain-vanilla web application is what I would call a lowest common denominator solution. The difference between Ajax and the plain-vanilla web application is the amount of dynamics and interaction. Both use a web browser, but there is less interaction and fewer dynamics with a plain-vanilla web application. Generally speaking, a plain-vanilla web application is controlled using server-side interactions. The client is there only to display the data that is generated by the server, and provides links or simple GUI elements to determine what the next step should be.

This architecture has the following problems:

- Interaction between the browser and consumer is simple and limited.

- The consumer is presented with an inferior user interface when compared with a rich client.

- The application requires recoding by the programmer to make the data fit the limited browser implementation. Some interactions result in hacks, which cause the consumer to be confused when they press the Back button, or reload, and so on.

The plain-vanilla web application model has suited us for a long time. It works and is successful. It is the application development model that created the Internet that we have and use today. The problem with the plain-vanilla web application model is that it is showing its age. Ajax is an evolution of this model.

Some Final Thoughts

Now that you know what Ajax is all about, at least at the higher architectural level, and how it compares to other architectures, here is a summation of principles:

- An Ajax application can be a traditional application such as a word processor. What is unique about an Ajax application is that it combines multiple data streams into a unique view that is natural from the perspective of the user. In the case of Map.search.ch, this unique view is the display of mapped data in combination with aerial photos to explain to the user where things are.

- Ajax applications solve a problem in a specific context. When going beyond that context, the Internet is exploited in that other websites are referenced transparently, without the client having to figure out what the other website could be. The example from Map.search.ch was the shifting of the `http://map.search.ch` website to the Swiss train `http://www.sbb.ch` website. Clients will notice the change of website, but they will not notice where one "application" starts and another "application" ends.

- Ajax applications are written to solve an immediate problem and do not attempt to generalize. You would generalize when writing horizontal software applications. Ajax applications, in contrast, are vertical in nature. For example, Google develops their own software for their own consumption. In contrast, companies such as Microsoft for the most part sell software that could be used by a Google-like company to provide Google-like services. Even if the software being written is horizontal in nature, the solution is vertical. For example, if I were to write an Ajax word processor, the idea behind the word processor would not be to sell licenses of the word processor, but to sell services associated with the word processor. These services could include document conversion, typesetting, editing, and other value-added services.

- There is no single state to an Ajax application. Whenever a state is captured in the form of an HTML page or file, then it is a snapshot. There is no guarantee that performing the same actions will result in the same snapshot. This makes testing more complicated because it means you need to test logic and not results.

- Ajax applications are not about the application, but the data. For example, when you install an application on a local computer, you care about the application, because most applications store the data in a proprietary format. If the application is lost, then so is your data. Over time, converters have been written so that losing an application is not as critical. With the advent of Ajax applications, what is critical is the data. In most cases, the data will be stored in formats that can be manipulated by other applications. Therefore, when writing Ajax applications, you are concerned with managing and providing an interface to the data.

- Ajax applications are generally "idiot proof" and do not require lengthy user manuals or explanations. This relates back to the scope of the Ajax application in that what you see is what you get. There are no hidden or extra features to confuse the user.

- Ajax applications are dynamic and exhibit behavior that is similar to a traditional client application that is executed from the local computer.

Everything is not rosy when writing Ajax applications, and the following problems can arise:

- The consumer is entirely dependent on the Internet. You can create an Ajax application that runs from a local server, but most likely that server will reference another server.

- A question of ownership with respect to the presented content arises because many Ajax applications combine streams from other websites. This referencing could be hostile or desired.

- The user must get used to the Internet way of doing things, which is not always identical to the traditional rich client's way.

The next chapter describes the essentials of an Ajax application. Before you learn about Ajax patterns, you need to learn more about the basics of Ajax.

CHAPTER 2

■ ■ ■

The Nuts and Bolts of Ajax

Ajax is simple and could be described as an 11-line piece of code. So, doing some mental math, describing Ajax and the XMLHttpRequest type[1] should take no more than four or five pages. Yet this chapter is more than four or five pages—in fact, quite a bit more. The reason is that knowing *how* to use the XMLHttpRequest type does not equate to making the *best* use of XMLHttpRequest.

The first purpose of this chapter is to introduce and explain a simple Ajax example. The second purpose is to explain a meaningful development strategy using the XMLHttpRequest type.

Ajax for the Impatient

The Ajax example illustrated in this chapter is an HTML page that has a single button. Clicking the single button makes an HTTP request that downloads some data that is then inserted into the HTML page. This example illustrates two techniques: getting data by using the REST architectural style, and dynamically adding/modifying an HTML page using Ajax techniques.

Understanding REST Theory

REST is an architectural style that provides guidance on how to send data between a client and a server. Client/Server communications is a ubiquitous computing paradigm, and REST abstracts that paradigm to the level of the Web. REST assumes that you will be using XML and the HTTP protocol. And—very important—REST assumes that you will be using currently available technologies to their fullest potential.

REST emphasizes the following architectural concepts:

- Resources are used to describe an identifier. A resource can have any identifier, but that identifier will be unique to that resource.

- Separating the resource from the representation so that a resource is referenced, but a representation is manipulated. A representation will contain references to other resources.

- Using the HTTP GET, PUT, DELETE, and other commands to manipulate resources and their associated representations.

---

1. A clear and concise explanation of the XMLHttpRequest object can be found at http://developer. apple.com/internet/webcontent/xmlhttpreq.html.

- Making self-descriptive representations using metadata technology such as XML schemas.

- Using hypermedia as the basis of the exposed resources and representations. Servers that serve RESTful data are stateless, data exchanged between client and server is independent of the server, and the client maintains the state. What is meant by the client maintaining the state is that a server will have state, but the client is responsible for managing which state is being manipulated.

REST is useful because it works with current HTTP server architectures. The irony of REST is that to adopt it as an architectural style, the server does not have to be changed, but our coding styles do have to change. Because of the way many web application frameworks are implemented, they conflict with REST. I will not give any specific examples of problems because the pattern implementations presented later in this chapter and book will highlight problems as they appear.

You will want to adopt REST in your architecture because it makes your web application framework flexible and adaptable. One of the problems with web applications is that they defy traditional development techniques. Figure 2-1 provides an example.

Figure 2-1. *An example web page*

In Figure 2-1, there is a middle brown section that has a picture and some text. To the left, right, and top are blue areas with text and pictures. The middle brown section is the *content section,* and the outer blue areas are the *common areas.* From the perspective of a web application architecture, every generated HTML page has the same common areas but different content areas. What is bad about this is that for each and every downloaded HTML page, the common area has to be sent.

If the website were to implement Ajax and REST, the change would be dramatic in that the overall HTML page (including the blue and brown areas) would be downloaded once. Then as the user clicked on links in the blue area, the content in the brown area would be updated. The common (blue) area would need to be downloaded only once, and the content (brown) area would be downloaded on an as-needed basis.

The advantage of the Ajax and REST approach is that the web application architecture is simplified. In a traditional web application architecture, each page would need code to generate the common blue areas while generating specific brown areas. In contrast, in an Ajax and REST application each piece of content is responsible only for what the content wants to portray. This means that the blue area information does not need to care about the brown content area, and vice versa. In a nutshell, Ajax and REST disassemble the complexities of a traditional web application into an application development paradigm similar to what traditional applications do. After all, when developing a locally installed application, does the list box care how the menu bar is generated?

Implementing the REST Data

For the scope of this chapter and this book, whenever data is being referenced by an Ajax application it will use the REST architectural style. The word "REST" will not be explicitly referenced in the patterns defined in this book, but it is implied.

Let's define an initial Ajax example that implements the REST architectural style. Using Ajax and REST implies the following:

- The data is XML.

- The resource is defined as a Uniform Resource Locator (or URL, for example, http://mydomain.com/cgross/books) that references the representation books.xml.

- The data is retrieved from the HTTP server by using the HTTP GET command.

The initial example implements a sample book query service that generates the following XML file:

```
<?xml version="1.0" encoding="UTF-8"?>
<User>
    <Book>
        <ISBN>1-59059-540-8</ISBN>
        <Title>Foundations of Object Oriented
          Programming Using .NET 2.0 Patterns</Title>
        <Author>Christian Gross</Author>
    </Book>
    <Book>
        <ISBN>0-55357-340-3</ISBN>
        <Title>A Game of Thrones</Title>
        <Author>George R.R. Martin</Author>
    </Book>
</User>
```

This retrieved XML content contains two books from a library. How the data is stored on the server side is the responsibility of the HTTP server. The data could be stored as an XML file or it could be dynamically generated. From the perspective of an external application, the data is based on XML. The description of the book is simple as there are three fields: ISBN, Title, and Author.

Implementing the Ajax Application

The HTML content that contains the Ajax technology is implemented as a single HTML page. The HTML page does not include the XML content when the HTML page is downloaded. You could be cynical and say, but that is the point of Ajax—for the XML content to be downloaded separately from the HTML page. This goes back to the example web page in Figure 2-1, where the XML file represents the brown area, and the downloaded page represents the blue areas.

Following is the implementation of the Ajax application to download the XML books data:

```
<html><head>
<title>Sample Page</title>
<script language="JavaScript" type="text/javascript">
var xmlhttp = null;

xmlhttp = new ActiveXObject("Microsoft.XMLHTTP");

function GetIt( url) {
    if( xmlhttp) {
        xmlhttp.open('GET', url, false);
        xmlhttp.send(null);
        document.getElementById('result').innerHTML = xmlhttp.responseText;
    }
}
</script>
</head>
<body>
<button onclick="GetIt('/cgross/books')">Get a document</button>
<p><table border="1">
    <tr><td>Document</td><td><span id="result">No Result</span></td></tr>
</table></p>
</body>
</html>
```

In the HTML content (the elements contained by the HTML body tags), a button is defined that when clicked will call the function GetIt. The parameter for the function GetIt is the URL for the resource that contains the XML book data. The data, when retrieved and processed, is presented in an HTML table, where one column (indicated by the td HTML tag) contains a span HTML tag. The span tag uses the attribute id to define a place where the retrieved data is displayed. The attribute id is a unique identifier that can be used by JavaScript to reference an HTML element.

When the HTML page is processed, the `script` tag identifies a place where JavaScript can be defined to execute the Ajax logic. For all scripts in this book, JavaScript or JScript (Microsoft variation) will be used on the client side.

The variable `xmlhttp` and the next line, `xmlhttp = new ActiveXObject...`, are not part of a function, meaning that they are executed when the HTML page is being loaded by the web browser. The executed lines of code instantiate an object instance of `XMLHttpRequest`, which is assigned to the variable `xmlhttp`. The variable `xmlhttp` will be used to download the resource `/cgross/books` or the associated representation `/cgross/books.xml` file that is stored on the server.

Some developers may comment that it would have been safer to contain the logic in a function that is called when the HTML page has been completely loaded (`window.onload`). That is often good coding style, but it was not used in this example because that would be unnecessarily complicated for this demonstration.

In the implementation of the function `GetIt`, the parameter `url` represents the URL of the document that will be downloaded (`books.xml`). Calling the method `open` creates a request that is sent by using the method `send`. The third parameter of `open` is the value `false`, which results in the HTTP request being executed synchronously. This means that when calling the method `send`, the method will return after the results have been retrieved from the server. The results are accessed in the script by using the property `responseText` and then assigned using dynamic HTML to the `span` element.

Putting Together Ajax and REST

When creating an Ajax application, the HTML page and the referenced data files must be downloaded from the same domain. This requirement is part of the *same origin policy,* which prevents cross-site scripting vulnerabilities (more about this policy will be discussed later in this chapter). It is not possible to retrieve the HTML page from one domain and then retrieve the data from another domain. So, for example, if the HTML were stored at `http://www.devspace.com`, the data file could not be stored at `http://www.amazon.com`. This is because the `XMLHttpRequest` object instance executes in a sandbox. In certain situations, the sandbox complicates putting together an Ajax application.

Having a sandbox means that an Ajax application and its associated REST data must reside on the same domain. For the current example, the Ajax HTML page is stored at the URL `http://localhost:8080/example.html`, and the data file is stored at the URL `http://localhost:8080/cgross/Books` and thus are both part of the same domain.

Figure 2-2 shows a browser that has loaded the page `/example.html`.

The HTML page in Figure 2-2 is fairly simple; it displays a button and a table. To illustrate the use of `XMLHttpRequest`, the Get a Document button is clicked, resulting in an output similar to Figure 2-3.

In the updated page shown in Figure 2-3, the text No Result has been replaced with the text 1-59059 . . .. This is the "11-line" `XMLHttpRequest` example that was hinted at, at the beginning of the chapter, which illustrates how Ajax works.

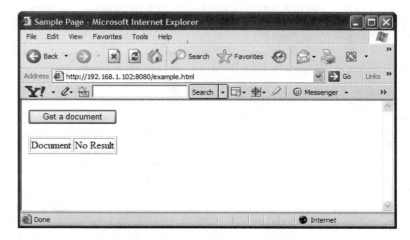

Figure 2-2. *Initial generation of the Ajax page*

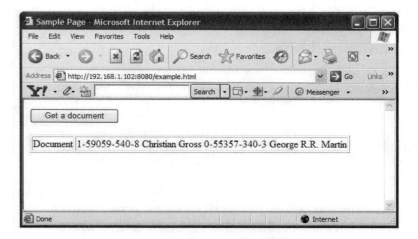

Figure 2-3. *The resulting generated page after the button has been pressed*

Understanding the Ramifications of Ajax and REST

The preceding example is simple and illustrates that Ajax is indeed an 11-line solution. However, there are many ramifications; the first and most notable is that the simple example will run only on Microsoft Internet Explorer. When using another browser such as Mozilla Firefox or Apple's Safari, the sample will not work. When writing Ajax applications, you need to think in a cross-platform, cross-browser manner because you will be confronted with these problems right from the beginning.

Extending the first ramification, it means when writing Ajax applications that Dynamic HTML is your user interface toolkit. Some individuals may extend the functionality by including Java applets or ActiveX controls, or even Macromedia Shockwave or Flash,[2] but in essence Ajax

---

2. http://en.wikipedia.org/wiki/AFLAX

requires that you understand Dynamic HTML. I highly recommend that all Ajax developers purchase the book *Dynamic HTML: The Definitive Reference* by Danny Goodman (O'Reilly Media, 2002). It is a thick book, but it provides answers to all browser issues—what works and does not work.

The second ramification is that all content should be referenced by using REST URLs. If REST is not used, then referencing the data within the brown areas of Figure 2-1 will result in using remote procedure calls (RPCs). Using RPCs is not recommended, because additional overhead is required, such as method name encoding, parameter encoding, and data decoding. Programmers may like using RPCs, but they are intended for classical programming techniques and not for Ajax or Internet applications.[3]

The third and final ramification is that to keep things simple. It is possible to reference other websites, but that will introduce security issues that will need to be resolved. For example, using Internet Explorer to make the domain trusted where the HTML page was downloaded allows XMLHttpRequest to download content from other domains. Keeping things simple includes using techniques that work across all browsers on all platforms. It is possible to do more "neat" and "cool" tricks, but those tricks need to be maintained and extended.

It is important to understand these ramifications because they define from an architectural perspective our boundaries on what patterns and best practices can and cannot be applied.

XMLHttpRequest Details

Regardless of how the XMLHttpRequest type is instantiated, and regardless of which browser and platform are used, a set of methods and properties is associated with XMLHttpRequest. Table 2-1 defines the methods.

Table 2-1. *Methods of XMLHttpRequest*

Method	Description
abort()	Stops a request that is being processed.
getAllResponseHeaders()	Returns the complete set of HTTP headers from the HTTP request as a string.
getResponseHeader(label)	Returns the associated HTTP header identified by the variable label.
open(method, URL, asyncFlag, username, password)	Opens and prepares an HTTP request identified by the HTTP method and URL. The variable asyncFlag can either be true or false, where true means to make an asynchronous request. The variables username and password are used to access a protected HTTP resource.
send(content)	Executes the HTTP request, where the variable content represents data that is posted if applicable.
setRequestHeader(label, value)	Assigns an HTTP header before the HTTP request is made.

---

3. `http://www.tbray.org/ongoing/When/200x/2004/04/26/WSTandP`, Web Services Theory and Practice, Tim Bray

You'll be using these methods throughout the book, so more details are not necessary at this moment. What does need some special attention are the properties. When a request has retrieved data, four properties are used to indicate how the request fared. Consider the following HTML code that references the four properties and would be called after the send method had completed:

```
document.getElementById('httpcode').innerHTML = xmlhttp.status;
document.getElementById('httpstatus').innerHTML = xmlhttp.statusText;
document.getElementById('result').innerHTML = xmlhttp.responseText;
document.getElementById('xmlresult').innerHTML = xmlhttp.responseXML;
```

The four properties can be subdivided into two subcategories: result and HTTP status. The properties status and statusText retrieve the HTTP result codes. The property status contains an integer value, such as 200 for success. The property statusText contains a textual representation of the HTTP result code, such as OK. The properties responseText and responseXML contain the result of the HTTP request. The difference between the two properties is that responseText contains a string buffer of the results, and responseXML references an XML Document Object Model (DOM) representation of the results. If responseXML does reference an XML DOM instance, then responseText references a valid XML text buffer.

Adding the property code to a modified version of the simple Ajax application and executing the HTML page results in Figure 2-4.

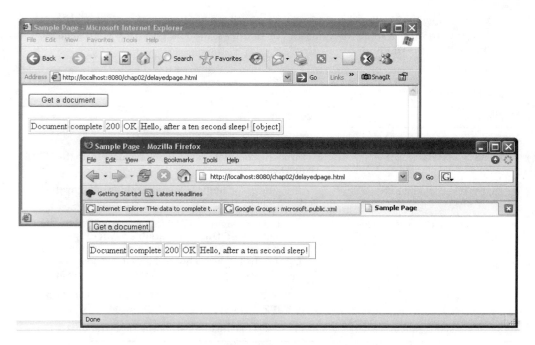

Figure 2-4. *Output of XMLHttpRequest properties in two web browsers*

The results in Figure 2-4 are generated for two browsers: Mozilla Firefox and Microsoft Internet Explorer. The values for status, statusText, and responseText are identical across most browsers (Internet Explorer, Firefox, and Safari). The difference is the value for responseXML.

For Firefox a textual representation does not exist, for Internet Explorer it is text with square brackets, and finally for Safari it is the text undefined. The reason for the difference is that the script is trying to convert an object into a piece of text. There is no defined result, and as such, different browsers generate different representations. To use the XML DOM node, you must use XML operations.

Using the Factory Pattern

The Factory pattern[4] is used to instantiate a type. When coding in C# or Java, the instantiated type would be manipulated as an interface. The Factory pattern is called by a client to instantiate a class that implements the interface. From a coding perspective, that code looks like the following:

```
public interface MyInterface {
    void SomeMethod();
}

class MyClass : MyInterface {
    public void SomeMethod() { }
}

class MyAnotherClass : MyInterface {
    public void SomeMethod() { }
}

public class Factory {
    public static MyInterface Create() {
        return new MyClass();
    }
}
```

In this code, there is a single interface (MyInterface), and two classes (MyClass and MyAnotherClass) that implement that interface. When a client wants to use either implementation, the client does not instantiate MyClass or MyAnotherClass directly. Instead, the client expects to call a method to do the instantiation. In this example, that would mean the method Factory.Create is responsible for instantiating either MyClass or MyAnotherClass. The advantage of the Factory.Create method is that the method implementation can decide to instantiate MyClass or MyAnotherClass. Clients do not need to concern themselves with those details. This makes it possible to change the implementation type without having to change the code of the client. The client interacts only with the interface MyInterface and not the types MyClass or MyAnotherClass.

So, let's relate this back to JavaScript and decide whether we need to use a Factory pattern, and if so, how it is implemented. First, JavaScript is a dynamic language, which very simply put means there is no such thing as an interface and implementation. In JavaScript, everything is dynamic and hence the existence of a method is determined when the method is called. In JavaScript,

---

4. Erich Gamma et al., *Design Patterns: Elements of Reusable Object-Oriented Software* (Boston, MA: Addison-Wesley Professional, 1995), p. 107.

the purpose of the Factory pattern is to determine which type to instantiate at runtime. That way, when the resulting object is referenced, the methods being queried should exist.

The downside to dynamic languages is that you don't know whether your code works until you actually test it.

There is no such thing as a JavaScript compiler, and hence it is not possible to know if your code works or does not work. This is partially what can make developing with JavaScript tedious as you may have to wade through a series of syntax errors before being able to test and debug your source code. However, do not think that JavaScript is an environment where you need to use printouts to see what the code is doing. Mozilla includes a very sophisticated and useful debugger that makes it simple to figure out what your JavaScript code is doing.

Defining an XMLHttpRequest Factory

Getting back to the Factory pattern and instantiation of XMLHttpRequest, the pattern is needed because each browser (for example, Firefox, Internet Explorer, and Safari) has a different way of instantiating the XMLHttpRequest object, and using the Factory pattern is the only way to mask the decision of the object instantiation.

If you search the Internet (query "XMLHttpRequest factory"), you'll find a multitude of techniques proposed to abstract the instantiation of XMLHttpRequest. As much as I would like to reference a toolkit or factory, there is a problem with doing so. A web browser is by default a cross-platform end client, or at least mostly a cross-platform end client. Using a comprehensive toolkit to create cross-browser applications is like creating a cross-platform toolkit for the Java environment. Like the Web, Java is cross-platform, and adding a layer on top complicates development and distribution of the application. The aim of this book is to focus on those methods, properties, and objects that are cross-browser compatible and when necessary introduce very lightweight functions or classes.

The instantiation of the XMLHttpRequest object is an example where it is necessary to introduce a lightweight function. The XMLHttpRequest Factory pattern is illustrated as follows:

```
function FactoryXMLHttpRequest() {
    if(window.XMLHttpRequest) {
        return new XMLHttpRequest();
    }
    else if(window.ActiveXObject) {
        var msxmls = new Array(
            'Msxml2.XMLHTTP.5.0',
            'Msxml2.XMLHTTP.4.0',
            'Msxml2.XMLHTTP.3.0',
            'Msxml2.XMLHTTP',
            'Microsoft.XMLHTTP');
        for (var i = 0; i < msxmls.length; i++) {
            try {
                return new ActiveXObject(msxmls[i]);
            } catch (e) {
            }
        }
    }
    throw new Error("Could not instantiate XMLHttpRequest");
}
```

The Factory pattern is implemented as a single method, FactoryXMLHttpRequest, which returns an XMLHttpRequest object instance. In the implementation of the method are two if statements. The first if statement tests whether the window.XMLHttpRequest object exists. If window.XMLHttpRequest exists, then the object XMLHttpRequest can be instantiated, which most likely includes all browsers except Microsoft Internet Explorer. The second test, window.ActiveXObject, is used if the browser is Internet Explorer. When instantiating the XMLHttpRequest object for Internet Explorer, multiple versions are tested and instantiated. If the instantiation does not work, an exception is generated and caught by the try...catch block. If the if statement does not work or the XMLHttpRequest type could not be instantiated, the function does not return null, but an exception.

It is important to throw an exception so that a developer diagnosing why a script had problems knows where the problem occurred. Many developers would be inclined to return a null value, but that is an incorrect response. When a script calls the FactoryXMLHttpRequest method, it is expected to return an instance of XMLHttpRequest. If an instance cannot be returned, it is an error and an exception must be thrown.

Rewriting the Ajax Application to Use a Factory

In this section, the minimal Ajax application shown previously is rewritten to use the FactoryXMLHttpRequest method so that all browsers can run the Ajax application. Following is the rewritten HTML page:

```
<html><head>
<title>Sample Page</title>
</head>
<script language="JavaScript" src="/lib/factory.js"></script>
<script language="JavaScript" type="text/javascript">
var xmlhttp = FactoryXMLHttpRequest();

function GetIt(url) {
    if( xmlhttp) {
        xmlhttp.open('GET', url, false);
        xmlhttp.send(null);
        document.getElementById('result').innerHTML = xmlhttp.responseText;
    }
}
</script>
</head>
<body>
<button onclick="GetIt('/cgross/books')">Get a document</button>
<p><table border="1">
    <tr><td>Document</td><td><span id="result">No Result</span></td></tr>
</table></p>
</body>
</html>
```

The rewritten page loads the `XMLHttpRequest` Factory pattern implementation by using a `script` tag, and assigning the attribute `src` to be the name of the file containing the Factory pattern implementation. Then, to instantiate and assign the `XMLHttpRequest` instance to the variable `xmlhttp`, the function `FactoryXMLHttpRequest` is called. The remaining code remains identical to the previous example because regardless of the browser, the methods of `XMLHttpRequest` are identical.

Making Asynchronous Requests

The Ajax examples used the `XMLHttpRequest` object in a synchronous manner, meaning that the moment `send` is called, the browser stops processing other messages and waits for an answer. To illustrate that a browser locks while processing synchronous requests, the previous Ajax application will retrieve a page from a server that will wait 10 seconds before returning the content. Following is the ASP.NET source code (note that this book will focus on both Java and ASP.NET):

```
<%@ Page Language = "C#" %>
<html>
<head>
<title>Hanging page</title>
</head>
<body>
    <%
      System.Threading.Thread.Sleep( 10000);
     %>
    Hello, after a ten second sleep!
</body>
</html>
```

The ASP.NET sample is written by using the C# programming language. The single statement, `System.Threading.Thread.Sleep`, causes the current thread on the server to sleep for 10 seconds, which means that the browser will be waiting 10 seconds for its content to be retrieved.

Modifying the previous Ajax application and clicking the button to retrieve the hanging page causes the browser to appear similar to Figure 2-5.

In Figure 2-5, the clicked button remains pressed because it is waiting for the content to be returned. While the browser is waiting, the user cannot switch to another tab to process other HTTP requests. A hanging browser is a problem and will make the Ajax experience potentially painful for the user.

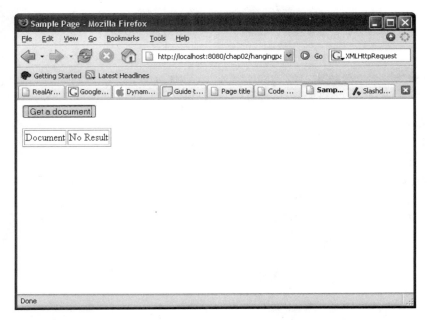

Figure 2-5. *Hanging browser waiting for content to be retrieved*

The solution is to use an asynchronous Ajax XMLHttpRequest request. An asynchronous request will not block the browser, and the user could continue clicking or using other tabs of the browser. The following source code rewrites the simple Ajax application to use an asynchronous request:

```
<html>
<head>
<title>Sample Page</title>
</head>
<script language="JavaScript" src="/lib/factory.js"></script>
<script language="JavaScript" type="text/javascript">
var xmlhttp = FactoryXMLHttpRequest();

function AsyncUpdateEvent() {
    switch(xmlhttp.readyState) {
    case 0:
        document.getElementById('status').innerHTML = "uninitialized";
        break;
    case 1:
        document.getElementById('status').innerHTML = "loading";
        break;
    case 2:
        document.getElementById('status').innerHTML = "loaded";
        break;
```

```
        case 3:
            document.getElementById('status').innerHTML = "interactive";
            break;
        case 4:
            document.getElementById('status').innerHTML = "complete";
            document.getElementById('result').innerHTML = xmlhttp.responseText;
            break;
    }
}

function GetIt(url) {
    if(xmlhttp) {
        xmlhttp.open('GET', url, true);
        xmlhttp.onreadystatechange = AsyncUpdateEvent;
        xmlhttp.send(null);
    }
}
</script>
</head>
<body>
<button onclick="GetIt('/chap02/serverhang.aspx')">Get a document</button>
<p><table border="1">
    <tr>
        <td>Document</td>
        <td>
            <span id="status">No Result</span>
        </td>
        <td>
            <span id="result">No Result</span>
        </td></tr>
</table></p>
</body>
</html>
```

There are several new additions to the rewritten Ajax application, and they deal with the technical issues of loading content asynchronously. Let's start by focusing on the function GetIt. The implementation of GetIt is similar to previous Ajax application examples, except that the third parameter of the method open is true to indicate that the request will be asynchronous. This means that when the method send is called, the method will send the request, start another thread to wait for the response, and return immediately.

Whenever XMLHttpRequest operates in asynchronous modes, feedback is given to the caller on the state of the request. The property onreadystatechange is a function that receives the feedback. It is important to note that the feedback function must be assigned before each send because upon completion of the request, the property onreadystatechange is reset. This is evident in the sources of the Mozilla-based browsers.

The property onreadystatechange is assigned the function AsyncUpdateEvent. In the implementation of AsyncUpdateEvent is a switch statement that tests the current state of the request. When an asynchronous request is made, the script is free to continue executing other code.

This could cause problems if the script attempts to read the request results before the request has been completed. Using the property readyState, it is possible to know the stage of the HTTP request. The property readyState can contain one of five values, each representing a request state:

- 0: The XMLHttpRequest instance is in an inconsistent state, and the result data should not be referencing.

- 1: A request is in progress, and the result data should not be retrieved.

- 2: The request has downloaded the result data and is preparing it for reference.

- 3: The script can interact with the XMLHttpRequest instance even though the data is not completely loaded.

- 4: The request and result data are completely downloaded and loaded as an object model.

The request states seem to indicate that it is possible to manipulate various properties at different states. The problem is that not all browsers support the same property states at the same state codes. The only cross-platform solution is to reference the XMLHttpRequest result properties (status, statusText, responseText, and responseXML) when the request state is equal to 4. When the request state is 4, you can be sure that the result properties contain a valid value.

Executing the asynchronous Ajax application results in a call being made, and the browser is not locked. You can click the button, open a new browser, and surf to another website. After the 10 seconds have expired, the generated HTML page should resemble Figure 2-6.

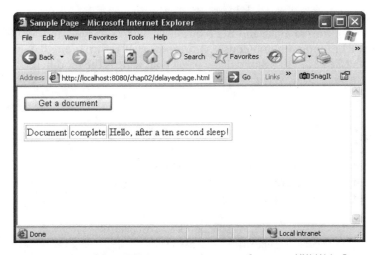

Figure 2-6. *Resulting HTML page using asynchronous* XMLHttpRequest

The asynchronous approach solves the problem of the hanging browser. The Ajax application could continue processing other data, and in fact multiple requests could be made.

What is not optimal is that there is no busy indicator. You have no idea whether anything is working when you click the OK button. There should be some form of indicator that something is happening.

Another problem is that some browsers will cache the results of the XMLHttpRequest. This is an age-old problem because caching can result in unpredictable behavior, and caching still happens even if the Ajax HTML page is reloaded.

Making Practical Use of XMLHttpRequest

The Factory pattern implementation that was used to abstract the instantiation of XMLHttpRequest was a good first step. Using an asynchronous request is a good second step, as it improves the Ajax experience, but other problems remain, such as user feedback and how to use security that falls in the context of same origin policy.

Implementing an Asynchronous Calling Mechanism

When executed in the context of a web browser, JavaScript is not a multithreaded programming language, and therefore it is not possible to instantiate a thread that processes some data, while the main Ajax application is executing. Using an asynchronous XMLHttpRequest instance is sort of multithreading in that the application can continue execution while waiting for a response. Asynchronous programming means writing event-driven code, and that requires a different way of programming with JavaScript. Yet writing code with JavaScript is not like writing code in an object-oriented language. JavaScript is more or less a procedural language that has some hand-wired extensions that make it appear object oriented.

The Modified Ajax Application

In this section, I'm going to again modify the Ajax application that has been illustrated multiple times, except this time I'll add a button to make another request. To illustrate asynchronous programming, two requests will be made simultaneously. One request will return immediately with the data, and the second will call the 10-second delay page. Following is the modified HTML code:

```
<html>
<head>
<title>Sample Page</title>
</head>
<script language="JavaScript" src="/lib/factory.js"></script>
<script language="JavaScript" src="/lib/asynchronous.js"></script>
<script language="JavaScript" type="text/javascript">

function AsyncUpdateEvent(status, statusText, responseText, responseXML) {
    document.getElementById('httpcode').innerHTML = status;
    document.getElementById('httpstatus').innerHTML = statusText;
    document.getElementById('result').innerHTML = responseText;
    document.getElementById('xmlresult').innerHTML = responseXML;
}
```

```
function AsyncUpdateEvent2(status, statusText, responseText, responseXML) {
    document.getElementById('httpcode2').innerHTML = status;
    document.getElementById('httpstatus2').innerHTML = statusText;
    document.getElementById('result2').innerHTML = responseText;
    document.getElementById('xmlresult2').innerHTML = responseXML;
}

var asynchronous = new Asynchronous();
asynchronous.complete = AsyncUpdateEvent;
var asynchronous2 = new Asynchronous();
asynchronous2.complete = AsyncUpdateEvent2;

</script>
</head>
<body>
<button onclick="asynchronous.call('/chap02/serverhang.aspx')">
Get a document</button>
<button onclick="asynchronous2.call('/books/cgross')">
Get a document2</button>
<p><table border="1">
    <tr><td>Document</td>
        <td><span id="httpcode">No Http Code</span></td>
        <td><span id="httpstatus">No Http Status</span></td>
        <td><span id="result">No Result</span></td>
        <td><span id="xmlresult">No XML Result</span></td></tr>
    <tr><td>Document</td>
        <td><span id="httpcode2">No Http Code</span></td>
        <td><span id="httpstatus2">No Http Status</span></td>
        <td><span id="result2">No Result</span></td>
        <td><span id="xmlresult2">No XML Result</span></td></tr>
</table></p>
</body>
</html>
```

Going through the HTML code from the top to the bottom, near the top of the HTML code are three script tags. The first two reference the files factory.js and asynchronous.js. The file factory.js contains the XMLHttpRequest factory used for instantiation purposes. The file asynchronous.js is new and it contains the code to make asynchronous HTTP requests. For the moment, ignore the exact details of this file and just assume it is a black box that works. The last script tag contains the JavaScript code to update the HTML page.

In the JavaScript code are two functions: AsyncUpdateEvent and AsyncUpdateEvent2, which are similar but not identical. Each of the functions updates one of rows of the HTML table and is wired to be called when the HTTP request completes.

In the middle of the HTML code, near the end of the last script tag, is the instantiation of the variables asynchronous and asynchronous2. Each of these variables is of the type Asynchronous, which is a class that encapsulates the XMLHttpRequest asynchronous functionality. When the buttons call Asynchronous.call, an HTTP GET request is made. When the request completes, the Asynchronous class calls the functions AsyncUpdateEvent and AsyncUpdateEvent2 with the retrieved data. The Asynchronous class calls the functions because in the JavaScript code the functions are wired to Asynchronous via the property complete. In the example HTML code, instantiating two instances allows two simultaneous HTTP requests.

The Asynchronous Class

The Asynchronous class is a JavaScript class that encapsulates the XMLHttpRequest functionality. The user of a class is expected to assign specific properties to receive feedback on the status of a request. In the modified Ajax application, the property complete was assigned to the functions AsyncUpdateEvent and AsyncUpdateEvent2 to process the request's returned data.

Following is the implementation of the asynchronous.js file:

```
function Asynchronous( ) {
    this._xmlhttp = new FactoryXMLHttpRequest();
}

function Asynchronous_call(url) {
    var instance = this;
    this._xmlhttp.open('GET', url, true);
    this._xmlhttp.onreadystatechange = function() {
        switch(instance._xmlhttp.readyState) {
        case 1:
            instance.loading();
            break;
        case 2:
            instance.loaded();
            break;
        case 3:
            instance.interactive();
            break;
        case 4:
            instance.complete(instance._xmlhttp.status,
                instance._xmlhttp.statusText,
                instance._xmlhttp.responseText, instance._xmlhttp.responseXML);
            break;
        }
    }
    this._xmlhttp.send(null);
}
```

```
function Asynchronous_loading() {
}
function Asynchronous_loaded() {
}
function Asynchronous_interactive() {
}
function Asynchronous_complete(status, statusText, responseText, responseHTML) {
}

Asynchronous.prototype.loading = Asynchronous_loading;
Asynchronous.prototype.loaded = Asynchronous_loaded;
Asynchronous.prototype.interactive = Asynchronous_interactive;
Asynchronous.prototype.complete = Asynchronous_complete;

Asynchronous.prototype.call = Asynchronous_call;
```

To declare a class in JavaScript, you need to declare a function with the name of the class. The declared function is called a *constructor*. In the case of the class Asynchronous, you would declare a function with the identifier Asynchronous. When a class is instantiated by using the new keyword, the object instance is empty, or more simply put, it has no methods or properties.

You can define default properties and methods by using the prototype property. When using the prototype property, each defined method and property is shared by all instances of the type. For the class Asynchronous, there are four shared methods. The methods—loading, loaded, interactive, and complete, are called whenever the asynchronous request updates its status. For the default case, all the status methods do nothing and are placeholders so that no exceptions are generated. If the prototype property were not used and the methods were assigned in the constructor, each instance would have its own copy of a function.

When the Asynchronous class is instantiated, an object with five methods is created. To be able to reference the data of the object instance, the this keyword must be used. In the Asynchronous constructor, the data member _xmlhttp is assigned an instance of XMLHttpRequest by using the factory function FactoryXMLHttpRequest. This means that for every instantiated Asynchronous class, an instance of XMLHttpRequest is associated.

Cross-referencing the Asynchronous class with the HTML code, the class method complete is assigned to reference the methods AsyncUpdateEvent and AsyncUpdateEvent2. When an asynchronous request is finished, the property method complete is called, and it calls the functions AsyncUpdateEvent and AsyncUpdateEvent2. The client script uses the method call to execute an asynchronous request.

The Problem of Multiple Requests and Multiple Callbacks

Before I discuss the function Asynchronous_call, I need to explain the problem that Asynchronous_call solves. In the previous section, assigning the property onreadystatechange a function makes it possible to know when the result data is available. For the initial asynchronous XMLHttpRequest request example, the property onreadystatechange was assigned a global function. Now imagine that you want to create multiple requests. That would encompass creating multiple instances of XMLHttpRequest, where each instance was assigned its own function. A more efficient approach would be to use object-oriented principles and the this keyword.

Consider the following source code that seems correct, but will work incorrectly:

```
function AsyncUpdateEvent() {
    window.alert( "Who's calling (" + this.myState + ")");
}

function GetIt(xmlhttp, url) {
    if( xmlhttp) {
        xmlhttp.open('GET', url, true);
        xmlhttp.onreadystatechange = AsyncUpdateEvent;
        xmlhttp.send(null);
    }
}

var xmlhttp1 = FactoryXMLHttpRequest();
xmlhttp1.myState = "xmlhttp1";
var xmlhttp2 = FactoryXMLHttpRequest();
xmlhttp2.myState = "xmlhttp2";

GetIt(xmlhttp1, '/chap02/serverhang.aspx');
GetIt(xmlhttp2, '/books/cgross');
```

The functions GetIt and AsyncUpdateEvent are like previous examples in which asynchronous function calls were made. New to the function GetIt is the additional parameter xmlhttp. This was added so that multiple XMLHttpRequest instances could be used with GetIt. The variables xmlhttp1 and xmlhttp2 represent two different instances of XMLHttpRequest, and assigned to each instance is the data member myState. To make two separate HTTP requests, GetIt is called twice with different XMLHttpRequest instances and different URLs.

When the asynchronous XMLHttpRequest returns, the function AsyncUpdateEvent is called. The function AsyncUpdateEvent is assigned to the instance of either xmlhttp1 or xmlhttp2, and therefore in the implementation of the function, the this keyword should work. What happens is that the this.myState reference in the function is undefined, and therefore AsyncUpdateEvent has no idea to which XMLHttpRequest instance it is assigned.

A solution would be to create two callback functions, AsyncUpdateEvent and AsyncUpdateEvent2, and assign them individually to the instances xmlhttp1 and xmlhttp2. The function GetIt would be updated to include an additional parameter that represents the callback where the request results are processed. Creating two callback functions would work but is not elegant because for three independent requests you would need three callbacks. The real context of this problem is that JavaScript in this instance has lost its object-oriented features. What needs to be solved is the association of an XMLHttpRequest instance with a callback, and that is solved in the next section.

The Magic of the Asynchronous Class

Let's focus on how the Asynchronous class solves the instance and callback problem. The specific code is illustrated again as follows:

```
function Asynchronous_call(url) {
    var instance = this;
    this._xmlhttp.open('GET', url, true);
    this._xmlhttp.onreadystatechange = function() {
        switch(instance._xmlhttp.readyState) {
        case 1:
            instance.loading();
            break;
        case 2:
            instance.loaded();
            break;
        case 3:
            instance.interactive();
            break;
        case 4:
            instance.complete(instance._xmlhttp.status,
                instance._xmlhttp.statusText,
                instance._xmlhttp.responseText, instance._xmlhttp.responseXML);
            break;
        }
    }
    this._xmlhttp.send(null);
}
```

Asynchronous_call is associated with an instance of Asynchronous because of the prototype definition. Then when the HTML code calls asynchronous.call, the function Asynchronous_call is called and the this instance references the instantiated class. The variable this.xmlhttp is an instance of XMLHttpRequest, and the property onreadystatechange needs to be assigned a function. There is a peculiarity with JavaScript in that if a property is assigned the value of this.somefunction, then what is assigned is a function and not a function associated with a class instance, as was shown by the code that looked like it would work, but didn't.

When the method Asynchronous_call is called, the this variable references an instance of Asynchronous. What is happening is that JavaScript is associating a function with an instance. Logically then, if the property onreadystatechange were assigning a function associated with an instance of Asynchronous, then when a callback is made, the this variable should reference an instance of Asynchronous. Figure 2-7 shows that there is no reference to an instance of Asynchronous.

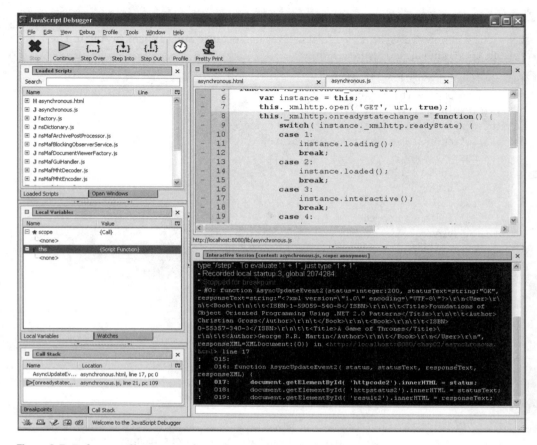

Figure 2-7. *Debugger illustrating that a function does not reference a class instance*

The debugger shown in Figure 2-7 is distributed with Mozilla, and in the middle window on the left side is a reference to the this variable. The watch window illustrates that this does not reference an instance and is a plain, simple ScriptFunction. This means that even though the original function was associated with an instance of Asynchronous, when used as a callback the reference disappears.

A solution would be to cross-reference a request with an Asynchronous instance that is stored in an array that is accessed to identify the request. Such a solution is complicated and relies on some global array.

The solution is not a complex cross-referencing algorithm, but the use of a unique implementation detail of JavaScript. Look back at the implementation of Asynchronous_call, illustrated briefly as follows:

```
function Asynchronous_call(url) {
    var instance = this;
    this._xmlhttp.open('GET', url, true);
    this._xmlhttp.onreadystatechange = function() {
        switch(instance._xmlhttp.readyState) {
```

First, the `this` variable is assigned to the `instance` variable The assignment is important because it is a variable that is managed by JavaScript. Second, the property `onreadystatechange` is assigned a dynamic anonymous function. An anonymous function is a function without an identifier, which contains only a signature and implementation. Using an anonymous function in the context of a function allows the referencing of variables in the anonymous function that were defined in the function itself. This means the variable `instance` is available for referencing in the anonymous function. What makes this feature a big deal is that when the anonymous function is called, the caller of `Asynchronous_call` will already have exited the function and be doing something else. The reason the local variable `instance` is still available is because JavaScript sees a reference and does not garbage-collect it until the `this_xmlhttp` instance is garbage-collected.

Putting all of this together in the HTML code, the `Asynchronous` property `complete` is assigned the functions `AsyncUpdateEvent` and `AsyncUpdateEvent2`. Whenever any of these functions are called, the `this` references a valid instance of `Asynchronous`. Then the code that was referencing `myState`, which should have worked, would work. Looking at the HTML code, you can see that the `AsyncUpdateEvent` `this` references the variable `asynchronous`, and `AsyncUpdateEvent2` `this` references the variable `asynchronous2`. Figure 2-8 shows the proof that the `this` variable is assigned.

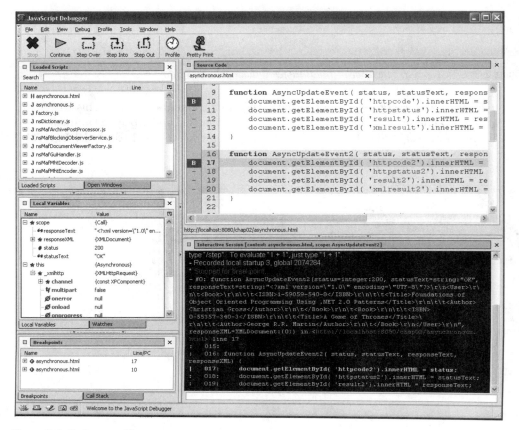

Figure 2-8. *Debugger illustrating that a function does reference a class instance*

In Figure 2-8 the debugger shows that `this` references an instance of `Asynchronous`. In the example HTML code, the methods `AsyncUpdateEvent` and `AsyncUpdateEvent2` do not use the `this` variable, but they could.

Now you're ready to put it all together and execute the HTML code. Click the Get a Document button and then click the Get a Document2 button. The HTML page in Figure 2-9 is generated.

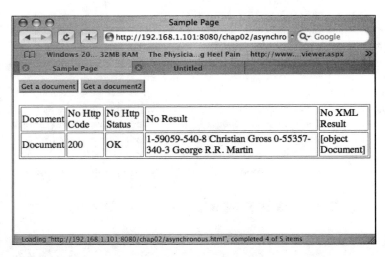

Figure 2-9. *HTML page state after immediate feedback of the second row*

In Figure 2-9 the second row contains data, whereas the first row does not. This is because the second row references a static document that is downloaded and processed immediately. The first row is not yet filled out because there is a 10-second delay. After 10 seconds, the HTML page appears similar to Figure 2-10.

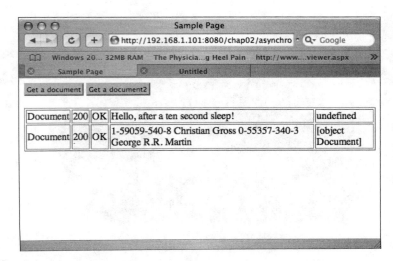

Figure 2-10. *HTML page state after all requests are finished*

In Figure 2-10 the page is in its final state with both rows containing data. The processing occurred at different times, and the two requests ran concurrently. Using the defined Asynchronous class, multiple requests could be running at the same time.

Providing Feedback from Asynchronous Requests

When an HTML page makes an asynchronous request, the request will return immediately and the JavaScript will not know whether the request worked. Right after making the call, the JavaScript has to assume that the HTTP request worked. The feedback from the server to the JavaScript is a *callback*. Between the call and callback, 1 second, 10 seconds, or 3 minutes could transpire. If 3 minutes pass, the user will become impatient as nothing will be happening on the HTML page. If there is no feedback whatsoever, people get nervous and think something went wrong and will press the button again. This is why it is important to provide some form of feedback.

To provide feedback, a timer is used. The timer periodically checks the state of the HTTP request by querying the readyState property. While the user is waiting, a turning hour clock is generated or progress bar incremented. How you provide the feedback is up to you, but to provide feedback you will need a timer.

One-Shot Timers

A *one-shot timer* in JavaScript counts down a period of time and then executes some JavaScript. There is no repetition when using a one-shot timer. A one-shot timer is implemented by using the following HTML code:

```
<html>
<head>
<title>Sample Page</title>
<script language="JavaScript" type="text/javascript">
var counter = 0;

function StartIt() {
    document.getElementById('result').innerHTML = "(" + counter + ")";
    counter ++;
    if( counter <= 10) {
        window.setTimeout("StartIt()", 1000);
    }
}

</script>
</head>
<body>
<button onclick="StartIt()">One Shot Counter</button>
<p><table border="1">
    <tr><td>Counter</td><td><span id="result">No Result</span></td></tr>
</table></p>
</body>
</html>
```

In the example HTML code, there is a button that when pressed calls the function StartIt. The function StartIt generates output in the HTML code of the variable counter. The *variable counter* is a counter that is incremented. To start the timer, the method window.setTimeout needs to be called. The method setTimeout starts a one-time timer that executes the JavaScript represented by the first parameter. The second parameter represents the number of milliseconds that should pass before the JavaScript is executed. It is important to realize that the JavaScript executed is a text-based script and should not reference variables that are not in scope.

To generate a repeating timer, the JavaScript calls the function StartIt. Then for each time-out (1 second), the timer countdown is started again. The timer is not started after the counter has reached a value of 10.

Periodic Timers

The other type of timer is a *periodic timer* that executes every *n* milliseconds. Using a periodic timer in JavaScript is similar to using a one-shot timer except the method call is different. Following is the HTML code used to run a periodic timer:

```
<html>
<head>
<title>Sample Page</title>
<script language="JavaScript" type="text/javascript">
var intervalId;
var counter2 = 0;

function NeverEnding(input) {
    document.getElementById('result').innerHTML =
        "(" + input + ")(" + counter2 + ")";
    counter2 ++;
    if( counter2 > 10) {
        window.clearInterval(intervalId);
    }
}

function StartItNonEnding() {
    intervalId = window.setInterval(NeverEnding, 1000, 10);
}

</script>
</head>
<body>
<button onclick="StartItNonEnding()">Get a document</button>
<p><table border="1">
    <tr><td>Counter</td><td><span id="result">No Result</span></td></tr>
</table></p>
</body>
</html>
```

In this example, the button calls the function StartItNonEnding. In the function StartItNonEnding, there is a single method call, window.setInterval. The method setInterval has multiple variations, and a valid variation is like setTimeout illustrated previously. The variation illustrated in the HTML code uses three parameters, even though only two are necessary. The first parameter is a reference to a function that is called for each periodic event. The second parameter is the length of the period. And the third parameter is an argument that is passed to the function NeverEnding. The third parameter does not work in Internet Explorer, but works on other browsers such as Firefox and Safari.

As in the one-shot timer, the timer output is inserted into the HTML document. The counter is incremented for each call to the function NeverEnding. What is different is that NeverEnding has a parameter that can be used to uniquely identify an instance of the timer. To stop a periodic timer, the method clearInterval is used. The parameter for clearInterval is the value of the instantiated timer that is returned when calling the method setInterval.

After running the HTML code, the generated output is similar to Figure 2-11. The value 10 in the lower-right corner of the HTML table is the value passed to the function NeverEnding. The 0 value is the counter.

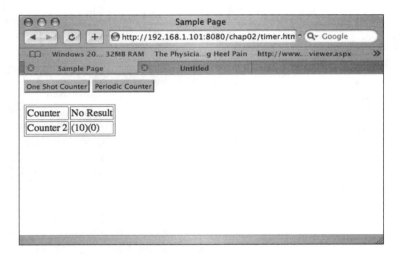

Figure 2-11. *Generated HTML document*

Calling Domains Other Than the Serving Domain

When an HTML page is downloaded from one domain, the XMLHttpRequest object can download content only from that domain. So if the page is downloaded from devspace.com, content can be downloaded only from devspace.com. Attempting to download content from another domain will generate an error similar to that in Figure 2-12—regardless of the browser.

The error is permission related and is a consequence of the same origin policy, and not a programmatic error. A permission error indicates that something is being attempted that may be possible under different circumstances. The error is used to prevent the cross-site scripting vulnerability. What needs to be modified are the permissions on the browser.

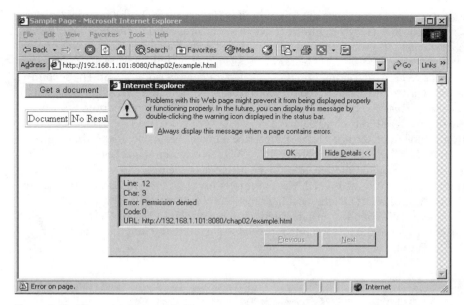

Figure 2-12. *Generated error after attempting to load content from another domain*

Before learning how to change permissions to get around the same origin policy, you need to understand what the policy is. Let's say that I retrieve a document from the server `http://localhost:8080/chap02/factory.html`. The same origin policy states that only requests to the same origin can be retrieved. The defined origin is the protocol `http`, and the host `localhost` with the port 8080. If any of these values change, any document that is referenced will result in a permission exception. The file `http://localhost:8080/rest/cgross/books.xml` could be downloaded. The same origin policy exists so that other sites cannot be referenced, as many hackers have used the technique for their malware.

Apple Safari

Using the Apple Safari browser is a problem in that there is no way to get around the same origin policy. The browser does not have any preferences that can be used to assign trust to a site or web page. Nor is it possible to sign an HTML page to allow cross-domain HTTP requests, or at least that was the status at the time of this writing.

Microsoft Internet Explorer

Microsoft Internet Explorer is one of the two browsers mentioned in this book that allow cross-domain HTTP requests if the permission has been granted. Internet Explorer grants permissions only if the site has been assigned as trusted. An algorithm is implemented so that trusted sites do not apply the Same Origin Policy.

So, for example, to set the site http://192.168.1.101:8080 as trusted, you would use the following steps:

1. Open Microsoft Internet Explorer and from the menu select Tools ➤ Internet Options. A dialog box similar to Figure 2-13 is generated.

Figure 2-13. *Internet Options dialog box used to define a trusted site*

2. Select the Security tab and then the Trusted Sites icon, resulting in a dialog box similar to Figure 2-14.

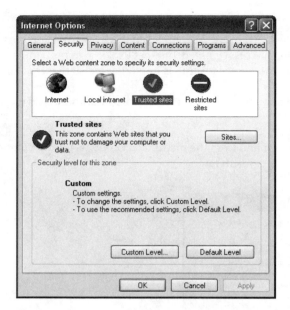

Figure 2-14. *Security tab and Trusted Sites icon selected*

3. Click the Sites button, and the dialog box changes, as shown in Figure 2-15.

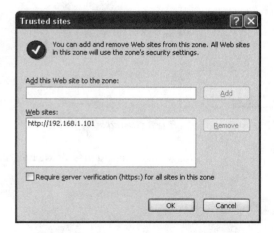

Figure 2-15. *Dialog box used to define a trusted site*

4. In the text box, add the website http://192.168.1.101 and click the Add button. Remember to deselect the check box labeled Require Server Verification. The added site will include all ports and is not necessary to specify.

After adding the trusted site, you can perform a cross-domain call, as illustrated in Figure 2-16.

Figure 2-16. *Cross-domain HTTP request that retrieves* http://www.cnn.com

Mozilla Firefox

Mozilla Firefox does not have any dialog boxes for defining a site as trusted. There are two solutions to enable cross-domain HTTP requests. The first is to use signed HTML pages,[5] which is beyond the scope of this book. The second solution is a programmatic solution that will be illustrated.

Documented at many locations is use of the security manager, as illustrated by the following source code:

```
netscape.security.PrivilegeManager.enablePrivilege('UniversalBrowserRead');
```

---

5. http://www.mozilla.org/projects/security/components/jssec.html

Using this line enables cross-domain calls. Yet if you were to run this JavaScript code, you would get a security failure because an additional security item has to be enabled. The security item could be added to the file [Mozilla or Firefox installation]\defaults\pref\ browser-pref.js, or the user's prefs.js file. The security item is defined as follows:

```
pref("signed.applets.codebase_principal_support", true);
```

The security item enables a set of security descriptors, where one item includes the same origin policy descriptors.

Then, calling the netscape.se... method from a JavaScript file results in a security warning as illustrated in Figure 2-17.

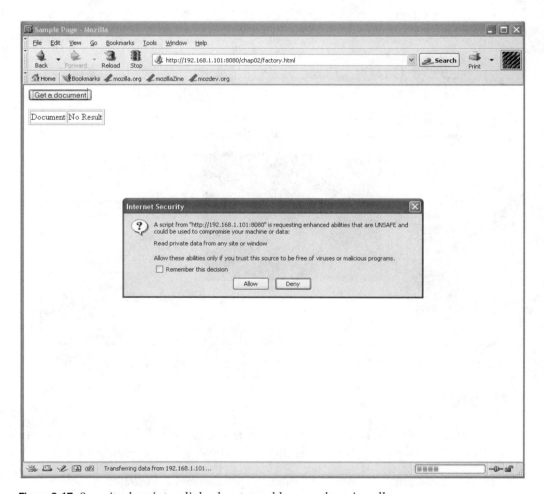

Figure 2-17. *Security descriptor dialog box to enable cross-domain calls*

The user can click the Allow button of the dialog box for each time the method netscape.se... is called on the HTML page. Or the user can select the Remember This Decision check box to enable an automatic acceptance of the security policy. After the policy has been accepted, calling the XMLHttpRequest.open method with a cross-domain URL will download the contents. There is a catch in that the security descriptors are enabled only in the function where the security call is made. This means you cannot define a function to call the security descriptors, and another function to make the cross-domain call. Both calls need to be in the same function.

Having fulfilled all requirements, the content can be downloaded as in Internet Explorer and is illustrated in Figure 2-18.

Figure 2-18. *Cross-domain request that downloads* http://www.cnn.com

Some Final Thoughts

The mechanics of the XMLHttpRequest type are simple, but the ramifications are not. When using XMLHttpRequest, you should keep three points in mind: use a Factory pattern to enable cross-browser support, use asynchronous requests to avoid browser lockup, and enable security to allow cross-domain calls.

Using a Factory pattern is obvious and necessary, but some may balk at using asynchronous requests because it means reacting to events. Asynchronous programming when done improperly can result in an erratically behaving Ajax application. However, I tend to think that because we are already used to writing event-driven GUI code, most people will not have any problems.

The security issue is a bigger concern. When learning about how to circumvent a security measure, administrators may become nervous. This is not because they are worried about the security, but worried that many problems relating to security are often related to the Internet. Hence, getting an administrator to play along might become difficult. A solution is using the REST-Based Model View Controller pattern, described in Chapter 11.

Overall the purpose of this chapter was to introduce the nuts and bolts of an Ajax application and the `XMLHttpRequest` type. You can build on this basic knowledge to create more-complicated applications.

CHAPTER 3

■ ■ ■

Content Chunking Pattern

Intent

The Content Chunking pattern makes it possible to incrementally build an HTML page, thereby allowing the logic of an individual HTML page to be distributed and the user to decide the time and logic of the content that is loaded.

Motivation

Originally, when the Web was in its infancy, HTML content designers created documents that were incomplete. The incomplete pages were made complete by using document links. The completeness of a document was the sum of the pages in the document tree.

Think of it as follows: instead of creating a book in which you follow through the content in a sequential manner, for the Web you would paste materials together like a bunch of magazine articles. But unlike a magazine that required you to go through one page after another, the Web allowed you to click a link and jump to different content. As time passed, websites moved away from this distributed web structure to a strictly hierarchical self-contained structure.

An example of a strictly hierarchical self-contained website is illustrated in Figure 3-1.

In Figure 3-1, the website is split into two areas: blue-background navigation and brown-background content. When a user clicks on a navigational link, the content is changed. But the problem is that the entire page is reloaded even though the user is only interested in the brown-background content. One way to get around this problem is to use HTML frames so that the navigational area is one frame, and the content area is another frame. When a link in the navigational area is clicked, only the frame containing the content is altered. However, as time has shown, although frames solve the problem of loading content individually, they are problematic from a navigational and user interface perspective. Thus websites have used fewer and fewer frames.

Ideally, what a website developer wants is the ability to alter the content that needs to be altered and to leave the rest of the content as is. After all, untouched content is content that stays the same and works.

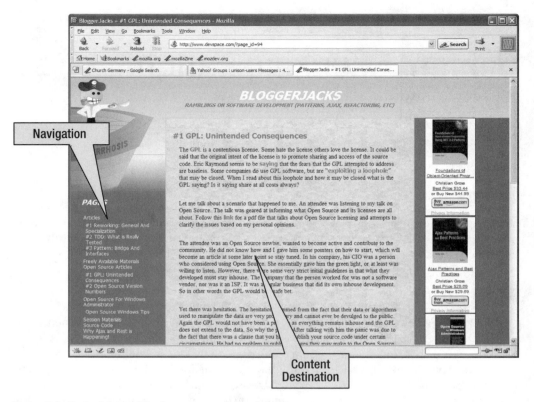

Figure 3-1. *Strict hierarchical structure of a website*

Applicability

Use the Content Chunking pattern in the following contexts:

- When it is not known what the HTML page should look like because of the nature of the website. In Figure 3-1, there is a blue-background navigational area and a brown-background content area. The content of each area is unknown, but what is known is the area where the content is destined.

- When the content to be downloaded is too large and would cause an excessive wait for the user. For example, doing a search and waiting for all found elements to be collected as a result set is not an option because the user would have to wait too long. A better approach would be to keep a search executing while displaying whatever is found.

- When the displayed content is not related. Yahoo!, MSN, and Excite are portal applications displaying content side-by-side with other content that has no relation to it. If the content is generated from a single HTML page, the server-side logic would have to contain a huge decision block to know which content is loaded and not loaded. A better approach would be to consider each block of content as a separate piece that is then loaded separately.

Associated Patterns

The Content Chunking pattern is a core pattern to any Ajax application. You could even make the assertion that the Content Chunking pattern is implicit to Ajax. Be that as it may, it is still necessary to identify and define the context of the Content Chunking pattern. What makes the Content Chunking pattern unique is that it always follows the same steps: generated event, request, response, and chunk injection. The other patterns covered in this book are similar, but do take deviations such as sending a request and not getting an immediate response (for example, the Persistent Communications pattern).

Architecture

The architecture of the Content Chunking pattern is relatively simple. A URL is called by the client. The server responds with some content that is received and processed by the client. An implementation of the Content Chunking pattern always follows these steps:

1. An event is generated that could be the result of a button being clicked or of an HTML page being loaded.

2. The event calls a function that is responsible for creating a URL used to send a request to the server.

3. The server receives the request and associates the request with some content. The content is sent to the client as a response.

4. The client receives the response and injects the response in an area of the HTML page.

Implementing Order in a Web Application

Looking back at Figure 3-1, the strict hierarchical nature of the website is not a bad thing. With respect to HTML, the result of the strictness is to generate the content in one step, and this all-in-one generation causes problems. Traditional applications do not function in such a manner, as illustrated in Figure 3-2.

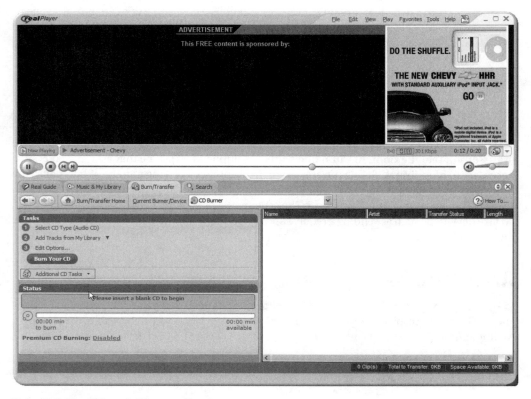

Figure 3-2. *Traditional client application*

In Figure 3-2, the RealPlayer is an example of a traditional client application that mixes newer HTML-type technologies with traditional user interface elements. Clicking the Burn Your CD button causes RealPlayer to burn your CD but does not affect the advertisement that is running at the top half of the application. The logic associated with the advertisement and the logic associated with burning the CD are two separate, distinct pieces of logic that happen to be sharing the same window area.

Figure 3-3 dissects the web application of Figure 3-1 into distinct pieces of logic.

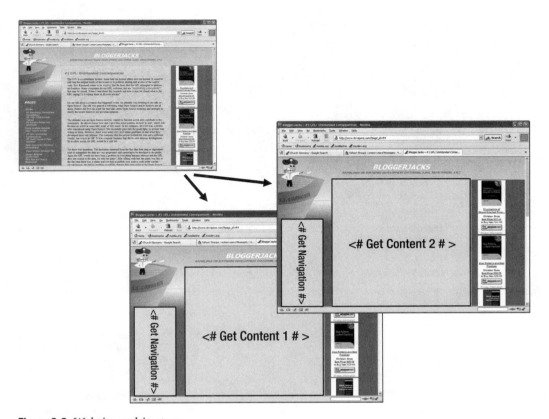

Figure 3-3. *Website architecture*

In Figure 3-3, the original HTML page has links to two other pages that represent an example blog and article content. The example content has two execution blocks: Get Navigation and Get Content (1,2). The logic used to generate Get Content 1 is distinct from the logic used to generate Get Content 2. In the context of generating an HTML page, when either Get Content 1 or Get Content 2 is executed, the logic Get Navigation is executed. This means the logic Get Navigation is executed multiple times, generating the same data each time. Some readers might argue that different data is generated by Get Navigation (e.g., different folders are opened), but in fact it is the same data formatted a different way. In a nutshell, there is an inherent data-generation redundancy that should be avoided.

The solution is to distribute the logic so that an HTML page is generated, by using an architecture similar to Figure 3-4.

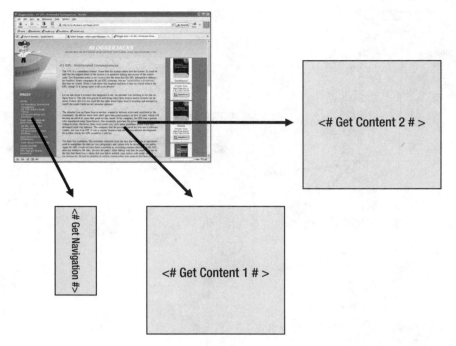

Figure 3-4. *Improved website architecture*

In Figure 3-4, the HTML page is the result of multiple pieces of server-side logic. When the main outline of the HTML page has been loaded, the XMLHttpRequest object retrieves the content blocks Get Navigation, Get Content 1, and Get Content 2. When and how the individual content blocks are retrieved depends on the events and links created by the content blocks. Each content block is a separate request that needs to be called by the XMLHttpRequest type.

The proposed architecture has the following advantages:

- The client downloads only what is necessary, when it is necessary. There is no need to re-retrieve a content block unless necessary.

- The architecture is separated into different code blocks that can be assembled dynamically in different contexts.

- The architecture resembles that of a traditional client in that only those elements that pertain to the event are manipulated.

- The overall look and feel is not affected because the generated code blocks delegate the look and feel to the parent HTML page retrieving the content blocks.

Figure 3-4 shows how the Content Chunking pattern got its name: a single HTML page is the sum of its chunks of content, which are referenced and loaded separately.

Defining the Content Within a Content Chunk

The content chunks referenced by the `XMLHttpRequest` object can be in any form that both the client and server can understand. Whatever the server sends must be understood by the client. In Figure 3-4, the content chunks would be in HTML because the chunks would be injected directly into the HTML page. HTML, though, is not the only format that can be sent to and from the server.

The following formats are covered in this chapter:

- *HTML:* The server can send HTML to the client directly. The received HTML would not be processed, but injected directly into the HTML page. This is a blind processing approach in that the client has no idea what the HTML does, and knows only that it should be injected into a certain area of the HTML document. Injecting HTML directly is a very simple and foolproof way of building content. The client has to do no processing and needs to know only the destination area of the HTML content. If processing is necessary, the received content (if it is XML compliant) would also be available as an instantiated object model. Using the instantiated object model, it is possible to manually manipulate the received HTML content. It is advised that the HTML content sent to the client be XHTML compliant (HTML that implements a particular XML schema) or at least XML compliant.

- *Images:* It is not possible to directly send images because images are binary, and the `XMLHttpRequest` object cannot process binary data. Typically, image references are sent as HTML tags that are injected into the HTML document, resulting in the remote image to be loaded. It is possible to download and reference binary data if the data has been encoded and decoded by using Base64 encoding. However, manipulating binary data directly is not recommended because that will create more problems than it solves.

- *JavaScript:* The server can send JavaScript to the client that can be executed by using the JavaScript `eval` statement, and the client can send persisted JavaScript objects to the server for further processing. A first impression may be that executing arbitrary JavaScript presents a security problem. It is not typically a problem because the JavaScript engines in all browsers use the same origin and sandbox policies. Sending arbitrary JavaScript to execute could be a security problem if there is a bug in the JavaScript engine. Sending JavaScript is desirable if you want to dynamically execute and add logic on the client that was not loaded when the initial HTML page was loaded. It is a very powerful method of enhancing the functionality of a client without the client having to be aware of that. For example, let's say an HTML form element needs validation. Because different users have different validations, it would not be desirable to send all validation implementations to the client. A solution would be to let the user decide which HTML form element they are presented with, and then dynamically download the validation of the form element as a content chunk. Be forewarned, though, that sending JavaScript chunks could open up your application to hackers. So think before using this technique.

- *XML:* The preferred approach is to send and receive XML. The XML can be transformed or parsed on the client side by manipulating the XML object model, or an Extensible Stylesheet Language Transformations (XSLT) library can be used to transform the XML into another object model such as HTML. The reason XML is preferred is that XML is a known technology and the tools to manipulate XML are well defined, working, and stable. XML is a very well established technology that you can search, slice, dice, persist, and validate without having to write extra code. Some do consider XML heavy because of the angle brackets and other XML character tokens. The advantage, though, is that when a server-side application generates XML, it can be processed by a web-browser-based client or a non-GUI-based browser. The choice of how to parse the XML and what information to process depends entirely on the client, so long as the client knows how to parse XML. XML is flexible and should be used. Throughout this book, XML will be used extensively and is considered the premier data exchange format.

There are other data exchange formats, such as JavaScript Object Notation (JSON).[1] However, I advise when those formats are chosen that you carefully consider the ramifications. It is not that I find them badly designed or improper. What concerns me about these other data exchange formats is that they do not provide as extensive an environment as XML for processing, searching, validating, and generating. For example, using XPath I search for specific elements in XML without having to parse the entire XML document. Granted, XML might in certain conditions not have the same performance levels as, let's say, JSON. For those readers who do not care whatsoever for the diversity of XML and are sure that they will never need it, JSON might be the right technology. However, I do not cover other technologies such as JSON in the scope of this pattern or in the rest of the book.

Now that you understand the architecture, you're ready to see some implementations that demonstrate how that architecture is realized.

Implementation

When implementing the Content Chunking pattern, the sequence of steps outlined earlier needs to be followed (event, request, response, and injection). The logic is easily implemented by using the Asynchronous type, because the Asynchronous type can be called by an HTML event and there is an explicit response method implementation. The example implementations that follow will illustrate how to generate the events by using HTML, call the functions, generate requests by using XMLHttpRequest, and process responses by using Dynamic HTML and JavaScript techniques.

Implementing the HTML Framework Page

The implementation of the Content Chunking pattern requires creating an HTML page that serves as the framework. The idea behind the framework page is to provide the structure into which content can be chunked. The framework page is the controller and provides a minimal amount of content.

The following HTML code is an example HTML framework page that will dynamically inject HTML content into a specific area on the HTML page:

---

1. http://www.crockford.com/JSON/index.html

```html
<html>
<head>
<title>Document Chunk HTML</title>
<script language="JavaScript" src="/lib/factory.js"></script>
<script language="JavaScript" src="/lib/asynchronous.js"></script>
<script language="JavaScript" type="text/javascript">
var asynchronous = new Asynchronous();
asynchronous.complete = function(status, statusText, responseText, responseXML) {
    document.getElementById("insertplace").innerHTML = responseText;
}
</script>
</head>
<body onload="asynchronous.call('/chap03/chunkhtml01.html')">
<table>
    <tr><td id="insertplace">Nothing</td></tr>
</table>
</body>
</html>
```

In the HTML code, the class Asynchronous is instantiated and the asynchronous.complete property is assigned a function callback. How the Asynchronous class works and which properties need to be assigned was discussed in Chapter 2. The instantiation of asynchronous occurs as the HTML page is loading. After the page has loaded and is complete, the event onload is executed—which is the event step of the pattern implementation. The onload event calls the asynchronous.call method to execute an XMLHttpRequest request to download an HTML chunk—which is the request step of the pattern implementation.

After the request has completed, a response is generated that when received by the client results in the method asynchronous.complete being called. The received response is the response step of the pattern implementation. In the example, the method asynchronous.complete is assigned an anonymous JavaScript function. In the implementation of the anonymous function, the method getElementById is called to insert the XMLHttpRequest results into an HTML element. The HTML element is located by the identifier insertplace, which happens to be the HTML tag td. The referencing of the Dynamic HTML element and its assignment using the innerHTML property is the HTML injection—which represents the injection step of the pattern implementation.

In the example, it is odd that after the HTML page is downloaded, processed, and considered complete, another piece of logic is called. The other piece of logic is used to retrieve the rest of the content in the form of a chunk. The server-side code could have generated the complete page in the first place. However, it was illustrated in this fashion to show how simple the implementation of the Content Chunking pattern can be. The example illustrated reacting to the onload page event, but any event could be used. For example, examples in Chapter 2 used the button onclick event. A script could even simulate events by using the Click() method.

This example illustrated separation of the HTML page's appearance from its logic. The framework HTML page could be realized by an HTML designer. For the area where content is injected, the HTML designer would need only to add a placeholder token identifier such as Nothing. A server-side web application programmer creates the generated content that replaces the placeholder. The HTML designer would not need to be concerned with any server programming technology because the framework HTML page would contain only client-side instructions.

The server-side web application programmer would not need to be concerned with the look of the HTML page, because the generated content does not contain any information that affects the look and feel. For testing purposes, the web application programmer focuses on logic, whereas the HTML designer focuses on look and workflow.

Injecting Content by Using Dynamic HTML

The magic of the example is the ability of Dynamic HTML to dynamically insert content in a specific location. Before Dynamic HTML, you would have to use frames or server-side logic to combine the multiple streams. In recent years, Dynamic HTML has been formally defined by the World Wide Web Consortium (W3C) in the form of the HTML Document Object Model (DOM). The W3C HTML Document Object Model is not as feature rich as the object models made available by Microsoft Internet Explorer and Mozilla-derived browsers. For the scope of this book, the object model used is a mixture of the W3C HTML Document Object Model and functionality that is available to most browsers (for example, Mozilla-derived browsers and Microsoft Internet Explorer).

Going back to the previous example, the attribute id uniquely identifies an element in the HTML page. Using the uniquely identified element, a starting point is described from where it is possible to navigate and manipulate the HTML object model. The other way to find a starting point is to explicitly retrieve a type of tag and then find the HTML element that provides the starting point. Regardless of which approach is used, one of these two ways must be used to retrieve a starting point. Some readers may say that you could use other properties or methods, but those properties and methods are considered non-HTML-DOM compliant and hence should be avoided.

The following HTML code illustrates how to find a starting point using the two approaches:

```
<html>
<head>
<title>Document Chunk HTML</title>
<script language="JavaScript" src="/lib/factory.js"></script>
<script language="JavaScript" src="/lib/asynchronous.js"></script>
<script language="JavaScript" type="text/javascript">
var asynchronous = new Asynchronous();
asynchronous.complete = function(status, statusText,
    responseText, responseXML) {
    document.getElementsByTagName("table")[ 0].rows[ 0].cells[ 0].innerHTML
        = responseText;
    document.getElementById("insertplace").innerHTML = responseText;
}
</script>
</head>
<body onload="asynchronous.call('/chap03/chunkhtml01.html')">
<table>
    <tr><td>Nothing</td></tr>
    <tr><td id="insertplace">Nothing</td></tr>
</table>
</body>
</html>
```

In the implementation of the anonymous function for the `asynchronous.complete` method, two methods (`getElementsByTagName`, `getElementById`) are used to inject content into a Dynamic HTML element. The two methods retrieve an element(s) that represents a starting point.

The method `getElementsByTagName` retrieves all HTML elements of the type specified by the parameter to the method. In the example, the parameter is `table`, which indicates to search and retrieve all `table` elements in the HTML document. Returned is an instance of `HTMLCollection` of all HTML elements, and in the case of the example contains all of the `table` elements. The class `HTMLCollection` has a property, `length`, that indicates how elements have been found. The found elements can be referenced by using the JavaScript array notation (square brackets), where the first element is the zeroth index.

In the example, right after the method identifier `getElementsByTagName("table")` is a set of square brackets (`[0]`) used to retrieve the first element from the collection. The zeroth index is arbitrarily referenced, meaning the first found table is referenced. In the example, some index was used. The correct index is referenced because the example HTML page only has a single table; therefore, the zeroth index will always be the correct index, meaning that the correct table, row, and cell are referenced. However, imagine a scenario of multiple tables. Then, referencing an arbitrary index may or may not retrieve the correct table. Even worse, if the Content Chunking pattern were called multiple times, the order of the found element collection could change and reference elements that were not intended to be referenced.

The method `getElementsByTagName` is best used when operations are executed on all found elements without trying to identify individual elements. Examples of such operations include the addition of a column in a table and modification of a style. The method `getElementById` is best used when an individual element needs to be manipulated.

It is possible when using the method `getElementsByTag` to retrieve all elements in the HTML document, as illustrated in the following example:

```
var collection = document.getElementsByTag("*");
```

When the method `getElementsByTag` is called with an asterisk parameter, it means to return all elements of the HTML document. Some may note that using the property `document.all` does the exact same thing. Although this is true, it is not DOM compliant and will generate a warning by any Mozilla-based browser.

Focusing on the following code from the example:

```
document.getElementsByTagName("table")[ 0].rows[ 0].cells[ 0].innerHTML
```

The identifiers after the square brackets of the method `getElementsByTagName` represent a series of properties and methods that are called. These properties and methods relate directly to the object retrieved, which in this case is a table that contains rows, and the rows contain cells. Had the retrieved element not been a table, the calling of the properties and methods would have resulted in an error.

Again from the example source code, let's focus on the following:

```
document.getElementById("insertplace").innerHTML = responseText;
```

The method `getElementById` retrieves an HTML element with an `id` attribute identical to the parameter of the method. The `id` attribute and parameter are case-sensitive. The result of the method `getElementById` is to retrieve the `td` tag with the `id` attribute value `insertplace`. When using the method `getElementById`, if there are multiple items with the same identifier on the HTML page, then only the first found element is retrieved. The other elements are not returned nor accessible because the method getElementById returns only a single HTML element instance. Unlike the getElementsByTagName method, the returned element is not guaranteed to be a certain type other than having the parameter identifier equal to the id attribute. As a result, the object model referenced after the getElementById method may or may not apply to the found element. In the case of the property innerHTML, that is not a problem because virtually all visible elements have the innerHTML property. What could be more problematic is if the identifier assumed the retrieved element were a table when in fact the element is a table cell. At that point, the object model referencing would result in an exception.

When writing JavaScript code that dynamically retrieves an HTML element(s), it is a good idea to test the found element before manipulating it. As a rule of thumb, when using getElementsByTag, you know what the HTML elements are but do not know where they are or what they represent. When using getElementById, you know what the found HTML element represents and where it is, but do not know the type and hence the object hierarchy.

Understanding the Special Nature of innerHTML

The property innerHTML is special in that it seems simple to use but can have devastating consequences. To illustrate the problem, consider the following HTML code:

```html
<html>
<head>
<title>Document Chunk HTML</title>
<script language="JavaScript" type="text/javascript">
function GoodReplace() {
    document.getElementById("mycell").innerHTML = "hello";
}
function BadReplace() {
    document.getElementById("mytable").innerHTML = "hello";
}
function TestTable() {
    window.alert(document.getElementsByTagName(
        "table")[ 0].rows[ 0].cells[ 0].innerHTML);
}
</script>
</head>
<body>
<button onclick="GoodReplace()">GoodReplace</button>
<button onclick="BadReplace()">BadReplace</button>
<button onclick="TestTable()">TestTable</button>
<table id="mytable" border="1">
    <tr id="myrow"><td id="mycell">Nothing</td><td>Second cell</td></tr>
</table>
</body>
</html>
```

In this example, there are three buttons (GoodReplace, BadReplace, and TestTable), and the HTML elements table, table row, and row cell have added identifiers. The GoodReplace button will perform a legal HTML injection. The BadReplace button will perform an illegal HTML injection. And the TestTable button is used to test the validity of an object model. The TestTable button is used as a way of verifying the result of the HTML injection performed by either GoodReplace or BadReplace. Downloading the HTML page and presenting it in the browser results in something similar to Figure 3-5.

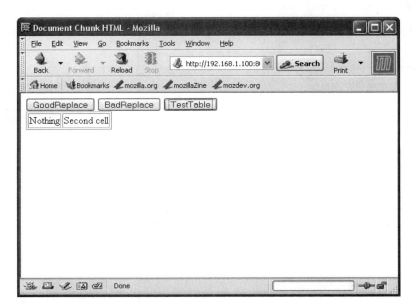

Figure 3-5. *Initial generation of the HTML page*

To check that the HTML page is in a valid state, the button TestTable is clicked. Clicking the button calls the function TestTable, which tests whether the content within a table cell exists by outputting the content in a dialog box. The generated output appears similar to Figure 3-6.

The dialog box in Figure 3-6 confirms that the table cell contains the value Nothing. This means our HTML page is in a stable state. If the GoodReplace button is clicked, the function GoodReplace is called, which changes the table cell contents from Nothing to Hello. To verify that the HTML page is still valid, the TestTable button is clicked. If the HTML page is valid, a dialog with the text Hello should appear, and it does, as is illustrated in Figure 3-7.

Figure 3-6. *Displaying the contents of the cell* `mycell`

Figure 3-7. *Modified contents of the cell*

For interest, let's add some complications by clicking the button BadReplace. Clicking BadReplace calls the function `BadReplace`, and that assigns the property `innerHTML` of the HTML table with other text. This means that the HTML content `<table><tr><td>...</table>` is changed to `<table>Nothing</table>`. The changed HTML is not legal and is displayed as shown in Figure 3-8.

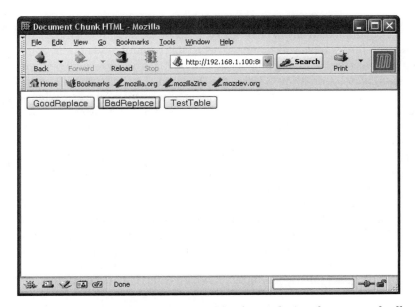

Figure 3-8. *Modified contents of the table after replacing the rows and cells*

Figure 3-8 illustrates that the table rows have been replaced with nothing. If the TestTable button is clicked to validate the state, an error is generated, as illustrated in Figure 3-9.

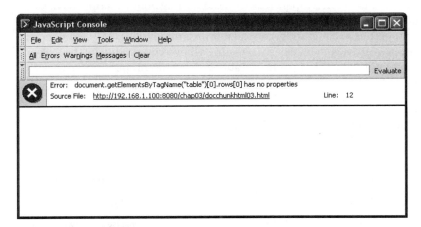

Figure 3-9. *Object model exception*

The exception is important and relates to how the property innerHTML operates. When HTML content is assigned using the innerHTML property, the data is text based. When retrieving the value of the innerHTML property, child elements are converted into a text buffer. Assigning the innerHTML property means replacing the child elements with the HTML text defined by the assignment. Then that new HTML text is converted into a series of HTML elements that are presented to the user. The functions GoodReplace and BadReplace are examples of manipulating the innerHTML property. However, things can run amok if the innerHTML property is manipulated when it should not be manipulated or when doing so will violate the structure of the HTML. For instance, as illustrated in the example you cannot create a table without rows or cells.

Another way to interact with the HTML Document Object Model is to use individual elements that are instantiated, manipulated, and deleted. Using the Document Object Model, it is much harder to mess up because this model supports only certain methods and properties. When using the HTML Document Object Model, it is not as simple to arbitrarily remove all the rows and replace them with text. There are no methods on the table object model to create a construct, as illustrated in Figure 3-8.

It is important to remember that entire chunks of HTML content are replaced when using the Content Chunking pattern. So even though the property innerHTML is powerful and flexible, replacing the wrong chunk at the wrong time will result in an incorrectly formatted HTML page. What you need to remember is that when referencing HTML elements in the context of the pattern, only framework HTML elements used to contain content chunks should be referenced. As a pattern rule, script in the HTML framework page should not directly reference injected elements, as that would create a dynamic dependency that may or may not work. If such a dependency is necessary, encapsulate the functionality and call a method on the injected elements. JavaScript allows the assignment of arbitrary functions on HTML elements.

Identifying Elements

It was previously mentioned that when finding elements by using a tag type, it is not possible to know the identifier; and when finding elements using the identifier, it is not possible to know the tag type. Regardless of how the elements have been found, they are considered a starting point from which manipulations can happen. Based on the starting point, a script can navigate the parent or the child elements by using a number of standard properties and methods.

These standard properties and methods are available on virtually all HTML elements, and script writers should focus on using them when navigating a hierarchy, modifying the look and feel, or attempting to identify what the element is. Table 3-1 outlines properties that are of interest when writing scripts.

Table 3-1. *HTML Element Properties Useful for Writing Scripts*

Property Identifier	Description
attributes[]	Contains a read-only collection of the attributes associated with the HTML element. An individual attribute can be retrieved by using the method getAttribute. To assign or overwrite an attribute, the method setAttribute is used. To remove an attribute, the method removeAttribute is used.
childNodes[]	Is an instance of NodeList that most likely is referenced by using an array notation, but the array is read-only. To add a child node to the current element, the method appendChild is used. To remove a child node, the method removeChild is used; and to replace a child node, replaceChild is used.
className	Assigns a stylesheet class identifier to an element. A class type is very important in Dynamic HTML in that the look and feel of the element can be dynamically assigned.
dir	Indicates the direction of the text, either left to right (ltr) or right to left (rtl).

Table 3-1. *HTML Element Properties Useful for Writing Scripts*

Property Identifier	Description
disabled	Enables (false) or disables (true) an element. Useful when the script does not want a user to click a certain button or other GUI element before completing a required step.
firstChild, lastChild	Retrieves either the first child node or the last child node.
id	Is the identifier of the element used to find a particular element. For example, this property is referenced when a script calls the method getElementById.
nextSibling, previousSibling	Retrieves either the next or previous sibling. When used in combination with firstChild and lastChild, can be used to iterate a set of elements. This approach would be used to iterate a list in which the element is responsible for indicating what the next element should be—for example, when implementing a Decorator pattern or similar structure.
nodeName	Contains the name of the element, which in HTML means the tag (for example, td, table, and so on).
nodeType	Contains the type of element but is geared for use when processing XML documents. With respect to HTML, this property has very little use.
nodeValue	Contains the value of the data in the node. Again, this property has more use when processing XML documents. With respect to HTML, this property cannot be used as a replacement for innerHTML.
parentElement	Retrieves the parent element for the current element. For example, can be used to navigate to the table that contains a row cell.
style	Identifies the current style properties associated with the element and is an instance of CSSStyleDeclaration type.
tabIndex	Defines the tab stop of the element with respect to the entire HTML document.
tagName	Identifies the tag of the current element. Use this property when attempting to figure out the element type after the element has been retrieved via the method getElementById.

Binary, URL, and Image Chunking

Chunking binary or images in their raw form using the XMLHttpRequest object is rather complicated because the data that is read turns into gibberish. The XMLHttpRequest properties responseText and responseXML expect either text or XML, respectively. Any other data type is not possible. Of course there is an exception: Base64-encoding binary data that is encoded as text, and then retrieving the text by using the XMLHttpRequest object. Another solution is not to manage the binary data but to manage the reference of the binary data. In the case of the img tag, that means assigning the src attribute to where an image is located.

Images are downloaded indirectly. To understand how this works, consider an application that uses XMLHttpRequest to retrieve a document containing a single line. The single line is a URL to an image file.

Here is the implementation of the example program:

```
<html>
<head>
<title>Document Chunk Image HTML</title>
<script language="JavaScript" src="/lib/factory.js"></script>
<script language="JavaScript" src="/lib/asynchronous.js"></script>
<script language="JavaScript" type="text/javascript">

var asynchronous = new Asynchronous();
asynchronous.complete = function(status, statusText, responseText, responseXML) {
    document.getElementById("image").src = responseText;
}

</script>
</head>
<body>
<button onclick="asynchronous.call('/chap03/chunkimage01.html')">Get Image</button>
<br>
<img id="image" />
</body>
</html>
```

The img tag is used to reference an image. The img tag is in most cases defined by using a src attribute that references an image location. In the example, the src attribute does not exist, and instead an id attribute exists. When the HTML page is downloaded and presented, a broken image is displayed because there is no image associated with the img tag. To make the img tag present an image, the Get Image button is clicked to make a request to retrieve the single-line file containing the URL of the image. When the XMLHttpRequest has downloaded the single-line file, the function implementation for complete is called and the attribute/property src is assigned to the URL of the remote image. Thus the browser updates itself, loading the image and displaying it.

The single-line file is stored at the URL /chap03/chunkimage01.html, and its content is defined as follows:

```
/static/patches01.jpg
```

When the previously outlined HTML page with an undefined src attribute is loaded, Figure 3-10 is generated.

Figure 3-10 shows a small box below the Get Image button that indicates a broken img tag, because there is no loaded image. When the Get Image button is clicked, the link of the image is downloaded and assigned to the img tag, which causes the image to be loaded. Figure 3-11 is the regenerated HTML page.

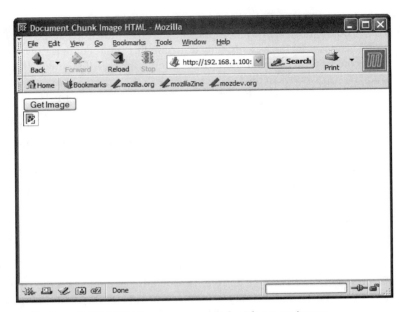

Figure 3-10. *Initial HTML page generated without an image*

Figure 3-11. *The HTML page after the image has been downloaded*

It seems a bit odd to download and assign links that are then processed by the web browser. This indirect approach is done not to illustrate how complicated a web application can be made. The indirect technique is necessary because directly downloading binary data is not possible. But all is not lost, because of the way that the browser caches images. If an image is referenced and downloaded, the image stays in the browser's cache. If the image is referenced a second time, the image is retrieved from the cache. Of course this happens only if the HTTP server implements caching. There is a downside: If a request is made for a URL that references an image, two HTTP requests are required: one to download the content that contains the URL of the image, and the image itself. If both requests are using HTTP 1.1, which most likely is the case, the requests will be inlined using a single connection.

Another variation of the illustrated strategy is to download not a URL but the entire HTML to create an image. The strategy does not save a request connection, but provides a self-contained solution that involves no additional scripting. The following HTML code snippet illustrates how the entire img HTML tag is downloaded:

```
<img src="/static/patches01.jpg" />
```

When injecting both the img tag and its appropriate src attribute, the browser will dynamically load the image as illustrated in the previous example. The advantage of injecting the HTML is that the server side could inject multiple images or other types of HTML. Additionally, by injecting the entire img tag, there is no preliminary stage where a broken image is generated. However, either approach is acceptable, and which is used depends on the nature of the application. When injecting HTML, there might be a flicker as the HTML page resizes. When you assign the src property, there is no flicker, but an empty image needs to be defined or the image element needs to be hidden.

JavaScript Chunking

Another form of chunking is the sending of JavaScript. Sending JavaScript can be very effective because you don't need to parse the data but only execute the JavaScript. From a client script point of view it is very easy to implement. For reference purposes, do not consider downloading JavaScript faster than manually parsing and processing XML data and then converting the data into JavaScript instructions. JavaScript that is downloaded needs to be parsed and validated before being executed. The advantage of using the JavaScript approach is simplicity and effectiveness. It is simpler to execute a piece of JavaScript and then reference the properties and functions exposed by the resulting execution.

Executing JavaScript

Consider the following HTML code that will execute some arbitrary JavaScript:

```
<html>
<head>
<title>JavaScript Chunk HTML</title>
<script language="JavaScript" src="/lib/factory.js"></script>
<script language="JavaScript" src="/lib/asynchronous.js"></script>
<script language="JavaScript" type="text/javascript">
```

```
var asynchronous = new Asynchronous();
asynchronous.complete = function(status, statusText, responseText, responseXML) {
    eval(responseText);
}

</script>
</head>
<body>
<button onclick="asynchronous.call('/chap03/chunkjs01.html')">Get Script</button>
<table>
    <tr><td id="insertplace">Nothing</td></tr>
</table>
</body>
</html>
```

When the user clicks the Get Script button, an XMLHttpRequest request is made that retrieves the document /chap03/chunkjs01.html. The document contains a JavaScript chunk that is executed by using the eval function. The following chunk is downloaded:

```
window.alert("oooowweee, called dynamically");
```

The example chunk is not very sophisticated and pops up a dialog box. What would concern many people with arbitrarily executing JavaScript code is that arbitrary JavaScript code is being executed. An administrator and user might be concerned with the security ramifications because viruses or Trojans could be created. However, that is not possible because JavaScript executes within a sandbox and the same origin policy applies. Granted, if a developer bypasses the same origin policy, security issues could arise.

When receiving JavaScript to be executed, a simple and straightforward implementation is to dynamically create a JavaScript chunk that executes some methods. The JavaScript chunks make it appear that the web browser is doing something. For example, the JavaScript chunk downloaded in the previous example could be used to assign the span or td tag as illustrated here:

```
document.getElementById("mycell").innerHTML = "hello";
```

The generated script is hard-coded in that it expects certain elements to be available in the destination HTML page.

Generating a JavaScript That Manipulates the DOM

Earlier you saw the image generation solution in which an image was broken and then made complete by downloading a valid link. It is also possible to download an image by modifying the Dynamic HTML object model. You modify the object model by using a JavaScript chunk to insert the img tag. The following is an example image JavaScript chunk that creates a new img tag and chunks it into the HTML document:

```
var img = new Image();
img.src = "/static/patches01.jpg";
document.getElementById("insertplace").appendChild(img);
```

In this example, the variable img is an instance of an Image, which cross-references to the HTML tag img. The property src is assigned the URL of the image. The last line of the code chunk uses the method appendChild to add the instantiated Image instance to the HTML document. Not associating the variable img with the HTML document will result in an image that is loaded but not added to the HTML document, and hence not generated. The resulting generated HTML page is shown in Figure 3-12.

Figure 3-12. *Generated HTML page after image has been inserted*

Figure 3-12 is not that spectacular because it illustrates yet again how an image can be added to an HTML page. What is of interest is that the text Nothing has remained and is not replaced as in previous examples. The reason is that the method appendChild was used (and not replaceChild or removeChild, and then appendChild).

The advantage of using the Dynamic HTML object model approach is that it enables images or arbitrary actions to be downloaded in the background that can at the script's choosing be displayed.

Instantiating Objects

Another type of JavaScript chunk that can be downloaded are object states. By using an object state, you can add a level of indirection, allowing functionality to be added during the execution of the HTML page. In all of the past example HTML code pieces, the initial HTML page had to have all the scripts and know the URLs of the resources that were retrieved. Using an indirection, the JavaScript on the client side does not need to know the specifics of a URL or data structure. The client references a general piece of code that is executed. The general piece of code is managed by the server, and contains specific instructions to do something that the client was not programmed to do. Using indirection, it is possible to add functionality to the client that the client did not possess at design time.

Consider the following example HTML page:

```
<html>
<head>
<title>JavaScript Chunk HTML</title>
<script language="JavaScript" src="/lib/factory.js"></script>
<script language="JavaScript" src="/lib/asynchronous.js"></script>
<script language="JavaScript" type="text/javascript">
var asynchronous = new Asynchronous();
asynchronous.complete = function(status, statusText, responseText, responseXML) {
    eval(responseText);
    dynamicFiller.makeCall(document.getElementById("insertplace"));
}
</script>
</head>
<body>
<button onclick="asynchronous.call('/chap03/chunkjs04.js')">Start Process</button>
<table>
    <tr><td id="insertplace">Nothing</td></tr>
</table>
</body>
</html>
```

As in previous examples, a variable of type Asynchronous is instantiated. The button is wired to make an asynchronous method call with the URL /chap03/chunkjs04.js. When the request receives the JavaScript chunk, it is executed via the eval statement. After the eval statement has returned, the method dynamicFiller.MakeCall is made. The call to the method dynamicFiller.MakeCall is a general piece of code. In the implementation of the dynamicFiller.MakeCall method is the specific code managed by the server. Referencing the dynamicFiller.MakeCall method is done using an incomplete variable; that is, the initial script includes no definition of the variable dynamicFilter. Of course, a loaded and processed script cannot reference an incomplete variable because that would generate an exception. But what a script can do is load the implementation just before an incomplete variable is used. That is what the example HTML page has illustrated. For those wondering, there is no definition of dynamicFilter in the files factory.js or asynchronous.js. Incomplete variables, types, and functions are possible in JavaScript, allowing a script to be loaded and processed without generating an exception.

The following source code implements the incomplete dynamicFiller variable:

```
var dynamicFiller = {
    generatedAsync : new Asynchronous(),
    reference : null,
    complete : function(status, statusText, responseText, responseXML) {
        dynamicFiller.reference.innerHTML = responseText;
    },
    makeCall : function(destination) {
        dynamicFiller.reference = destination;
        dynamicFiller.generatedAsync.complete = dynamicFiller.complete;
        dynamicFiller.generatedAsync.call('/chap03/chunkjs05.html');
    }
}
```

The example JavaScript source code is formatted using object initializers. An object initializer is the persisted form of a JavaScript object. You should not equate an object initializer with a JavaScript class definition; they are two entirely separate things. When an object initializer is processed, an object instance is created, and the identifier of the object instance is the variable declaration. In the example, the variable dynamicFiller is the resulting object instance.

The variable dynamicFiller has two properties (generatedAsync and reference) and two methods (complete and makeCall). The property generatedAsync is an instantiated Asynchronous type and is used to make an asynchronous call to the server. The property reference is the HTML element that will be manipulated by the method complete. The method makeCall is used to make an XMLHttpRequest, and the parameter destination is assigned to the property reference.

Putting all the pieces together, the HTML framework code contains general code that references an incomplete variable. To make a variable complete, the JavaScript content is downloaded and executed. The complete variable contains code to download content that is injected into the framework page. Figure 3-13 illustrates the execution sequence of events.

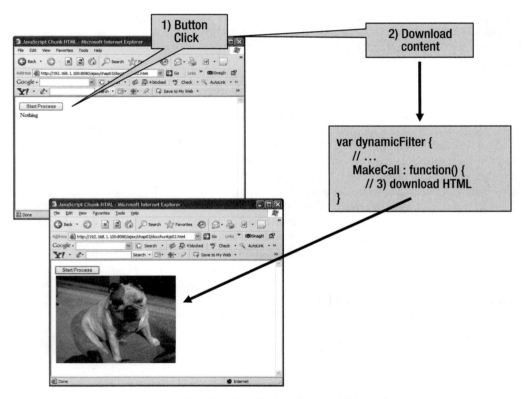

Figure 3-13. *Sequence of events when downloading and executing JavaScript*

In Figure 3-13, the initial page is downloaded by clicking the button. The downloaded content is JavaScript, and the initial page has no idea what the content does. When the content has been downloaded, it is executed. The HTML framework page has coded the referencing of the variable `dynamicFilter` and the calling of the method `MakeCall`. The `MakeCall` method does not exist when the HTML framework page is executed, and is available when the downloaded content is executed. The downloaded content that is executed downloads yet another piece of content that is injected into the HTML page. The result is the loading of an image where the text Nothing was.

The role of the HTML framework page has changed into a bootstrap page that loads the other code chunks. The other code chunks are purely dynamic and contain references and code that the HTML framework page does not know about. The advantage of this implementation is that the document can be loaded incrementally by using pieces of dynamic code that are defined when they are loaded. The Content Chunking pattern defines the loading of content dynamically. But the additional use of JavaScript makes it possible to dynamically define the logic that is used by the HTML framework page.

Pattern Highlights

The following points are the important highlights of the Content Chunking pattern:

- An HTML page is the sum of an HTML framework page and content chunks.

- The HTML framework page is responsible for organizing, referencing, and requesting the appropriate chunks. It should act as a mediator for the individual chunks. The HTML framework page delegates the processing of the chunks to another piece of code.

- The content chunks are uniquely identified by a URL. Content chunks that are distinct do not use the same URLs. Content chunks are used to implement functionality that is determined by the user.

- Content chunks should be one of three types: XML (preferred), HTML (preferred XHTML), or JavaScript. There are other formats, but they are not covered in this book and their use should be carefully considered.

CHAPTER 4

Cache Controller Pattern

Intent

The Cache Controller pattern provides the caller a mechanism to temporarily store resources in a consistent manner, resulting in an improved application experience for the caller.

Motivation

There are many forms of web applications, and one form is a data-mining application. There are different types of data-mining applications, but they all have one thing in common: they query a repository, and the repository responds with data. This means an application will retrieve data based on a query that in structure is identical over the multiple queries.

Figure 4-1 shows a data-mining application that has a series of maps as a database.

Looking a bit closer at the MapQuest application, there are a number of links and advertisements. What is of interest in the context of this pattern are the navigational and zooming controls. The navigational controls are used to pan the map left, right, up, and down. The zooming controls are used to zoom in to or out of the map. These controls are necessary, of course, because the user will want to focus in on various parts of the map.

What is more important about the navigational and zooming controls is that they are predefined operations used to retrieve values from the same repository. This is in stark contrast to the links surrounding the controls, which will result in the execution of some query on an unrelated repository (unrelated, that is, to the map database). The predefined queries can be converted into standard operations such as zoom in, zoom out, pan left, pan right, pan up, and pan down.

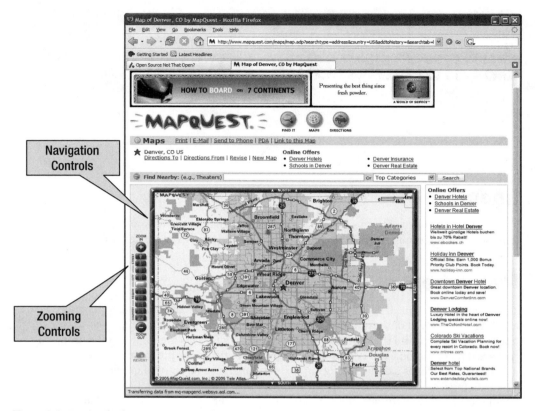

Figure 4-1. *Example data-mining application*

The predefined queries also can be converted into look-ahead queries; for example, to pan left, you want to preload the map left of Denver. Preloading the map by using a background task will make the map application appear fluid. Figure 4-2 is an example application that uses preloading.

Like MapQuest, Maps.google.com is another mapping web application that provides the capability to pan and zoom. What makes Maps.google.com unique is that the map pieces that could be referenced as a result of one of the predefined operations are preloaded. If you experiment with the mapping application, you'll see that it is fluid. The application stops becoming fluid if you pan or zoom too quickly and the preloading task is busy loading other map pieces.

The Maps.google.com application is using a cache to preload map pieces. A cache can also be used to remember old pieces of data so that if they are referenced multiple times, they are not loaded multiple times.

A nontechnical reason for using a cache is for legal reasons. When creating web applications, very often you will be integrating other data sources. Those other data sources reference very large databases (for example, Amazon.com). The data contained within those very large databases is not yours, and you cannot store the data locally in your database for future reference. Most end-user license agreements will specifically state that the data that is retrieved does not belong to you. Having a cache will increase the performance of your application without having to illegally store the data locally.

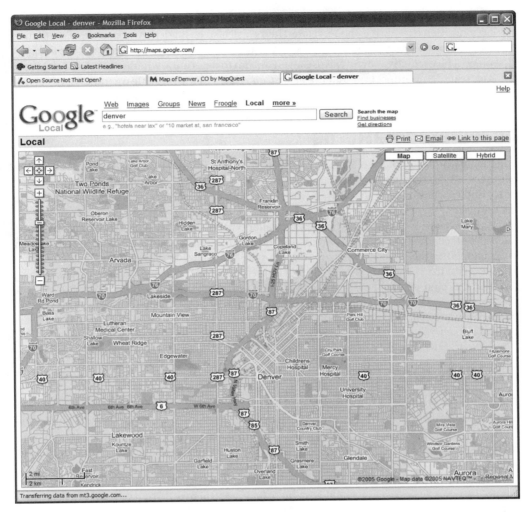

Figure 4-2. *Example data-mining application that preloads map pieces*

Applicability

The Cache Controller pattern in all cases is a request proxy that makes a decision as to whether information should be retrieved from the cache or a request should be made. This pattern is used in the following contexts:

> *Passive caching:* Passive caching occurs when the request proxy manages the resources but does not preload any data. The purpose of creating a passive cache is to keep a list of data that has already been loaded and will not be unnecessarily reloaded. An example of passive caching is the referencing of configuration information. Configuration information does not change for the most part and is considered read-mostly. Additionally, configuration information does not have any other data to preload, as illustrated in the mapping examples. There is typically only one piece of configuration information, and it can be loaded as a single block.

Predictive caching: Predictive caching implements passive caching but has an additional action: when a request is made, related items will also be loaded. An example of predictive caching is the Google Maps mapping application. The client makes a request for a map piece. The predictive cache will use an algorithm to determine whether related map pieces are loaded. It is important that the algorithm relates to the possible operations, which in the mapping example would be zooming and panning operations.

Associated Patterns

The Cache Controller pattern is used with other patterns. It is not used on its own because the pattern does not do anything by itself. As previously stated, the Cache Controller pattern is a proxy implementation that sits between the caller making the request and the server processing the request.

This does not mean that the Cache Controller pattern can be used with all patterns. The Cache Controller pattern can be used only in those situations where HTTP validation has been implemented on the server side. As you will see in the "Implementation" section of this chapter, validation on the server side is not typically implemented for custom functionality. As is illustrated in this chapter, it is possible to add HTTP validation for all situations, but there are still situations when HTTP validation does not make sense. That is usually when the data is not under the management of the web application or when the REST Based Model-View-Controller pattern is used.

Architecture

The essence of the Cache Controller pattern is the Proxy pattern. The Cache Controller pattern is a proxy to `Asynchronous` and implements the interface exposed by `Asynchronous`. The implementation of the Proxy pattern for the Cache Controller pattern is the implementation of a caching strategy. The focus of this section will be the definition and explanation of that caching strategy.

There are two ways to implement caching: let the Internet infrastructure do as much as possible for you, or write code to help the Internet infrastructure do its work. As much as I find writing a caching algorithm interesting and fun, doing so would be a waste of time. Doing your own caching is hard because so many elements in the HTTP request chain are already caching data that you have a good chance of re-caching already cached data. By caching yet again, you are providing no added value.

HTML and HTTP Cache Directives

Letting the Internet infrastructure manage the caching is called using the *HTTP Expiration model.* There are two ways to control the caching by using the Internet infrastructure: adding HTML tags or adding HTTP identifiers.

When you want to use HTML tags to control the cache, the following HTML uses the necessary HTML tags:

```
<html>
<head>
<title>Hanging Page</title>
<meta http-equiv="Cache-Control" content="max-age=3600">
<meta http-equiv="Expires" content="Tue, 01 Jan 1980 1:00:00 GMT">
</head>
<body>
...
```

The HTML tag meta has two attributes, http-equiv and content, that are used to mimic HTTP identifiers. The problem with using HTML meta tags is that they are intended to be consumed by a web browser. It is not possible to add the meta tag to an XML data stream. Therefore, it is not possible to use HTML-based cache control tags when streaming data other than HTML.

The second way to control caching by using the Internet infrastructure is to generate a set of HTTP tags, as illustrated by the following HTTP request result:

```
HTTP/1.1 200 OK
Cache-Control: Public, max-age=3600
Expires: Wed, 10 Aug 2005 10:35:37 GMT
Content-Type: text/html;charset=ISO-8859-1
Content-Length: 39
Date: Wed, 10 Aug 2005 09:35:37 GMT
Server: Apache-Coyote/1.1

<html><body>Hello world</body></html>
```

The HTTP identifiers Cache-Control and Expires manage how the page is supposed to be cached. The Cache-Control identifier specifies a caching of the content for 3600 seconds, or one hour. The Expires identifier defines when the retrieved content is considered expired. Both identifiers make it possible for proxies or browsers to cache the HTTP-retrieved content by using the HTTP Expiration model.

When used in the context of a script, the HTTP identifiers can be programmatically generated by using the following ASP.NET code:

```
<%@ Page Language = "C#" %>
<%@ Import Namespace="System" %>
<%
Response.Cache.SetExpires(DateTime.Now.AddMinutes( 60 ) ) ;
Response.Cache.SetCacheability(HttpCacheability.Public) ;
%>
<html>
<head>
<title>Cached Page</title>
</head>
<body>
    Hello world!
</body>
</html>
```

Using .NET, the methods SetExpires and SetCacheability will add the Expires and Cache-Control identifiers. To achieve the same effect by using a Java servlet, you would use the following code:

```
import javax.servlet.http.*;
import javax.servlet.*;
import java.io.*;
import java.util.*;

public class GenerateHeader extends HttpServlet {
    protected void doGet(HttpServletRequest req, HttpServletResponse resp)
        throws ServletException, IOException {
        resp.addHeader("Cache-Control", "Public, max-age=3600");
        resp.addHeader("Expires", "Fri, 30 Oct 2006 14:19:41 GMT");
        resp.setContentType("text/html");
        PrintWriter out = resp.getWriter();
        out.println("<html><body>Hello world</body></html>");
    }
}
```

HTTP Expiration Caching Is a Bad Idea (Generally)

It is generally not a good idea to use the HTTP Expiration model, but to use the second way of managing caching by writing code to help the Internet infrastructure do its work. The second way is called the *HTTP Validation model.*

To understand why the HTTP Expiration model is problematic, consider the following scenario. You are running a website hosting news. So that there is less traffic on the website, you enable HTTP caching and assign an expiry of 30 minutes. (The expiry time is an arbitrary value used for illustrative purposes.) This means that when a browser downloads some content, the next version of the content will be available in 30 minutes. Indicating a wait period of 30 minutes is a bad idea because in that 30 minutes news can dramatically change. A client who has downloaded some content is then restricted to retrieving news in 30-minute cycles. Of course the client could ignore or empty the cache, resulting in downloads of the latest information. If the client always empties the cache, the client will always get the latest news, but at a cost of downloading content that may not have changed. The resource cost should not surprise anyone because always getting the latest content means using no caching whatsoever. Scripts such as Java servlets/JSP or ASP.NET pages very often use this strategy, and the administrator managing the website wonders why there are performance problems.

A Better Approach: Using HTTP Validation

The better approach is to use the HTTP Validation model. This model sends each response with a ticket that references the uniqueness of the data. If the client wants to download the content again, the client sends the server a ticket from the last download. The server compares the sent ticket with the ticket that it has; if the server notices the tickets are identical, it sends an HTTP 304 to indicate no changes have occurred. At that point, the client can retrieve the old content from the cache and present it to the user as the latest and greatest. The HTTP Validation model still requires an HTTP request, but does not include the cost of generating and sending the content again.

In terms of an HTTP conversation, the HTTP Validation model is implemented as follows. This example illustrates a request from a client and the response from the server.

Request 1:

```
GET /ajax/chap04/cachedpage.html HTTP/1.1
Accept: */*
Accept-Language: en-ca
Accept-Encoding: gzip, deflate
User-Agent: Mozilla/4.0 (compatible; MSIE 6.0; ➡
Windows NT 5.1; SV1; .NET CLR 2.0.50215)
Host: 127.0.0.1:8081
Connection: Keep-Alive
```

Response 1:

```
HTTP/1.1 200 OK
ETag: W/"45-1123668584000"
Last-Modified: Wed, 10 Aug 2005 10:09:44 GMT
Content-Type: text/html
Content-Length: 45
Date: Wed, 10 Aug 2005 10:11:54 GMT
Server: Apache-Coyote/1.1

<html>
<body>
Cached content
</body>
</html>
```

The client makes a request for the document /ajax/chap04/cachedpage.html. The server responds with the content, but there is no Cache-Control nor Expires identifier. This seems to indicate that the returned content is not cached, but that is not true. The server has indicated that it is using the HTTP Validation model, and not the HTTP Expiration model. The page that is returned has become part of a cache identified by the unique ETag identifier. The ETag identifier, called an entity tag, could be compared to a unique hash code for an HTML page. The letter W that is prefixed to the entity tag identifier means that the page is a weak reference and the HTTP server may not immediately reflect updates to the page on the server side.

The next step is to refresh the browser and ask for the same page again. The HTTP conversation is illustrated as follows.

Request 2:

```
GET /ajax/chap04/cachedpage.html HTTP/1.1
Accept: */*
Accept-Language: en-ca
Accept-Encoding: gzip, deflate
If-Modified-Since: Wed, 10 Aug 2005 10:09:44 GMT
If-None-Match: W/"45-1123668584000"
```

```
User-Agent: Mozilla/4.0 (compatible; MSIE 6.0;
    Windows NT 5.1; SV1; .NET CLR 2.0.50215)
Host: 192.168.1.100:8081
Connection: Keep-Alive
```

Response 2:

```
HTTP/1.1 304 Not Modified
Date: Wed, 10 Aug 2005 10:11:58 GMT
Server: Apache-Coyote/1.1
```

When the client makes the second request, the additional identifiers If-Modified-Since and If-None-Match are sent in the request. Notice how the identifier If-None-Match references the identifier of the previously sent ETag value. The server queries the URL and generates an entity tag. If the entity tag is identical to the value being sent, the server returns an HTTP 304 code to indicate that the content has not changed.

When using entity tags, the client can send an If-Match or an If-None-Match. If the client sends an If-Match, and the data on the server is out-of-date, the server returns a cache miss error, and not the new data. If the client sends an If-None-Match identifier when the server data is unchanged, the server sends an HTTP 304 return code. If the data is out-of-date, new data is sent.

The advantage of using the HTTP Validation model of caching is that you are always guaranteed to get the latest version at the time of the request. The clients can make the request every couple of seconds, hours, weeks, or whatever period they choose. It is up to the client to decide when to get a fresh copy of the data. Granted, there is still some HTTP traffic due to the requests, but it has been reduced to a minimum.

Having said all that, there are situations when using the HTTP Expiration model does make sense—for example, when the HTML content is static and changes rarely. For the scope of this book and this pattern, it does not make sense to use the HTTP Expiration model because Ajax applications are inherently using data that does change.

Implementing HTTP validation is simple because the most popular web browsers and HTTP servers already implement it. In this chapter, I will discuss the details of implementing HTTP validation because there are some things the web browser and HTTP server do not do. However, building a more sophisticated infrastructure that supposedly enhances HTTP validation is not recommended because that would be defeating the facilities of HTTP 1.1.

Using the HTTP 1.1 infrastructure means that the server you are communicating with must have implemented the HTTP 1.1 protocol properly. If you are using Microsoft Internet Information Server, Apache Tomcat, or Jetty, you will have no problems. If you are using anything else, check that the server fully understands the HTTP 1.1 protocol. Otherwise, you will have problems with excessive network communications. As an example recommendation, it you plan on using Mono, then use mod_mono with Apache, and not just XSP. Although XSP (1.0.9) is a promising web server, it is not quite ready for prime time, at least at the time of this writing.

Some Findings Regarding Server-Side Caching

There is a fly in the soup of HTTP validation: when implementing the server side of a web application, there is an inconsistency. Any file that the HTTP server manages directly has entity tags. But for content managed by an external application such as Java Servlet, ASP.NET, or script, there are no entity tags nor HTTP cache control directives. Consider the following request and response, which is an HTTP conversation of a JSP page.

Request:

```
GET /ajax/chap04/index.jsp HTTP/1.1
Host: 127.0.0.1:8081
User-Agent: Mozilla/5.0 (Windows; U; Windows NT 5.1; ➥
en-US; rv:1.7.10) Gecko/20050716 Firefox/1.0.6
Accept: text/xml,application/xml,application/xhtml+xml,
      text/html;q=0.9,text/plain;q=0.8,image/png,*/*;q=0.5
Accept-Language: en-us,en;q=0.5
Accept-Encoding: gzip,deflate
Accept-Charset: ISO-8859-1,utf-8;q=0.7,*;q=0.7
Keep-Alive: 300
Connection: keep-alive
```

Response:

```
HTTP/1.1 200 OK
Set-Cookie: JSESSIONID=1B51C170A3F24A376BF2C3B98CF1C2C9; Path=/ajax
Content-Type: text/html;charset=ISO-8859-1
Content-Length: 333
Date: Thu, 11 Aug 2005 12:25:41 GMT
Server: Apache-Coyote/1.1
```

Additionally, for illustration purposes, consider the following HTTP conversation that retrieves an XML data set from the Amazon.com catalog.

Request:

```
GET /onca/xml?Service=AWSECommerceService&SubscriptionId=aaaaaaaa&Operation= ➥
ItemSearch&Keywords=Stephen+King&SearchIndex=Books HTTP/1.1
User-Agent: Wget/1.9.1
Host: webservices.amazon.com:8100
Accept: */*
Connection: Keep-Alive
```

Response:

```
HTTP/1.1 200 OK
Date: Thu, 11 Aug 2005 15:26:55 GMT
Server: Stronghold/2.4.2 Apache/1.3.6 C2NetEU/2412 (Unix) mod_fastcgi/2.2.12
x-amz-id-1: 1VQ2V7MESPAC6FNGFGDR
x-amz-id-2: lpxEwchCrLJfO3qopULlUMYzbcVx1QmX
Connection: close
Content-Type: text/xml; charset=UTF-8
```

In both responses, there was neither an ETag nor HTTP cache control directives. This means that if the same HTTP request is repeatedly made, there will be multiple HTTP identical requests with multiple identically generated response sets. As web application developers, we are trained to write server-side applications that generate content dynamically, and that has a ramification:

Content can never, ever, ever be cached. This is ironic because for many of our web applications the supposed dynamic data is in fact static data, or at least mostly static data, that is converted from one form (for example, a database) into another form (for example, HTML).

It must be questioned whether the HTTP server is taking the right approach by not doing anything. The HTTP server cannot validate the content and therefore cannot know when the content has changed or not changed. With respect to the server-side application framework (for example, JSP), the assumption is completely correct. What is incorrect is that a script does not do anything to implement HTTP validation. When a script generates content, the script has an understanding of the underlying data structures and hence can determine whether the data has changed. Therefore, the server-side application can implement HTTP validation.

There are two ways to implement HTTP validation: dynamic and static validation.

Defining Static HTTP Validation

In static HTTP validation, the HTTP server does the difficult work of calculating the entity tag. An HTTP server, when it encounters a file that is not processed by some framework (for example, .html or .png), will read the file and calculate a number that uniquely identifies the content of the file. Suppose a server-side framework were to generate a static form of the content that is generated. If the server-side framework were JSP, a Java filter could convert the generated JSP content into a static HTML file that is managed by the HTTP server and retrieved by the client. This requires that the server-side application know the difference between posting and retrieving data, as there is an updated state and saved state. In technical implementation terms, it means a state that previously existed only in a database form must also be saved in the form of a file or another persistent storage medium that the HTTP server manages. When the state is modified, the server application is responsible for modifying the database and file at the same time.

When the HTTP server manages the entity tag calculations, each resource has two separate representations. The retrieving representation is static and is managed by the HTTP server. The posting representation is dynamic and is managed by the server application framework. Technically speaking, from a browser perspective HTTP GET results in a file being retrieved, and HTTP POST or PUT results in data being posted to a JSP or ASP.NET file.

From a URL perspective, a static HTTP validation application would be similar to Figure 4-3.

An individual book is retrieved by using its ISBN number, which is unique for every book. When retrieving a book, the static URL /ajax/books/[ISBN].xml is used. The URL maps to a file managed by the HTTP server. Because the file is managed by the HTTP server, when the client attempts to retrieve the document, the HTTP server will send an ETag identifier based on the file.

To update the file, the dynamic URL /ajax/servlet/LibrarianServlet is used. It is impossible to update the data by using the static URL because the static URL is a file that when posted to results in nothing being updated. That a static file does nothing is fairly logical and is the reason why server application frameworks were created in the first place. The defined URL will be processed by a Java servlet, but could just as easily have resulted in the activation of an ASP.NET page or some other web application framework. To update the content, the URL uses an HTTP POST or an HTTP PUT, but in the case of the example an HTML form was used to update the content and hence HTTP POST is required.

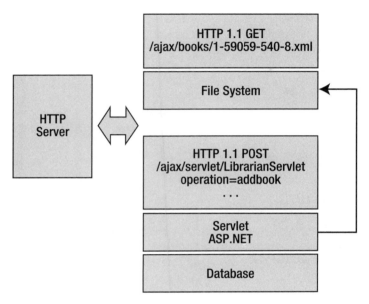

Figure 4-3. *URL architecture implementing HTTP server-based HTTP validation*

In a typical HTTP POST, a query string represents the variables to update the static content. The data does not need to be a query string, but could just as easily be XML content. Within the posted data is an operation identifier used to determine the action to be completed. This action will accomplish two things: update the underlying storage medium that usually is a database, and generate a new file (for example, HTML) with the new data.

The static HTTP validation works well when the data is read-mostly. Read-mostly data is being retrieved and read for most of the time, and is being updated only sometimes.

Defining Dynamic HTTP Validation

For those websites that read data as often as it is written, the static HTTP validation approach would be wrong because updating the file takes too many resources. In the case of dynamic HTTP validation, the server application framework has to manage everything, which includes the generation and verification of the entity tag.

The major problem to solve is the generation of the entity tag (ETag) identifier. Traditionally, web developers do not write an ETag identifier. But what is an entity tag for dynamic content? Calculating the entity tag for the generated content does not make sense because there could be small changes in the generated content that do not quantify as changed content. There is a solution, and one that functions like an entity tag but is not called that.

The proposed solution uses a hash code that is assigned as an entity tag value. A hash code is a reasonably unique value for a given state of an object. In .NET and Java, each object has a hash code method that can be overridden. Imagine the following Book class that represents a book. Ignore the details of the book definition, but understand that the book represents some type. To calculate the hash code for the book, you could write the following source code:

```
public class Book {
    private String _ISBN;
    private String _author;
    private String _title;
    private int _staticHashCode;
    private boolean _isHashCodeAssigned = false;

    public int hashCode() {
        if( _isHashCodeAssigned) {
            return _staticHashCode;
        }
        else {
            return new HashCodeBuilder()
                .append( _ISBN)
                .append( _author)
                .append( _title)
                .append( _comments).toHashCode();
        }
    }
    public void assignHashCode(int hashcode) {
        _staticHashCode = hashCode();
        _isHashCodeAssigned = true;
    }
    public void resetAssignedHashCode() {
        _isHashCodeAssigned = false;
    }
}
```

In the implementation of Book, there are several methods and data members. The data member _staticHashCode represents an old hash code value. The old hash code value is needed to verify whether content has changed. Consider the following context. The client makes a request for a resource. The server instantiates the needed objects and from those objects generates a hash code that is stored in the object state itself (staticHashCode). The client comes back and asks for the same resource, sending the hash code as an entity tag. As a quick check technique, the server does not load all of the objects, but loads the saved hash code (staticHashCode) and compares the sent entity tag with the hash code. If they match, the server generates an HTTP 304 error or sends the new state. What makes this architecture work is that whenever the objects are updated, the saved hash code must be updated. Otherwise, the saved hash code will reflect an old state.

The method assignHashCode assigns a predefined hash code that will be used by the caller to test for change. The method resetAssignedHashCode resets the flag so that the hash code is computed from the state. The example used in the Book class is to declare a local data member, but *that is not the only way to implement the optimization.* You can implement it however you want. What is important is to associate the hash code with the data members that uniquely represent the object. The Builder pattern could be applied that accepts as a parameter the entity tag and then either constructs the object hierarchy or generates a result code to indicate no change. How you would implement this logic is left to you. In the case of the Book class, the unique identifier is the ISBN number. As an alternative, a SQL table with two columns (ISBN and Hash Code) could be created.

Wrapping up the architecture, it is obvious that the best way of caching data is to complement the Internet infrastructure and use HTTP validation. HTTP validation is not a task left for the HTTP server to implement, but is part of implementing any resource. The following section illustrates how to implement static and dynamic HTTP validation.

Implementation

As the Cache Controller pattern uses HTTP validation that is already implemented by the browser or HTTP server, implementing the Cache Controller pattern requires writing code that is needed. It might be necessary for a given content to write only client code, or maybe only server code, or maybe both client and server code. The point is that what you need to write depends on the context. When writing either the client or server caching code, it is important to implement the HTTP validation contract. Implementing the HTTP validation correctly ensures that either your client or server fits into an already existing Internet infrastructure. The important piece of the implementation is that both the client and server when implemented follow the contract of HTTP validation.

The example application manages books, as illustrated in the "Architecture" section. The focus of the application is to illustrate the state of a type and how it affects the entity tag. On the client side, the Cache Controller code is a minimal implementation and is receiving a reference number that is used by the server to indicate whether new content needs to be sent. More complicated is the server side, which needs to generate and validate the reference number, resulting in a larger explanation of the server-side code.

Implementing the Passive Cache

On the client side, there are two implementations of the cache: passive and predictive. The *passive cache* happens as the request and response are being made. A *predictive cache* watches for specific requests and makes further requests in anticipation of having been asked. A predictive cache grows on its own and is used to implement functionality, like Google Maps.

Implementing the predictive cache requires implementing the passive cache. However, it is not in your best interest to implement something that the browser may already do quite well (for example, passive cache). When a web browser retrieves an image, the image is usually added to the browser cache. Therefore, writing a cache for images does not make any sense.

Because the browser manages a cache, the quickest and simplest solution is to let the browser manage the passive cache. Ideally, this is the best solution, but it will not always work because cache implementations are very inconsistent across the various browsers. At the time of this writing, when using Microsoft Internet Explorer, the HTTP validation with a passive cache worked both with the browser and the XMLHttpRequest object. However, any Mozilla-based or Apple Safari browsers when using the XMLHttpRequest object did not implement the passive cache, and would not take advantage of entity tags. A really peculiar situation is that a request for an HTML document is passively cached by the browser. If instead the same requests were made by using XMLHttpRequest, the contents of the passive cache would be ignored.

I am not going to debate who is right or who is wrong because every browser has implementation problems and this one is only the tip of the iceberg. If a JavaScript script manages the HTTP headers for validation, the passive cache is consistently managed whether it is used by the browser or XMLHttpRequest. The only browser that is inconsistent—and this problem has been registered as a bug at the time of this writing—is Safari in that when the HTTP 304 code is returned, Safari fills in the properties status and statusText as undefined.

Defining the Client HTML Page

I am not going to illustrate the implementation of the HTTP validation cache just yet. First, I will show you the HTML code used by the client so that you will understand where the responsibilities lie. I don't want to show the HTTP validation cache code because doing so would confuse you and make you wonder, "Okay, so why is this code doing this?"

From the perspective of the HTML code, the cache would operate transparently, just like what happens when using a browser. When implementing a predictive cache, the HTML code should need to provide only a function that is used for prefetching URLs. The following HTML code illustrates an ideal implementation:

```html
<html>
<head>
<title>Cached Content</title>
<script language="JavaScript" src="../lib/factory.js"></script>
<script language="JavaScript" src="../lib/asynchronous.js"></script>
<script language="JavaScript" src="../lib/cache.js"></script>
<script language="JavaScript" type="text/javascript">

CacheController.prefetch = function(url) {
    if( url == "../chap03/chunkhtml01.html") {
        CacheController.getCachedURL( "../chap03/chunkimage02.html");
    }
}

var cache = new CacheProxy();

cache.complete = function(status, statusText, responseText, responseXML) {
    document.getElementById("insertplace").innerHTML = responseText;
    document.getElementById("status").innerHTML = status;
    document.getElementById("statustext").innerHTML = statusText;
}

function clearit() {
    document.getElementById("insertplace").innerHTML = "empty";
    document.getElementById("status").innerHTML = "empty";
    document.getElementById("statustext").innerHTML = "empty";
}

</script>
</head>
<body>
<button onclick="cache.get('../chap03/chunkhtml01.html')">Get Content 1</button>
<button onclick="cache.get('../chap03/chunkimage02.html')">Get Content 2</button>
```

```
<button onclick="clearit()">Clear Fields</button>
<table>
    <tr><td id="insertplace">Nothing</td></tr>
    <tr><td id="status">Nothing</td></tr>
    <tr><td id="statustext">Nothing</td></tr>
</table>
</body>
</html>
```

The example uses four `script` tags, and the third tag references the cache script code file `cache.js`. In the implementation of the `cache.js` file is an instantiation of the variable `CacheController`. Because a cache must operate on all requests made by the browser, there is a single variable instance containing all cached content. Because `Asynchronous` is a type that can be instantiated for the Cache Controller pattern to properly implement the Proxy pattern, the type `CacheProxy` is defined.

The method `CacheController.prefetch` is used by the predictive cache code to prefetch other HTTP content. What happens in the implementation of the cache code is that when a request for content is made, the `prefetch` function is called with the URL that is being fetched. The prefetching implementation can then preload a single piece or multiple pieces of HTTP content based on the URL currently being retrieved. How much content is preloaded depends entirely on the `prefetch` function implementation.

Let's step back for a moment and think about `prefetch`. The HTML page defines a `prefetch` function, which contains the logic of what to get and when. The exact logic contained within the `prefetch` implementation reflects the possible operators associated with the data to `prefetch`. In the context of a mapping application, that means the `prefetch` logic must incorporate the resources that can be loaded using the zooming and panning functionality. Where the `prefetch` logic becomes complicated is if there are two areas on the HTML page where content can be preloaded. Then, as in the example, it is important to figure out what the URL is requesting and to preload the required resources.

In a nutshell, when writing `prefetch` implementations, the URLs should be fairly logical and easy to deduce. Using the mapping example, if the URL is `http://mydomain.com/0/0`, panning up would reference the element `http://mydomain/0/1`. The numbers in the URL represent latitude and longitude, and moving up means shifting from longitude 0 to longitude 1. The URL numbers don't include the zooming factor, but that can be calculated. As a rule of thumb, if in your `prefetch` implementation you cannot logically deduce what the associated resources are based on the URL being requested, then most likely you have a passive cache only.

Getting back to the example HTML page, the variable `cache` is an instance of `CacheProxy`, which acts as a proxy for the `Asynchronous` class. This means whatever methods and properties exist for `Asynchronous` also exist for `CacheProxy`. As with `Asynchronous`, to process a response the `cache.complete` function is assigned. Note that when the content is prefetched by the predictive cache, the `complete` method is not called. This is because data that is fetched by the predictive cache is considered in a raw state and not a processed state. Only when the client makes a request for prefetched content will `complete` be called. As with `Asynchronous`, multiple `CacheProxy` instances can be created; however, there is only a single instance of `CacheController`.

The function `clearit` is used to clear the results so that when testing the HTML code it is possible to reset the Dynamic HTML fields `insertplace`, `status`, and `statustext`. To retrieve the code that is inserted into the Dynamic HTML fields, the buttons Get Content 1 and Get Content 2 are clicked. The method that is called is `CacheController.getURL`, which requires two parameters. The first parameter is the URL that is downloaded, and the second URL is the complete function that receives the results.

To illustrate how the HTML content is cached, it is not helpful to show the pages after they have been downloaded. Showing images after the fact illustrates that content is available and presented but does not illustrate where the content came from—whether it was from the cache or from an HTTP request. A better way to show that there is a cache with content is to set a breakpoint in the code and illustrate the contents of the cache with a debugger. Figure 4-4 shows the variable CacheController and the cache that it contains.

Figure 4-4. *Mozilla debugger illustrating that there are two items in the cache*

In Figure 4-4, the this variable in the middle-left window is the CacheController instance. The property _cache is an Array instance that contains the cached objects. Notice that stored in the cache are the objects chunkhtml01.html and chunkimage02.html, which happen to be the HTTP content retrieved by the buttons.

Implementing CacheController and CacheProxy

Implementing CacheController requires implementing a script-defined passive cache. It would seem that writing a passive cache is a bad idea because the browser already does this. The script-defined passive cache is necessary because of the browser-defined passive cache inconsistencies. The script-defined passive cache does not implement any sophisticated cache algorithm. However, if you wanted to extend the functionality of the cache, you could. The variable CacheController implements the client side of the HTTP Validation model. Implementing the HTTP Validation model on the client side requires the client to receive, store, and send entity tags when sending requests and receiving responses. Then based on the HTTP return codes, the cache controller receives, stores, and returns new content, or returns old content to the consuming script of the passive cache.

The following is the implementation of CacheController (the details of the getURL function are missing because that function is fairly complicated and will be explained in pieces later in the chapter):

```
var CacheController = {
    cache : new Array(),
    prefetch : function( url) { },
    didNotFindETagError : function(url) { }
    getCachedURL : function(url) {
        var func = function(status, statusText, responseText, responseXML) { }
        CacheController.getURL(url, func, true);
    },
    getURL : function(url, inpCP, calledFromCache) {
    }
}
```

At first glance, the cache seems to expose one property and three functions. The reality is that CacheController is making extensive use of JavaScript anonymous functions, making the implementation contain more functions than illustrated. The effectiveness of CacheController depends completely on the HTTP server; if the server does not use entity tags, no caching will occur and CacheController will pass all requests directly to the user's complete function implementation.

The property _cache is an Array instance that contains a series of objects representing the cache. Each entry in the cache is associated with and found by using a URL. HTTP content is added to the array when the CacheController internally-defined complete method's parameter status has a value of 200, indicating a successful downloading of HTTP content. The CacheController internally-defined complete method is an anonymous function assigned to asynchronous.complete.

The property prefetch is a function that is assigned by the HTML code to preload HTML content pieces into the cache. If the default prefetch function implementation is used, the predictive cache becomes passive because the prefetch function does nothing.

The function getCachedURL retrieves HTTP content from a server, and is called by the prefetch function defined by HTML code. The implementation of getCachedURL passes three parameters to getURL. The first parameter is the URL that is being retrieved. The second parameter is the complete function implementation, which for the prefetch implementation is neither required nor desired and hence is an empty function declaration. The third parameter, and the only one required to be passed by the getCachedURL function, stops the prefetch function from being called again. Otherwise, a recursive loop of calling getURL that calls prefetch that calls getURL and so on could be initiated.

The method getURL retrieves HTTP content that is added to the cache. The method is called by the still undefined CacheProxy. Following is an implementation of getURL without the implementation of the anonymous functions:

```
getURL : function(url, inpCP, calledFromCache) {
        var asynchronous = new Asynchronous();
        var cacheProxy = inpCP;
        asynchronous.openCallback = function(xmlhttp) {
        }
        asynchronous.complete = function(status,
            statusText, responseText, responseXML) {
        }
        asynchronous.get(url);
        if( calledFromCache != true) {
            CacheController.prefetch(url);
        }
    }
```

Within the implementation of getURL, the anonymous function has been used several times. The anonymous function solves the problem of associating variables with object instances, as explained in Chapter 2. In the abbreviated implementation, each time getURL is called, an instance of Asynchronous is created. This was done on purpose so that multiple HTTP requests could retrieve data concurrently. Remember that CacheController is a single instance. The function openCallback is new and is used to perform a callback operation after the XMLHttpRequest.open method has been called. The implementation of openCallback is called by Asynchronous after the XMLHttpRequest.open method has been called. The function openCallback is required because it is not possible to call the method XMLHttpRequest.setRequestHeader until the XMLHttpRequest.open method has been called.

The anonymous function assignment of asynchronous.complete is needed so that when a URL has been retrieved, the data can be processed. In the implementation of asynchronous.complete are the details of the Cache Controller pattern implementation. The method asynchronous.get calls XMLHttpRquest and the server. After the call has been made and the getURL method is not called from a prefetch implementation (calledFromCache != true), the prefetch implementation is called.

In this implementation of CacheManager, the prefetch function is called before the request has a chance to return with the data. The prefetch function is called before a response can be generated because it is assumed that the prefetch logic can deduce from a URL what an associated URL is. However, in some situations a URL cannot be deduced because the associated URLs are defined in the response of the request. This happens when the Decoupled Navigation pattern is implemented. In that case, the CacheManager prefetch-calling functionality has to be called in the anonymous function implementation assigned to asynchronous.complete. The modification of the prefetch functionality is beyond the scope of this book, but is mentioned as a potential extension that you may need to implement.

Focusing now on the incomplete anonymous functions, and specifically the anonymous openCallback function:

```
asynchronous.openCallback = function(xmlhttp) {
    var obj = CacheController._cache[url];
    if(obj != null) {
        xmlhttp.setRequestHeader("If-None-Match", obj.ETag);
    }
    cacheProxy.openCallback(xmlhttp);
}
```

In the implementation of openCallback, the _cache array that contains all of the object instances is referenced, and the element associated with the variable url is retrieved and assigned to obj. If the URL exists, obj will not be equal to null and will have an associated ETag identifier. The associated ETag is assigned to the request by using the method setRequestHeader, with the HTTP header identifier If-None-Match. This process of retrieving the URL object instance and assigning the ETag identifier is the essence of HTTP validation.

Let's focus on the complete anonymous function implementation:

```
asynchronous.complete = function(status, statusText, responseText, responseXML) {
    if(status == 200) {
        try {
            var foundetag = this._xmlhttp.getResponseHeader("ETag");
            if(foundetag != null) {
                CacheController._cache[url] = {
                    ETag : foundetag,
                    Status : status,
                    StatusText : statusText,
                    ResponseText : responseText,
                    ResponseXML : responseXML
                };
            }
            else {
                CacheController.didNotFindETagError(url);
            }
        }
        catch(exception) {
            CacheController.didNotFindETagError(url);
        }
        if(calledFromCache != true) {
            cacheProxy.complete(status, statusText, responseText, responseXML);
        }
    }
```

```
    else if(status == 304) {
        var obj = CacheController._cache[ url];
        if(obj != null) {
            cacheProxy.complete(obj.Status, obj.StatusText,
                obj.ResponseText, obj.ResponseXML);
        }
        else {
            throw new Error("Server indicated that this ➡
         data is in the cache, but it does not seem to be");
        }
    }
    else {
        if(calledFromCache != true) {
            cacheProxy.complete(status, statusText, responseText, responseXML);
        }
    }
}
```

In the implementation, three possible actions can be carried out: HTTP return code value 200 for success, HTTP return code value 304 for a state that has not changed, and the default.

If the server returns an HTTP 200 value, the ETag is searched for in the returned HTTP headers. This condition results either when the request has never been issued before or if the already issued cached content has changed. Regardless of whether the local cache instance exists, if there is an entity tag value, then the variable CacheController._cache[url] is assigned with the new object that has five properties: ETag, Status, StatusText, ResponseText, and ResponseXML.

The entire ETag retrieval and assignment is wrapped in a try catch exception block and if statement to ensure that only objects that have an associated ETag identifier are added to the cache. If there is no ETag, the method CacheController.didNotFindETagError is called with the URL. The purpose of the method is to get the user to stop using the prefetch function. Remember that if there is no ETag, there is no caching, and hence doing a prefetch is silly. There is a default method implementation for the method didNotFindETagError, but the HTML page can implement its own.

Still focusing on the complete anonymous function implementation, if the status is 304 (indicating unchanged content that the client already has), the cache is queried using the URL, and the associated content is sent to the client. There will always be content in the cache because if an ETag was generated, there is a value in the _cache variable. The retrieved content is assigned to the variable obj, and then the userComplete method is called with cached content. If in the function implementation a status code other than 200 or 304 is generated, it is passed directly to the client for further processing.

The class CacheProxy is the Proxy pattern implementation, and its implementation determines whether the call is to Asynchronous or CacheController. The following is a partial implementation of CacheProxy, with the redundant pieces removed:

```
function CacheProxy() {
}

function CacheProxy_get(url) {
    CacheController.getURL(url, this, false);
}

function CacheProxy_post(url, mimetype, datalength, data) {
    var thisreference = this;
    asynchronous = new Asynchronous();

    asynchronous.openCallback = function(xmlhttp) {
        thisreference.openCallback(xmlhttp);
    }
    asynchronous.complete = function(status, statusText, ➥
        responseText, responseXML) {
        thisreference.complete(status, statusText, ➥
            responseText, responseXML);
    }
    asynchronous.post(url, mimetype, datalength, data);
}
CacheProxy.prototype.openCallback = CacheProxy_openCallback;
CacheProxy.prototype.complete = CacheProxy_complete;
CacheProxy.prototype.get = CacheProxy_get;
CacheProxy.prototype.put = CacheProxy_put;
CacheProxy.prototype.del = CacheProxy_delete;
CacheProxy.prototype.post = CacheProxy_post;
```

To act as a full proxy for Asynchronous, CacheProxy needs to expose the methods that Asynchronous exposes. This means CacheProxy needs to implement the get, put, del, and other such methods. Implementing a proxy means delegating functionality. In the case of the client calling an HTTP GET, it means the function CacheProxy_get needs to delegate to CacheController. For all of the other functions (for example, CacheProxy_post), CacheProxy delegates to Asynchronous. Doing a full proxy implementation of Asynchronous also requires implementing openCallback and callback, which then delegates to the method CacheProxy.openCallback or CacheProxy. complete that will call the user-defined implementations, if the user defined an implementation.

Putting It All Together

When the HTML code is combined with CacheController and CacheProxy, a cache is created that uses HTTP validation. Using the CacheController HTML code is quicker than not using a cache. Multiple instances of CacheProxy instantiate multiple instances of Asynchronous to allow concurrent downloads. Do not confuse multiple instances with multiple threads. When writing web-browser-based JavaScript applications, there is no such thing as threads, because the JavaScript code in the web browser runs within a single thread. The asynchronous downloads might be running on individual threads, but the point is that when using JavaScript it is not possible to create threads nor use any synchronization mechanisms. Having said all that, the cache code was written to be as thread-friendly as possible in case an individual web browser decides to optimize the JavaScript code.

As a side note, many may comment that threading is possible when using JavaScript timers. Again, timers are not threads, but they allow multiple tasks to be executed. Be forewarned that if your script is executing, there is no way to manipulate to the HTML page because the HTML page will be frozen for the length of the request. The example of freezing the browser was illustrated in Chapter 2.

Implementing the Server Side of the HTTP Validator

As mentioned in the explanation of the variable CacheController and the type CacheProxy, it is expected that the server send entity tags and perform the heavy work when comparing these tags. When implementing a server-side HTTP validator, that does not mean implementing a cache. The cache is on the client side, the proxy, or somewhere along the chain of Internet infrastructure. Implementing HTTP validation on the server side means processing entity tags only.

Defining the Book

Let's begin the book application with the definition of the Book class. The Book class was briefly illustrated in the "Architecture" section, but the details were not discussed, just the hash code feature. The Book class is relatively undemanding and has only data members. It is important to not have any built-in serialization defined in the class because two persistence techniques will be used: file system and general storage. If the general storage were a relational database, an object to relational mapper could be used (Hibernate for Java, or NHibernate for .NET).

Using Java, the Book class is defined as follows:

```java
public class Book {
    private String _ISBN;
    private String _author;
    private String _title;

    public void setISBN(String iSBN) {
        _ISBN = iSBN;
    }
    public String getISBN() {
        return _ISBN;
    }
    public void setAuthor(String author) {
        _author = author;
    }
    public String getAuthor() {
        return _author;
    }
    public void setTitle(String title) {
        _title = title;
    }
```

```
    public String getTitle() {
        return _title;
    }
}
```

The Book class has three data members: _ISBN, _author, and _title. The three data members represent the unique state of the Book.

Implementing the Action Classes

For every operation, there is an action set interface. The action set interface is responsible for retrieving, updating, and performing other operations on the data set. The following is an example definition:

```
public interface Librarian {
    public Book checkOutBook(String isbn) throws Exception;
    public void checkInBook(Book book) throws Exception;
}
```

The Librarian interface has two methods, checkOutBook and checkInBook, that are used to retrieve and add a book, respectively. An interface is preferred because to implement the operations, the Decorator pattern is going to be used. In a nutshell, the purpose of the Decorator pattern is to dynamically add responsibilities to already existing classes. Relating the Decorator pattern to the Librarian interface means that when the checkInBook method is called, multiple implementations will be called with the same calling parameters.

Implementing the Decorator pattern is appropriate because, as you saw in the "Architecture" section, when implementing static HTTP validation it is necessary to save content to a file and the database. The file was consumed by the HTTP server, and the database for the application. So a calling sequence could be first saving to a file and then saving to the relational database. The Decorator pattern masks these two steps as one. The client thinks only one call is being made. The underlying Decorator pattern implementation handles the details of chaining together the various action set interface implementations.

The following example classes implement the static HTTP validator, which saves to a file and a database. Note that the classes have not been fully implemented from a persistence point of view because doing so would detract from the discussion of the pattern implementations:

```
public class LibrarianSaveToFile implements Librarian {
    private static String _rootPath;
    private Librarian _next;

    public LibrarianSaveToFile(Librarian next) throws InstantiationException {
        if( _next == null) {
            throw new InstantiationException("Next element cannot be null");
        }
        _next = next;
    }
    public static void setRootPath(String path) {
        _rootPath = path;
    }
```

```
    public Book checkOutBook(String isbn) throws Exception {
        // Ignore nothing to do and continue to next element
        return _next.checkOutBook( isbn);
    }
    public void checkInBook(Book book) throws Exception{
        String path = _rootPath + "/books/" + book.getISBN() + ".xml";

        // Save the data to a file ...
        _next.checkInBook(book);
    }
}
public class LibrarianSaveToStorage implements Librarian {
    public LibrarianSaveToStorage() {

    }
    public Book checkOutBook(String isbn) throws Exception {
        // Retrieve from the storage mechanism
        return null;
    }

    public void checkInBook(Book book) throws Exception {
        // Save to the storage mechanism
    }
}
```

The class LibrarianSaveToFile implements the Librarian interface and is responsible for saving changed content to the file retrieved by using the URL /ajax/books/[ISBN].xml. The class LibrarianSaveToStorage also implements the Librarian interface and is responsible for retrieving and saving the Book data to a relational database. The two classes are separate, and when they are wired together they form the basis of the Decorator pattern.

The way that LibrarianSaveToFile works is that if the class is used, the constructor requires an instance of Librarian. The instance is assigned to the data member next, which is used by LibrarianSaveToFile to delegate Librarian method calls. Looking closer at the abbreviated method implementation LibrarianSaveToFile.checkinBook, the building of a string will be used to save the content to a file on the hard disk. After the file has been saved, the next Librarian instance is called with the exact same parameters and method. The class LibrarianSaveToFile is responsible only for saving the data to a file, and the next instance is responsible for doing its work. In our example, the next instance references the type LibrarianSaveToStorage, which means that the content is saved to the relational database. The advantage of this approach is that each class (LibrarianSaveToFile and LibrarianSaveToStorage) can do what it is best at and leave the rest of the work to another class. The advantage of using the Decorator pattern is that classes can be dynamically wired together without changing the functionality of the other.

To instantiate the classes LibrarianSaveToFile and LibrarianSaveToStorage and to wire them together, the Builder pattern is used, as illustrated in the following example:

```java
public class LibrarianBuilder {
    public static Librarian create(String rootPath) throws InstantiationException {
        LibrarianSaveToFile.setRootPath(rootPath);
        return new LibrarianSaveToFile(new LibrarianSaveToStorage());
    }
}
```

The Builder pattern is an extension of the Factory pattern. It is used to instantiate multiple instances of different types that are arranged in a specific configuration. In the case of our example class LibrarianBuilder, that would mean assigning the root directory by using the method setRootPath, instantiating LibrarianSaveToFile, instantiating LibrarianSaveToStorage, and wiring the two Librarian instances together. The returned Librarian instances would appear to the caller to be a single Librarian instance. However, when a Librarian method is called, two different instances are called.

Implementing Static HTTP Validation

The last step to implementing static HTTP validation is to put the entire solution together to build a web application. The following example uses Java servlets, but other implementations such as ASP.NET could have easily been used:

```java
public class LibrarianServlet extends HttpServlet {
    protected void doPost(HttpServletRequest req, HttpServletResponse resp)
        throws javax.servlet.ServletException, java.io.IOException  {
        if(req.getContentType().compareTo( ➡
          "application/x-www-form-urlencoded") == 0) {
            String operation = req.getParameter("operation");
            if(operation != null && ➡
                operation.compareTo("addBook") == 0) {
                Librarian librarian = LibrarianBuilder.create( ➡

        getServletContext().getInitParameter("generatepath"));
                try {
                    Book book = new Book();
                    String isbn = req.getParameter("isbn");
                    if(isbn != null) {
                        try {
                            book = librarian.checkOutBook(isbn);
                        }
                        catch(Exception ex) {
                            book.setISBN(isbn);
                        }
                    }
                    String author = req.getParameter("author");
                    if(author != null) {
                        book.setAuthor(author);
                    }
```

```
                    String title = req.getParameter("title");
                    if(title != null) {
                        book.setTitle(title);
                    }
                    resp.setContentType("text/html");
                    PrintWriter out = resp.getWriter();
                    librarian.checkInBook(book);
                    out.println( ~ ➥
                    "<html><body>Did update</body></html>");
                }
                catch(Exception ex) {
                    throw new ServletException( ➥
                       "LibrarianServlet generated error", ex);
                }
            }
        }
     }
   }
}
```

The servlet LibrarianServlet has implemented the method doPost, meaning that the servlet will react to only HTTP POST requests. As per the "Architecture" section, when implementing the static HTTP validation, the servlet is used to only update data and not to retrieve data. The servlet will process only those requests that post the content as being the type application/x-www-form-urlencoded. Other data types could have been processed, but for the scope of this example only CGI-encoded data is supported. It is important that the server check which content type is sent because the Permutations pattern calls for the server to be able to react to different types.

Because the content type is CGI encoded, there exists an action to carry out, and it is retrieved by using the method req.getParameter("operation"). Then, based on the operation, the remaining parameters are retrieved: isbn, author, and title. If the isbn parameter exists, the method librarian.checkOutBook is called to retrieve a book instance. This is done on purpose because an already existing book may be updated. The design is to let the servlet incrementally update the contents of the book if it already exists.

Contrast the incremental update to an update in a traditional software language. In traditional software development, when a method requires three parameters, the caller must supply three parameters. This means that to update an object with a single method, all parameters must be supplied. A solution is to create multiple methods with multiple parameters, or to create a structure and then determine which properties are populated. Regardless of which approach is chosen, using a URL is simpler, because the client needs to provide only those details that need to be updated.

When the updated parameters have been retrieved and assigned to the Book instance, the book needs to be saved. The book is saved by using the method librarian.checkInBook. When calling the method checkInBook, the Decorator pattern is called that will then call both LibrarianSaveToFile and LibrarianSaveToStorage. As illustrated earlier, calling the Librarian instance saves the book to the file and to the relational database. Because the HTTP server is managing the entity tag, a new entity tag will be created.

Implementing Dynamic HTTP Validation

Implementing dynamic HTTP validation is not that difficult if static HTTP validation has been implemented, because static HTTP validation provides a base for dynamic HTTP validation. When implementing dynamic HTTP validation, the LibrarianSaveToStorage is kept identical as is the use of the Decorator pattern. What changes is the implementation of the Builder pattern: the class LibrarianSaveToFile is replaced with LibrarinHTTPValidation, and the class Book has some additional properties.

What is different in this instance of using the Decorator pattern is that the LibrarianHTTPValidation class is used to figure out whether LibrarianSaveToStorage has to be called. Additionally, LibrarianSaveToStorage is a bit misnamed because when using dynamic HTTP validation LibrarianSaveToStorage is used for both retrieval and saving of data.

Modifying the Decorator Pattern Implementation

In the static HTTP server validation, the Decorator pattern was used. For the dynamic HTTP server validation, the implementation LibrarianHTTPValidation is used to manage the hash codes of the individual book instances:

```
public class LibrarianHTTPValidation implements Librarian {
    private Librarian _next;
    private String _etag;
    public LibrarianHTTPValidation(String etag, Librarian next)
        throws InstantiationException {
        if( _next == null) {
            throw new InstantiationException("Next element cannot be null");
        }
        _next = next;
        _etag = etag;
    }
    public Book checkOutBook(String isbn) throws Exception {
        if(isSameState( _etag, isbn)) {
            Book book = new Book();
            book.assignHashCode(Integer.parseInt( _etag));
            book.setISBN( isbn);
            return book;
        }
        else {
            return _next.checkOutBook( isbn);
        }
    }
    public void checkInBook(Book book) throws Exception {
        saveHashCode(book);
        _next.checkInBook(book);
    }
}
```

In the instantiation of the LibrarianHTTPValidation, the constructor has two parameters. The first parameter identifies the ETag, and the second parameter is the next Librarian instance, which is LibrarianSaveToStorage. The method checkOutBook has an incomplete method isSameState that is used to test whether the input etag parameter and the to-be-retrieved book instance associated with the isbn number are identical. The method isSameState is incomplete because the way that the cross-referencing of the client-supplied ETag identifier and the current hash code value is done depends on how the old hash code value is stored. It's an implementation detail that is beyond the scope of this book.

If the method isSameState indicates that the state has not changed, Book is instantiated and the hash code is assigned to the input ETag value. The instantiated value is returned. If the method isSameState indicates that the state has changed, then the checkOutBook is delegated to the next Librarian instance (_next.checkOutBook).

In the implementation of checkInBook, a call is made to an incomplete method implementation, saveHashCode. The incomplete method saveHashCode saves the current hash code value and its associated unique ISBN identifier. After the values have been saved, the next Librarian instance is called to persist the value to the underlying storage mechanism.

To instantiate the new Decorator pattern structure, the Builder pattern has to be modified and would appear similar to the following:

```
public class LibrarianBuilder {
    public static Librarian create(String etag)
        throws InstantiationException {
        if(etag != null && etag.length() > 0) {
            return new LibrarianHTTPValidation(etag, new LibrarianSaveToStorage());
        }
        else {
            return new LibrarianSaveToStorage();
        }
    }
}
```

The modified method create requires a parameter that is passed in etag from the client. If the etag value is null, the class LibrarianSaveToStorage is instantiated without any parameters, indicating that either the content sent to the client is called for the first time or HTTP validation is not used. If there is an etag value and its length is greater than zero, a validation using LibrarianHTTPValidation is performed. The class LibrarianSaveToStorage is still instantiated, but the instance is a parameter to the constructor of LibrarianHTTPValidation, and both instances are chained together.

Putting It All Together

In dynamic HTTP validation, it is necessary to implement multiple HTTP verbs. In the example, the verbs GET and PUT are implemented. Note that the same code used for PUT could also be used for POST to make the servlet HTML form-friendly.

The implementation of the hash code calculation has been shown in the "Architecture" section and will not be reiterated because doing so would provide no value. The hash code would be calculated on the state of the object that is saved to a file or a relational database.

The servlet implementation is defined as follows:

```java
public class ValidationLibrarianServlet extends HttpServlet {
    protected void doGet(HttpServletRequest req, ➥
        HttpServletResponse resp)
        throws javax.servlet.ServletException, ➥
        java.io.IOException  {
        String isbn = getISBNFromURL(req.getRequestURI());
        try {
            String etagvalue = req.getHeader("If-Match");
            Librarian librarian = ➥
                LibrarianBuilder.create(etagvalue);
            Book book = librarian.checkOutBook(isbn);
            if(etagvalue != null && book.hashCode() == ➥
                Integer.parseInt(etagvalue)) {
                resp.setStatus(304, "Not modified");
                return;
            }
            resp.setHeader("ETag", Integer.toString( ➥
                book.hashCode()));
            generateGetContent(resp, book);
        }
        catch (Exception ex) {
            throw new ServletException( ➥
                "LibrarianServlet generated error", ex);
        }
    }
    protected void doPut(HttpServletRequest req, ➥
        HttpServletResponse resp)
        throws javax.servlet.ServletException, ➥
        java.io.IOException  {
        try {
            Librarian librarian = ➥
                LibrarianBuilder.create("empty");
            Book book = getDetailsFromRequest(req);
            librarian.checkInBook(book);
            generatePutContent(resp, book);
        }
        catch (Exception ex) {
            throw new ServletException( ➥
                "LibrarianServlet generated error", ex);
        }
    }
}
```

In the example code, a number of incomplete methods are beyond the scope of this pattern because they are implementation details specific to a code base. Starting with the method goGet, which is called when the HTTP GET method is called, the ISBN is retrieved. At the beginning of this chapter, the URL /ajax/books/[ISBN].xml was used to uniquely identify a book. The method getISBNFromURL will parse the URL and retrieve the desired ISBN. Having multiple

URLs associated with a single servlet is not difficult. Specifically for Java, the administrator would change the web.xml file to associate the base URL /ajax/books with the ValidationLibrarianServlet.

After having extracted the ISBN number, the ETag identifier is retrieved from the request by using the method req.getHeader("If-Match"). The retrieved instance is passed as a parameter to the method LibrarianBuilder.create. Depending on the value of the ETag, a decorated LibrarianSaveToStorage class is created.

The method checkOutBook is called, and an instance will be retrieved that indicates either that an HTTP 304 should be returned, or that a new instance has been instantiated and output should be generated. If output is generated, an ETag identifier is generated and added to the HTTP output.

The method doPut is called whenever an HTTP PUT is called. The implementation is relatively simple in that the decorated Librarian classes are instantiated, and the Book class parameters are retrieved and added to the underlying storage mechanism by using the method checkInBook. Because the Librarian classes are decorated, the hash code value will be automatically identified with the ISBN of the book.

The examples illustrated a relatively simple HTTP GET and PUT. Let's say that you want to search for a book based on the title. Then the URL /ajax/books/search?author=[name] could be used, and ValidationLibrarianServlet would need to be extended to include the functionality.

Pattern Highlights

Let's wrap all of this up and consider what the Cache Controller pattern accomplishes. The purpose of the Cache Controller pattern is to provide a temporary cache by complementing the Internet infrastructure. The idea is not to re-create yet another caching infrastructure, because the Internet already does that very well. In the scope of writing web applications, the cache infrastructure to use is HTTP validation. Even though HTTP validation is not typically used for scripts, it can and should be.

The following points are important highlights of the Cache Controller pattern:

- When using a cache, it is preferable to use the HTTP Validation model. The HTTP Expiration model is less useful because expiration says content is good for a certain time frame regardless of what happens to the server.

- When using HTTP validation for writing a cache, only the client actually caches the information. The server is responsible for generating the entity tags and for comparing old with new entity tags. This means that the server has to keep a sense of history with respect to the changing state of the objects.

- There are two ways to implement HTTP validation: letting the HTTP server do the heavy lifting, or creating a server-side processor that does everything.

- When letting the HTTP server do the heavy lifting, the server framework (for example, JSP, Servlet, ASP.NET) is responsible for updating the static content pieces managed by the HTTP server.

- The server framework manages the state completely, and the entity tag is calculated by using the hash code of the state of the objects. The hash code should never be taken based on the HTML content that is sent because that would conflict with the Permutations pattern.

- A predictive cache that preloads data is based on the ability of associating a URL or its response with one or more URLs. If the predictive cache cannot logically associate URLs, a predictive cache cannot be created. Very often the logic used in the predictive cache is directly related to the operations that can be carried out on the data presented to the user. In the case of mapping, this means zooming and panning.

CHAPTER 5

Permutations Pattern

Intent

The Permutations pattern is used by the server to separate the resource (URL) from the representation (for example, HTML or XML). Separating the resource from the representation makes it possible for an end user to focus on the resource and not have to worry about the content associated with the URL. For example, if a client's bank account is at the URL `http://mydomain.com/accounts/user`, the same URL can be used regardless of device (phone, PC, and so on).

Motivation

In the early days of the Web, there were applications called price comparison services. Price comparison services compared prices between multiple online vendors. The price comparison services were made possible by using screen-scraping technologies. Essentially, screen scraping involves the deciphering of the HTML content to extract the price and product information. What made screen scraping complicated was that the generated HTML content was intended for consumption by an HTML browser. Because screen scraping was inefficient, another idea arose: to create a web service that must be explicitly called by a device other than a browser. The web service and HTML content provided two different content streams for the same content.

The web service example illustrates how the same data can have multiple representations. Extrapolating the illustration a bit further, an idea would be to consider the data as a resource that can be associated with a representation. As much as we would like to have data associated with a single representation, it is not possible because each end device has its own way of representing information. A web browser loads Dynamic HTML that results in the user being presented with images, text, and links. To get more content, a user will click on a link that will load more Dynamic HTML content in the browser. Typically, you create links in Dynamic HTML by using the HTML tag `<a href="somelink" />`. The a tag is a built-in mechanism used by HTML to replace the currently loaded HTML content with the content referenced by the `href` attribute.

The preceding two paragraphs discuss the problem in relatively abstract terms, and it would be better to illustrate the problem. The problem of not getting the right content can be practically illustrated by using three browsers to visit two websites. Specifically, for this example I will visit the websites http://www.google.com and http://www.yahoo.com. The three browsers used are *not* Mozilla Firefox, Microsoft Internet Explorer, and Apple Safari. The three browsers are indeed three completely different browser types, namely a GUI browser, a text-based browser, and a Wireless Access Protocol (WAP) browser. Each browser represents a different segment of the browsing public. The graphical browser is used by most people, text-based browsers are used by those who cannot or do not want to see the graphical HTML representations (for example, a blind or a host-terminal–based user), and the WAP browser is used by those operating cell phones. Figures 5-1, 5-2, and 5-3 show snapshots of the three browsers visiting the website http://www.google.com.

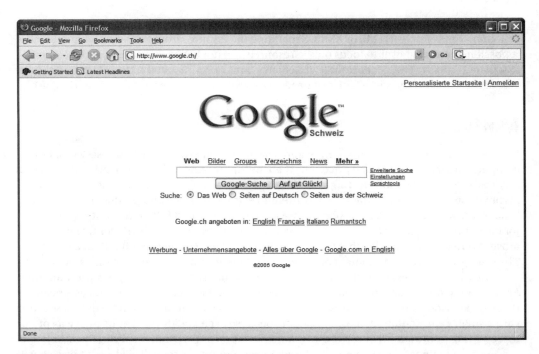

Figure 5-1. *Graphical browser presentation of* http://www.google.com

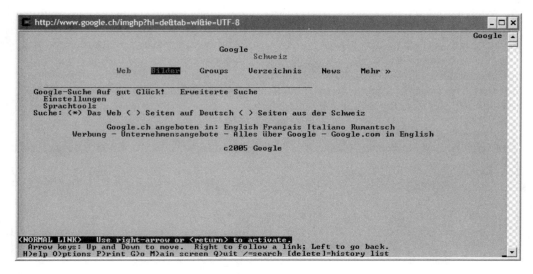

Figure 5-2. *Textual browser presentation of http://www.google.com*

Figure 5-3. *WAP browser presentation of http://www.google.com*

What you should notice is that the resource is the Google search engine, but the representation of each resource is different. You might be tempted to believe that there is nothing special going on because `http://www.google.com` is a simple website and hence the representation of the content is relatively simple. However, look closely at each of the figures and you will see that although the pages look similar, there are differences. Downloading the content from `http://www.yahoo.com` illustrates the different representations. Figures 5-4 and 5-5 show two of the browsers at the Yahoo! site.

Figure 5-4. *Graphical browser presentation of* `http://www.yahoo.com`

Yahoo! has a fairly complicated portal website and will present one of three formats depending on the browser making the request. This means that a user can call the URL `http://www.yahoo.com` and be presented with the appropriate content. This is how most people want their websites to function because users expect that kind of web experience. What users do not expect are experiences such as that illustrated in Figure 5-6.

In Figure 5-6, the user uses a nondefault browser and receives an error message and a message about launching another HTML content type.

Let's take the example of the WAP content. Imagine needing to transfer some money into a bank account and being confronted with a message to launch another application that does not happen to exist on your cell phone. That would be frustrating and entirely unnecessary. Maybe some websites have other URLs for the nondefault devices, but is it the responsibility of the user to figure that out? The answer is a definite no; it is the responsibility of the website to figure that out. Frankly, it would have been better for the website to just not offer the content than to have a customer grumble and panic midway through a transaction.

Figure 5-5. *WAP browser presentation of* http://www.yahoo.com

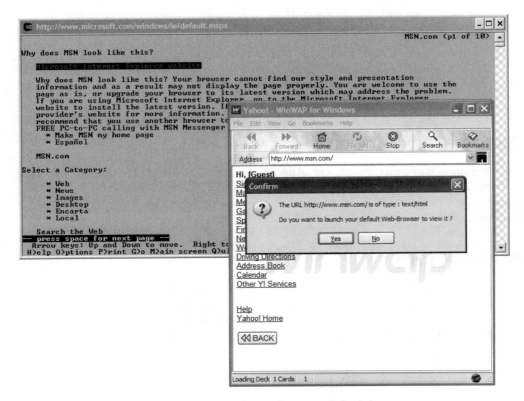

Figure 5-6. *Incorrect web user experience when using a nondefault browser*

The main idea behind the Permutations pattern is to present the right content at the right time. It is about creating content and presenting it appropriately based on the requirements of the end browsing device. By using the Permutations pattern, content is created like that of Google and Yahoo! From an end user perspective, that means users will need to remember only a single URL such as `http://mydomain.com/bank/account/cgross`, and then be assured regardless of device that they will be presented with similar content.

Applicability

The Permutations pattern is a core pattern that can and should be used as much as possible. However, it is a pattern that requires extra work, and that extra work should not be underestimated. For example, both Yahoo! and Google provide a similar, but different, user interface for their mobile clients. When implementing multiple user interfaces, a significant amount of work is associated with creating each one of them. Also understand that the Permutations pattern is not only user-interface related, but should be considered device related. With respect to current URLs used by current web application frameworks, the Permutations pattern may require redefinition. This means this pattern will revisit topics that seem already solved, such as session identification and authorization.

The following contexts define when the Permutations pattern should be used:

- For the main entry points of a web application (such as `http://mydomain.com/application`) or for a specific user (for example, `http://mydomain.com/account/user`). The idea is that if the end device and/or user has been identified, you don't have to keep re-identifying what or whom the device is.

- For web applications that are more Internet than intranet in nature. Controlling the end devices accessing an intranet web application is easy. In contrast, it is not possible to control the end devices accessing an Internet web application, nor should any attempt be made to control them.

Associated Patterns

The Permutations pattern is the basis of all patterns defined in this book. The Content Chunking and Persistent Communications patterns use the Permutations pattern directly, and the remaining patterns use it indirectly. The only pattern that does not explicitly use this pattern is Cache Controller.

Architecture

The big-picture architecture idea behind the Permutations pattern is to separate the resource from the representation. This means that when a URL is referenced, the data that is returned from the URL is not bound to the resource. This section explains the details of why you should separate the resource from the representation and how to do that.

Understanding Why the Resource Is Separated from the Representation

The need to separate the resource from the representation has not been adequately explained, and some developers may wonder why it is necessary at all. After all, many websites work well and nobody has complained too loudly. The reason why many websites work well is because they have probably implemented the separation of resource from representation. And those that have not done so have received complaints. Separating the resource from the representation is not complicated, but it is associated with quite a bit of grunt work. What makes matters more complicated is that many of today's web application frameworks get it completely wrong as they bind resource with representation. It's not that today's web application technologies cannot manage resources and representations properly, but the fact is that they don't do it.

To illustrate the separation of resource from representation, consider the following C# code:

```
interface IBase {
    void Method();
}

class Implementation1 : IBase {
    public void Method() { }
}

class Implementation2 : IBase {
    public void Method() { }
}
```

The interface IBase defines a method and is implemented by two classes, Implementation1 and Implementation2. This is called *interface-driven development* because when the client uses either of the implementations, the client doesn't use the implementations but the interface of the implementations, as illustrated by the following source code:

```
class Factory {
    public static IBase Instantiate() {
        return new Implementation1();
    }
}

class UseIt {
    public void Method() {
        IBase obj = Factory.Instantiate();
        // ...
    }
}
```

In the example source code, the class Factory has a static method, Instantiate, that creates an instance of IBase by instantiating Implementation1. In the class method UseIt.Method, an instance of IBase is instantiated by calling the method Factory.Instantiate. The class UseIt has no idea whether Implementation1 or Implementation2 is instantiated. The class UseIt uses the interface as defined by IBase and expects the interface methods to be implemented correctly. Those users of dynamic programming languages such as Ruby or Python do not implement interfaces. Dynamic programming languages use contracts where functionality is implied.

Let's relate this to URLs and separate the resource from the representation. The resource is the interface, and the representation is the implementation. Right now most web technologies bind together resource and representation or use implementations directly, as the URLs http://mydomain.com/item.aspx and http://mydomain.com/item.jsp illustrate. The direct bindings are the extensions .aspx, and .jsp, and the proper interface-defined URL would have been http://mydomain.com/item.

Ironically, all web technologies implement the separation of resource from representation for the root URL /, as illustrated by the following HTTP conversation. (Note that the conversation has been abbreviated for explanation purposes).

Request:

```
GET / HTTP/1.1
Host: 192.168.1.242:8100
User-Agent: Mozilla/5.0 (Macintosh; U; PPC Mac OS X Mach-O; ➥
    en-US; rv:1.7.8) Gecko/20050511
```

Response:

```
HTTP/1.1 200 OK
Server: Apache/2.0.53 (Ubuntu) PHP/4.3.10-10ubuntu4
```

The requested URL is /, and it is returned by the server as index.html or index.jsp or index.php or even default.aspx. If web technologies are capable of separating the resource from the representation for the root URL, why can't they carry this throughout the entire web application? It is a truly puzzling question. The root URL implements the Permutations pattern, and many other URLs would implement the pattern, but the pattern does not need to be used everywhere, as illustrated in Figure 5-7.

The URL /account[user] has two representations, HTML and XML. Which representation is returned depends on the preference of the client. The preference of the client is determined by the Accept header. Let's say that the client wants the HTML content. Contained within the HTML content is a link to the file details.aspx. If the URL were theoretically pure, the URL /account/[user]/details.aspx should have been /account/[user]/details. However, in some situations being theoretically pure is the wrong approach. Just as with interface-driven development, you do not always reference interfaces. However, in the content of details.aspx, the resource-based URL /account/[user]/transactions is referenced. The resource-based URL is referenced by two representations: details.aspx and details.xml.

When implementing the Permutations pattern, what you are implementing is interface-driven development for the Web. A resource is an interface, and the representations are implementations. The current batch of web technologies supports web application components, but their granularity is too coarse.

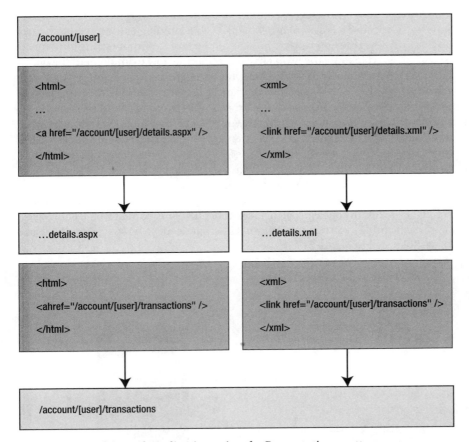

Figure 5-7. *Rearchitected application using the Permutations pattern*

Using Cookies and HTTP Authentication to Authorize Access Only

A problem with URLs is that they associate a user with a URL based on some extra information. It is a bad practice because it does not allow a URL to be copied. For example, I issue the URL `http://mydomain.com/~cgross`. The tilde character (~) indicates, "Please download the content from a user's directory." The user's directory is specified after the tilde character, and in this example is `cgross`. If I do not happen to be `cgross`, I can still access the information from `cgross`. If `cgross` implements authentication, then I as a user other than `cgross` need to be authorized to view the contents of `cgross`.

Let's take another example URL: `http://mydomain.com/~`. Does the HTTP server know which user's directory is being specified? The answer is no, because the HTTP server cannot know who is being referenced. The HTTP server could resolve which user is being referenced by asking the user to log in. So if, for example, I logged in as `cgross`, the HTTP server could resolve the URL from `http://mydomain.com/~` to `http://mydomain.com/~cgross`. This example is what most websites do. Most websites give you a generic URL that gives user-specific content only if you are authenticated.

The generic URL approach with specific content on authentication is promoted by web application frameworks because it is easy to implement. Web technologies are not constructed to process URLs in a manner more appropriate for Ajax applications. Without going into a deep URL design discussion, let's illustrate the problem by considering how to implement the home pages of the individual users who use the tilde character. When using Apache on the Linux operating system, the mapping of the tilde character and `cgross` identifier to a directory would be `/home/cgross/public_html`. If the user `maryjane` existed, the mapping would be `/home/maryjane/public_html`. These two individuals have two separate mappings. Now imagine you are building a web application and you want `cgross` and `maryjane` to have identical default pages that are implemented by the ASP.NET page `default.aspx`. To achieve the goal, you would have to copy the ASP.NET page to the directories `/home/cgross/public_html` and `/home/maryjane/public_html`. The `default.aspx` page has to be copied because the URLs `/~cgross` and `/~maryjane` are two distinct URLs, even though the default page functionalities are identical. Current web technologies cannot cope with such a scenario. Therefore, current web technologies take the other approach and say you have a common URL that needs to be specialized by using authentication, as illustrated in Figure 5-8.

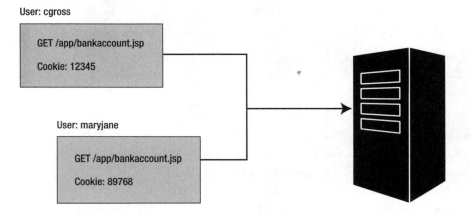

Figure 5-8. *Associating a bank account with a user*

Figure 5-8 shows the JSP page `/app/bankaccount.jsp`. If either `maryjane` or `cgross` wanted to access their bank account, each would perform a login, and an HTTP cookie would be associated with each login. Then both `cgross` and `maryjane` would access their bank account information from the same URL. This is a bad way of designing a URL for the following reasons:

- A user can use only one data set because there is no way for a super user to exist. For example, if resource-based URLs were used, a user could be authenticated but be able to access multiple resources.

- Security is put into the hands of the web application developer. To ensure that only authorized people are allowed access to certain pieces of information, the web application developer has to add barriers. The barriers are written into the web application, which all too often results in security problems. HTTP security is well known, well defined, and stable, and those who manage it—administrators—are well aware of any security holes. Programmers, although capable and intelligent, are not security specialists.

- Resources can be assigned individual representations, meaning that multiple versions of data can coexist with each other.

When URLs become resources, some developers become hesitant because it means added complexity. For example, imagine sending out an e-mail saying, "Hey, buy this and you will get credited with 1000 points in your bank account." Forget for the moment that this is a famous phishing attack. Just take the sentence at face value and assume you will be sending out e-mails to people who can access their bank accounts. The question a developer has is, what URL will be sent in the e-mail? The answer is a general URL that after a login becomes specific, as illustrated in Figure 5-9.

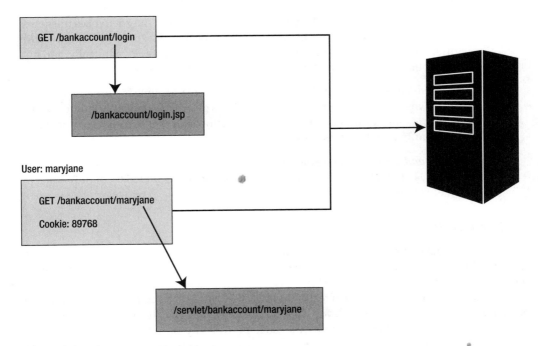

Figure 5-9. *URLs used to access a bank account*

In Figure 5-9, the Permutations pattern is used twice, but in two different contexts. To understand the URLs, let's relate them back to the e-mail example. The bank sends out an e-mail that includes the URL /bankaccount/login. When a user receives the e-mail, the user clicks on the link. The HTTP server uses the Permutations pattern to load the appropriate content, which is HTML, and that means the URL /bankaccount/login.jsp. The URL /bankaccount/login is an interface, and the URL /bankaccount/login.jsp is its implementation. The login could be carried out by using HTTP authentication or an HTTP cookie. What you should notice is that the login is a separate process from the application itself.

After being authenticated, the user is redirected to the URL /bankaccount/maryjane with an associated HTTP cookie. When the HTTP server sees the request for /bankaccount/maryjane, it checks for either HTTP authentication information or HTTP cookie information. The information is required to verify that the request can be carried out. The HTTP server sees that the request is maryjane and therefore allows access to the URL. Like the login, the resource /bankaccount/maryjane has an associated representation, /servlet/bankaccount/maryjane.

Comparing Figure 5-9 to Figure 5-8, you can see that the authorization, resource, and representation have been separated from each other. The solution in Figure 5-9 is better because it allows a developer or administrator to update one component (for example, authorization) without having to update the other components (for example, resource and representation).

There are multiple ways to authorize a user, and they are defined as follows:

- *Cookies:* Cookies are identifiers sent in the HTTP header between the client and the server. The server is responsible for generating a cookie, and the client is responsible for sending the cookie to the server for a given URL and its descendents.

- *URL rewriting:* To identify the client, the URL is rewritten, and the client uses the new URL for all requests. For example, instead of requesting the URL /bank/account, the URL is rewritten to /session12345/bank/account. The URL is rewritten dynamically, and a router component will capture the rewritten URL to identify the user.

- *HTTP authentication:* By using HTTP authentication, it is possible to authenticate a user. Then, whenever the user requests content for a given URL realm, the authorization information is sent by the client. HTTP authentication is similar to a cookie, except that users must authenticate themselves.

- *HTML form addition:* Another variation of URL rewriting is not to rewrite the URL but to rewrite the HTML forms that send content. Hidden fields are added to identify who is sending the content.

Using Cookies

HTTP cookies[1] have a bad reputation, partially undeserved, and therefore many will argue that you should not use cookies. The problem with cookies is not their theory, but their implementation and their ramifications.

To compare the use of cookies to real life, consider entering a shopping mall. At the entrance somebody gives you a token, which you can refuse. After you refuse the token, all of a sudden all the store doors close. You can wander the mall, but can only look at the merchandise through the windows. You can still view the content and everything that the store offers, but it is behind glass. Now imagine that you accept the token. The store doors remain open, and you can browse all the products. To be helpful, the store clerks offer recommendations and best offers in the mall. Yet there is a dark underside: the shopping mall is watching every step you make, and everything you look at is being tracked. Of course, the shopping mall assures you that the information will not be used for other purposes, but the question is, where did those recommendations come from? Or how about the best offers? The tokens—or in the real world, cookies—are being used to track people.

I am split regarding the use of cookies. I find nothing extremely disturbing about them, nor am I enthused about them. HTTP cookies are a means to an end.

---

1. http://en.wikipedia.org/wiki/HTTP_cookie

An Example Book Application

Assuming that you do not need to implement the Permutations pattern, there are some rules of thumb with respect to URL design. When a URL is a resource, it references a piece of data and you need to design a URL. For URL design purposes, let's go through a library example. In terms of functionality, books can be added, manipulated, and deleted. An individual can add books to a list and have comments associated with them. Additionally, a user can create a wish list that contains the books that he would like to have in his library.

Defining the URLs

When defining URLs, the idea is not to define everything but to define the operations that the web application exposes. The URL is defined in the same way that a JavaScript function is defined, in that specifics are bound when used. The following URLs would be used to realize this application:

- `http://mydomain.com/books/[ISBN]`: Associates the URL with a book that has the indicated ISBN number.

- `http://mydomain.com/books/[ISBN]/comments`: Associates the URL with the comments of a book identified by the ISBN number.

- `http://mydomain.com/books/[ISBN]/comments/[username]`: Associates the URL with a user's comments about a book identified by the ISBN number. The user is identified by `username`.

- `http://mydomain.com/users/[username]`: Associates the URL with a user identified by `username`.

- `http://mydomain.com/users/[username]/books`: Associates the URL with the books owned by the user identified by `username`.

- `http://mydomain.com/users/[username]/comments`: Associates the URL with the comments made by the user identified by `username`.

- `http://mydomain.com/users/[username]/wishlist`: Associates the URL with the wish list of books wanted by the user identified by `username`.

- `http://mydomain.com/search/books`: Associates the URL with a search for a specific book.

- `http://mydomain.com/search/users`: Associates the URL with a search for a specific user.

Looking at the different URLs, you can see that what is being illustrated is the logical organization of data associated with a URL. The first URL returns a representation of the book that may include comments about the book. Yet the comments associated with a book have their own URLs. A bit of thought about the implementation of the book URL would have the returned content include the comments of the book. What happens is not the inclusion of the comments in the book, but the inclusion of links to the comments of the book. When multiple items are being requested, do not create a URL that represents a list of resources. As in the example, associate the list of resources with a root-like URL (for example, `/[ISBN]/comments`). The included comments links would be associated with a description.

To understand this way of linking, consider the following example book definition retrieved from the URL `http://mydomain.com/books/12345` that has been abbreviated to illustrate the referencing of comments:

```
<Book ISBN="12345" xmlns:xlink="http://www.w3.org/1999/xlink">
    <Title>My Book</Title>
    <Author>Joe Smith</Author>
    <Comment
        xlink:href="/comments/maryjane"
        xlink:label="My Comment On Joe Smith"
        xlink:title="This book is not great">
        <!-- Optional but here a short description could be added -->
    </Comment>
</Book>
```

The book is defined by using the `Book` XML tag and the child tags `Title` and `Author`. The important tag in this example is the `Comment` XML tag, which uses XML XLink attributes (`href`, `label`, `title`) to define references to the full comments. Defined as a child element within the `Comment` XML tag is an XML comment that says extra descriptive information could be added. The reason for the extra descriptive information is to allow a richer temporary descriptor of the `Comment`. However, under no circumstances should the description information be manipulated by the client and assigned to the book URL. If a comment is to be updated or manipulated, the comment URL referenced by the `Comment` tag is used.

Consider the URLs `http://mydomain.com/books/[ISBN]/comments` and `http://mydomain.com/users/[username]/comments`. Both URLs reference a set of comments, but the comments displayed are different. These URLs provide an example of filtering URLs that illustrate different perspectives of the same underlying data. The problem with these URLs is, who owns the comment? Is the comment owned by the book or by the user? The answer is that it does not matter, because the underlying data will be referenced by using an individual URL. An example of this is the following URLs: `http://mydomain.com/books/[ISBN]/comments/12345` and `http://mydomain.com/users/[username]/comments/12345`. Notice how the individual comment is referenced by using a unique comment identifier. This is important because the comment `12345` should be identical when found by navigating to a book or navigating to a user.

Now consider the URLs `http://mydomain.com/search/books` and `http://mydomain.com/search/users`. These are action URLs that are used to generate a result set that depends on the HTTP query string. This means doing an HTTP `PUT` and `DELETE` will have no effect, and an error should be generated. If the URL `http://mydomain.com/search/users` is requested, all users are returned. If, however, the URL `http://mydomain.com/search/users?username=J*` is requested, all users that have a username starting with `J` are returned. The format of the query string should always be flexible and should not require all parameters to be specified. For example, if you can search for users by using a username and age, you don't have to always specify a username *and* age. Maybe sometimes only the username is specified, other times an age, and sometimes both a username and age. It is even possible in the URL to add a request for a specific formatting of the data (for example, `format=xml`). This is useful when the returned data should be in one format even though the client requesting the data usually gets another format.

When defining a resource URL, it is important to consider what the URL is being used for. Is it being used to represent a user (for example, `http://mydomain.com/user`)? Is it used to represent information (for example, `http://mydomain.com/news/column/jack`)? Is the information created in a time-dependent fashion (for example, http://mydomain.com/news/column/jack/current for current news and http://mydomain.com/news/column/jack/2005-10-10 for an archived news item)? You must remember that the URL represents a resource that the HTTP server is responsible for converting into a representation. The client is not responsible for knowing what technologies or files are stored on the server side, because that is a complete dependency of the HTTP server.

Identifying the Resource and Representation

Taking a closer look at the URL http://mydomain.com/books/[ISBN], let's work through how it would be implemented. The URL refers to a specific book with the identified ISBN number. When the URL is sent to an HTTP server, a response is generated. The problem is determining which content the server should send to the client. Separating the resource from the representation means that a single URL will have separate representations. The representation that is sent depends on the value of the HTTP Accept-* header, but that header need not be the only one. As was just mentioned, the user using a query variable could specify the representation. More about other HTTP headers will be discussed shortly. For now, let's focus on the Accept HTTP header and consider the following HTTP conversation that returns some content.

Request:

```
GET /books/3791330942 HTTP/1.1
Host: 192.168.1.242:8100
User-Agent: Mozilla/5.0 (Macintosh; U; PPC Mac OS X Mach-O; ➥
    en-US; rv:1.7.8) Gecko/20050511
Accept: text/xml,application/xml,application/xhtml+xml, ➥
    text/html;q=0.9,text/plain;q=0.8,image/png,*/*;q=0.5
Accept-Language: en-us,en;q=0.5
Accept-Encoding: gzip,deflate
Accept-Charset: ISO-8859-1,utf-8;q=0.7,*;q=0.7
Keep-Alive: 300
Connection: keep-alive
```

Response:

```
HTTP/1.1 200 OK
Date: Sun, 21 Aug 2005 14:51:40 GMT
Server: Apache/2.0.53 (Ubuntu) PHP/4.3.10-10ubuntu4
Last-Modified: Wed, 11 May 2005 17:43:45 GMT
ETag: "41419c-45-438fd340"
Accept-Ranges: bytes
Content-Length: 69
Keep-Alive: timeout=15, max=100
Connection: Keep-Alive
Content-Type: text/html; charset=UTF-8
```

The request is an HTTP GET, which means the HTTP server needs to retrieve the data associated with the resource. The operation becomes specific due to the request-provided HTTP headers Accept, Accept-Language, Accept-Encoding, and AcceptCharset. These HTTP headers are accepted by the HTTP server and indicate what content to send.

Focusing on the HTTP header `Accept`, you can see that the values are a series of MIME-encoded identifiers that the client can accept and process. The order and type of the identifier are important because they specify the priority of the content that the client wants to receive from the server. The logic is to send the best content available that has the best priority defined by the client. This, for example, forces the server to send HTML content before plain text content. As per the HTTP specification, the priority of the example request-provided MIME types is as follows:

1. `application/xhtml+xml`

2. `text/xml`

3. `application/xml`

4. `image/png`

5. `text/html;q=0.9`

6. `text/plain;q=0.8`

7. `*/*;q=0.5`

The ordering of the identifiers depends on the identifier specialization and its q value. When a MIME-type identifier has no q value, it means a default value of 1.0. When there is a q value, it means to lower the priority of the MIME-type identifier to the value specified by the q value. Identifier specialization occurs when one identifier is a higher priority because the content specified is more specific than the other identifier. In the list of priorities, the identifier `text/xml` is more specific than `*/*` because `*/*` means everything. Additionally, `text/xml` is more specific than `text/*`, and hence `text/xml` is a higher priority.

What you should notice is that the first MIME identifier from the HTTP conversation is `text/xml`, and the second is `application/xml`. Yet in the priority ordering, the first MIME identifier is `application/xhtml-xml`. This is an assumption I made after having read the HTTP and MIME specifications,[2] but I feel it's a bug that happens to be correct.

To understand why this bug happens to be correct, the example request needs to be dissected. The MIME-type identifiers `application/xml`, `text/xml`, and `application/xhtml-xml` are considered specific, and each has a q value of 1. If the order of the MIME types as issued by the browser is followed, it means that the browser prefers receiving XML content to HTML or XHTML content. From the specifications, `application/xml` and `text/xml` MIME types contain XML content, although the XML content could be XHTML content. Reading the specification solves the problem because it indicates that a more specific MIME type is ordered before a less specific MIME type. This means `application/xhtml-xml` is ordered before `application/xml` and `text/xml` because `application/xhtml-xml` is specifically formatted XML.

Having solved this bug (which could be considered an interesting feature) and having sent the proper representation, figuring out what to send with respect to the `Accept` HTTP header does not get any better. Following is another HTTP request that asks for some content.

---

2. `http://www.w3.org/TR/xhtml-media-types/`

Request:

```
GET /books/3791330942  HTTP/1.1
Accept: */*
Accept-Language: en-ca
Accept-Encoding: gzip, deflate
User-Agent: Mozilla/4.0 (compatible; MSIE 6.0; ➥
    Windows NT 5.1; SV1; .NET CLR 2.0.50215; .NET CLR 1.1.4322)
Connection: Keep-Alive
```

Some browsers send the Accept type identifier */*, which essentially means, "Send me whatever you've got; I will accept it." Such a request is extremely unhelpful and makes it difficult to implement the separation of the resource from the representation. The solution to this problem is to define a default representation for the identifier */*. It's not an ideal solution, but a solution created from the necessity to send something. A good default is HTML because those clients that send */* are most likely HTML-based web browsers.

Knowing the preferences of the client, and combining those preferences with the URL, it is possible to send a representation. The decisions are encapsulated into a component that routes the content. The component when called can contain the logic to do one of two things: send the appropriate content, or rewrite the URL that will send the appropriate content. The preferred approach is to rewrite the URL to something that will send the appropriate content. So, for example, if a web browser is interested in the document /book, the representation is /book/[document].html. If an XML-based REST client is interested in the content /book, the representation is /book/[content].xml.

The URL rewrite approach is used for the following reasons:

- Content editors such as Microsoft FrontPage, Macromedia Dreamweaver, or Altova XMLSpy require a specific URL that can be used to edit content. Content editors are not able to edit different representations associated with a single URL.

- A generic URL can be bookmarked, but a redirection to a specific URL can be downloaded.

- URLs can be dynamically routed to any content, which makes it possible to include application versioning capabilities.

The result is that the routing component will never know the details of the content sent to the client. The routing component knows only the URL of the content. The Accept header was illustrated as a way to provide a cue on how to redirect the request, but other HTTP headers can also be used. In the example HTTP headers, Accept-Language indicates the language that the content should be returned in. The routing component needs to consider both HTTP headers when rewriting the URL. The result could be HTML pages in multiple languages, XML content in a subset of languages and encodings, and so on. The routing component manages all the decisions and rewrites the URL to the appropriate representation. This frees the representation developer from having to figure out what content to send.

Now that you have read about the architecture of the Permutations pattern, it should be obvious why the pattern is called what it is. The idea is that a resource is transformed into a set of representations, and the client can choose one of those representations. The remaining part of this chapter is about implementing the Permutations pattern.

Implementation

In the implementation of the Permutations pattern, there are two concerns: associating a representation with a resource, and authorizing a user to access a resource or representation. The implementation of the two concerns requires the creation of a URL rewriter component. The purpose of the URL rewriter component is to inspect the request and decide which content should be generated.

Rewriting URLs

In Figure 5-9, the URL /bankaccount/login was redirected to reference the URL /bankaccount/login.jsp. The redirection in HTTP server terms is called *rewriting* the URL. By using URL rewriting, it is possible to alter the URL being requested without doing a physical HTTP redirect. Even though there are times to use a physical HTTP redirect (for example, after the bank account login), doing so for each URL is a waste of resources.

The URL rewriter component changes the URL to another value; this action is very common on many web servers. Some readers may want to point out that the Apache HTTPD web server has a very capable URL-rewriting module called mod_rewrite, which can be used in lieu of writing a separate URL rewriter component. The mod_rewrite module is a very good URL rewriter, but its ability to return content based on the Accept HTTP header is limited. Hence for most cases it is necessary to write a URL rewriter component. Conceptually, though, writing a URL rewriting component is identical to the functionality being offered by the module mod_rewrite.

When rewriting URLs, the logic to rewrite them needs to be put into something an HTTP server calls a *filter*. Filters are not handlers, in that filters are not responsible for generating the output of a specific request. Filters process all requests, and they will modify input streams, output streams, HTTP parameters, or whatever a filter needs to accomplish. Filters are often used for logging or authentication purposes.

In ASP.NET, a filter can be defined in two places. The first place is in the file global.asax, and the second place is a component that is referenced by the web application configuration file. HTTP servers have multiple phases in which a filter can process the HTTP request. There are phases before the handler processes the request, phases to manage authentication, and phases after the handler has processed the request. The reason for the different phases is that the HTTP request has different states at each phase.

In the case of ASP.NET, the filter phase used to implement the URL rewriting component is OnBeginRequest. The phase OnBeginRequest occurs before any of the other filters are called. The phase is ideally suited for rewriting a URL because the authentication, logging, and so on have not been executed. When performing HTTP authentication, it is important to authenticate by using the rewritten URL, and not the original. This is because depending on the content requested, a client may or may not be granted access.

For simplicity purposes, the URL rewriter component is added to the file global.asax. Additionally, when adding filters to an ASP.NET application, the filter applies to that ASP.NET application only, and not other ASP.NET applications. If instead you wanted a global filter, you would need to write an Internet Server API (ISAPI) filter.

The URL rewriter component will have two definitions: URL rewriter component and rewrite component. The purpose of the URL rewriter component is to provide an entry point and identify a URL that needs to be rewritten. The purpose of the rewrite component is to rewrite a given URL. In C# interface terms, both components are defined as follows:

```
public interface IURLRewriter {
    bool IsResource(HttpRequest request);
    void WriteRedirection( HttpRequest request);
}
public interface IRewriter {
    bool WriteRedirection(string mimetype);
}
```

The interface IURLRewriter is the URL rewriter component and has two methods: IsResource and WriteRedirection. The method IsResource is used to recognize a resource URL, such as http://mydomain.com/account/joesmith. The method WriteRedirection is used to rewrite the URL. Even though it is not obvious, the IRewriter component is wired to the internals of the IURLRewriter component.

The interface IRewriter also has a single method, WriteRedirection, that is used to rewrite the URL. The interface IRewriter is responsible for converting the resource into an appropriate representation. Relating the interface IRewriter to Figure 5-9, it would mean converting the URL /bankaccount/login to the URL /bankaccount/login.jsp. The way that the URL is rewritten is not based on the URL itself but on the MIME type. However, an IRewriter and IURLRewriter implementation could be coded to rewrite the URL based on multiple HTTP headers. When rewriting a URL by using multiple HTTP headers, a priority ordering is used (for example, Accept before Accept-Language). Getting back to the IRewriter interface, if the URL is rewritten, then the WriteRedirection method returns true; otherwise, a false is returned.

As will shortly be illustrated, the URLRewriterASPNet class implements the IURLRewriter interface, and DefaultRewriter implements the IRewriter interface. Based on the implementation types, the interface instances of IRewriter and IURLRewriter are wired together in the OnBeginRequest filter phase of an ASP.NET application. The following source code illustrates the implementation of OnBeginRequest in the global.asax file:

```
void Application_OnBeginRequest(Object sender, EventArgs e) {
    HttpApplication app = (HttpApplication)sender;
    IRewriter rewriter = new DefaultRewriter( app);
    IURLRewriter router = new URLRewriterASPNet( rewriter);
    if (router.IsResource(app.Request)) {
        router.WriteRedirection(app.Request);
    }
}
```

The OnBeginRequest function is named and defined based on the requirements of ASP.NET. When implementing any of the filter phases in ASP.NET, they are propagated as .NET events; therefore, the signature of the method is fixed to the first parameter being an Object instance, and the second parameter being an EventArgs instance. Sender is an instance of HttpApplication, which represents the ASP.NET application. Looking closer at the instantiation of URLRewriterASPNET, you can see that it is wired to an IRewriter instance by using the URLRewriterASPNet constructor. After the instantiations, the first if statement uses the method IsResource to test whether the HTTP request is a resource. If the HTTP request is a resource, the method WriteRedirection is called to rewrite the URL.

Implementing the Details of URL Rewriting

Looking a bit closer at the wiring of the IURLRewriter and IRewriter interface instances, you can see that some details were not explained in the OnBeginRequest function. These details indicate the logic of how to convert a resource into a representation and are described as follows:

1. Verify that the URL is referring to a resource.

2. If the URL is a resource, process the URL. Otherwise, ignore the URL and let the HTTP server process the request.

3. Read the Accept HTTP headers from the request and store them in an array.

4. Sort the array so that the highest-priority Accept header is at the beginning of the list.

5. Iterate the array and attempt to rewrite the URL for each item.

6. If during the looping the URL could be rewritten, exit the loop and let the other filters continue their processing.

The class RouterASPNet is responsible for steps 1, 2, 3, and 5. Step 4 is delegated to another yet-to-be-described class, and step 6 is implemented by DefaultRewriter.

The implementation of URLRewriterASPNet is defined as follows:

```
class URLRewriterASPNet : IURLRewriter {
    IRewriter _defaultRewriter;

    public URLRewriterASPNet( IRewriter rewriter) {
        if (_defaultRewriter == null) {
            throw new Exception( "Rewriter cannot be null");
        }
        _defaultRewriter = rewriter;
    }
    public bool IsResource(HttpRequest request) {
        FileAttributes attributes;
        try {
            attributes = File.GetAttributes(request.PhysicalPath);
        }
        catch (FileNotFoundException ex) {
            return false;
        }
        if ((attributes & FileAttributes.Directory) != 0) {
            return true;
        }
        else {
            return false;
        }
    }
```

```
    public void WriteRedirection(HttpRequest request) {
        string[] elements = (string[])request.AcceptTypes.Clone();
        Array.Sort( elements, new CompareMimeTypes());
        Regex semiColon = new Regex(";");
        foreach (string type in elements) {
            String[] buffers = semiColon.Split(type);
            if (_defaultRewriter.WriteRedirection(buffers[0])) {
                break;
            }
        }
    }
}
```

When implementing step 1 in the method IsResource, the challenge is to figure out whether the URL is a resource or a file reference. A file reference, simply put, would have an extension in the URL indicating the referencing of a specific file type. The decision chosen by the URLRewriterASPNet implementation is to test whether the absolute path of the URL refers to a directory. If a directory is referenced, the URL is a resource; otherwise, the URL is something else. In other IURLRewriter implementations, other logic might be used. Maybe a regular expression is used to validate the URL to see whether a reference to a file exists. Whatever logic is used, a true is returned to indicate a URL resource, and false is used to indicate the URL is something else. If there are multiple IURLRewriter implementations, they are wired together and called by using the Chain of Responsibility pattern.

If the URL needs to be rewritten as per step 2, the method WriteRedirection is called. In the implementation of WriteRedirection, which executes steps 3 and 4, the Accept headers are sorted from highest priority to lowest priority. The sorting is carried out by cloning the Accept headers (request.AcceptTypes) and then calling the method Array.Sort. The default algorithm used by Array.Sort will not work, and therefore the class CompareMimeTypes is used. I will explain that class in a moment. After the Accept identifiers have been sorted, they are iterated, and for each one the method defaultRewriter.WriteRedirection is called. As each identifier is called from highest to lowest priority, the IRewriter implementation tests to see whether the URL can be rewritten. If the test returns a true value, an identifier is found and the URL is rewritten. If the URL has been rewritten, defaultRewriter.WriteRedirection returns true and all processing stops.

The sorting of the individual Accept identifiers will now be discussed. When using a custom sorting routine with Array.Sort, the custom sorting routine would have to implement the IComparer interface. The IComparer interface has a single method that compares two values from the list to be sorted. The single method implementation returns a positive, negative, or zero integer value indicating which value is greater than the other. Following is the implementation of CompareMimeTypes:

```
class CompareMimeTypes : IComparer {
    Regex _wildcard = new Regex(@"/\*");
    Regex _semiColon = new Regex(";");
    public void CalculateValue(string val, out int level, out double qvalue) {
        String[] buffers = _semiColon.Split(val);
        double multiplier = 1.0;
```

```
            if (buffers.Length > 1) {
                multiplier = double.Parse(buffers[1].Substring(2));
            }
            qvalue = multiplier;
            level = 0;
            if (String.Compare(buffers[0], "*/*") == 0) {
                level = 1;
            }
            else if (_wildcard.IsMatch(val)) {
                level = 2;
            }
            else if (String.Compare(buffers[0], "application/xhtml+xml") == 0) {
                level = 4;
            }
            else {
                level = 3;
            }
        }
        public int Compare(object x, object y) {
            int levelx = 0, levely = 0;
            double qvaluex = 0.0, qvaluey = 0.0;
            CalculateValue((string)x, out levelx, out qvaluex);
            CalculateValue((string)y, out levely, out qvaluey);
            if (levelx < levely) {
                return 1;
            }
            else if (levelx > levely) {
                return -1;
            }
            else {
                if (qvaluex < qvaluey) {
                    return 1;
                }
                else if (qvaluex > qvaluey) {
                    return -1;
                }
                else {
                    return 0;
                }
            }
        }
    }
}
```

CompareMimeTypes has two methods: CalculateValue and Compare. The Compare method is required by the IComparer interface and compares two Accept header identifiers. CalculateValue converts the Accept header identifier into a value that can be used for comparison purposes. The calculation of the greater-than value of an individual item is based on the MIME-type specification and its q value. The method CalculateValue has three parameters. The first parameter is the MIME type to test. The second and third parameters are numeric values returned to the caller that indicate the priority of the MIME type. The priority calculation is based on levels and its associated q values. The levels result from the priority precedence of text/xml to text/*. The q values are associated with the Accept identifier.

In the implementation of the method Compare, there are two parameters: x and y. The method implementation has to figure out which value is greater than the other. To get a priority level, the method CalculateValue is called for each parameter. Then the levels (levelx and levely) are compared. If one of the levels is higher, the appropriate integer value is returned. If the levels are equal, the q values (qvaluex and qvaluey) are tested and the appropriate integer value is returned.

After the MIME types have been sorted, URLRewriterASPNet will call the rewriter DefaultRewriter to generate the return content, which is step 5. Following is the implementation of DefaultRewriter:

```
public class DefaultRewriter : IRewriter {
    protected HttpApplication _app;
    private Regex _xml = new Regex("xml");
    private Regex _html = new Regex("html");
    private Regex _text = new Regex("plain");

    public DefaultRewriter(HttpApplication app) {
        _app = app;
    }
    private bool DoesFileExistAndRewrite(string filename) {
        string path = _app.Request.PhysicalPath + filename;
        FileAttributes attributes;
        try {
                attributes = File.GetAttributes(path);
        }
        catch (FileNotFoundException ex) {
            return false;
        }
        if ((attributes & FileAttributes.Directory) == 0) {
            _app.Context.RewritePath(filename);
            return true;
        }
        else {
            return false;
        }
    }
    public virtual bool WriteRedirection(string mimetype) {
        if (_xml.IsMatch(mimetype)) {
            return DoesFileExistAndRewrite("default.xhtml");
        }
        if (_html.IsMatch(mimetype)) {
            return DoesFileExistAndRewrite("default.html");
        }
```

```
            if (_text.IsMatch(mimetype)) {
                return DoesFileExistAndRewrite("default.txt");
            }
            if (String.Compare(mimetype, "*/*") == 0) {
                return DoesFileExistAndRewrite("content.html");
            }
            return false;
        }
}
```

The implementation of the method WriteRedirection will iterate a series of if statements to test which MIME type has been passed in. If any one particular MIME type matches the type, the method DoesFileExistAndRewrite is called. The method DoesFileExistAndRewrite will test whether the proposed rewritten URL references a file that exists, and if so the URL is rewritten. The big idea of the operation for the URL rewriter is to generate a potential URL and test whether there is a file available on the storage medium. If the file exists, the URL can be rewritten; otherwise, another MIME type is tested for availability. If a representation exists, WriteRedirection will return true and consider the URL rewritten, which causes an exit, thus implementing the last step, step 6.

The defined DefaultRewriter will work for static content, but not for dynamic content such as PHP, JSP, or even ASP.NET because the redirections always reference static extensions such as XML, HTML, and XHTML. Suppose PHP is used for generating XML and HTML content. If a request (for example, /content) requires generation of XML content, the generated filename will end with .php (for example, /content.php). Yet if the request requires dynamic generation of HTML, the generated filename will end with .php again (for example, /content.php). One solution would be to append the dynamic script extension and type (for example, HTML would be /content.html.php). The appending of two extensions is used by Apache when sending language-specific content.

Generating the Content

When the rewriting component executes its code, the rewriting of the URL /bankaccount/login to the URL /bankaccount/login.jsp occurs transparently. The next step is to test whether the URL is indeed rewritten, so let's watch Firefox's decision process as it calls the URL. Figure 5-10 illustrates how the browser loads the appropriate document, and that the server tests what the appropriate document would be.

The bottom window of Figure 5-10 is a Secure Shell (SSH) console window of the Mono XSP ASP.NET server running on Linux. The asterisks represent the beginning and ending of an HTTP request. The first line, which starts with Path, is the absolute path of the ASP.NET application's physical path appended with the URL. The next line, which reads Is routable, indicates that a resource has been requested. Then the HTTP Accept header sent by Mozilla is reorganized and then tested to see whether the content can be downloaded. Notice how the various MIME types are iterated and tested. The last MIME type tested is text/html, because the path associated with the MIME type exists. There are other MIME types, but they are not iterated because a MIME type has been found.

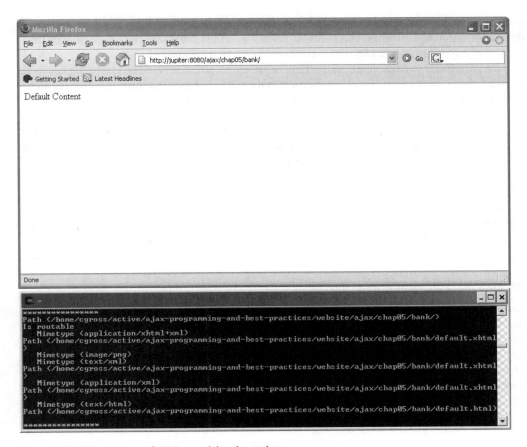

Figure 5-10. *Illustration of URL rewriting in action*

Using the Accept Header on the Client Side

By default, all browsers send the content that they are interested in. It is possible when using the XMLHttpRequest type to specify the Accept HTTP header, as illustrated by the following source code example:

```
var xmlhttp = FactoryXMLHttpRequest();
xmlhttp.open( "GET", "/url", true);
xmlhttp.setRequestHeader( "Accept", "application/xml");
```

The method setRequestHeader is used to specify the Accept HTTP header. Based on the HTTP header, the server can generate the proper source code and send it to the client.

An Example Shopping Cart Application

Back in Figure 5-9, you saw the second URL, /bankaccount/maryjane, which is rewritten, performs an authorization, and references the bank account resource of maryjane. This sort of scenario is commonplace; a simple example is a shopping cart. A shopping cart is a resource, requires the identification of some user, and uses URL rewriting. Additionally, the shopping cart adds the complexity of performing a URL redirection to an unknown resource.

Imagine that I will be buying something at Amazon.com. The Amazon shopping cart will contain what I want to buy. What is unknown is the shopping cart that Amazon uses to reference the items that I want to buy. Shopping carts can be associated with and authorized by only a single person. From a logic perspective, while shopping at Amazon, I do not want somebody to add or remove items from my shopping cart. Additionally, I do not want somebody to be able to create a shopping cart in my name and ship it to another address. So in the end, even though it is not obvious, a shopping cart is a very personal resource.

If the user is authenticated, the shopping cart is associated with the authenticated user. If the user is not authenticated, the shopping cart is associated with the client using a cookie. In either case, a cookie could be used to authorize who is allowed to manipulate the shopping cart. The URL for the shopping cart would be /shoppingcart/12324, but the shopping cart can be accessed only by the authenticated user or cookie of the anonymous user. What is never done is the association of the URL /shoppingcart with a specific authenticated user or cookie.

Defining the User Identification Interfaces

Authenticating a user is the process of creating a user identifier, and there are multiple ways to create a user identifier. This means that when implementing HTTP authentication, some thought should be given to keeping everything neutral so that other user identification implementations could be switched at runtime without affecting how authentication is managed. The solution is to use the Bridge and Factory patterns to define an intention of identifying the user and then define the implementations that technically identify the user.

The following source code defines the interfaces for the intention of identifying a user:

```
public interface IUserIdentificationResolver<WebReference> {
    IUserIdentification Resolve(WebReference reference);
}
public interface IUserIdentificationFactory {
    IUserIdentification Create( string identifier);
    IUserIdentification Create();
}
public interface IUserIdentification {
    string Identifier { get; }
    bool IsIdentified { get; }
}
```

The interface IUserIdentificationResolver<> is defined by using .NET Generics and has a single method, Resolve. .NET Generics are used to define the interface, allowing the interface to be used in multiple user identification implementation contexts. When using Generics, the interface is saying, "Given the WebReference type, I will resolve what the user identification mechanism is."

The interface `IUserIdentification` is returned by the method `IUserIdentificationResolver<>.Resource` and has two properties, `Identifier` and `IsIdentified`. The `Identifier` property is used to identify the user, and `IsIdentified` to indicate whether a user has been identified. In the definition, the interface `IUserIdentification` has only two properties, but depending on your particular context could have more properties or methods. The purpose of the interface is to provide enough information to uniquely identify who is making the called request and to allow the application to use that information for managing the authorization of a resource.

The interface `IUserIdentificationFactory` is used by `IUserIdentificationResolve<>` to instantiate an `IUserIdentification` instance whenever a user identity has been found.

The interfaces make up an important basis of user identification and should be used regardless of the user identification scheme used.

Using HTTP Authentication

The first user identification implementation is HTTP authentication. Using HTTP authentication is probably one of the most underused techniques of creating a user identifier. Most web applications tend to prefer HTTP cookies, but HTTP authentication offers some yet-to-be-discussed options that HTTP cookies do not.

In the early nineties, HTTP authentication was not well known and considered generally insecure because the client would constantly be sending the username and password to the server whenever an authorization was performed. To get around the security issue, a more secure form of HTTP authentication was created, called HTTP digest authentication. HTTP digest authentication in the early Web days was not widely distributed. Of course today that is not the case as every browser, or at least most browsers, support HTTP digest authentication.

Understanding How HTTP Authentication Functions at a Practical Level

HTTP authentication is a very good way of creating a user identifier because the authentication mechanism is formal and requires participation by the user. If the user declines, authentication will not occur, and no information is sent to the server. The user can remain anonymous. Granted, the user might not be able to access all of the content, but there is anonymity and some people treasure their anonymity. Figure 5-11 illustrates how HTTP authentication is presented to the user via current browsers.

Also illustrated in Figure 5-11 is the ability of current browsers to remember past HTTP authentication sessions. HTTP authentication is both a blessing and curse in that users must authenticate themselves whenever they exit and restart the browser. The blessing is that authentication information is not sent automatically, and the curse is that the user must authenticate themselves before starting a session at a website. Some may consider requiring authentication a downside, but when security is important, using HTTP authentication ensures giving the correct rights to the identified user.

At a technical level, HTTP authentication is a mechanism whereby a user requests the contents of a resource and the server issues a challenge, asking for identification. The browser converts the challenge into something similar to Figure 5-11. After the user enters the appropriate information, the server will authenticate the user. If the authentication works, the representation of the resource is downloaded by the browser.

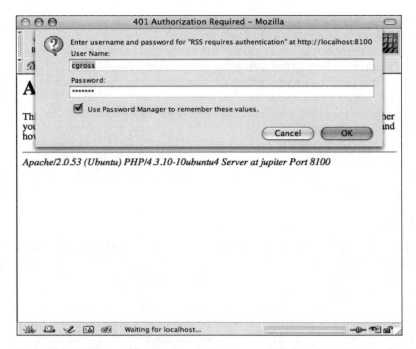

Figure 5-11. *HTTP authentication dialog box prefilled with authentication information*

A typical HTTP digest authentication conversation is described in the following steps. The process starts with the client requesting a resource:

```
GET /test/ HTTP/1.1
Host: jupiter:8100
User-Agent: Mozilla/5.0 (Macintosh; U; PPC Mac OS X Mach-O; ➡
    en-US; rv:1.7.8) Gecko/20050511
Accept: text/xml,application/xml,application/xhtml+xml,text/html;q=0.9, ➡
    text/plain;q=0.8,image/png,*/*;q=0.5
Accept-Language: en-us,en;q=0.5
Accept-Encoding: gzip,deflate
Accept-Charset: ISO-8859-1,utf-8;q=0.7,*;q=0.7
Keep-Alive: 300
Connection: keep-alive
```

The resource is protected, and therefore the server will challenge for an authentication:

```
HTTP/1.1 401 Authorization Required
Date: Sat, 27 Aug 2005 14:00:05 GMT
Server: Apache/2.0.53 (Ubuntu) PHP/4.3.10-10ubuntu4
WWW-Authenticate: Digest realm="Private Domain", nonce="0hvlrVH/
AwA=8225d4804076a334d81181695204fee405adaaee", ➡
algorithm=MD5, domain="/test", qop="auth"
```

```
Content-Length: 497
Keep-Alive: timeout=15, max=100
Connection: Keep-Alive
Content-Type: text/html; charset=iso-8859-1
```

The client receives the HTTP error code 401 and looks for the HTTP header WWW-Authenticate. The value of HTTP WWW-Authenticate contains which authentication mechanism is being requested. In this example, HTTP digest authentication is requested. As a side note, it is possible to use basic authentication, but because it is not considered secure, it is avoided. As a response to the challenge, the browser generates a dialog box similar to Figure 5-11 asking for a username and password. The user types in the username and password, which causes the browser to reissue the original request with the added user authentication information, as shown here:

```
GET /test/ HTTP/1.1
Host: localhost:8100
User-Agent: Mozilla/5.0 (Macintosh; U; PPC Mac OS X Mach-O; ➥
    en-US; rv:1.7.8) Gecko/20050511
Accept: text/xml,application/xml,application/xhtml+xml, ➥
    text/html;q=0.9,text/plain;q=0.8,image/png,*/*;q=0.5
Accept-Language: en-us,en;q=0.5
Accept-Encoding: gzip,deflate
Accept-Charset: ISO-8859-1,utf-8;q=0.7,*;q=0.7
Keep-Alive: 300
Connection: keep-alive
Authorization: Digest username="cgross", realm="Private Domain", ➥
nonce="0hvlrVH/AwA=8225d4804076a334d81181695204fee405adaaee", ➥
uri="/test/", algorithm=MD5, ➥
response="fc4ec419438f87a540d8898a537ea401", qop=auth, ➥
nc=00000001, cnonce="01b6730aae57c007"
```

The resulting request is similar to the initial request, except that there is an additional HTTP header, Authorization. When confronted with the same URL request, the server will search for the Authorization HTTP header. If the server finds the header, the server will verify the information and then, depending on the verification, either return another HTTP 401 error causing the browser to generate a dialog box that asks the user to authenticate himself, or consider the user authenticated. If the provided authentication information is correct, the associated representation is downloaded.

When using HTTP authentication, the Authorization HTTP header is sent for all URLs and their dependents that were specified by the WWW-Authenticate header sent by the server. In this example, the value domain="/test" refers to the single URL /test and its dependencies.

Implementing HTTP Authentication

A programmer should not write any code that manages HTTP authentication. All web servers are capable of managing HTTP authentication, and it should be left as an administrative exercise. This does not mean that the programmer does not use HTTP authentication. The programmer still needs to know whether a user is authenticated and needs to associate user identifier information.

When developing a server-side application, the approach taken to HTTP authentication is to add the user identifier code to a filter, as illustrated previously in the Accept HTTP header example. The filter will search for the Authorization HTTP header and attempt to create a user identifier. The example used ASP.NET code to extract the Authorization header. Some readers who know ASP.NET code will consider this a wrong approach because ASP.NET has methods and properties that manage authentication. I agree that the ASP.NET methods and properties would be a better solution, but because not all readers will be using ASP.NET, the approach that I took is one that can be applied to all platforms. If there are optimizations, then I say, "Good, use them." The implementation does not matter anyway because interfaces are used and the applications using the implementations will not care how the user identification information is extracted. In fact, this is why interfaces are used—so that you are not dependent on a particular implementation.

The following source code starts the implementation of the IUserIdentification interface:

```
public class UserIdentification : IUserIdentification {
    private string _identifier;
    private bool _isIdentified;

    public UserIdentification() {
        _isIdentified = false;
    }
    public UserIdentification( string identifier) {
        _identifier = identifier;
        _isIdentified = true;
    }
    public string Identifier {
        get {
            return _identifier;
        }
    }
    public bool IsIdentified {
        get {
            return _isIdentified;
        }
    }
}
```

The implementation of UserIdentification has two constructors, with and without parameters. There are two constructors to indicate the two states of user identification: found and not found. The constructor without parameters indicates that no user has been identified. The other constructor, which has a single parameter, indicates that user identification has been found; the single parameter is the state of the identified user. In the implementation of either constructor, the private data member isIdentified is assigned a value of true or false to indicate whether or not, respectively, a user identification has been found.

The properties of UserIdentification define the state of the user identification, and it is important to understand that UserIdentification is a state object. A *state object* is one where the primary focus is to store data that is used by other processes to make decisions. A state object is very versatile because it does not have other type dependencies and does not manipulate other classes; thus the UserIdentification implementation would be similar for all IUserIdentificationResolver<> implementations.

The interface IUserIdentificationResolver<> is used to extract the user identifiers. For HTTP authentication, the implementation is illustrated as follows:

```
public class HttpAuthenticationResolver :
    IUserIdentificationResolver<HttpRequest> {
    IUserIdentificationFactory _factory;
    public HttpAuthenticationResolver(IUserIdentificationFactory factory) {
        _factory = factory;
    }
    public IUserIdentification Resolve(HttpRequest app) {
        if (request.Headers["Authorization"] != null) {
            string identifier = "";
            // Do some operations to find out who it is
            return _factory.Create(identifier);
        }
        else {
            return _factory.Create();
        }
    }
}
```

The class HttpAuthenticationResolver implements the interface IUserIdentificationResolver<>, and for the Generics parameter defines the type HttpRequest. What this declaration is saying is that the resolver will extract the user identification information from the type HttpRequest. In ASP.NET, HttpRequest contains all the information that is sent by the request. The constructor for HttpAuthenticationResolver has a parameter, which is an instance of the Factory pattern interface IUserIdentificationFactory. The Factory pattern interface is used by any IUserIdentificationResolver<> implementation whenever an instance of IUserIdentification needs to be instantiated. A Factory pattern implementation is used to instantiate an IUserIdentification instance because the IUserIdentificationResolver<> does not need to know about the type that implements IUserIdentification.

In the implementation of Resolve, the Request.Headers property is referenced to extract the value of the Authorization header. If the HTTP header exists, an identifier is extracted and assigned to the variable identifier, which is passed to the method Create. Using the method Create with parameters indicates that a user has been identified. If the HTTP header is not found, the method Create without parameters is called to instantiate an IUserIdentification instance that indicates that the user has not been identified.

The implementation of Resolve is fairly incomplete and simple because the details are beyond the scope of this discussion; different platforms and environments will be implemented in different techniques. What is complete is the theory of the Resolve method. The theory is that first a check must be made to see whether the HTTP request contains any HTTP authentication headers. If the HTTP headers contain authentication information, the headers must be processed. Regardless of whether or not authentication information is found, Resolve is required to instantiate an IUserIdentification instance.

The processing of the HTTP headers cross-references the authorization information with some local information. The local information represents the user identity as defined by the server and could be stored in a database, a Lightweight Directory Access Protocol (LDAP) server, or some other repository. In the example, the variable identifier represents the local information, but the local information does not need to be a single variable, and it could be a structure, class, or some other hierarchy. The form of the local information really depends on the server implementation and nature of the web application. What this results in is a modified version of IUserIdentification, and the factory Create methods. If your local application has a class to represent the local information, the Create method with a parameter would be modified to pass in a class instead of a simple string buffer. If the local information consisted of two classes, the Create method and IUserIdentification definition would consist of those two classes. The examples proposed are only rules of thumb, but two Create factory methods are needed to indicate an identified user and an unidentified user.

The last step is to wire everything together in the global.asax file. As in the Accept HTTP header example, the user identification code is placed in the BeginRequest handler, which is the first phase called when handling a request. Before the code is shown, let's ask ourselves whether that is the best place to put the user identification code. Regardless of platform, there are various phases, and one of them is before an authentication phase. As it stands right now, the wiring is happening before the server performs the authentication, which might mean that the authentication by the server is not complete. This in turn might mean that if certain authentication properties and methods are used, they will not be complete. Hence, a better place to wire the user identification routines when using HTTP authentication is after the authentication phase. For ASP.NET, that is the OnAcquireRequestState phase.

Following is the implementation of the method Application_OnAcquireRequestState:

```
void Application_OnAcquireRequestState(Object sender, EventArgs e) {
    HttpApplication app = (HttpApplication)sender;
    IUserIdentificationResolver<HttpApplication> resolver =
        new HttpAuthenticationResolver(new UserIdentificationFactory());
    IUserIdentification user = resolver.Resolve(app);
    app.Context.Items["identifier"] = user;
}
```

In the implementation of Application_OnAcquireRequestState, the object instance sender is typecast to an instance of HttpApplication. The resolver variable references an instance of the HttpAuthenticationResolver type. The implementation of the factory UserIdentificationFactory has not been shown, but is an implementation of the Factory pattern and instantiates the UserIdentification type. Then the method Resolve is called, and an instance of IUserIdentification is returned. These steps can be performed on any platform because they are generic. What is specific to ASP.NET and will be on other platforms is how to hand the user identification information (IUserIdentification instance) to the handler. In the case of ASP.NET, the user identification is assigned to the Context.Items property. On other platforms, it will be some other property that is common to all handlers and filters throughout the life cycle of the HTTP request and response.

As it stands, the server has been wired, and the individual handler needs to reference the user identification whenever content should be accessed or not. To make the HTTP authentication application work, the client has to provide the username and password. Figure 5-11 showed how to send a username and password via the browser, but the following example illustrates how to do the same thing via the XMLHttpRequest object:

```
var xmlhttp = FactoryXMLHttpRequest();
xmlhttp.open( "GET", "/url", true, username, password");
```

The only change is the addition of the fourth and fifth parameters of the open method. The fourth parameter represents the username, and the fifth parameter is the password. When given those parameters, XMLHttpRequest will use the username and password when XMLHttpRequest is challenged. If there are no authentication challenges, the username and password are ignored. Therefore, when using HTTP authentication and the XMLHttpRequest object, you could always pass the username and password to XMLHttpRequest and let XMLHttpRequest handle the details.

Authenticating When It Is Not Necessary

One of the side effects of HTTP authentication is that content usually is either protected or not protected. Traditionally—and this is why cookies are used—HTTP authentication cannot be off for a resource and then on again for the same resource. That would confuse users because, as it stands right now, HTTP authentication is a global setting and not an individual setting. In other words, if authentication is required for one, then it is required for all. That poses a problem in that if a user wants to browse a site and is purchasing something, that user will need a shopping cart. But to implement a shopping cart, a user identifier is needed. To create a shopping cart, unprotected resources need to be protected. But the protection is global and hence it would mean everybody would need to get a shopping cart after browsing the first page of a shopping site and start buying something. Nice idea to jump-start an economy, but it is not going to happen. To get around this issue of sometimes protection, you can use an HTTP authentication technique.

The technique is as follows:

1. Let the user browse the site as usual (for example, `http://mydomain.com/browse`).

2. On each browsed page, add a protected link to indicate that the user wants to be authenticated (`http://mydomain.com/browse/authenticate`).

3. When the user clicks on the authentication link after the authorization, the HTTP realms (domains) that include the nonprotected content are assigned in the response (`http://mydomain.com/browse`).

4. Then when the user browses the URL `http://mydomain.com/browse`, user identification information is sent even though it is not required.

This trick works extremely well if you use HTTP digest authentication. Following is an example Apache HTTPD configuration that uses this technique:

```
<Directory "/var/www/browse/authenticate">
        AllowOverride AuthConfig
        AuthType Digest
        AuthDigestDomain /browse /browse/authenticate
        AuthDigestFile "/etc/apache2/digestpasswd"
        AuthName "Private Domain"
        Require valid-user
</Directory>
```

The technique is implemented by the configuration item AuthDigestDomain, where both the URLs /browse and /browse/authenticate are referenced. Because the configuration item Directory references the URL /browse/authenticate, only the URL /browse/authenticate will be challenged for an authentication. To illustrate that the technique actually works, consider the following HTTP conversation.

First, a request is made for an unprotected resource:

```
GET /browse/ HTTP/1.1
Host: jupiter:8100
User-Agent: Mozilla/5.0 (Windows; U; Windows NT 5.0; en-US; ➡
    rv:1.7.5) Gecko/20041220 K-Meleon/0.9
Accept: text/xml,application/xml,application/xhtml+xml,text/html;q=0.9, ➡
    text/plain;q=0.8,image/png,*/*;q=0.5
```

The server responds as usual with an HTTP 200 return code, which causes the client to load the resulting page. Then the client makes another request to the protected link because the user wants to shop and needs to be authenticated. The client makes the following request for the protected content:

```
GET /browse/authenticate HTTP/1.1
Host: 192.168.1.103:8100
User-Agent: Mozilla/5.0 (Windows; U; Windows NT 5.0; en-US; ➡
    rv:1.7.5) Gecko/20041220 K-Meleon/0.9
Accept: text/xml,application/xml,application/xhtml+xml,text/html;q=0.9, ➡
    text/plain;q=0.8,image/png,*/*;q=0.5
```

The server responds with an authentication challenge:

```
HTTP/1.1 401 Authorization Required
Date: Sun, 28 Aug 2005 16:08:28 GMT
Server: Apache/2.0.53 (Ubuntu) PHP/4.3.10-10ubuntu4
WWW-Authenticate: Digest realm="Private Domain", ➡
nonce="yiLhlmf/AwA=e1bafc57a6151c77e1155729300132415fc8ad0c", ➡
    algorithm=MD5, domain="/browse /browse/authenticate", ➡
    qop="auth"
Content-Length: 503
Content-Type: text/html; charset=iso-8859-1
```

In the server response for the domain identifier, a nonprotected resource is defined. This is the technique used to send authorization information for nonprotected content. The client responds with user authentication as follows:

```
GET /browse/authenticate HTTP/1.1
Host: 192.168.1.103:8100
User-Agent: Mozilla/5.0 (Windows; U; Windows NT 5.0; en-US; ➡
    rv:1.7.5) Gecko/20041220 K-Meleon/0.9
Accept: text/xml,application/xml,application/xhtml+xml,text/html;q=0.9, ➡
    text/plain;q=0.8,image/png,*/*;q=0.5
Authorization: Digest username="cgross", realm="Private Domain", ➡
nonce="yiLhlmf/AwA=e1bafc57a6151c77e1155729300132415fc8ad0c", ➡
```

```
uri="/browse/authenticate", algorithm=MD5, ➡
response="c9b5662c034344a06103ca745eb5ebba", qop=auth, ➡
nc=00000001, cnonce="082c875dcb2ca740"
```

After the authentication, the server allows the downloading of the protected content. Now if the client browses the unprotected URLs again, the authorization information is passed to the server, as illustrated by the following request:

```
GET /browse/morecontent / HTTP/1.1
Host: jupiter:8100
User-Agent: Mozilla/5.0 (Windows; U; Windows NT 5.0; en-US; ➡
    rv:1.7.5) Gecko/20041220 K-Meleon/0.9
Accept: text/xml,application/xml,application/xhtml+xml,text/html;q=0.9, ➡
    text/plain;q=0.8,image/png,*/*;q=0.5
Authorization: Digest username="cgross", realm="Private Domain", ➡
nonce="yiLhlmf/AwA=e1bafc57a6151c77e1155729300132415fc8ad0c", ➡
    uri="/browse/morecontent/", algorithm=MD5, ➡
    response="18ccd32175ce7a3480d5fbbc24de8889", qop=auth, ➡
    nc=00000005, cnonce="0d448aca73b76eb1"
```

For this request, the client has sent authorization information for a URL that does not require authentication. Simply put, the authentication mechanism has become an "HTTP cookie" mechanism that is controlled by the client. The client is in full control of when to become authenticated and when to remain anonymous.

Using HTTP Cookies

The other way of creating a user identifier is to use an HTTP cookie, as illustrated in Figure 5-9. Frameworks such as ASP.NET have made it very comfortable to implement user identifiers that are cross-referenced with an HTTP cookie. The cross-referencing of the HTTP cookie with the authorization of a resource is not implemented by default in ASP.NET, but it is not difficult to implement.

Generating the Cookie

It is possible to generate an HTTP cookie[3] without using any help from a library. Because of the prevalence of cookies, most server-side libraries have classes or functions to generate cookies based on a few parameters. Using the available server-side libraries is highly recommended.

Generating the cookie by using the server-side libraries is not difficult. When using ASP.NET, the following source code would be used:

```
HttpCookie mycookie = new HttpCookie("Sample", "myvalue");
mycookie.Path = "/ajax/chap05";
Page.Response.Cookies.Add(mycookie);
```

A cookie is instantiated (HttpCookie) and at a minimum the key (Sample) and value (myvalue) are specified. The combination key-value pair is sent between the client and server. The cookie property mycookie.Path specifies for which URL and its descendents the cookie is valid. Comparing

---

3. http://www.ietf.org/rfc/rfc2965.txt

this to HTTP authentication, the cookie path is equal to the HTTP authentication realm. The newly created cookie is added to the response by using the method `Page.Response.Cookies.Add`. When a cookie is added, the HTTP response will generate a cookie using the `Set-Cookie` HTTP header, as illustrated by the following HTTP server response:

```
HTTP/1.0 200 OK
Server: Mono-XSP Server/1.0.9.0 Unix
X-Powered-By: Mono
Date: Sun, 28 Aug 2005 17:31:14 GMT
Content-Type: text/html; charset=utf-8
Set-Cookie: Sample=myvalue; path=/ajax/chap05
Content-Length: 388
Keep-Alive: timeout=15, max=99
Connection: Keep-Alive
```

The cookie `Sample` has a value of `myvalue` and is valid for the path `/ajax/chap05`. Because there is no expires value, the cookie is valid only for the lifetime of the browser. If the browser is closed, the cookie is deleted, thus behaving like an HTTP authentication-based user identifier.

Understanding How the Client Manages the Cookie

When the client receives the cookie, the cookie will automatically be saved if the client is a browser or the `XMLHttpRequest` object of the browser. In fact, the JavaScript on the client side has to do absolutely nothing with the assigned cookie because everything occurs transparently. For example, if a browser loads a page and a cookie is assigned for the entire domain, and then when the `XMLHttpRequest` object calls a page within the domain, the cookie will be sent.

One thing that is not recommended is the storing of sensitive information within the cookie. Storing passwords or any kind of personal information is not recommended. A cookie is a reference to information, not a repository for information. When a user has been authenticated by using other means, a cookie should be used only as a token to identify the user.

Identifying a User with a Cookie

When the server generates a cookie, it means nothing because a cookie is just a token. Going back to the shopping mall example, it is equivalent to giving each person a token that provides a reference to that person, and as that person wanders the mall, data is generated. To cross-reference the token, an authentication mechanism has to be applied. Two authentication mechanisms could be used. The first is to tie the cookie with HTTP authentication. The second is to create an HTML page that associates the cookie with a user.

Using HTTP authentication to associate a user with a cookie would involve protecting a file that requires an explicit authentication. When the user is authenticated by using HTTP authentication the protected file is responsible for associating the cookie and authentication information.

Implementing HTTP authentication in the context of a cookie is similar to the pure HTTP authentication example. The URL used to authenticate the user has a slightly modified implementation. The same interfaces are used in the HTTP authentication example except that the `IUserIdentificationResolver<>` implementation resolves the authorization and associates it with the cookie. Other than the slight modification of `IUserIdentificationResolver<>`, the exact same source code as was illustrated in the HTTP authentication can be used. The difference is where the association of user identification to cookie occurs. For the example using ASP.NET, the protected URL would be authentication.aspx, and the implementation of authentication. aspx would be as follows:

```
<%@ Page Language="C#" %>
<%@ Import Namespace="Component.Authentication" %>
<script runat="server">
    public void Page_Init( Object source, EventArgs ev) {
        IUserIdentificationResolver< HttpRequest> resolver =
            new HttpAuthenticationToCookieResolver(
                new UserIdentificationFactory());
        IUserIdentification user = resolver.Resolve(Page.Request);
        if (!user.IsIdentified) {
            Page.Response.StatusCode = 500;
            Page.Response.StatusDescription = "No authorization information";
            Page.Response.SuppressContent = false;
            Page.Response.End();
        }
        else {
            Session["useridentifier"] = user;
        }
    }
</script>

<html>
<head runat="server">
    <title>Protected</title>
</head>
<body>
    Success!
</body>
</html>
```

In the ASP.NET page, the function Page_Init implements the initialization phase of the page loading. The init phase is called before the page is processed, and is ideal to test whether the user is authorized. In the implementation, the first two lines, which instantiate the HttpAuthenticationToCookieResolver type and call the method Resolve, are identical to the user identification examples using HTTP authentication.

What is different from the HTTP authentication examples is that the instantiated IUserIdentification instance is tested to see whether the user is identified. If the user is not identified (!user.IsIdentified), an HTTP 500 error is generated with the message that there is no authorization information. It might be tempting to return an HTTP 401 error to indicate an unauthorized access to the document, but that would be incorrect. It would be incorrect because authentication.aspx is not responsible for implementing HTTP authentication. That is the job of the administrator. If an HTTP 500 error has been generated, what has happened is that the administrator did not protect the URL.

If authorization information is associated with the request, the user variable will reference an authenticated user instance that could be assigned to the Session variable. In ASP.NET, the Session variable is the session information associated with the cookie sent by ASP.NET. Then whenever any handler is called, the Session will contain a reference to the identified user.

The user does not have to be authenticated using HTTP authentication. An HTML form could be used instead. Using the HTML form, the developer is responsible for providing code that manages a user. Because of this added code, the HTTP authentication mechanism is preferred because it is the basis of the HTTP protocol.

Implementing the Shopping Cart

Now that you can authenticate a user, you can associate a shopping cart with a user. When creating a shopping cart, do not consider the shopping cart to be available at one URL. There will be many users of a site, and they will each need their own shopping cart. This means each user gets an individual shopping cart at a unique URL. This is a chicken-and-egg scenario, because if there is an individual URL for a shopping cart, how does the user get that individual URL if they do not know it in the first place? Comparing it to the mall example, it is like saying, "Yeah, we have shopping carts, but they are somewhere in this mall." Logically all malls put their shopping carts in easy-to-reach locations. This is what has to happen online. The result is the creation of a URL that acts as a directory listing.

If the URL http://mydomain.com/shoppingcart were the easy-to-reach location, calling it would result in the following being generated:

```
<dir xmlns:xlink="http://www.w3.org/1999/xlink">
    <cart
        xlink:href="example12345"
        xlink:label="unlabelled"
        xlink:title="Unlabelled Shopping Cart" />
</dir>
```

The generated result is an XML file that contains a number of contained links defined by using the XML XLink notation. Each generated link represents an available cart. Because each client requires a cart, the generated result does not need to contain all available shopping carts. The generated result needs to contain only one unique available cart. When referencing the shopping cart, the client needs to remember only the links generated in the result.

If the client is operating in anonymous mode, has not been authenticated, and has turned off cookies, the client JavaScript only needs to remember the provided shopping cart link. If the client is authenticated or has allowed cookies, the projected shopping cart links can be associated with the cookie.

Another solution that allows complete anonymity and could be used very effectively is not to save the state on the server side, but on the client side. So whenever the client decides to purchase something, the shopping cart on the client is filled. To check out the items in the cart, the client references a URL and passes the cart to the server. The cart state would be volatile, but it would be a true shopping cart in that no authentication is necessary until the user is ready to check out.

If the shopping cart is based on the generated link, the cart is server side. The shopping cart could be kept for a long time, and implementing the Permutations pattern would allow users to switch devices, browsers, or locations to view their shopping carts. To make the shopping cart work properly, you need to define the Accept and Authorization headers, as illustrated by the following HTTP request:

```
GET /shoppingcart HTTP/1.1
Host: 192.168.1.103:8100
User-Agent: Mozilla/5.0 (Windows; U; Windows NT 5.0; en-US; ➥
    rv:1.7.5) Gecko/20041220 K-Meleon/0.9
Accept: application/xml
Authorization: Digest username="cgross", realm="Private Domain", ➥
nonce="yiLhlmf/AwA=e1bafc57a6151c77e1155729300132415fc8ad0c", ➥
    uri="/browse/authenticate", algorithm=MD5, ➥
    response="c9b5662c034344a06103ca745eb5ebba", qop=auth, ➥
    nc=00000001, cnonce="082c875dcb2ca740"
```

The request is an illustration of doing multiple things at the same time and contains both authorization and representation information. The server would generate a response similar to the following:

```
<dir xmlns:xlink="http://www.w3.org/1999/xlink">
    <cart
        xlink:href="cgross/cart1"
        xlink:label="cart1"
        xlink:title="Shopping Cart 1" />
    <cart
        xlink:href="cgross/cart2"
        xlink:label="cart2"
        xlink:title="Shopping Cart 2" />
    <cart
        xlink:href="cgross/cart3"
        xlink:label="unlabelled"
        xlink:title="Unlabelled Shopping Cart" />
</dir>
```

The newly generated response contains a directory listing of all shopping carts associated with the individual user cgross. The links cgross/cart1 and cgross/cart2 represent already created and manipulated carts. The link cgross/cart3 is a new cart that could be used to buy other items. The already existing carts could be old shopping experiences or shopping carts that are waiting for checkout. The big idea is that it is possible to have multiple carts that could be manipulated at different times. Or the server could implement repeat purchases based on a past shopping cart, wish lists, and so on. Using server-based carts allows a website to perform automations.

The example illustrated the available carts being generated for those who want to manipulate XML. If a browser references the shopping cart URL link, the following HTML content would be generated:

```
<html>
    <body>
        <a href="cgross/cart1" label="cart1">Shopping Cart 1</a>
        <a href="cgross/cart2" label="cart2">Shopping Cart 2</a>
        <a href="cgross/cart3" label="unlabelled">Shopping Cart 1</a>
    </body>
</html>
```

Notice how the generated content is HTML, but that a directory listing is still generated similar to the generated XML.

Shopping carts are personal items that do not need to be associated with a generic link. Shopping carts have unique URLs that can be entirely anonymous or be associated with a user. The shopping cart illustrates how it is unnecessary to have generic URLs yet still be able to offer the same functionality, even if the user has turned off cookies.

Pattern Highlights

The purpose of the Permutations pattern is to define a component-type structure for Web applications that can be associated with a user identifier. Web applications can implement an interface-driven architecture, where the resource mimics an interface, and representation mimics an implementation. The added benefit for the developer is the ability to modularize a web application in a consistent structure.

The benefit of the pattern is best illustrated by looking at Figure 5-7, where some URLs implement the Permutations pattern, and others do not. The URLs that implement the Permutations pattern are the reference URLs that clients use when accessing their functionality. A reference URL would be a user's bank account, shopping cart, and so on. Those URLs that are part of the implementation are specific and will generally not be bookmarked by the user.

The following points are the important highlights of the Permutations pattern:

- There are two aspects of the Permutations pattern: resource separated from representation, and the definition of URLs that reference specific resources.

- Separating a resource from a representation means providing a generic URL that can be used on multiple devices or browser types. The end user needs to remember only the URL, and the appropriate content will be generated by the server, depending on the HTTP headers of the HTTP request.

- When implementing the separation of the resource from the representation, URL rewriting is commonly used. For example, the resource URL `http://mydomain.com/resource` is redirected to a potential representation URL `http://mydomain.com/resource/content.html`.

- Redirected resources such as `content.html` do not need multiple representations. When a resource has an extension such as `html`, it is implied that the representation is HTML.

- When defining resource URLs, they will often reference data resources such as users or bank accounts. The resource URLs are noun based, for example, `http://mydomain.com/bankaccount/maryjane`. The URL rewriting component then has the additional responsibility of ensuring those who access a noun-based, resource-based URL have the security clearance. Security clearance is determined by the user identifier. User identifiers are not used to generate content, but to allow or disallow access to a resource.

- Cookies and HTTP authentication mechanisms are the preferred means used to implement user identification.

- Sometimes when implementing the Permutations pattern it is not possible or desirable to return content solely based on the Accept HTTP header. In those instances, it is possible to specify the content that is retrieved by using a parameter in the query. An example is `http://mydomain.com/mybooks/1223?accept=text/xml`. The query parameter accept is an arbitrary value and has no special value other then being illustrative in this example.

- Even though all of the examples used HTTP GET to retrieve the correct content, the same rules apply for HTTP POST because an HTTP POST can generate data.

- A URL rewriter component need not use only a single HTTP header such as Accept. A more sophisticated URL rewriter component will base its decisions on all information passed to it by the HTTP request and then make a single URL rewrite decision.

CHAPTER 6

Decoupled Navigation Pattern

Intent

The Decoupled Navigation pattern defines a methodology for decoupling client-side code and navigation into smaller modular chunks, making the client-side content simpler to create, update, and maintain.

Motivation

The basis of any web application is its capability to link together two pieces of content. An HTML link, for example, is a one-way link in that clicking it sends you from content A to content B. There is no built-in HTML mechanism that provides a bidirectional link to connect content B with content A. In theory, when clicking on a link that loads another page, there is no way to get back to the original page. A web browser solves that problem by providing a history of navigated pages. Pressing the Back button on the web browser causes the web browser to look in the history and load the previously visited page.

The link is the basis of the web application, and without the link the Web would not be the Web. However, the link that was the default navigation mechanism in 1995 is not the same link more than a decade later. Let me rephrase that statement: the technical implementation of the link has not changed, but what has changed is how the link is used. With the advent of Dynamic HTML, Ajax, REST, and all the other technologies, the link has taken on a new kind of importance.

For most of the other patterns in this book, the link was a URL that was loaded. The patterns focused on defining a good URL and using the URL, but did not consider how to process a URL or a link on an HTML page.

The classical link that links one HTML page to another is illustrated in Figure 6-1.

Figure 6-1 shows two types of links: the classical link and the static GUI link. A *classical link* is a construct that has some defined text surrounded by special HTML tags that when processed by a web browser cause the text to be highlighted. The special HTML tags for the classical link include an a tag that contains a reference to a URL. A *static GUI link* is like a classical link except that an image is used instead of some defined text.

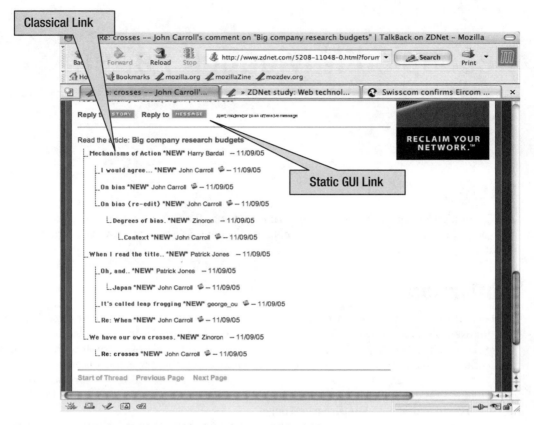

Figure 6-1. *Example of a classical link and a static GUI link*

Clicking the classical link or static GUI link causes the current HTML page to be replaced with a new HTML page. The links are obvious to the human eye, because they tend to be distinguished from other content on the HTML page by using boldface or underlining. When a search engine processes a link, the link is used to provide connection to other content that is indexed. Figure 6-2 illustrates what a search engine sees when processing an HTML page.

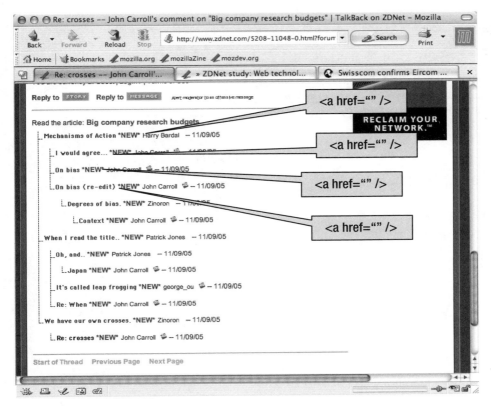

Figure 6-2. *HTML page structure with respect to a search engine*

In Figure 6-2, the links of Figure 6-1 have been explicitly highlighted and illustrate that most HTML pages have a multitude of links. A search engine sees many more links than we realize. The point is that links have changed in their nature, complexity, and sheer number.

Figure 6-3 illustrates a more complicated GUI with links that do more than provide a way to navigate content as a classical link does.

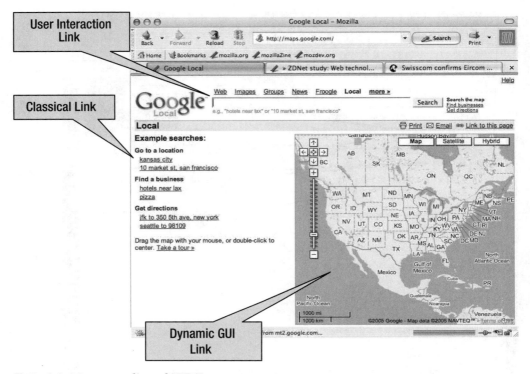

Figure 6-3. *More-complicated HTML page structure*

Figure 6-3 shows three types of links: classical, user interaction, and dynamic GUI. A classical link has already been explained. A *user interaction link* is used when the result of content navigation depends on what the user provides as data. In Figure 6-3, the user interaction link is a text box used to define a query that executes a search. The results of the search depend on the content of the query string. The *dynamic GUI link* is a short-circuited link that when clicked will execute some logic resulting in the navigation of content, generation of images, or some other visual effect.

Figures 6-1 and 6-2 show links of the traditional or initial Web, and Figure 6-3 shows links of the modern Web. The modern Web has changed what it means to navigate content, in that information is navigated. Navigating information is more complicated because determining what information is navigated requires client-side logic. In Figure 6-3, not all links are created equal from a logic perspective. Some links are more complicated, and that is the focus of the Decoupled Navigation pattern.

Figure 6-4 dissects the HTML content of Figure 6-3 into individual content chunks.

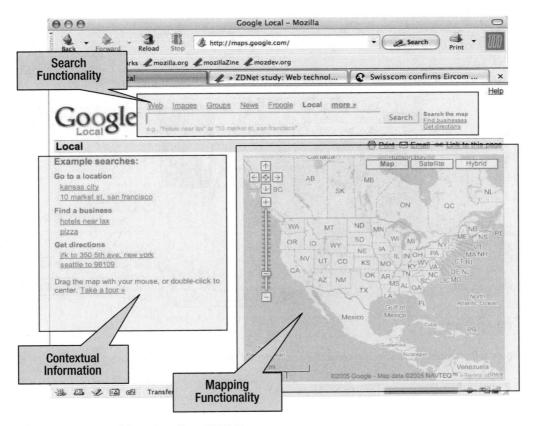

Figure 6-4. *Dissected functionality of HTML page*

This HTML page has three types of content chunks: searching, mapping, and contextual. The content chunks are not—and do not need to be—independent of each other. In Figure 6-4, the contextual information is generated based on what is displayed in the mapping chunk. And the searching chunk, when executed, generates content for the mapping and contextual chunks. What is interesting about these chunks is that they are related, because each chunk generates links that depend on the context of the content in the other chunk.

Applicability

The Decoupled Navigation pattern is used when content is navigated. The statement is obtuse and does not really say anything because HTML content is always navigated. However, because of the way Dynamic HTML is used, content navigation is sometimes used to generate an effect. When links are used to generate effects, the Decoupled Navigation pattern does not apply.

To clarify this explanation, Figure 6-5 provides a snapshot of a website that illustrates where the Decoupled Navigation pattern is applicable and not applicable.

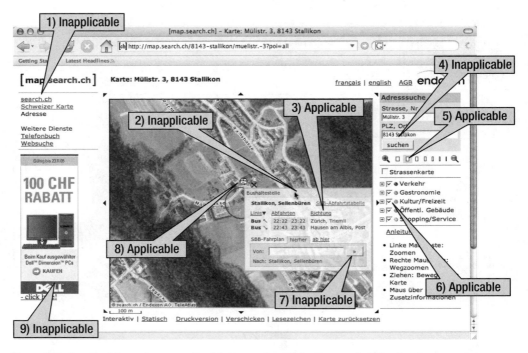

Figure 6-5. *Applicable and not applicable scenarios of the Decoupled Navigation pattern*

The individual scenarios are explained as follows:

1. Inapplicable: The link is inapplicable because it references another link that wishes to start a new context unrelated to the current content. This scenario is comparable to when a user runs one application and then starts another application.

2. Inapplicable: The pop-up dialog box has a title bar that in some cases allows the pop-up to be dragged by using a mouse. The act of dragging is purely a user interface action that at the technical level uses HTML events and navigation techniques.

3. Applicable: The link referenced in the pop-up dialog box is visually identical to scenario 1, but when clicked the actions are not. This link-click is caught as an event and processed by using a JavaScript function. The JavaScript function processes the link context and loads content that relates to the context. In a sense, this scenario and the first scenario are related because under normal circumstances the referenced content is unrelated to the current content. The difference is that the JavaScript function intelligently decides what should be loaded, thus relating the current context to the new context.

4. Inapplicable: The link referenced by this scenario is an HTML form. By its nature an HTML form is designed to change contexts and replace the old context with a new context. However, HTML forms can function like the link in scenario 3. To make this scenario applicable, the form event onsubmit would need to be processed.

5. Applicable: The images as they are presented are visually similar to the classical and static graphic links. The difference is that the onclick events are captured and processed by using JavaScript.

6. Applicable: This scenario would usually be inapplicable because the check boxes would be part of an HTML form. In this scenario, the check boxes are applicable because selecting and deselecting the boxes causes some JavaScript filtering code to make circles appear or disappear on the map.

7. Inapplicable: This example HTML form would typically be applicable because a JavaScript script would execute to change the contents of the pop-up. However, in this scenario the Decoupled Navigation pattern is inapplicable because the resulting navigation causes another web browser window to appear.

8. Applicable: The graphic on the map is a so-called *hot spot* because when a mouse moves over the graphic, a pop-up box (like the yellow dialog box) appears. This scenario is applicable because a JavaScript script has to wire the onmousemove event with the appearance of the pop-up box.

9. Inapplicable: The advertisement is inapplicable because in most cases the content used to generate the advertisement has absolutely nothing to do with the content of the HTML page.

From the different scenarios there are a few rules of thumb indicating when the Decoupled Navigation pattern applies and does not apply:

- When applying the pattern, there will be some JavaScript that represents some application logic. This is one of the main considerations as it indicates some intelligent decision-making process is required.

- Each application of the pattern involves an event, a URL, application data, and some form of presenting that data.

- If the navigation requires any type of data processing, the Decoupled Navigation pattern can be applied. Do not confuse this with data gathering, as that is what a plain-vanilla HTML form does.

Associated Patterns

The Decoupled Navigation pattern is an extension of the Content Chunking pattern. The Content Chunking pattern outlines a strategy whereby areas of an HTML page are defined to be filled with chunks of content. The Content Chunking pattern does not define what content is injected into the areas or how. The role of the Decoupled Navigation pattern is to define that what and how.

When the Content Chunking pattern is implemented, a function calls XMLHttpRequest, which generates some data that is then injected into the current HTML content. The Decoupled Navigation pattern does chunk content, but does so with a strategy in mind. The strategy involves the execution of the following sequence of steps: an HTML event is generated, a URL is usually executed, some data is manipulated, and that data is converted into a user interface representation.

The Decoupled Navigation pattern can be confused with the Persistent Communications pattern. The confusion stems from the fact that a timer event is an HTML event, and that the timer event could be used to kick off the Decoupled Navigation. The main difference between the Decoupled Navigation and Persistent Communications patterns is that Persistent Communications is used for "ticker tape" type applications. This means content is being generated in larger quantities, and it is more important to get information flowing from server to client, and not the usual client to server.

Architecture

The Decoupled Navigation pattern is an attempt to organize the possible navigations on an HTML page. The average HTML page has at least 30 links, and more than 50 is not out of the norm. If an HTML page has 30 links, those links need to be managed by using a strategy. And if 15 of those 30 links require some amount of JavaScript, the average HTML page will be very complex. Complexity requires organization because otherwise chaos and maintenance problems can result. The Decoupled Navigation pattern is used to provide organization to the chaos.

Technically, classical navigation is the result of clicking a link that results in some content being downloaded. The process of navigation can be disassembled into three functionalities, as illustrated in Figure 6-6.

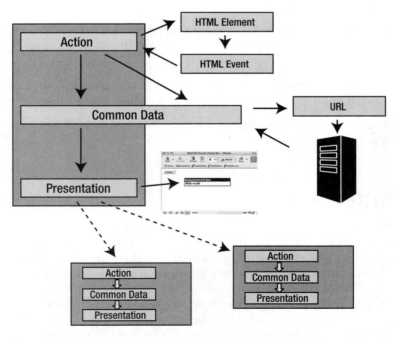

Figure 6-6. *Navigation disassembled into three functionalities*

The three functionalities are described as follows:

- *Action:* Represents the HTML element and the associated HTML events. A link with an implementation of the `onclick` event is an example of Action functionality. The purpose of the Action functionality is to instantiate the navigation process and prepare the data.

- *Common Data:* The Common Data functionality does two things: define a common data structure called state, and provide a function to manipulate the state. The state is a data structure shared by all functionalities. The function to manipulate the state may be purely local or may involve a remote `XMLHttpRequest` object call. One example of using a state function is to manipulate the state by using an XSL transformation.

- *Presentation:* Represents the physical representation of the state. The Presentation functionality transforms the state into something that the user can see and potentially interact with. The transformation may be a pop-up box, window, or HTML injection. It is important to realize that the Presentation functionality only reads—and does not change—the state.

Considering the Decoupled Navigation pattern and its functionalities, you can see that the pattern is concerned primarily with the client side. The Decoupled Navigation pattern is responsible for defining, calling, and processing the URLs. From the perspective of the Decoupled Navigation pattern, the server side is some other functionality that implements the appropriate patterns such as the Permutation pattern.

Figure 6-6 illustrates the Decoupled Navigation pattern in abstract terms, and that is good for understanding what needs to be implemented. However, to get an idea of what is involved technically, Figure 6-7 illustrates the three functionalities and their associated implementations.

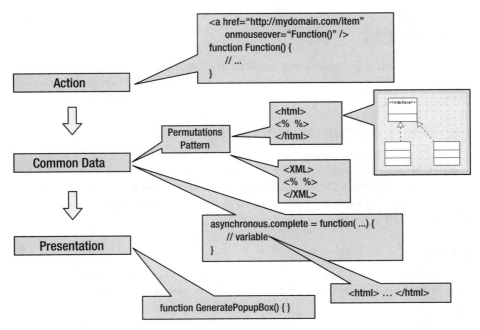

Figure 6-7. *Three functionalities and their associated technical implementations*

In Figure 6-7, the three functionalities are converted into technical implementation counterparts. For the Action functionality, there is a link that captures the onmouseover event and calls Function. The Action functionality in implementation terms will have an HTML element that triggers some HTML event that is captured by a JavaScript function. The JavaScript function Function, in turn, requests content from a URL, which is a resource implemented by the server. The JavaScript function may or may not involve a remote call, as that depends on the needs of the Decoupled Navigation pattern implementation. There are many pieces to the pattern that exchange information requiring some common attributes. This is why the Common Data functionality is so important: it provides the decoupling of functionality between all pieces of code while sharing common state.

If for the Common Data functionality a remote call is made, the server implements the Permutations pattern and decides what content the caller wants to receive. The content is generated by using some server-side framework implemented by using a series of classes, interfaces, or functions. The server-side-generated content is processed by the asynchronous. complete method and assigned to a variable. The assigned variable is used by the function GeneratePopupBox to generate some content that the user can interact with.

The overall objective of the Decoupled Navigation pattern is to decouple the HTML element and event from the processing of the data and from the presentation of the data. When the individual pieces are decoupled from each other, it is possible to change one of the pieces without affecting the others. You can change one piece and still have a well organized and maintainable web application. The Decoupled Navigation pattern gets its name from the fact that the pieces are modularized and are used to navigate content in a web application. When implementing the Decoupled Navigation pattern, you are working with data that is generated, processed, and presented.

Implementation

Implementing the Decoupled Navigation pattern requires defining independent pieces of code that are wired together to navigate some content. This section will cover the technical details of the three functionalities and will present a special discussion on designing a URL.

Implementing the Action Functionality

When implementing the Action functionality, most likely what you will be doing is implementing some HTML event. The event could be the result of a mouse click, timer event, HTML form being submitted, or other HTML event. Regardless of what event it is, it needs to be processed. When processing events, the challenge is to define which element captures the event, and what event to capture.

A Simple Example

The simplest of all navigations is the link, which in the default case will replace the current content with the content of another URL. The notation of the link is defined as follows:

```
<a href="http://www.apress.com">Apress</a>
```

The a HTML element has an href attribute, which indicates the destination URL that the web browser will navigate to. Clicking on a link results in whatever content you have loaded being replaced with the content that the URL http://www.apress.com contains. With respect to writing Ajax applications, these types of links are dangerous because they will replace the current content that has a state with brand new content that has no state. Pressing a Back button does not reload the old state, but loads a new state. The described simple link is akin to killing an application and then starting a new application.

One way to save the content and state is to use the State Navigation pattern, which saves the state of the content before loading the new content. Another way of getting around the content deletion problem is to redirect the content to another window, as illustrated by the following link example:

```
<a href="http://www.apress.com" target="external">External Link</a>
```

The additional attribute target references an identifier that represents another window identifier. If the window identifier does not exist, a brand new window is opened and the content is loaded into that separate window. If the content needs to be loaded locally, a frame is used. Following is an example that uses a floating frame:

```
<a href="http://www.apress.com" target="external">External Link</a></p>
<iframe name="external"></iframe>
```

A *floating frame* is a document within a document. Figure 6-8 shows an example.

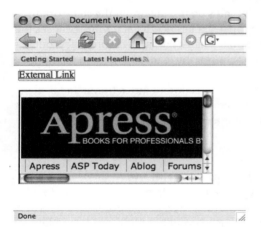

Figure 6-8. *A floating frame, or document within a document*

Using a frame creates a document-within-a-document architecture and has been a way for web application developers to mimic the XMLHttpRequest object behavior. The following example mimics the XMLHttpRequest object behavior by using a floating iframe with a pixel size of 1 by 1 in a small corner to the side of the document:

```
<html>
<head>
    <title>Document Within a Document</title>
</head>
<script language="JavaScript" type="text/javascript">
function LoadedContent( frame) {
    window.alert( "Location (" + frame.contentWindow.location.href + ")");
}
</script>
<body>
    <a href="http://www.apress.com" target="external">External Link</a></p>
    <iframe name="external" onload="LoadedContent( this)"></iframe>
</body>
</html>
```

In the example HTML, the `iframe` has an attribute, `onload`, that represents an event that is triggered when the document within `iframe` has been loaded. In the example, the function `LoadedContent` is called, which will generate a pop-up box displaying the URL of the loaded document.

What is of special interest is the `frame.contentWindow.location.href` reference, which crosses domain boundaries. Remember from Chapter 2 there was an explanation of the same origin policy. The property `frame.contentWindow` is considered one domain, and `location.href` is considered another domain. If both domains fall under the same origin policy, the `window.alert` pop-up box can execute. If, however, both domains do not fall under the same origin policy, a permission exception is generated. The property reference `location.href` causes the permission exception. It is possible to load content that violates the same origin policy, but it is not possible to manipulate that content, nor is it possible for the loaded content to manipulate the caller.[1]

What has not been illustrated, but is possible, is to load content into a frame that is then used to manipulate content in the caller. In that situation, the frame behaves like the Content Chunking pattern as the frame provides a chunk of content that is injected.

Event Bubbling

HTML events can be associated with any HTML element. The HTML event can be triggered in two ways: the HTML element triggers the event, or the HTML element contains another element that triggers the event. HTML has a unique characteristic in that events can pass up a hierarchy of elements in a process called *event bubbling*. In event bubbling, an HTML element triggers an event that is sent from one HTML element to another HTML element. The idea is to pass the HTML event from the child to the parent, and to continue that event-chaining process until the last parent is called. Typically, the last parent to process a bubbling HTML event is the HTML document.

Consider the following HTML, which illustrates event bubbling:

---

1. At the time of this writing, there exists a "hack" that makes it possible to load a script that violates the same origin policy. The technique is considered a hack because it is a loophole that most likely will be closed at some later point and is a security issue.

```
<body>
    <h1>Decoupled Navigation Pattern: Action Examples</h1>
    <div id="div" onclick="OnClick( event)" style="background:yellow;">
        <p id="paragraph">Hello</p>
        <table border="1">
            <tr id="Row 1">
                <td id="Row 1 Cell 1">OnClick</td>
            </tr>
            <tr id="Row 2">
                <td id="Row 2 Cell 1">
                    <input type="button" value="Button" id="Row 2 Button 1"/>
                </td>
            </tr>
            <tr>
                <td id="eventDestination">Nothing yet</td>
            </tr>
        </table>
    </div>
</body>
```

The example HTML content has a header (h1), block division (div), paragraph (p), table (table), table row (tr), and table cell (td). Each element is embedded in another element. Put simply, there is a block division element embedding a table, which is embedding a table row, and so on. Graphically, the structure would be similar to Figure 6-9.

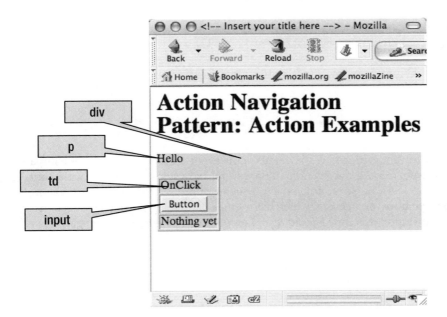

Figure 6-9. *HTML page structure*

Even though this discussion of the HTML structure might seem basic and long-winded, it is important to realize that there is a nested structure because HTML event bubbling and how it occurs is directly related to this structure.

Looking back at the HTML code, you can see that the div HTML element has the onclick attribute, which implements the onclick event. From a traditional programming perspective, the defined onclick event would capture only click events that relate directly to the div element. With event bubbling, the defined event will be triggered for all click events that involve the div element and one of its descendent elements. This means that if the nested button is clicked, the OnClick function is called. Event bubbling is a clever way to define collecting-type events that can be triggered by multiple HTML elements. However, event bubbling works only if the event bubbles. There are some HTML events that will not bubble and are specific to the HTML element.

Let's say that an event has been triggered and is bubbling up the chain. If the event is caught and processed, the caught event can be canceled. The way to cancel the event is to return false, as illustrated by the following example:

```
<div onclick="return false" />
```

Canceling an event that is bubbling works only if the event can be canceled. Canceling every onclick event is a solution when you don't want the browser to process certain events to disable functionality. In the example HTML, the event called the OnClick function will process the click event for multiple HTML elements. The implementation of the function is as follows:

```
function OnClick( evt) {
    evt = (evt) ? evt : ((event) ? event : null);
    if( evt) {
        var elem = (evt.target) ? evt.target :
            ((evt.srcElement) ? evt.srcElement : null);
        if( elem) {
            document.getElementById( "eventDestination").innerHTML =
                "Click (" + elem.id + ")";
        }
    }
}
```

When an HTML event is triggered, the details of the event are not cross-browser compatible. To make the event cross-browser compatible, several extra steps need to be carried out. The function OnClick has a single parameter, evt, which is supposed to represent the event. But the function signature for an event, which has a single parameter, is not recognized in all browsers. The following source code is used to extract the event object instance regardless of browser used:

```
evt = (evt) ? evt : ((event) ? event : null);
```

The statement tests whether the variable evt is null. If the value evt is not null, evt is assigned to evt, which in effect does nothing. The assignment is a placeholder assignment to provide an option to evt being null. However, if evt is null, most likely Microsoft Internet Explorer is being used. Then the variable evt needs to be assigned to the event variable, which is always defined in Internet Explorer.

The test is not necessary if the method is called as illustrated in the example. The reason has to do with how the OnClick function is called, which is illustrated again here:

```
<div id="div" onclick="OnClick( event)" style="background:yellow;">
```

Notice that OnClick is called with the event object instance and is compatible with Microsoft Internet Explorer. What is important to realize is that the event object instance is valid only in the context of the attribute onclick when using Mozilla-compatible browsers.

When an HTML event is caught by a parent of the HTML element that triggers the event, the parent does not have immediate knowledge of the source of the event. This is the case of the OnClick function example implementation in that it can be called in multiple contexts, such as clicking the button, table cell, and so on. You will want to know the source element for manipulation purposes, but like the HTML event object, the property for the source element depends on the browser used. The source element can be found by referencing either the target or srcElement property. The following source code from OnClick illustrates how to retrieve the element that originally triggered the event:

```
if( evt) {
    var elem = (evt.target) ? evt.target :
        ((evt.srcElement) ? evt.srcElement : null);
```

In the source code example, it is assumed that the evt variable instance is valid. The variable elem references the HTML element responsible for the event. After the assignment character, there is an existence test of either evt.target or evt.srcElement. If the browser is Mozilla based, the property evt.target exists, and if the browser is Microsoft Internet Explorer, the property evt.srcElement exists. Other browsers will have a valid instance for one of the two properties.

After both the event and target object instances have been retrieved, you can assign an HTML element innerHTML property to the identifier of the element that generated the event. Because all the HTML elements have been associated with an identifier, clicking on a cell of a table generates the identifier in the last row of the table, as illustrated in Figure 6-10.

Figure 6-10 shows two balloons highlighted. The first balloon with the number 1 shows where a user clicked. This user clicked on the first row of the table. This generates an onclick event, which is given first to the td element, then to the tr element, then to the table element, and then finally to the div element—which implements the onclick and generates the output. The generated output is highlighted in the second balloon.

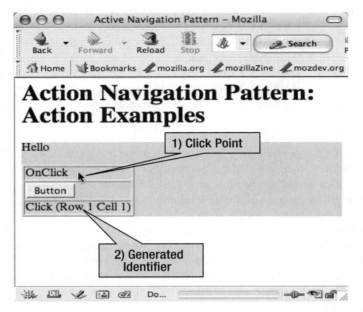

Figure 6-10. *Sequence of steps: clicking on an HTML element and identifying the results*

Canceling Bubbled Events

Events that are bubbled can be canceled, but there is a caveat in that not all events can be canceled. However, let's put off that caveat for the moment. When an event—let's say a click—is bubbled, it can be canceled. Canceling an event is appropriate if you don't want a link clicked under certain circumstances. Or another example is an HTML form that should not be submitted after the validation has failed.

Consider the following HTML:

```
<div onclick="return MonitorLinks( event)">
    <a href="http://www.apress.com" target="external">Apress is not allowed</a>
    <a href="http://www.google.com" target="external">Google is not allowed</a>
    <a href="http://www.slashdot.org" target="external">Slashdot is allowed</a>
</div>
```

The example shows three links: apress, google, and slashdot. The three links are nested within a div element that has implemented the onclick event. Notice in this example how the implementation of the onclick event prefixes the return keyword before the function MonitorLinks. Using the return keyword is essential in canceling the click event, and in general those events that can be canceled. If an event is captured and processed, the functionality can return true to continue the event bubbling, or false to cancel the event bubbling.

The purpose of the function MonitorLinks is to selectively allow a clicked link to navigate to its destination. Logically, the MonitorLinks function will allow navigation to the slashdot link, but not the apress or google links. The implementation of MonitorLinks is illustrated as follows:

```
function MonitorLinks( evt) {
    evt = (evt) ? evt : ((event) ? event : null);
    if( evt) {
        var elem = (evt.target) ? evt.target :
            ((evt.srcElement) ? evt.srcElement : null);
        if( elem) {
            if( elem.href == "http://www.apress.com/") {
                window.alert( "Not allowed on Apress");
                return false;
            }
            else if( elem.href == "http://www.google.com/") {
                window.alert( "Not allowed on Google");
                return false;
            }
            else if( elem.href == "http://www.slashdot.org/") {
                return true;
            }
        }
    }
    return false;
}
```

In the implementation of MonitorLinks, there is the usual code to retrieve the source HTML element (elem) and event (evt). If the variable elem is not null, the property elem.href is tested. The property is tested against three tests to see which link has been clicked. For the cases of having clicked on apress or google, a window.alert pop-up box appears, indicating that the link cannot be clicked. After the user clicks the OK button, the MonitorLinks function returns a value of false to indicate that the event bubbling should be canceled. Canceling the onclick event causes the navigation to be halted, with the HTML content staying as is.

You need to make a mental note that the function MonitorLinks assumes that the elem variable references a link element. The assumption is due to the property reference elem.href, because the href property is applicable only to a link element. It is not a bad thing to assume, but you must remember it because MonitorLinks is a function that captures the click event for all child HTML elements. If there were a button that generated a click event, MonitorLinks would fail and potentially cause undesired side effects. A solution is to use the elem.nodeName property and test whether the source element is a link. From the example, the if statement would be rewritten to the following:

```
if( elem && elem.nodeName == "A")
```

Another solution is to reference a common property such as id when testing for a specific link identifier. Using the id property is a useful solution because the property is type agnostic and is a unique identifier. The unique identifier is a good way to compare and distinguish HTML elements because there is no possibility of making a by-accident failure. A *by-accident failure* is illustrated by the following source code:

```
<a href="http://www.apress.com" target="external">Apress is not allowed</a>
// ....
if( elem.href == "http://www.apress.com/") {
```

In the example source code, the href property is http://www.apress.com, but the comparison is the value http://www.apress.com/. Between the two buffers, there is a missing slash character. When the web browser processes the link element written as HTML, a slash is added to the href property. The added slash is not obvious to the script author and leads to a by-accident error, where by debugging you find out that a slash has been added. Using the id property, there is no translation by the web browser causing a by-accident error.

Following is the rewritten HTML that uses id properties to identify each link:

```
<div onclick="return MonitorLinks( event)">
    <a href="http://www.apress.com" id="apress"
        target="external">Apress is not allowed</a>
    <a href="http://www.google.com" id="google"
        target="external">Google is not allowed</a>
    <a href="http://www.slashdot.org" id="slashdot"
        target="external">Slashdot is allowed</a>
</div>
```

Following is the MonitorLinks function rewritten to use the id property:

```
function MonitorLinks( evt) {
    evt = (evt) ? evt : ((event) ? event : null);
    if( evt) {
        var elem = (evt.target) ? evt.target :
            ((evt.srcElement) ? evt.srcElement : null);
        if( elem) {
            if( elem.id == "apress") {
                window.alert( "Not allowed on Apress");
                return false;
            }
            else if( elem.id == "google") {
                window.alert( "Not allowed on Google");
                return false;
            }
            else if( elem.id == "slashdot") {
                return true;
            }
        }
    }
    return false;
}
```

The HTML and the function implementation stay relatively the same, with the only real change being the addition and comparison of the id property.

Other Ways to Define Events

There are other ways to wire events. One popular other way is to retrieve the HTML element and then associate a function to that element. So, for example, if you were capturing the click event, you would assign the onclick property to a function. Then when a click occurs, an event is generated and the element captures it. Consider the following example that illustrates how to capture an event by using a property to wire the event:

```
function DoAssociation() {
    (document.getElementById(
        "manualassociation"))[ 'onclick'] = MonitorLinksId;
    document.getElementById(
        "manualassociation").attachEvent( 'onclick', MonitorLinksId);
}
</script>
<body onload="DoAssociation()">
```

In the example, the wiring of the methods to an HTML element should happen in the HTML element body onload event. It is important that only when the onload event is being fired that the events can be wired. If the wiring occurs before the document has been loaded, some HTML elements might not exist and cannot be referenced. The onload event ensures that the HTML content has been loaded and can be referenced.

After the method DoAssociation is called, there are two ways to wire an event to an HTML element. In either way, it is important to call the document.getElementById method to retrieve an HTML element instance.

The first way to assign an event is to assign the array index of the event that is to be wired. In the example, that means assigning the onclick array index. This assignment illustrates a fundamental feature of JavaScript: there are no differences made between properties, functions, and so on.

The second way to assign an event is to use the method attachEvent (as illustrated) or addEventListener. When calling the methods attachEvent or addEventListener, you will need two parameters. The first parameter is the event to be captured, and the second parameter is the function to be associated with the event. In both cases, it is not necessary to use function variables or identifiers, because an anonymous function would be acceptable. You would use attachEvent with Microsoft Internet Explorer, and addEventListener when using a Mozilla-based or Safari browser.

The advantage of using the array index approach is that it works on all browsers without any special requirements. However, it works because it is a special case of how the JavaScript language is constructed. The official approved way would be to use either addEventListener or attachEvent. After the events have been wired, they will function identically to the MonitorLinks function of previous examples.

If you do not want to associate the event to the HTML element in the body onload event, it can be done after the element has been declared, as illustrated by the following source code:

```
<div id="manualassociation"></div>
...
<script>
    (document.getElementById(
        "manualassociation"))[ 'onclick'] = MonitorLinksId;
...
```

In the example source code, the div element with an ID manualassociation is declared completely. After a complete declaration, the div HTML element exists in the Document Object Model, making the element accessible for referencing.

Of course, it goes without saying that a good programming practice in the implementation of MonitorLinks would be to test whether the evt variable is null. This is because when the events are wired together by using programmatic terms, the first parameter may or may not be the event.

Defining and Implementing the Common Data Functionality

As outlined earlier in this chapter, the Common Data functionality requires defining a state and potentially some function that processes the state. When processing the state, the data may be locally processed or may involve some remote processing. If the state is processed remotely, a URL is involved and the process requires URL design. Therefore, this section presents materials relating to URL design.

The Purpose of the State and State Manipulations

Some may perceive the Common Data functionality as unnecessary overhead. The Common Data functionality is a necessity, albeit (as described in the "Applicability" section) only when the Decoupled Navigation pattern is a necessity. The purpose of the Common Data functionality is to provide a wedge between the Action and Presentation functionalities, enabling a decoupling of functions.

Consider Figure 6-11, which illustrates the steps that occur when an HTML button is clicked, generating an event that causes a JavaScript function to be called.

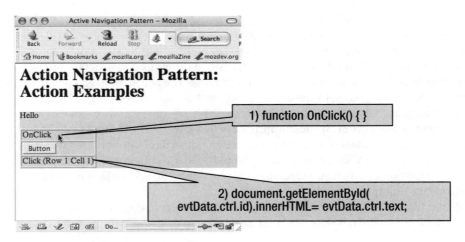

Figure 6-11. *Steps resulting from clicking a button*

Figure 6-11 represents the simple button click as two steps. The first step is the HTML event, which processes the mouse click. The second step is the content generation in the table row below the button. The content uses HTML injection by assigning the innerHTML property. From this simple example, there would be no need for the Common Data functionality because that would add an unnecessary layer.

Let's continue building on this example. Imagine that the same user interface is used to make a remote call via the XMLHttpRequest object. Figure 6-12 illustrates the steps needed in the remote case.

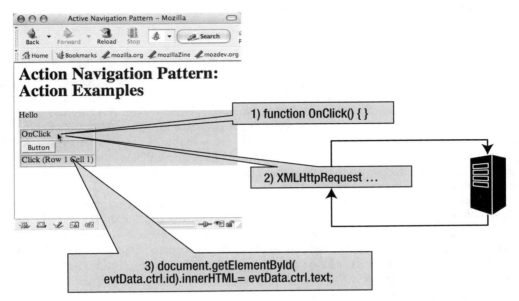

Figure 6-12. *Steps resulting from clicking a button when using an extra* XMLHttpRequest *call*

Figure 6-12 shows an added step (step 2), in which a request is made by using the XMLHttpRequest object that then generates some data that is processed in step 3.

Looking at Figures 6-11 and 6-12, you might be wondering where the need for the Common Data functionality is. The need arises because often an application is converted from the state depicted in Figure 6-11 to that in Figure 6-12, or vice versa. Implementing the conversion can require some major restructuring of the code, or a completely new implementation that needs to be tested and maintained. The Common Data functionality decouples the steps so that an application that executed as in Figure 6-11 could be converted without major surprises into an application that executes as in Figure 6-12. The intention is to decouple, allowing the fewest number of changes and yielding the largest user benefit.

Consider the following code, which mimics the implementation of Figure 6-11:

```
function OnClick( event) {
    document.getElementById( "myDiv").innerHTML = "data";
}
```

The code is a problem because what was defined as two steps in Figure 6-11 is one step in technical terms. The code is a function with an implementation. The problems of the function OnClick are that the text identifier myDiv is hard-coded, and so is the assigned value data. Imagine that the assignment code is used in multiple places, and imagine that the text has to be converted to uppercase before doing the assignment. Then the code would have to be updated in multiple places.

The solution is to decouple the steps of Figure 6-11, which was illustrated as a single piece of code, into two code pieces. The decoupled code would be as follows:

```
function InjectHTML( elementId, text) {
    document.getElementById( elementId).innerHTML = text;
}
function OnClick( event) {
    InjectHTML( "myDiv", "data");
}
```

There are now two functions (`InjectHTML` and `OnClick`). The function `InjectHTML` requires an element identifier and some text, and will perform an HTML injection. The function `InjectHTML` is a business-logic-specific implementation that operates on an HTML element reference defined by the client. The function `OnClick` reacts to the event and is responsible for gathering the data used to call the `InjectHTML` function. Each function has its responsibilities and each function is decoupled from the other. The only shared information is the data gathered by `OnClick` and processed by `InjectHTML`.

Figure 6-11 has been implemented by using a decoupled solution, but now Figure 6-12 needs to be implemented. This means that an additional step of using the `XMLHttpRequest` object needs to be added. For simplicity, assume that the `XMLHttpRequest` object functionality is encapsulated in the function `CallXMLHttpRequest`, which accepts a single parameter. As the function `CallXMLHttpRequest` is used to gather information, the function is called by `OnClick`, and the returned data is passed to the `InjectHTML` function. The modified source code is as follows:

```
function InjectHTML( elementId, text) {
    document.getElementById( elementId).innerHTML = text;
}
function OnClick( event) {
    InjectHTML( "myDiv", CallXMLHttpRequest( "data"));
}
```

In the modified source code, the second parameter of the `CallXMLHttpRequest` function has been replaced with the function `CallXMLHttpRequest`. Looking at the solution technically, you can see that the three steps have been decoupled from each other, and each can vary without affecting the other. What is still kludgy is how the data is gathered and passed to the function `InjectHTML`. This is the reason for creating Common Data functionality.

The Common Data functionality replaces the kludgy calling of the functions with some common state. The problem at the moment is that the `OnClick` function relies on the functions `InjectHTML` and `CallXMLHttpRequest`. The reliance cannot be avoided, but what can be avoided is the calling convention. Imagine that instead of `InjectHTML` being used, the function `InjectTextbox` is used due to a business logic decision. And then imagine that `InjectTextbox` requires an extra parameter, as illustrated by the following source code:

```
function InjectTextbox( convert, elementId, text) {
    // ....
}
function OnClick( event) {
    InjectTextbox( false, "myDiv", CallXMLHttpRequest( "data"));
}
```

Even though InjectTextbox and InjectHTML are similar, calling InjectTextbox requires a change in the logic of the OnClick function. The OnClick function has to make an additional decision of whether or not a conversion has to occur. You might say, "Well, duh, the OnClick function has to change if the called function changes." But the reply is, "Why must the OnClick function change?" The purpose of the OnClick function is to gather the data necessary to call either the InjectHTML or InjectTexbox function. The purpose of the OnClick function is not to make decisions, because decisions can change if a user interface does not, and vice versa. The data gathering and decisions made about the data need to be decoupled.

In an ideal world where everything is decoupled, you would write the following source code:

```
<button onclick="Call( OnClick, null, InjectHTML)" />
<button onclick="Call( OnClick, CallXMLHttpRequest, InjectTextbox)" />
```

The modified source code has added the function Call, which has three parameters that are three function references. The first function reference, OnClick, is the Action functionality responsible for gathering the data into a state. The second function reference is either null or CallXMLHttpRequest and represents the Common Data functionality that is responsible for processing the state. And finally, the third function references, InjectHTML and InjectTextbox, are responsible for displaying the state.

The resulting calling sequence illustrates that the first button click event gathers the data, does not process the data, and displays the data. The second button click event gathers the data, calls a remotely located server, and displays the data. The OnClick functions used in either button click event are identical, meaning that the OnClick event is not dependent on whether the processing of the common data is local or remote. So now the functions are decoupled, as is the calling sequence. The exact details of this decoupling and the calling of the functions is the topic of the following sections.

Implementing a Decoupled Library

The core of the Common Data functionality is a decoupled library, which is responsible for managing and processing the state. The decoupled library is called DecoupledNavigation and is defined as follows:

```
function DecoupledNavigation() {
}
DecoupledNavigation.prototype.call = DecoupledNavigation_call;
DecoupledNavigation.prototype.initializeRemote =
    DecoupledNavigation_InitializeRemote;
```

The definition of DecoupledNavigation has no properties and two methods. There are no properties because the common state object instance is defined in the implementation of the DecoupledNavigation methods. The method DecoupledNavigation_call is used to make a Decoupled Navigation pattern call as illustrated in the example Call(OnClick...). The method DecoupledNavigation_initializeRemote is used when the Common Data functionality wants to make a call to a remote server.

The function DecoupledNavigation_call, exposed as DecoupledNavigation.call, wires together the Action, Common Data, and Presentation functionalities as illustrated by the following implementation:

```
function DecoupledNavigation_call( evt, action, data, presentation) {
    evt = (evt) ? evt : ((event) ? event : null);
    if ( evt) {
        var elem = (evt.target) ? evt.target :
                    ((evt.srcElement) ? evt.srcElement : null);
        if ( elem) {
            var obj = new Object();
            obj.event = evt;
            obj.parent = this;
            obj.element = elem;
            obj.state = new Object();
            obj.presentation = presentation;
            if ( (action) != null) {
                if ( action( obj) != true) {
                    return false;
                }
            }
            obj.isRemote = false;
            if ( (data) != null) {
                if ( data( obj) != true) {
                    return false;
                }
            }
            if( obj.isRemote) {
                return true;
            }
            if (presentation != null) {
                if ( presentation( obj, obj.state) != true) {
                    return false;
                }
            }
            return true;
        }
    }
    return true;
}
```

The implementation of `DecoupledNavigation_call` has four parameters. The first parameter, evt, is the event object. Whether the first parameter has a valid value goes back to the event problem outlined in the "Event Bubbling" section. The second parameter, action, is a function reference to an Action functionality (for example, `OnClick`). The third parameter, data, represents the function reference that performs a state manipulation. The fourth parameter, presentation, is a function reference to a Presentation functionality, which usually is some HTML control. All of the lines up to `if( elem)` were outlined in the "Event Bubbling" section and are used to extract the HTML event and HTML source element.

The lines thereafter are the important lines and represent the technical details of the Common Data functionality. These lines represent the state as an object instead of a series of parameters, as illustrated by the example that had the `OnClick` function call either `InjectHTML` or `InjectTextbox`. So let's look at those lines in more detail:

```
var obj = new Object();
obj.event = evt;
obj.parent = this;
obj.element = elem;
obj.state = new Object();
obj.presentation = presentation;
```

The variable `obj` is the common object that is shared by the `action`, `data`, and `presentation` function references. The idea is to convert the parameters gathered by the example function `OnClick` and to convert them into an object instance. Based on that idea, the `action` function implementation manipulates `obj` and assigns the state. The state is then manipulated and processed by the `data` function reference. The state structures can be anything, and most likely will partially resemble the parameters used to call the example `InjectHTML` or `InjectTextbox` functions. It is essential that the `action`, `data`, and `presentation` function implementations know what the structure of the state is. The advantage of manipulating an object structure is that the calling code as illustrated by `OnClick` does not need to be modified. Only the functions that modify the object structure need to be modified, preserving a proven and testing navigation structure.

Getting back to the explanation of the `obj` properties, `event` and `element` reference the HTML event and source HTML element, respectively. The property `state` is the state that is manipulated by the various functionalities. The reason for using the `state` property is to provide an entry point for the common state that will not conflict with the other properties of `obj`. And the reference `obj.presentation` is required if a remote call is made; this need will be illustrated in a little bit.

Going back a bit further in the example source code, let's look at the implementation of `DecoupledNavigation_call`. After `obj` has been instantiated, the calling of the `action` function reference is called, as illustrated again here:

```
if( (action) != null) {
    if( action( obj) != true) {
        return false;
    }
}
```

Before the `action` function reference can be called, a decision is made that ensures that the `action` variable is not `null`. If the `action` variable is `null`, there is no implementation for the Action functionality. This is useful, for example, if you're creating a splash screen and you don't need to generate a state but only some presentation information when the document has finished loading.

If the `action` variable is not `null`, the `action` function reference is called, where the parameter is the common object `obj`. The `action` function implementation can query and manipulate `obj`, and then return either a `true` or `false`. If the `action` function implementation is successful, `true` is returned. Returning `false` indicates a failure, which will cause `DecoupledNavigation_local` to return `false`, causing the event bubbling to quit, if applicable.

After the Action functionality has been executed, the property `obj.state` will be assigned and will be ready to be processed by the `data` function reference. The details of using the data function reference are illustrated again here:

```
obj.isRemote = false;
if ( (data) != null) {
    if ( data( obj) != true) {
        return false;
    }
}
if( obj.isRemote) {
    return true;
}
```

The calling sequence of the data function reference is identical to the calling sequence of the action function reference. What is different is the assignment of the property `obj.isRemote = false`. The difference is due to the ability of the `data` function reference to process the state locally or remotely. If the data function reference processes the state remotely, an asynchronous call is made and further processing can continue only after the remote server has sent a response. The `DecoupledNavigation_call` function cannot continue and must return control to the web browser. The property assignment is used to indicate whether a remote server call is made. If a remote call is made, the `presentation` function reference cannot be called, and the function `DecoupledNavigation_call` returns a value of true.

This raises the question of whether a `true` or `false` value should be returned if the `obj.isRemote` property has a `true` value. Returning a value of `true` means that the event will continue to bubble, and depending on the context that might not be the best plan of action. The best plan of action depends on the context, and there is room for improvement in how the return value of the `data` function reference is handled.

If the data is processed locally, the Presentation functionality can be called. The calling sequence is illustrated as follows:

```
if( presentation != null) {
    if( presentation( obj, obj.state) != true) {
        return false;
    }
}
```

The calling of the Presentation functionality is identical to the Action and Data functionalities. The additional parameter `obj.state` is the state, and its presence makes it possible to recursively chain together multiple presentation functionalities, as illustrated in Figure 6-13.

Figure 6-13 illustrates how the function `MyPresentation` acts as a front processor for the functions `InjectHTML` and `InjectTextbox`. Because the state is a parameter, the front processor can filter out the appropriate state structure and then pass that state structure to the other Presentation functionalities. If `state` were not a parameter, the front processor would have to reassign the `state` property of the `common` variable.

The implementation of the function `DecoupledNavigation_InitializeRemote` has been delegated until a remote server call example is made. For now, the focus is on using the `DecoupledNavigation` class to perform a local call.

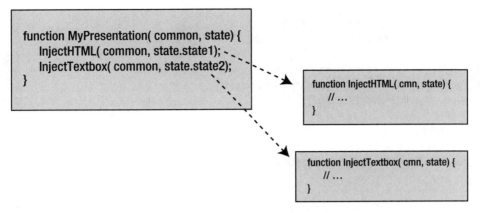

Figure 6-13. *Chaining Presentation functionalities together*

Illustrating a Local Call

Having defined the decoupled library, you can implement a simple example. Even though I have briefly mentioned the Presentation functionality, I haven't explained the details. Still, although the implementation may seem like we're jumping a bit ahead of ourselves, I am presenting it on purpose so that you understand the calling sequences.

To illustrate the Decoupled Navigation pattern, I have illustrated the copying of the contents from a text box into an HTML div element. The copied contents will be converted into uppercase. From a GUI perspective, the HTML page looks like Figure 6-14.

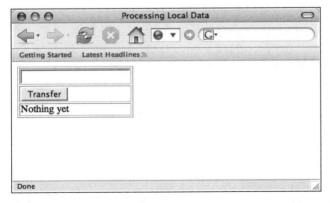

Figure 6-14. *Example HTML page used to transfer the contents of the text box to the div element, where the contents are converted into uppercase*

This HTML page is elementary, and the HTML and JavaScript code behind it are as well. The text box contains the data that is injected into the HTML page and replaces the text Nothing Yet. Following is the code used to create Figure 6-14:

```html
<html>
<head><title>Processing Local Data</title></head>
<script language="JavaScript" src="/ajax/lib/factory.js"></script>
<script language="JavaScript" src="/ajax/lib/asynchronous.js"></script>
<script language="JavaScript" src="/ajax/lib/events.js"></script>
<script language="JavaScript" type="text/javascript">
var nav = new DecoupledNavigation();

function OnClick( common) {
    common.state = new TextState( "divDestination",
        document.getElementById( "txtContent").value);
    return true;
}
function ConvertToUpperCase( common) {
    common.state.text = common.state.text.toUpperCase();
    return true;
}

</script>
<body>
    <div>
        <table border="1">
            <tr>
                <td><input type="text" id="txtContent"></td>
            </tr>
            <tr>
                <td>
                    <input type="button" value="Transfer"
                        onclick="return nav.call ( event, OnClick,
                            ConvertToUpperCase, InjectHTML)"/>
                </td>
            </tr>
            <tr>
                <td id="divDestination">Nothing yet</td>
            </tr>
        </table>
    </div>
</body>
</html>
```

In the HTML code, any HTML element that will be used by the JavaScript code is identified by using the id attribute. This is important so that when manipulations do occur, the Java-Script does not need to hunt for the HTML elements. The JavaScript code declares the variable nav, which is the Decoupled Navigation pattern implementation. The nav variable is used in the onclick event of the input HTML element. The action.local method call wires together the OnClick and ConvertToUpperCase functions with the undefined InjectHTML function. This means that when the button is clicked, the OnClick function is called to process the click, the ConvertToUpperCase function is called to convert the case of the text, and the InjectHTML function is called to update the user interface.

Looking closer at the OnClick function, you can see that the class TextState is instantiated. The purpose of TextState is to define a common state structure for a text buffer and an identifier. The TextState structure is passed to and from Action, Data, and Presentation functionalities. The constructor parameters to TextState are the contents of the text box and the destination identifier indicating where the contents are supposed to be injected. The instantiated TextState class is assigned to common.state, which is shared by the still-undefined function InjectHTML.

Consider the overall implementation and that the functions OnClick, ConvertToUpperCase, and InjectHTML are independent of each other. The functions share only the common state structure TextState. For example, to implement functionality whereby the contents of the text box are transferred whenever a letter is added to the text box, the OnClick function needs to be replaced. The OnClick function could be replaced by capturing the onchange event. The remaining functions would remain identical.

Converting the Local Call to a Remote Call

The power of decoupling the three functionalities was quickly explained by replacing the OnClick function. What would be more impressive, though, would be to actually go through an example of changing the processing of the data locally to remotely. The remote server call is a service that converts the local text into bold text. Calling the remote server to convert the text is overkill, but the conversion is meant to illustrate the steps of making a remote server call.

URLs Are Componentized Resources

Making a remote server call means using XMLHttpRequest, and that requires a URL. When calling a URL, it is important that the URL is well designed. When designing URLs, the objective is to design them as if they were components. Treating URLs as components makes it simpler to modularize the functionality.

Some server-side web frameworks—for example, ASP.NET and JavaServer Pages (JSP)— use the first identifier after the slash to identify an application. For example, the URL /application defines the web application application. The idea that the first identifier specifies an application is not a bad idea, and in fact it is a good idea. For example, imagine implementing both the REST-Based Model View Controller and State Navigation patterns. The two patterns require code that executes in the context of an HTTP server. The two patterns are orthogonal in that they offer different forms of functionality. Because they are orthogonal, there is no real reason why they should share variables, state, or code. The subdivision of applications does not need to stop with applications, but can be extended to components, as illustrated in Figure 6-15.

Figure 6-15 shows the root URL /. From the root there are the URLs /search and /state. Each of these URLs represents a resource to a component that implements searching and state navigation functionality. This means that any functionality that starts with /search must relate to search and only search. There cannot be any other type of functionality. Likewise with the URL /state, which means any related URL must relate to implementing state navigation functionality. If some functionality needs to be implemented that does not relate to the URLs, a new component URL is defined.

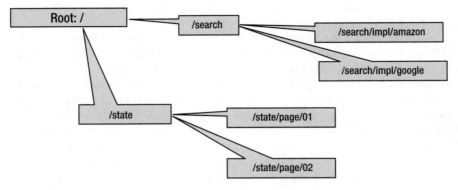

Figure 6-15. *Component architecture exposed as URLs*

In a nutshell, URLs begin with a general functionality definition and with each appended identifier to the URL the functionality becomes more specific. The URL /search is general, but the URL /search/impl/amazon is specific. The URL /search implements a searching component, whereas /search/impl/amazon relates to a search component specific to Amazon.com. This way of creating URLs is purely resource and state driven, and will conflict with those web applications that map directory structures to URLs for organizational purposes.

Referencing URLs in HTML Pages

When referencing a URL in an HTML page, do you really know what the URL is or should be? It has been explained that URLs should be components, but how are those components discovered? Consider the following link:

```
<a href="/search/impl/amazon">Amazon Implementation</a>
```

What does the URL /search/impl/amazon represent philosophically? How do you know that the Amazon.com implementation is at the URL /search/impl/amazon? Even more direct, how do you manage to download the content that references the URL in the first place? There is a German saying, "You can't smell it," which means that something needs to be defined somewhere because a URL does not have an odor to guide you to the proper location.

One way to define the URL is to use a JSP or ASP.NET page that generates the URL as follows:

```
<a href="<%=obj.getAmazonSearchURL()%>">
    Amazon Implementation</a>
```

In the generated code, a method call will generate the URL dynamically based on some logic contained within the method call. The logic could be the retrieval of the URL from a configuration file, or database, or some other persistent mechanism. This approach works well from a traditional application perspective; however, it is completely wrong. If you think abstractly about a URL, you know that a URL is nothing more than an indicator of functionality that you want to invoke. This means that a URL is your abstract resource, and adding an abstraction on an abstraction is wrong.

Therefore, in the original example of hard-coding the URL /search/impl/amazon, it is okay that it is hard-coded because the URL is an abstract resource. Many web application developers do not like to do this because it hard-codes an application. The problem is not the URL, but the framework. Imagine a developer using JSP. Then the URL /search/impl/amazon would be rewritten to the following:

```
<a href="/search/impl/amazon.jsp">Amazon Implementation</a>
```

The URL ends with the extension .jsp, indicating that amazon.jsp is a JavaServer page. And having the .jsp extension forces a JSP processor. Granted, it is possible to associate the .jsp extension with an ASP.NET page, or even PHP, but the fact is that the extension is a complication. The Permutations pattern explicitly dictates that externally exposed URLs are treated as components and require the use of a resource that does not tie into a representation like JSP.

This does not mean that URLs cannot be dynamically generated. What it means is that URLs that are exposed as resources as per the Permutations definition will not be dynamically generated. Those URLs will be hard-coded into the HTML page because they represent resources that are already abstracted. And as illustrated per the Permutations pattern, those URLs that are specific to the representation technology can be dynamically generated or hard-coded or retrieved from a configuration file. How the URL is inserted into the content depends on the representation technology.

Hard-coding a URL into an HTML page is difficult for a programmer to swallow. Programmers just don't like to hard-code any pieces of text, which is completely understandable. After all, programmers have been burned often enough. If you are a programmer who likes to be absolutely fail-safe, load the URL from a configuration file. However, it will not save that much work because the URLs are components, and if the URL is updated, many configuration files will need updating. Remember that we are entering an era of content that is retrieved, cached, archived, referenced, and stored. This means URLs should not change in the first place because changing them will cause problems with other HTTP-based applications. Therefore, think three times before creating the appropriate resource URL.

The one last bit that needs discussion is the referencing of the server. All of the URLs did not have an HTTP server reference. For example, to reference the Apress website, the HTTP server www.apress.com is used. How somebody knows www.apress.com is purely naming convention, as the URL some.cool.apress.server could have been used as well. The URL some.cool.apress.server is not very intuitive, as we have been trained to use www and .com or the appropriate country extension. Another way to discover a URL is through a search engine such as Google. Continuing on this thread, a single server is not appropriate for most HTTP servers; thus a web server farm is necessary.

The complications of figuring out the name of the server are extensive. The Decoupled Navigation pattern offers no solution to the HTTP server reference problem because it is a Domain Name Service (DNS), search engine, and load balancing problem. Today there are already very good implementations of each of these technologies, and writing a pattern about these technologies is futile because most people treat the technologies as black boxes that just happen to work all the time. Yes, I am hand waving and passing the buck, but talking about these technologies is like explaining the philosophy of the perfect garbage collector. We just assume that the garbage collector does their thing properly. Were this book about Internet infrastructure patterns, my answer would be completely different.

Restructuring the Application

Knowing what there is to know about URLs and the local application, the local processing application is converted to call a remote server that will convert the text into bold text.

Calling the remote server means using an asynchronous callback that makes a request and waits for a response. The HTML code remains almost identical, with a change in the ConvertToBolded function:

```
<html>
<head><title>Processing Local Data</title></head>
<script language="JavaScript" src="/ajax/lib/factory.js"></script>
<script language="JavaScript" src="/ajax/lib/asynchronous.js"></script>
<script language="JavaScript" src="/ajax/lib/events.js"></script>
<script language="JavaScript" type="text/javascript">
var nav = new DecoupledNavigation();

function OnClick( common) {
    common.state = new TextState( "divDestination",
        document.getElementById( "txtContent").value);
    return true;
}
function ConvertToBolded( common) {
    common.parent.initializeRemote( common);
    common.complete = function( cmdEmbedded, status, statusText,
        responseText, responseXML) {
        cmdEmbedded.state.text = responseText;
        return true;
    }
    var buffer = common.state.text;
    common.async.post( "/ajax/chap10/remotecontent",
        "application/text", buffer.length, buffer);
    return true;
}

</script>
<body>
    <div>
        <table border="1">
            <tr>
                <td><input type="text" id="txtContent"></td>
            </tr>
            <tr>
                <td>
                    <input type="button" value="Transfer"
                        onclick="return nav.call ( event, OnClick,
                            ConvertToBolded, InjectHTML)"/>
                </td>
            </tr>
```

```
        <tr>
            <td id="divDestination">Nothing yet</td>
        </tr>
    </table>
</div>
</body>
</html>
```

The changed content in the HTML page is bold. The changes are to only one function. This means that the change from processing data locally to remotely has been implemented transparently without updating the HTML elements responsible for the user interface, the OnClick or the InjectHTML function. The overall application still looks and feels the same, with the only noticeable change being the speed of converting the text to bold.

Let's focus on ConvertToBolded, which is illustrated again as follows:

```
function ConvertToBolded( common) {
    common.parent.initializeRemote( common);
    common.complete = function( cmdEmbedded, status, statusText,
        responseText, responseXML) {
        cmdEmbedded.state.text = responseText;
        return true;
    }
    var buffer = common.state.text;
    common.async.post( "/ajax/chap10/remotecontent.html",
        "application/text", buffer.length, buffer);
    return true;
}
```

In the implementation of the ConvertToBolded, there is a call to initializeRemote. The method initializeRemote sets up the functions and data members necessary to make a remote server call by using the Asynchronous type. The definition of the common.complete function is required by Asynchronous and is called when the remote call has completed. The existence of common.complete splits the Common Data functionality into two pieces. The first piece is the creation of the remote server call request, and the second piece is the processing of the results.

The last part of the ConvertToBolded method is to send the data to the server by using the method common.async.post (HTTP POST). Sending the data is the first step of the two-step Common Data functionality. The server will process the data and return a modified state to the caller. The modified state is then processed by the common.complete method, which is the second step of the two-step Common Data functionality. As the second step is part of the Common Data functionality, the Presentation functionality can be called thereafter.

Before the implementation of initializeRemote is started, a better way to explain the calling sequence is to illustrate it. Figure 6-16 makes it simpler to explain how the method initializeRemote is implemented.

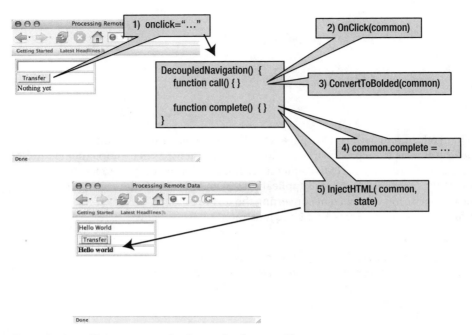

Figure 6-16. *Calling sequence for the method* `nav.call`

In Figure 6-16, when the user clicks the Transfer button, the event `onclick` is triggered. The `onclick` event calls the method `nav.call`, which is of the type `DecoupledNavigation`. `DecoupledNavigation` has two methods (`call` and `complete`) that are of interest when calling a remote server. Executing the `call` method will call the Action functionality (`OnClick`) and the Data functionality (`ConvertToBolded`). The Data functionality will wire up the asynchronous HTTP call, and call the remote server. At this point the Decoupled Navigation pattern gives up control and waits for a response from the server.

When the server receives a response, it is captured by `DecoupledNavigation.complete`, which then delegates to `common.complete`. Calling `common` restarts the Decoupled Navigation pattern and finishes the Data functionality part. Thereafter, the Presentation functionality starts, which calls the function `InjectHTML`. Calling `InjectHTML` causes the user interface to change and contains the bold code.

Now that you understand the sequence of events, let's look at the method `initializeRemote`, which is responsible for wiring together the various methods:

```
function DecoupledNavigation_InitializeRemote( common) {
    common.async = new Asynchronous();
    common.complete = function( obj, status, statusText,
        responseText, responseXML) {}
    common.openCallback = function( xmlhttp) {}
    common.async.openCallback = function( xmlhttp) {
        common.openCallback( xmlhttp);
    };
```

```
common.async.complete = function( status, statusText,
    responseText, responseXML) {
    if ( (common.complete) != null) {
        if ( common.complete( common, status, statusText,
            responseText, responseXML) == true) {
            if ( (common.presentation) != null) {
                common.presentation( common, common.state);
            }
        }
    }
}
common.isRemote = true;
}
```

The variable common is the object reference to the state that is passed across the various functionalities. The property common.async represents an Asynchronous instance. As explained in Chapter 2, Asynchronous requires an implementation for the property complete because that property is a function reference that will be called by Asynchronous when the server returns a response.

Look closer at the implementation common.async.complete. In the implementation, the user's complete (common.complete) is called if it exists. The user's complete is the second step of the Common Data functionality. If the complete function returns true, the common.presentation function reference (if it exists) is called.

Implementing the Presentation Functionality

When implementing the Decoupled Navigation pattern, the Presentation layer is where the output is generated. The examples thus far have been very simple; the output has been an HTML injection. In a more sophisticated Ajax application, the output would be more complicated and would involve the creation of pop-up boxes, as illustrated in Figure 6-17.

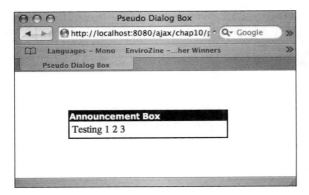

Figure 6-17. *A more complicated user interface that uses a pop-up box*

Figure 6-17 shows an HTML page containing a box that can be dragged around the page. To make the box work, and be "draggable," quite a bit of Dynamic HTML magic is going on. Here is the important fact: the HTML box is Dynamic HTML, and not Ajax per se. As per the original definition,[2] Ajax is not a technology, but the combination of several already-existing technologies.

The focus of the Ajax patterns is not to explain the Dynamic HTML components, but to use the components in the context of Ajax. Part of the reason why this book does not attempt to explain and illustrate the Dynamic HTML components is that plenty of scripts do those tasks very well.[3] The focus of this book is to integrate those already-existing components and make them Ajax aware. The aim of the Presentation functionality is to use the Dynamic HTML components to support the navigation.

What is interesting about Figure 6-17 is that the Dynamic HTML to make the draggable pop-up box work is fairly complicated, but the content within the box is rather simple. It shows that the author of the component took great effort to make it easy to use the draggable pop-up box. Consider the following abbreviated source code that creates the pop-up box:

```
<body>
<div id="showimage" style="position:absolute;width:250px;left:250px;top:250px">
    <table border="0" width="250" bgcolor="#000080" cellspacing="0" cellpadding="2">
        <tr>
            <td width="100%">
                <table border="0" width="100%" cellspacing="0" cellpadding="0"
                    height="36px">
                    <tr>
                        <td id="dragbar" style="cursor:hand; cursor:pointer"
                            width="100%" onMousedown="initializedrag(event)">
                            <ilayer width="100%" onSelectStart="return false">
                            <layer width="100%"
                onMouseover="dragswitch=1;if (ns4) drag_dropns(showimage)"
                            onMouseout="dragswitch=0">
                            <font face="Verdana"
                                    color="#FFFFFF">
                        <strong><small>Announcement Box</small></strong></font>
                            </layer>
                            </ilayer>
                        </td>
                        <td style="cursor:hand">
                            <a href="#" onClick="hidebox();return false">
                                <img src="close.gif" width="16px"
                                    height="14px" border="0"></a></td>
                    </tr>
```

---

2. http://www.adaptivepath.com/publications/essays/archives/000385.php

3. http://www.dynamicdrive.com, http://www.dhtmlcentral.com, http://scriptasylum.com, http:// www.hotscripts.com, http://www.howtocreate.co.uk, http://webdeveloper.earthweb.com, and so on. If I did not mention your website, I am sorry. Send me an e-mail at christianhgross@gmail.com, and I will create a reference list at the URL http://www.devspace.com:8080.

```
            <tr>
                <td width="100%" bgcolor="#FFFFFF" style="padding:4px" ➥
                    colspan="2">
                    <!-- PUT YOUR CONTENT BETWEEN HERE -->
                    Testing 1 2 3
                    <!-- END YOUR CONTENT HERE -->
                </td>
            </tr>
        </table>
    </td>
</tr>
</table>
</div>
</body>
```

After you look at the HTML source code, your first impression might be, "Okay, so what does this actually do?" The answer is, "No idea," and it is not really necessary to know. What you need to know is where to put the content, and that has been shown in bold. The place is marked, and if the table cell had an identifier attribute, the contents of the pop-up box could be injected. This is good because it means for the Presentation functionality you don't need to know how the HTML component works.[4] What you need to know is how to tweak the components, and specifically what you want to know are the following attributes:

- How to tweak the look and feel (for example, change font, background color, and so on)

- How to inject content and read content from the HTML component

- How to display, hide, and position the HTML component

The strategy of the Presentation functionality is to consider the HTML code as a component that is fit into the Decoupled Navigation pattern by using the Adapter pattern. Figure 6-18 illustrates this strategy.

Figure 6-18 shows two web browser snapshots. The upper snapshot shows the browser before clicking the button, and the lower snapshot shows it after clicking the button. All around the snapshots are oodles of balloons to indicate the calling sequence of making a remote call to a server that will generate a pop-up box. All balloons except three should be familiar, because they have already been explained in Figure 6-16.

The new callouts—5) PopupDialogBox, 7) Show Dialog, and Pop-up Box Component—are the Adapter implementation of the HTML component. The function PopupDialogBox implements the Presentation functionality and provides the adapter between the InjectHTML and pop-up box HTML component. The function PopupDialogBox redirects InjectHTML to inject HTML into a table row.

---

4. For a more detailed analysis of how Dynamic HTML components work, please refer to *JavaScript and DHTML Cookbook* by Danny Goodman (O'Reilly Media, 2003).

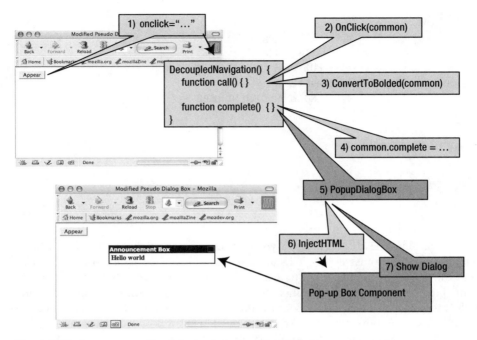

Figure 6-18. *A more complicated user interface that involves a pop-up box*

If you take a good look at Figure 6-18, what should be very apparent is the lack of changes necessary to switch the look and feel of the HTML content. The look of Figure 6-16 is entirely different from that of Figure 6-18, yet the same event structure is used, with a small change in the Presentation functionality. This is the real effectiveness of the Decoupled Navigation pattern, which decouples the various pieces of functionality.

As a thought experiment, imagine the conversion of the button click to a mouse event that pops up the dialog on an onmousemove event. It would not be a difficult change and would only require replacing the onclick event with the onmousemove event.

The following HTML code uses bold to show the pattern integration tweaks that need to be made to the pop-up box illustrated in Figure 6-17:

```
<body>
    <input type="button" value="Appear"
        onclick="return nav.call( event, OnClick,
            ConvertToUpperCase, PopupDialogbox)"/>
    <div id="showimage"
        style="position:absolute;width:250px;left:250px;
                top:250px;visibility:hidden;">
    <table border="0" width="250" bgcolor="#000080"
        cellspacing="0" cellpadding="2">
```

```
        <tr>
            <td width="100%">
                <table border="0" width="100%" cellspacing="0" cellpadding="0"
                    height="36px">
                    <tr>
                        <td id="dragbar" style="cursor:hand; cursor:pointer"
                            width="100%"onMousedown="initializedrag(event)">
                            <ilayer width="100%" onSelectStart="return false">
                            <layer width="100%"
        onMouseover="dragswitch=1;if (ns4) drag_dropns(showimage)"
                            onMouseout="dragswitch=0">
                                <font face="Verdana"
                                        color="#FFFFFF"><strong>
                                    <small id="title">Announcement Box</small>
                                </strong></font>
                            </layer>
                            </ilayer>
                        </td>
                        <td style="cursor:hand">
                            <a href="#" onClick="hidebox();return false">
                                <img src="close.gif" width="16px"
                                    height="14px" border="0"></a></td>
                    </tr>
                    <tr>
                        <td width="100%" bgcolor="#FFFFFF" style="padding:4px"
                            colspan="2"
                            id="destContent">
                            <!-- PUT YOUR CONTENT BETWEEN HERE -->
                            Testing 1 2 3
                            <!-- END YOUR CONTENT HERE -->
                        </td>
                    </tr>
                </table>
            </td>
        </tr>
    </table>
</div>
</body>
```

This HTML code has very few changes. The additional HTML element input is used to pop up the pop-up box defined by the div element. The div element is predefined, and the only real changes to it are to make the div element hidden (visibility=hidden), and to identify the HTML injection points for the pop-up box title bar (title) and pop-up box content (destContent).

For the event call `nav.call`, the new function is `PopupDialogbox` and it is defined as follows:

```
function PopupDialogbox( common, state) {
    InjectHTML( common, state);
    document.getElementById( "showimage").style.visibility = "visible";
    document.getElementById( "title").innerHTML = state.title;
}
```

The function `PopupDialogbox` is an adapter of the predefined pop-up box component. By using the function `InjectHTML`, you inject the text in the table cell destination, `destContent`. The first `getElementById` references the property visibility and is used to make the `div` HTML element appear. The second `getElementById` references the `innerHTML` property and is used to assign the title of the pop-up box. The title would be assigned in the `common.complete` function implementation.

In the example, `PopupDialogbox` is a function defined in the HTML page itself. But there is no reason why the function could not be reused in different contexts whenever a pop-up box is necessary. Additionally, the `PopupDialogbox` function needs other cosmetic changes, such as orientation and size of the pop-up box, that are not illustrated. The changes are not illustrated because they are application specific and do not help explain the Decoupled Navigation pattern.

Using HTML Components

When I was writing the details of this pattern, I was reluctant to repeat content that was written in great detail in other books or websites. After all, providing a bunch of widgets and their explanations without going into great detail is a very bad idea. However, I also knew that the Presentation functionality requires the explanation of HTML components.

My original idea was to spend pages and pages explaining some basic HTML components such as pop-up boxes, menus, and pop-up windows. So off I went to explore how other people were building these HTML components. During my exploration, I hit upon the website http:// www.dynamicdrive.com. At first I thought, interesting site and neat components. It did not have everything, but it was good. It was not until I had to start explaining how to create HTML components that I realized the brilliance of this website.

I thought I would have to spend hours integrating a pop-up box into the Decoupled Navigation pattern, when in fact it required only 20 minutes. At that point, it hit me that the best way to explain the Presentation functionality was to explain how to integrate HTML components. But as my exploration continued, I learned that there were good HTML components and bad HTML components. So as part of the implementation of the Decoupled Navigation pattern, I want to explain a good HTML component site so that when you are exploring for your own HTML components, you will be able to gauge a good or bad HTML component. After all, you do not want to write your own pop-up box. It has been done often enough.

Figure 6-19 is a snapshot of the http://www.dynamicdrive.com website, which lists the available HTML components for dynamic content.

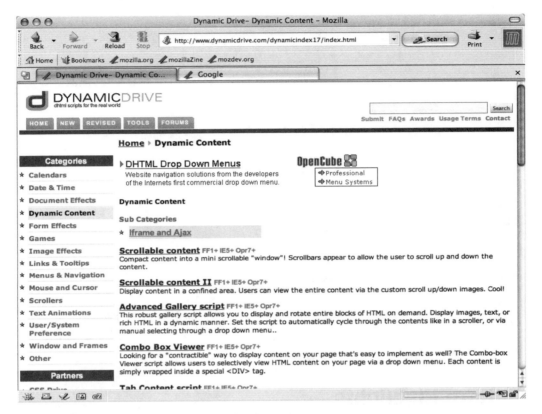

Figure 6-19. *Example HTML components for dynamic content*

Let's illustrate how to integrate the pop-up box HTML content and inspect the related HTML page (see Figure 6-20).

Figure 6-20 shows two text boxes that have been highlighted. The upper text box contains the common code that can be stored in a separate JavaScript file. The lower text box contains the user example code that is created as a prototype of how to invoke the common code. When implementing the Presentation functionality, the common code is not touched and is treated as its own module. What is touched and modified is the user example code.

The clear separation of the common code and the code used to invoke the common code is a very good HTML component. Such a definition of an HTML component indicates that the HTML component has been decoupled and can be plugged into an unrelated infrastructure. One of my pet peeves with many web application and Ajax frameworks is that they are not decoupled. Often the client-side technology relies on server-side technologies, and the client is coupled with other pieces on the HTML page. The result is a monolithic application that happens to function as a web application and Ajax application. However, these applications miss the main thrust of the Ajax and REST philosophies.

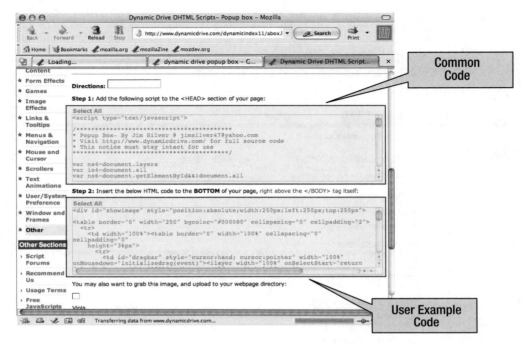

Figure 6-20. *Pop-up box HTML component details*

Pattern Highlights

Based on its description in the "Architecture" section, the Decoupled Navigation pattern might seem unnecessary. However, the usefulness of this pattern became obvious in the "Implementation" section. With Ajax, complex web applications are going to be written that navigate very sophisticated data. Navigating the content means using some type of link, and logic on the client side, and that is the heart of the Decoupled Navigation pattern in that it aims to organize and decouple the various pieces of the logic. All of this was illustrated by an example that became progressively more complex.

The essence of this pattern is to focus on the client side and to break apart the pieces of an HTML application so that maintenance, extensibility, and coding are simpler and can be overseen. The fact is that many HTML applications are complicated, and maintaining oversight of these applications is imperative.

For each of the functionalities, there are some rules of thumb.

For the Action functionality, the following rules are defined:

- Use the `id` property to uniquely identify all HTML elements that will be used in the application.

- The HTML event object instance should be abstracted for simplicity and robustness.

- Use HTML event bubbling to process multiple similar elements as a collection; otherwise, associate single events with single elements. When processing multiple elements, using the id property is imperative; otherwise, problems may occur.

- Use HTML event bubbling to perform validation and verification, potentially stopping the sending of an HTML form. Note that not all events can be canceled, and not all events bubble. When an event does not bubble, the event occurs only on the HTML element responsible for the event.

- For cross-browser compatibility, consider using only the events listed in Table 6-1.

Table 6-1. *Cross-Browser Events and Their Bubble and Cancelable Status*

Event	Bubbles	Cancel
onabort	No	No
onblur	No	No
onchange	Internet Explorer—No Mozilla—Yes	Internet Explorer—Yes Mozilla—No
onclick	Yes	Yes
ondblclick	Yes	Yes
onerror	No	Yes
onfocus	No	No
onkeydown	Yes	Yes
onkeypress	Yes	Yes
onkeyup	Yes	Yes
onload	No	No
onmousdown	Yes	Yes
onmousmove	Yes	No
onmouseout	Yes	Yes
onmouseover	Yes	Yes
onmouseup	Yes	Yes
onmove	Yes	No
onreset	No	Yes
onresize	Yes	No
onsubmit	Internet Explorer—No Mozilla—Yes	Yes
onunload	No	No

Here are some rules of thumb for defining URLs:

- URLs are resources that represent components and should be treated as such.

- URLs are general, and with each identifier appended to the URL, more details about the component are exposed.

- Application logic is related to the URL, and orthogonal application logic is distinctly separated by using the URL.

- As defined by the Permutations pattern, resource URLs exist until the end of time, or at least for a very long time, allowing a resource URL to be considered hard-coded.

Here are some rules of thumb about the Common Data functionality:

- Implementing the Common Data functionality means defining a common state structure that is shared by the Action, Common Data (functions that is), and Presentation functionalities.

- Implementing a common state structure is essential to decoupling the various functionalities from each other, making it possible to wire together predefined functionality.

- The common state structure should be decoupled from the functionalities by using classes and functions.

Here are some rules of thumb about the Presentation functionality:

- The Presentation functionality does not encompass all aspects of the user interface. For example, the details of creating and moving a pop-up box are managed by the routines of the pop-up box. The Presentation functionality is responsible for indicating what data to present and when to present that data.

- All Presentation functionalities should be adapters for HTML components. You do not want to write your own pop-up boxes, menus, or other more sophisticated HTML user interface components. Intelligent individuals have already done a good job, and you should take advantage of their generosity and intelligence.

- When implementing a function to generate the user interface, focus on creating general code that can be reused in multiple contexts.

CHAPTER 7

Representation Morphing Pattern

Intent

The Representation Morphing pattern is best described as a representation that implements a mini Model View Controller, where the model is a constant that can be substituted into other mini Model View Controllers. The uniqueness of this pattern is that the model, view, and controller are an all-in-one package. The result is a representation that is work-space oriented, allowing saving and reconstruction without having to use a large amount of JavaScript source code.

Motivation

The motivation for using this pattern relates to the desire to improve the usability of web applications. Web applications are not traditional client applications and require their own coding techniques. When implementing web applications, some will attempt to assign traditional client programming functionalities when the correct solution would be to concentrate on the Web and what it offers.

There are multiple types of web applications, two of which are informational and data gathering. *Informational* websites provide links and some HTML form elements to navigate the data. Search engines are an example of informational websites in which links and HTML form elements (for example, a text box) are used to navigate information. Figure 7-1 shows the Google search engine.

The Google search engine has multiple HTML form elements (text box, buttons, and radio buttons) illustrating sophisticated features in a simple-to-use representation. Most people probably do not use any of the HTML form elements except for the text box. Usually you enter your data into the text box, hit the Enter key, and get a listing of search results.

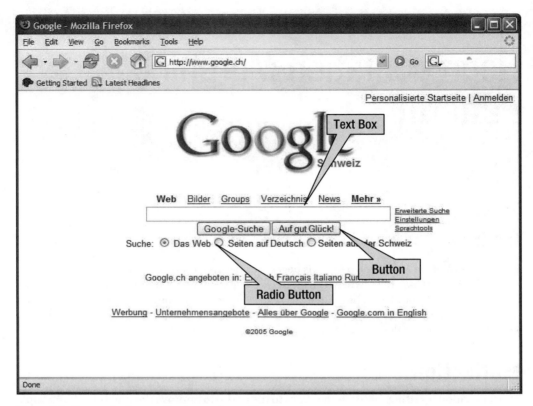

Figure 7-1. *Example data gathering web application*

A *data-gathering* web application is different in that the HTML elements are used to assemble data for reference purposes. Consider the data-gathering application illustrated in Figure 7-2.

In this data-gathering web application, all of the pieces of information are gathered by using HTML form elements. In Figure 7-2, all of the HTML elements are text boxes, which are compact and visually pleasing, but ill-suited for data entry. Two of the text boxes are incorrectly formatted and illustrate a fundamental problem. The topmost text box is too big for the task of entering the title of the message. The second text box, on the other hand, is completely under-sized for entering the message that will be sent. If the message causes scroll bars to appear, the little room that is available becomes even less. For any larger amounts of text, a user needs to constantly scroll from side to side or up and down. Users would be better off writing the text in another application and then copying the text into the text box.

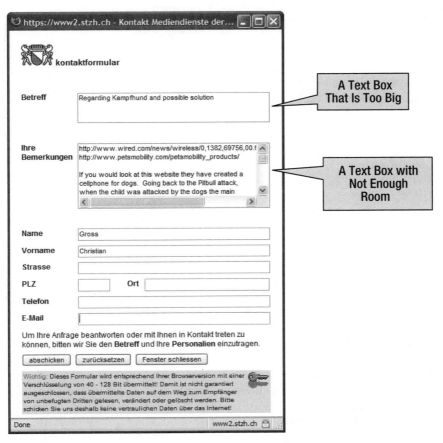

Figure 7-2. *Example data-gathering web application[1]*

The HTML form has an editing problem, and two factors are largely responsible: bad user-interface design, and not knowing how to deal with HTML forms. In contrast, Figure 7-3 illustrates how HTML can be organized to be both visually attractive and data-entry effective.

In Figure 7-3, Slashdot presents a very simple user interface that has a single-line text field for the subject and a generous text area for the comments. This is a good example of how to write a data-gathering application. However, there is a catch in that a well-organized HTML form takes a larger amount of screen real estate.

---

1. For those wondering, I sent a message to the Zurich regional government indicating how a pet collar that has GPS and cellphone capabilities could be used to control dogs such as pit bulls without resorting to drastic measures. This is a concern in Europe (also in other places such as the US) as fighting dogs have been responsible for many child deaths and critical injuries.

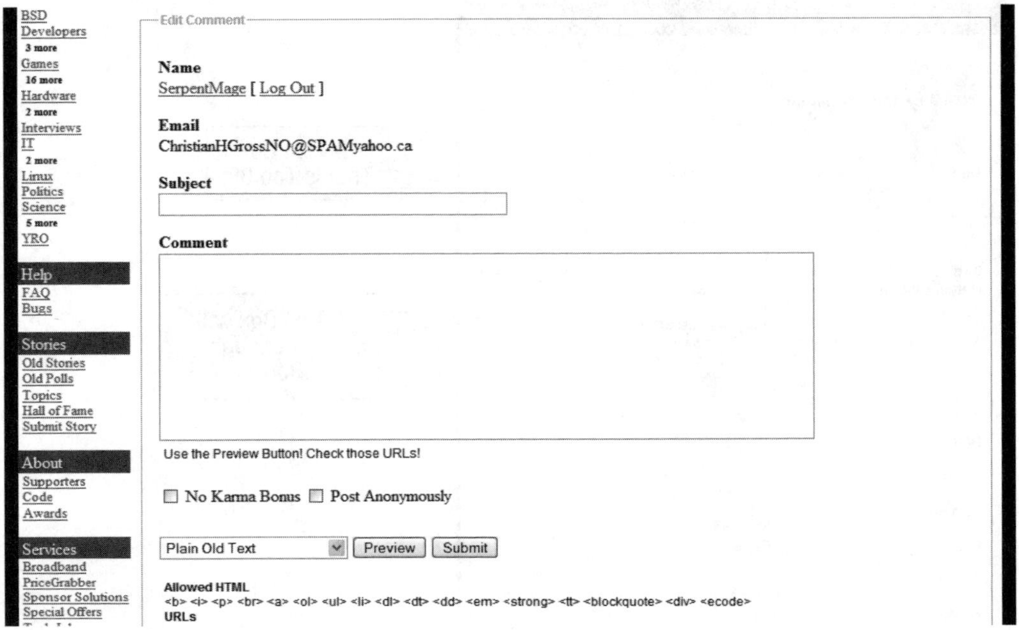

Figure 7-3. *A properly formatted text box*

This leads us to the question of whether it is even possible to write a compact and effective HTML form. And if it is not possible, does this mean web applications are ill-suited for data gathering and better suited for navigation? The answer lies in a change in thinking, where HTML offers capabilities that are beyond the reach of other technologies. Traditional user interfaces generally have predefined windows and dialog boxes, and are very static in nature (not dynamic). A traditional user interface application does not generate user interface elements dynamically from a few pieces of information. Traditional user interfaces are a "what you see is what you get" type of programming environment. Dynamic HTML, on the other hand, makes it possible to define the user interface as the application is being executed. It is possible to do the same sort of thing with traditional programming environments, but the effort required is not insignificant.

Static user interfaces are the result of creating a component that is a single block manipulated by a programming language. Figure 7-4 illustrates such a component, which is a combo box used to specify and purchase a plane ticket.

Figure 7-4 shows a combo box that when clicked will expose a list of available times that a person wants to fly. The combo box displays all available hours and is large enough to accommodate a large number of times with the least amount of scrolling required. The combo box is functional and represents the data in a format that JavaScript and a server application can easily process. Some developers consider this sort of user interface as being developer-convenient but user-inconvenient.

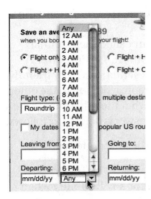

Figure 7-4. *Simple example of anchored state*

From a user interface perspective, the combo box is not optimal, but it is what we would use because of traditional programming habits. Another approach would be to create little sun and moon clocks and let the user click on the time. Creating the clocks would enable the user to make a choice more quickly and could even let the user specify quarter-hours. The combo box in Figure 7-4 cannot specify anything other than the hourly choices.

Another approach would be to use two separate components to select a value. Each component would represent a "best-of-breed" representation. For the time, the static representation could be a text box indicating the preferred time. The second component would present a user-friendly way to select the time. Such an example of using two separate components already exists today in the form of a calendar, as illustrated in Figure 7-5.

Figure 7-5. *Using two components to determine a single state*

Figure 7-5 shows a text box, representing the machine-friendly component, which contains an example of how the date should be formatted. The date-formatting specification is mm/dd/yy. The date formatting is cryptic, not obvious in the least, yet most of us seem to know what it means. The formatting is an example of incredible user idiosyncrasies that most of us accept because they are machine-friendly. The second component is user-friendly and is the larger calendar window. When the user selects a day in a month, the user-friendly component updates the contents of the machine-friendly component. The user does not have to understand the formatting; the date could even be formatted in seconds since 1970.

Most of us appreciate the two components as a single component called the calendar component, which is an example of the Representation Morphing pattern. The important message is that a calendar at its basic level has two best-of-breed representations (user friendly and machine friendly), where the model (date) is transferred from one representation to the other.

The calendar component is trivial and may lead you to wonder what the difference is between components and the Representation Morphing pattern. The answer is defined as follows:

- Traditional components are programmed so that the state of the component is determined at the component's runtime.

- Traditional components are hardwired together, not allowing for any flexibility when transferring the model from one representation to another.

- Traditional components have their model transferred by using external access mechanisms and consider the internals private.

In a nutshell, when implementing the Representation Morphing pattern, you are defining a structure in which the model, view, and controller are part of the representation.

The motivation for using the Representation Morphing pattern is as follows:

- To enable a programming model where the model, view, and controller are self-contained and can be saved and loaded. This makes it possible to create work spaces that a developer can save.

- To enable the flexible combination of representations so that a best-of-breed approach can be used when manipulating data. A simple example is the ability to transform an HTML form so that people who are blind or nearly blind can view content that suits their needs.

- To enable the definition of states that can be used in workflow applications without having to wire together an extensive number of objects.

The idea is to enable a programming model where the model, view, and controller can interact among themselves. A user of the model has the choice of manipulating the model directly or using helper functions, but the model is not hidden from the user of the representation. The idea of letting a script access the internal workings of a component does violate object-oriented programming. But the aim of the Representation Morphing pattern is not to abstract, but to standardize the model that makes up the component. In object-oriented programming techniques, the internal state is abstracted so that it can change without having to change the code of the user. With the Representation Morphing pattern, the intention is to keep the model constant and have the representation change.

Applicability

Technically speaking, the Representation Morphing pattern is used whenever data is transformed from one representation to another. This is useful when developing data-gathering applications that require two different representations for viewing the data and editing the data. In the "Implementation" section, the transformation of editing and viewing the data is illustrated.

A very appropriate example of where the Representation Morphing pattern is used is in a wiki-type application. A *wiki* is a web-based application used to manage documents that can be viewed and edited by individuals. A wiki is an ideal example of an application that has a common state but multiple distinct representations (editing, versioning, commenting, and viewing).

The Representation Morphing pattern is also very applicable in a navigation scenario, when navigated state should be presented by using different representations. A common navigation situation is the conversion of an HTML page into another HTML page that is printer-friendly.

With the Representation Morphing pattern, it is possible to send a representation to the server side for further processing. Such an approach gets around the limitations of HTML forms, allowing more complicated structures to be sent. The advantage of sending a representation directly to the server is that the client has to do no processing. A client can take advantage of the Content Chunking or Persistent Communications pattern without implementing extensive serialization routines.

The Representation Morphing pattern would be inappropriate if the data-gathering application were a *generate and forget* type of application. In a generate and forget application, somebody submits data that is sliced and diced into another state. After the state is transformed, implementing the Representation Morphing pattern becomes more complicated. The complication is the result of potentially losing a state that a representation needs. For example, imagine building a web application that adds two numbers. If the server side uses the two numbers to generate another number and then returns the generated number only, information is lost. The representation that generated the numbers needs the added numbers when generating its view.

Associated Patterns

The Representation Morphing pattern relies on blocks of content that can be either state or representation related. The blocks of content can be either sent or received, and therefore this pattern makes use of the Content Chunking pattern. When the content is received by using the Content Chunking pattern, the Permutations pattern does apply. The Representation Morphing pattern is a form of the Permutations pattern intended for the client side.

A more accurate description is that the Representation pattern imitates the Permutation pattern, except the Representation pattern has no URL. The URL is the model in the representation. The Representation Morphing pattern is used when the State Navigation pattern is implemented. The purpose of the Representation Morphing pattern is to define the state that is managed by the State Navigation pattern.

Architecture

Technically, the Representation Morphing pattern is used to define some representation that has some state that can be transferred to another representation, and back again with the state intact. The "Architecture" and "Implementation" sections will move away from the model-view-controller analogy because the analogy is good for presenting an initial impression of what the

Representation Morphing pattern does, but bad for explaining the nitty-gritty details. These nitty-gritty details, when critically considered, illustrate that there are some fundamental differences between the Representation Morphing pattern and the Model View Controller architecture.

Basic Theory

The architecture of the Representation Morphing pattern considers the state as the basis of the representation. The representation relies on the state, but not the state on the representation. This means that two representations can contain the same state but display the state differently. The state within a representation will be identical in literal terms. Figure 7-6 illustrates how this might work and provides a closer look at the calendar and its underlying HTML structure.

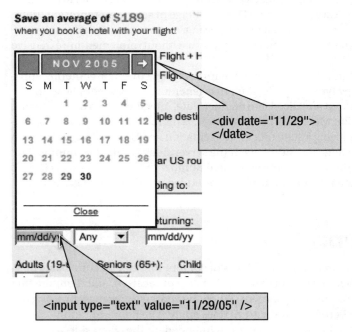

Figure 7-6. *Transformed state between text box and window*

In Figure 7-6, the common state is represented by the attributes value and date. The format of each attribute is identical; only the attribute identifier is not. What you want to avoid is the deciphering of the state into its base components, which for a date is month, day, and year. Deciphering state means that an external script accessing the state needs to understand how the state is deciphered. One could argue that because the calendar uses two different attribute identifiers, a state has already been deciphered. However, the point of the modified identifier was to illustrate that the Representation morphing pattern probably needs a bit of flexibility with respect to state identification, but not state value. Of course the ideal solution is to have 100 percent identical state identification across representations, but that is not always possible.

Having identical state values across representations makes it possible to apply transformations across representations without the loss of information. The moment state has to be deciphered, you are risking losing information. This is not to say that a representation cannot decipher the state. The point of the Representation Morphing pattern is to enable individual representations to decipher the state to something that is useful for their context. Additionally, embedding the state in the representation itself ensures that state is not lost when it exists temporarily in the context of an executing JavaScript document.

Why the Pattern Is Not an HTML Component

Considering the basic theory of the Representation Morphing pattern, you might question how the pattern is different from a component. The purpose of the component and the pattern are identical in that they provide multiple representations of the data.

Previously I discussed traditional components. Now, after having explained a bit of the pattern's architecture, I will define the attributes of the Representation Morphing pattern implementation:

- The representation and state are combined as a single piece of content.

- The "guts" of the component are exposed and can be manipulated by other representations.

- Transferring the representation means transferring a work space that is self-contained and allows for a later reinstantiation.

- A representation can be combined with other representations that evolve over time, and can create new pieces of functionality that the developers of the web application had not previously considered.

- The logic associated with the representation is used to manipulate state, and not keep state (for example, a JavaScript variable instance is not used to keep state).

In a nutshell, the big difference between most user interface–based components is that when the component is instantiated, it has no state. However, when a representation that implements the Representation Morphing pattern is instantiated, there is a state. The result is that potentially two instantiations of functionally identical representations will contain two entirely different states.

What the Representation Morphing pattern implements is one of the concepts made possible with dynamic programming. The entire architecture of the Representation Morphing pattern rests on the capabilities of dynamic languages and the Dynamic HTML object model. *Dynamic languages*[2] are known to some people as scripting languages. What makes a dynamic language unique is its ability to define, add, or delete functions, modules, or class types during the execution of the language and to have the ability to persist those changes as a work space for later execution. Languages such as Java and C# cannot do that, or at least not as simply as dynamic languages.

Consider the following example, which illustrates how a dynamic language operates:

```
function createTypeAndProperty() {
    var obj = new Object();
    obj.prop = 12345;
    return obj;
}
```

---

2. http://en.wikipedia.org/wiki/Dynamic_language

In the function createTypeAndProperty, the variable obj references the type Object, which has a minimal number of properties and methods. Dynamically, the property prop is assigned a value of 12345. There is no definition of prop in the Object type, but a dynamic language allows this arbitrary assignment. Had this example been coded using either Java or C#, there would be compilation problems due to the incomplete definitions. The dynamic assignment of the property is part of the basic design of a dynamic language. The result is that a dynamic language can assign properties that represent methods or data members on an as-needed basis. Putting this into the context of the pattern, it means that properties can be assigned to already-existing HTML elements. When implementing the Representation Morphing pattern, a dynamic language is needed because the state changes dynamically, including the type of state stored.

It also requires developers to stop coding using static programming techniques. Consider the following source code that illustrates two JavaScript functions; one uses static programming techniques, and the other uses dynamic programming techniques:

```
var value;

function AssignStatic() {
    value = document.getElementById( "form-element").value;
}

function AssignDynamic() {
    document.getElementById( "div-variable").innerHTML =
        document.getElementById( "form-element").value;
}
```

Let's say both functions are used to process a state that is entered in an HTML form element. The function AssignStatic transfers the state from the HTML form element to the variable value. The function AssignDynamic also transfers the state, but transfers the value to the div HTML element div-variable.

The ramification of storing the state directly in the representation is that you can transfer content by transferring the representation. From a traditional client perspective, it is as if somebody entered some text in a text box that is stored in another user interface element, and not the executing program. The representation is self-sufficient, and when it is transferred, the representation still continues to function—albeit with a few gotchas that will be explained in the "Implementation" section. It is not possible to transfer the contents of an HTML chunk without first explicitly transferring the state of the running JavaScript to some other content chunk.

Defining Blocks of State

Designing the Representation Morphing pattern requires defining blocks of state that are associated with a representation. A representation is a content chunk akin to that defined by the Content Chunking pattern. Figure 7-7 shows an initial HTML form that will be used to illustrate how an HTML form is converted into a number of content chunks representative of the Representation Morphing pattern.

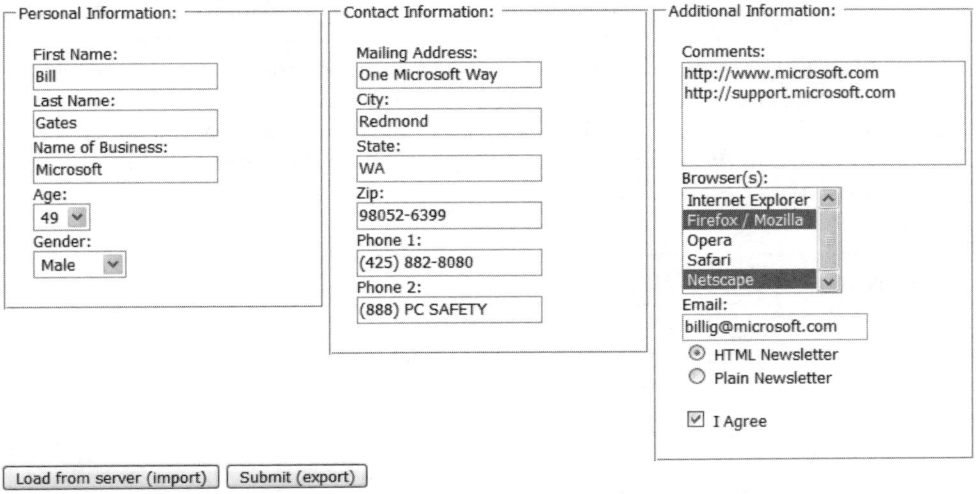

Figure 7-7. *Example HTML form[3]*

Figure 7-7 shows an HTML form with HTML form elements such as a text box, combo box, and the likes. The HTML form is used to enter some data, and is a classical example of a form that is machine-friendly, but in many aspects user unfriendly. The following points illustrate the user unfriendliness of the HTML form:

- What happens if you are older than 65? The Age combo box has a maximum of 65, which has been cited as the keyhole problem by Scott Meyers.[4]

- What happens if your naming pattern does not fit into the classical model of first name and last name? Many cultures on this planet have other naming conventions.

- What happens if the country does not have a state or a zip code?

- What happens if the phone number does not fit into the classical area code and seven digits? Where does the extension fit in?

- Why must the Comments text box have fixed rows and columns that always seem to be too narrow for anything but the simplest of information?

- Why must the Browser(s) list box contain elements that can be viewed only if the scroll bar is used?

- Why must abbreviations (such as WA for the state) be used that not everybody may understand?

- Why are the text boxes in the HTML form not wide enough?

---

3. The source of the HTML is `http://demo.xoad.org/examples/forms/`, which uses the XOAD toolkit.
4. `http://www.aristeia.com/`

The HTML form can be used to display the data, but when the data is edited a different representation should be used. Of course you could argue, why use an HTML form in the first place if a different representation is going to be used to edit the content? Even though that point is correct, most people today have HTML forms and it makes more sense to discuss how HTML forms and the Representation Morphing pattern can interact with each other. To convert the HTML form to use the Representation Morphing pattern, individual states have to be defined, as illustrated in Figure 7-8.

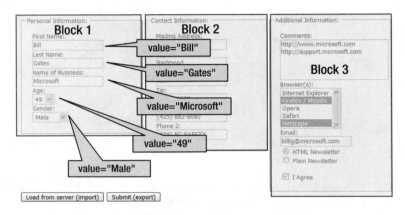

Figure 7-8. *Example HTML form converted into three state blocks*

Figure 7-8 shows three blocks of state. These blocks were defined based on the way that the elements were grouped. After all, if you group something, you have created an association between the grouped elements. However, it is not necessary to create one state per grouping, and there could be multiple groupings per state. The idea is to define a block of representation that contains a state. For this explanation, the focus is on Block 1 in Figure 7-8. Block 1 is a representation that contains a state made up of five pieces of information. Those five pieces of information make up the model that will be extracted and injected into different representations.

HTML form elements are useful for gathering data but hinder the user's comprehension of the data because the data's layout tends to be irregular. To improve the user's comprehension when viewing data, a better approach would be to use HTML without the form elements. Figure 7-9 illustrates what the state of Block 1 would look like without using HTML forms.

Figure 7-9, which presents a new representation of Figure 7-8, is more compact and easier to read at a glance. The representation is user friendly for reading purposes. The state in Figure 7-9 is contained within a series of span HTML tags. Each individual span tag has an identifier similar to the identifier in Figure 7-8. The state of Figure 7-9 is also the representation, as illustrated by the following HTML:

```
<td><span id="first-name">Bill</span>,
    <span id="last-name">Gates</span><br />
...
</td>
```

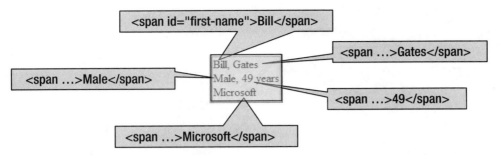

Figure 7-9. *Block of state morphed to a new representation*

One of the advantages of Dynamic HTML is that state can be embedded within a representation, thus making it unnecessary to store the state in a variable executing in the context of a JavaScript script. To assign or retrieve the state, the property `document.getElementById` (`"div").innerHTML` is used. This is one of the advantages of the Representation Morphing pattern: the state does not have to be converted from the memory of an executing script into a representation and back again. The only requirement is that the state needs to be stored in such a way that a script can easily extract the information.

Some readers may realize that the Representation Morphing pattern is similar to XForms.[5] Although the Representation Morphing pattern could be used like an XForm, the main thrust of this pattern is to create a state that is embedded in a representation. The state could represent a form, but it doesn't have to. The state could be an HTML document that is manipulated over time, such as a word processing document.

The Representation Morphing pattern comes into play when the state in Figure 7-9 is converted into an HTML form for user editing purposes. Then as the state has been edited, the representation changes back to Figure 7-9 with the new values. This transformation is a morphing of representation using a common state and is illustrated in Figure 7-10.

Figure 7-10 shows two states with two representations. The arrows indicate the direction of morphing. The transformation blocks are functionality used to morph the state from one representation to another representation. It is important to have bidirectional morphing capabilities, because only with bidirectional morphing can you be assured that no state is lost or corrupted. This bidirectional capability goes back to the argument of adding two numbers and getting a result. Consistent bidirectional behavior would require that the two numbers that are added and the addition result constitute a result.

---

5. http://www.w3.org/MarkUp/Forms/

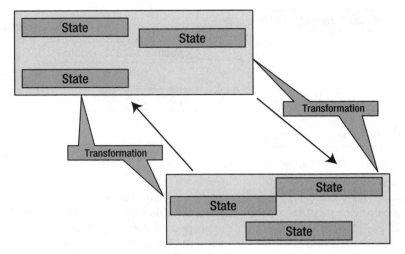

Figure 7-10. *Morphing from one state to another*

Figure 7-11 shows an example of implementing the Representation Morphing pattern: the wiki TiddlyWiki, which is considered an application that runs without a server.

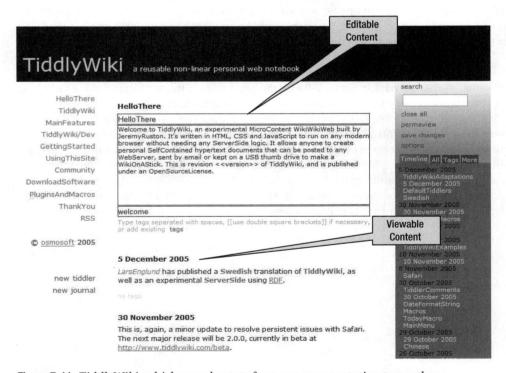

Figure 7-11. *TiddlyWiki, which morphs state from one representation to another*

TiddlyWiki may not completely implement the Representation Morphing pattern, but the concept is there. There is an editable representation that edits the state, and a viewable representation that views the state. Each representation is a best-of-breed representation useful for the context of viewing or editing the state. Between the two representations the state is identical, and converting from one representation to another does not add or remove data from the state.

Implementation

The implementation of the Representation Morphing pattern focuses on defining the state (as in Figure 7-8) and morphing the state (as in Figure 7-9). In this section, the first example implementation will focus on a purely JavaScript solution, and the second example will be a simplified implementation illustrating how XSLT could be used to morph content from one representation to another. Regardless of which solution is used, a complete Representation Morphing implementation requires some special techniques to get around the problems of Dynamic HTML.

Implementing the Framework

The aim of this example implementation is to fully implement the Representation Morphing pattern for the state of Block 1 in Figure 7-9. The example will convert the editable representation of the HTML form into a viewable representation, and then to another editable representation. The second editable representation morphing is the result of using XSLT. In total, there are three representations, but only one state. All of the representations displayed side by side without any state is identical to Figure 7-12. It goes without saying that in your HTML pages, the transition from one representation to another will be visually pleasing, as in Figure 7-11.

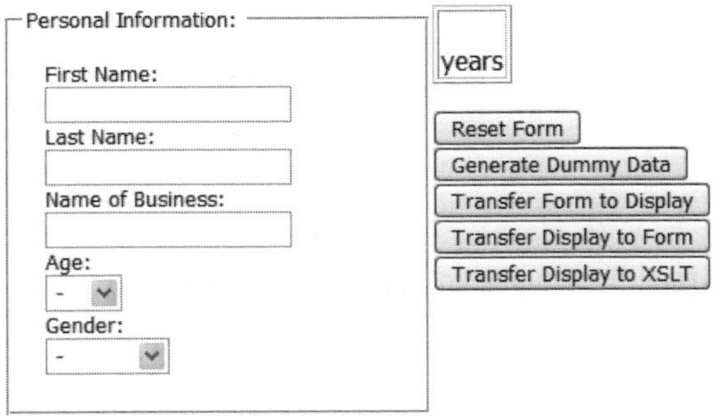

Figure 7-12. *Example HTML page without any state*

Figure 7-12 shows three representations with no state. The first representation is the Personal Information grouping, the second is the table labeled Years, and the third is the unseen div element between the second representation and the Reset Form button. If all of the representations are filled in with information, the HTML page will resemble Figure 7-13.

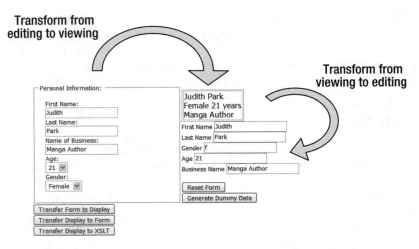

Figure 7-13. *Example HTML page with filled-in representations*

In Figure 7-13, the first editable representation is an HTML form that has been filled in with some information. The state from the first representation is transferred to the second representation, which is then transferred to the third representation. What is unique about the third representation is that it is plain-vanilla and is the raw machine-friendly information. Notice how the gender in the first and second representations is Female, but in the third representation is the letter *f*. The reason is that the raw state for gender is either f or m. The first and second representations convert the *m* or *f* to a more user-friendly Male or Female.

The abbreviated HTML code is similar to the following:

```html
<html>
    <body>
        <div id="htmlform">
            <script id="scripthtmlform" language="JavaScript"></script>
            <div>
            </div>
        </div>
        <div id="htmldisplay">
            <script id="scripthtmldisplay" language="JavaScript"></script>
            <div>
            </div>
        </div>
        <div id="htmlxslt">
            <div id="xsltFromSpan" style="visibility:hidden">
                <![CDATA[    ]]>
            </div>
            <script language="JavaScript"></script>
            <div id="htmlxsltdest">
            </div>
        </div>
    </body>
</html>
```

The abbreviated HTML code has three child `div` elements that are children to the `body` element. Each of those three `div` elements contain one representation. Each representation contains a number of HTML child elements, which can be directly related to the Model View Controller architecture. The state is the model and is contained in a child `div` element. The controller is contained within the `script` element, and the view is contained in another child `div` element. Having the model, view, and controller as child elements of a `div` element provides a JavaScript script a single reference point that is available for injection and extraction functionality.

Implementing the Representation Reference Points

There are two types of representation reference points: JavaScript and XSLT. A JavaScript representation reference point is used when the extraction and transformation of the state uses JavaScript. And an XSLT representation reference point is used when the injection of the state uses an XSLT sheet.

The Details of a JavaScript Representation Reference Point

When transferring state from one representation to another, some commonality between the two representations is required. The commonality could be an identical state as represented by an XML structure within the HTML content, or an identical set of methods. Using the commonality, the state is extracted from one representation and assigned to another representation. The commonality in this example is a set of methods called `assignState` and `extractState` and is illustrated as follows. For reference purposes, the function `el` maps to `document.getElementById`:

```
<html>
    <body>
        <div id="htmlform">
            <script id="scripthtmlform" language="JavaScript">
                el( "htmlform").assignState = function( state) { }
                el( "htmlform").extractState = function() { return state; }
            </script>
            <div>
            </div>
        </div>
        <div id="htmldisplay">
            <script id="scripthtmldisplay" language="JavaScript">
                el( "htmldisplay").assignState = function( state) { }
                el( "htmldisplay").extractState = function() { return state; }
            </script>
            <div>
            </div>
        </div>
    </body>
</html>
```

The bold code is code that is executed as the HTML page is being loaded. The bold code does two things: define the methods used to extract and assign state, and assign the methods to an HTML element. The code adds the functions `assignState` and `extractState` to the reference `div` elements `htmlform` and `htmldisplay`. What is unique about the method assignment is that the functionality of the div element is being extended dynamically. The method assignState accepts an object instance that contains the state from some other representation. The method extractState retrieves the state associated with the representation as an object instance. To transfer the state from one representation to another, the following method would be called:

```
el( "htmlform").assignState( el("htmldisplay").extractState());
```

What is common between multiple representations is the generated state object instance. It is important to realize that the generated state instances are used only for transformation purposes. The implementation of the assignState and extractState functions can be tricky because there are two implementation techniques. One technique is to write the code generically, and the other is to use specifics. Writing code *generically* means to store the state within a representation by using a consistent coding style that allows the creation of generic extraction and assignment routines. Writing code *specifically* means to explicitly define elements used to assign or extract the state.

Let's go through both approaches and develop an optimal solution. Consider the following implementation of the function extractState, which uses specifics:

```
el( "htmlform").extractState = function () {
    var obj = new Object();
    obj.firstName = el( "first-name").value;
    obj.lastName = el( " last-name").value;
    obj.businessName = el( " business-name").value;
    obj.age = el( "age").value;
    obj.gender = el( " gender").value;
    return obj;
}
```

In this example, an Object instance is created that represents the state instance. The properties firstName, lastName, and so on are then specifically referenced and assigned by retrieving the value from the HTML content. The manual referencing from the HTML content and then assignment is a traditional static-programming approach. The problem with using this approach is that if the HTML content is updated, the functions related to the specific referencing must be also updated. This results in a state being defined in the JavaScript, which is not the intention of the Representation Morphing pattern.

A better way to write the extractState function is to consider generic extraction routines that are tuned by the view of the representation. A generic implementation would iterate all of the child HTML elements within the view as defined by the div element. During the iteration, those elements that implement a coding standard represent state and would be copied to an object instance. The following is a generic implementation of the extractState function:

```
function parseElement( obj, element) {
    if( element.nodeType == 1) {
        if( element.nodeName.toLowerCase() == "input" ||
            element.nodeName.toLowerCase() == "select") {
            if( element.name) {
                obj[ element.name] = element.value;
            }
        }
```

```
        for( var i = 0; i < element.childNodes.length; i ++) {
            parseElement(obj,element.childNodes[ i]);
        }
    }
}
el( "htmlform").extractState = function () {
    var obj = new Object();
    parseElement( obj, el( "mainForm"));
    return obj;
}
```

In this example of extractState, the Object type is still instantiated, but the general function parseElement is called. The purpose of parseElement is to iterate HTML element nodes and to find all of the HTML form elements of type input and select. If an element node is found, the name and value of the element are copied to the Object instance. Let's look a little closer at that single line, because it is very important:

```
obj[ element.name] = element.value;
```

The square brackets indicate the referencing of an array, yet in the implementation of the extractState method an array was not created. What is happening is the dynamic association of a property with an object instance. The square brackets are used to identify a property that can be referenced at some later point. So if the value of element.name were firstName, the property could be referenced as follows:

```
obj.firstName = element.value;
```

Dynamic programming techniques that dynamically assign properties and methods, extending functionality of objects, tends to be frowned upon by static language programmers. The reason is that dynamically extending the functionality of an object tends to have the object exhibit a type of "now you see it, now you don't" behavior. The problem is that a programmer cannot be assured that functionality exists until the code is executed. However, with proper testing such worries are overblown.

Continuing the example, the state object instance is converted into a representation by using generic programming techniques. This means that the state from the editable representation is converted into a state for the viewable representation, as illustrated in Figure 7-13. In the viewing representation, the state is represented by using individual span elements. The following HTML provides a skeleton of how the state is stored in the view (ignore the bold code for the moment and consider the entire HTML):

```
<table border="1">
    <tbody>
        <tr>
            <td><span display="First Name" id="firstName"></span>
                <span display="Last Name" id="lastName"></span>
                <span display="Gender" id="gender" style="visibility:hidden;">
                </span><br />
                <span id="html-gender"></span>
                <span display="Age" id="age"></span> years<br />
                <span display="Business Name" id="businessName"></span>
```

```
                </td>
            </tr>
        </tbody>
    </table>
```

The HTML code is for a simple table with a single row and cell. Within the cell are a number of span elements with identifiers. The identifiers are identical to the properties defined in the JavaScript Object instance. The coincidence is not accidental; this was done on purpose so that a property on the state object instance could be cross-referenced with a span element.

The example code has two HTML span elements in bold. The span element with the identifier gender is cross-referenced with the JavaScript Object instance property gender. But the span element with the identifier html-gender does not cross-reference with a specific property on the state object instance. That span identifier is a field that is a transformation managed by the controller and represents the property gender. The transformation is necessary because the raw state for gender is an f or m, but when viewed, Female or Male, respectively, is preferred. The function of the controller is to convert the raw state into something that displays in a user-friendly manner.

Without considering the transformation, the following source code is used to provide a generic transformation of the state object instance to the model of the representation:

```
function processElement( obj, element) {
    if( element.nodeType == 1) {
        if( element.nodeName.toLowerCase() == "span") {
            if( obj[ element.id]) {
                if( element.callback) {
                    element.callback( obj)
                }
                element.innerHTML = obj[ element.id];
            }
        }
        for( var i = 0; i < element.childNodes.length; i ++) {
            processElement( obj,element.childNodes[ i]);
        }
    }
}
el( "htmldisplay").assignState = function( state) {
    processElement( state, el( "htmldisplay"));
}
```

The purpose of the assignState function is to assign the state, as discussed previously. In the implementation of assignState, the function processElement is called. The purpose of processElement is to iterate the individual HTML elements of the representation. If the HTML element is a span element, a cross-reference of the JavaScript state with the representation state is attempted and is bold in the example code.

The bold code illustrates how a dynamic language will automatically cross-reference an attribute with a property of an object instance. The HTML element property element.id represents the attribute id of the HTML element. This property provides a cross-reference of the object instance and HTML element. The property element.id is tested in obj to verify that a property exists. If the property does exist, the element.callback is tested to perform some fine-tuning that is associated with the state. After the element.callback test, the HTML span innerHTML property is assigned.

Getting back to the HTML callback property, the purpose of the property is to allow a customization operation. This goes back to the bold span elements for gender. One of the span elements is for the machine-friendly state, and the other is for the user-friendly view. The conversion works because a callback is associated with a span element by using the dynamic extension facilities used to assign the methods assignState and extractState. When the callback is called, the assigned machine-friendly state is inspected and converted into a user-friendly view. Figure 7-14 illustrates the sequence of events.

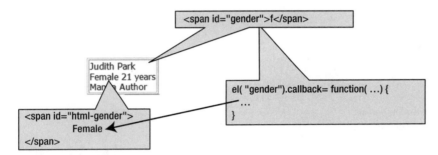

Figure 7-14. *Sequence of events for generating a custom output*

In Figure 7-14, the callback function is assigned dynamically to a span element. The assigned callback then manipulates another span element (html-gender) that contains the user-friendly representation. Extending an individual element allows the generic routines to generically extract or assign state, while still allowing fine-tuning. The implementation of the callback function is as follows:

```
locatel( "embedded", "gender").callback = function( state) {
    if( state.gender == "m") {
        locatel( "embedded", "html-gender").innerHTML = "Male";
    }
    else if( state.gender == "f") {
        locatel( "embedded", "html-gender").innerHTML = "Female";
    }
}
```

The definition of the callback function does not use the el function, but the localel function. The reason is that when using generic routines to process the state, each representation will have an identifier with the same name as the property. This means a single HTML page can have multiple identical identifiers, causing an identifier clash. If the function document. getElementById is used, the first found identifier will be returned. The function localel does two things: find the reference point to the representation, and then iterate the view to find the appropriately named element. In the example, that means the embedded parent HTML element has its children searched for an identifier gender. The embedded identifier is unique and is retrieved by using the function document.getElementById.

By combining the generic routines with the element assigned, fine-tuning makes it possible to develop representations that manipulate state in a general manner. From an HTML coder's perspective, the state is embedded in the HTML document and not in the JavaScript. Consider the following JavaScript, which illustrates how this would work:

```
<script language="JavaScript" type="text/javascript">
function ShowContent( element) {
    ddrivetip(
        document.getElementById( "txt" + element.title).innerHTML, 300);
}
</script>
<body>
...
<div>
    <span id="txtDecoupledNavigation"
        style="position:absolute;visibility:hidden;">
        ...
    </span>
    <span id="txtRestBasedMVC"
        style="position:absolute;visibility:hidden;">
        ...
    </span>
    <span id="txtRepresentationMorphing"
        style="position:absolute;visibility:hidden;">
        ...
    </span>
...
<map id="patterns" name="patterns">
        <area shape="rect"#DecoupledNavigation
            onmouseover="ShowContent( this)"
            coords="105,13,204,58" href="#null"
            title="DecoupledNavigation"
            onclick="return ShowLinks( this)">
        </area>
```

In the example, the function ShowContent implements the logic whereby the parameter content of a function is driven by the title attribute of an HTML element. The content of the parameter is the result of retrieving the content from a span element. In the example, the span contents are hard-coded, but they could also have been the result of doing a Content Chunking pattern call. Additionally, the span element and its contents are XML compliant, using XHTML element identifiers to delegate the hard work of processing the data to the web browser.

The Details of an XSLT Representation Reference Point

Another way to transform the state from one representation to another is to use Extensible Stylesheet Language Transformations (XSLT). XSLT is a technology that uses a programming language defined in XML to transform XML content into other text-based content. The state of the representation is stored as XML-compliant HTML. By using an XSLT transformation, the state is extracted from one representation and injected into another.

XSLT requires some content to transform. In the case of the Representation Morphing pattern, the content to transform is the other representation. The result is another transformation. What this means is that all of the representations need to use some common HTML tags such as HTML form elements, or span tags, or some other common tag. The common tags can be surrounded with unknown other tags because they are considered irrelevant. In a nutshell, the XSLT transformation accomplishes the same as the parseElement and processElement functions. The difference with the XSLT transformation is that it is accomplished all in one step, and not in two function calls. Furthermore, the entire processing is XML-based.

When using XSLT, the representation is not a classical Model View Controller architecture because the controller and the view are combined. Let's look back at the HTML framework and at how the XSLT reference point is defined:

```
<div id="htmlxslt">
    <div id="xsltFromSpan" style="visibility:hidden">
        <![CDATA[    ]]>
    </div>
    <script language="JavaScript"></script>
    <div id="htmlxsltdest">
    </div>
</div>
```

An XSLT reference point has at least three child elements. The first child element, div, with the identifier xsltFromSpan, contains the XSLT transformation that will be used to transform the HTML. Notice that embedded within the child div element is a CDATA section. The CDATA section is required because otherwise some escaped text will be unescaped. More about this will be illustrated shortly. The second child element, script, is used to execute the XSLT script. And the third child element, a div element, contains the representation generated by the transformation.

The example contains only a single XSLT sheet, representing a single transformation from one representation to another representation. This results in the necessity of having multiple XSLT sheets that represent a transformation from one representation to another. Typically this results in multiple transformations that are similar but not identical. One of the problems of using XSLT is that a certain starting and ending representation are required, which requires more coding and maintenance than using the JavaScript commonality approach.

The XSLT sheet that can be used to transform the span elements to the third representation in Figure 7-13 is as follows:

```
<div id="xsltTransformUsingSpan" style="visibility:visible">
<![cdata[
<xsl:stylesheet>
  <xsl:template match="/">
    <xsl:apply-templates select="//span"/>
  </xsl:template>
```

```
<xsl:template match="span">
  <xsl:if test="@display">
      <xsl:value-of select="@display" />
      <xsl:text disable-output-escaping="no">
      &lt;input type=&quot;text&quot; id=&quot;</xsl:text>
      <xsl:value-of select="@id" />
      <xsl:text disable-output-escaping="yes">&quot; value=&quot;</xsl:text>
      <xsl:value-of select="."/>
      <xsl:text disable-output-escaping="yes">&quot; /&gt; &lt;br /&gt;</xsl:text>
  </xsl:if>
</xsl:template>
</xsl:stylesheet>]]>
</div>
```

Describing how XSLT works is beyond the scope of this book, but I will explain the important pieces, which have been indicated in bold. The bold XML element xsl:template is a match instruction that will match a span element if it is encountered while iterating the HTML content. All of the other elements are ignored. If a span element is encountered, HTML content is generated by using the xsl:text tags. This is the crux of the problem when using XSLT, as the HTML is embedded within the XSLT document.

Earlier I mentioned that the CDATA section was necessary because of escaped sequences. The xsl:text tags embed the <, ", and < identifiers, which are escape sequences used to generate incomplete XML tags. If the CDATA instruction were not used, the escape characters would be unescaped and the generated representation would be incorrect.

To execute the XSLT stylesheet, the Google XSLT library[6] is used. The source code is as follows:

```
el( "htmlxslt").transfromFromSpan = function( src) {
    var xml = xmlParse( src);
    var xslt = xmlParse(trimBuffer( el('xsltTransformUsingSpan').innerHTML));
    var html = xsltProcess(xml, xslt);
    el( "htmlxsltdest").innerHTML = unescapeHTML( html);
}
```

The function xmlParse is used to convert a buffer containing XML into an object structure that can be used by the Google XSLT library. The xmlParse is called twice: once for the content to transform, and once for the XSLT sheet. To execute the XSLT, the function xsltProcess is called with the XML and XSLT content, resulting in a buffer of HTML. The HTML buffer is then assigned to the local representation reference node.

Overall, the XSLT solution is relatively straightforward so long you know how to write XSLT programs. The only real problem when using XSLT is the binding of the reading of the representation with the generation of the representation. This requires each representation to know which representation type that it will be reading from.

---

6. http://sourceforge.net/projects/goog-ajaxslt/

Some Implementation Details

Thus far, the pattern implementation has not illustrated the challenges that you will be confronted with. You might have noticed in previous examples that custom attributes and properties were assigned to the HTML object model. The HTML object model is flexible and allows it, although there are some gotchas. The gotchas are not critical because there are ways around them, but a developer needs to be aware of them.

I will use an abbreviated explanation when demonstrating the gotchas. I will illustrate them by using a single piece of HTML and then Figures 7-15 and 7-16. Finally, I will present a list highlighting each gotcha illustrated in the code and figures.

The code is as follows:

```
<html>
<title>Hello world</title>
<script language="JavaScript" type="text/javascript">
function el(id) {
  return document.getElementById(id);
}

function OnClickMe() {
    el( "txtArea1").value = el( "parentArea2").innerHTML;
}
function OnClickForMyProperty() {
    el( "txtArea2").value = el("txtArea2").directAssignedString;
    el( "txtBoxArea2").value = el( "txtArea2").directAssignedObject.prop;
}
function OnLoad() {
    el( "txtArea2").directAssignedString = "direct assigned string";
    var obj = new Object();
    obj.prop = "property on an object";
    el( "txtArea2").directAssignedObject = obj;
    el( "txtArea2").setAttribute( "attributeAssignedString",
        "attributed assigned string");
    el( "txtArea2").setAttribute( "attributeAssignedObject", obj);
}
</script>
<body onload="OnLoad()">
    <div id="element">
        Hello world
    </div>
    <div id="parentArea1">
        <textarea id="txtArea1" cols="60" rows="10">
            Nothing
        </textarea>
    </div>
```

```
    <div id="parentArea2">
        <textarea id="txtArea2" cols="60" rows="10">
            Nothing
        </textarea><br />
        <input type="text" id="txtBoxArea2" value="hello" />
    </div>
    <input type="button" value="Click For My Property First" onclick="OnClick-
ForMyProperty()" />
    <input type="button" value="Click Me Second" onclick="OnClickMe()" />
</body>
</html>
```

Figure 7-15. *Pattern specifics page loaded in Mozilla Firefox*

Figure 7-16. *Pattern specifics page loaded in Microsoft Internet Explorer*

Here are some specific implementation points about the HTML content:

- Properties assigned by using the notation el("txtArea2").directAssignedString are not visible when the HTML element is serialized using the innerHtml property.

- Properties that are assigned by using the method setAttribute are visible for both browsers when using the innerHTML property.

- Properties that are assigned with an object instance by using the method setAttribute are not visible as attributes for all browsers when using the innerHTML property.

- Properties (for example, el("txtArea2").value) that are assigned dynamically are not visible for all browsers when using the innerHTML property.

- Modified HTML content that is saved from the browser by using Save As is not stored consistently across all browsers.

What the specifics should illustrate is that the HTML document model is implemented consistently across both browsers. What is implemented inconsistently is whether the changes to the HTML page are visible when using the standard properties (for example, innerHTML). The rule of thumb is to assign properties to individual HTML elements by using the JavaScript property notation (for example, element.property) and not to use the setAttribute function. Then to get a consistent object model, the object model should be iterated by using a function that generates a true object model that innerHTML might not.

Pattern Highlights

The Representation Morphing pattern is used to enable a mechanism whereby content can be viewed, edited, or navigated by using best-of-breed user interfaces. When using the Representation Morphing pattern, state structure is a constant that is transferred from representation to representation.

This chapter focused on the following aspects:

- Defining a state in a representation.

- Transferring state from one representation to another.

- Using a representation as a state is acceptable so long as the state that is embedded is defined by using a clear and consistent manner. What you want to avoid is the defining of state that requires extra deciphering routines, making it more complicated to transfer a state from one representation to another.

- Even though the focus has been on transforming editable content into viewable content, there are other situations. The conversion of data from editable to read-only happens to be a clear example of when to use the Representation Morphing pattern.

- The JavaScript code associated with a representation is not used to store state but to manipulate state, and therefore must be stateless.

- It is possible to use XSLT to transform content from one representation to another, but the generic JavaScript solution is simpler.

CHAPTER 8

Persistent Communications Pattern

Intent

The Persistent Communications pattern provides a mechanism enabling the client and the server to communicate with each other on a persistent basis so that the client can send messages to the server, and the server can send messages to the client.

Motivation

Client-server programming, which HTTP is, requires that the client call the server to process a request. The server obliges, processes the request, and sends a response. This is a standard run-of-the-mill operation.

Now imagine writing a web application that acts like a bulletin board. Each individual has the ability to create a message and post it. One extension would be offering the capability, when the messages are displayed, to indicate whether the message poster is online. When a reader reads a posting and finds it of interest, the reader might want to ask further questions. If the reader knew that the poster was online, the reader could ask questions immediately. This capability is offered by Yahoo! and is illustrated in Figure 8-1.

In Figure 8-1, there are a number of rows that begin with a number followed by a title. Following the title is the name of the person who wrote the message. Below that name is the nickname of the person, and below that is a circle with either a smiley face or a face with another expression. The smiley face indicates that the person who wrote the message is available for discussion using Yahoo! instant messaging.

Associating the availability of a user with a posted message is a clever combination that integrates two distinctly separate solutions. The posted messages are generated from content in a database. The availability status of a user is from an instant messaging service. What makes the integration possible between the messaging service and the content from a database is the user who posted the message and is using the service.

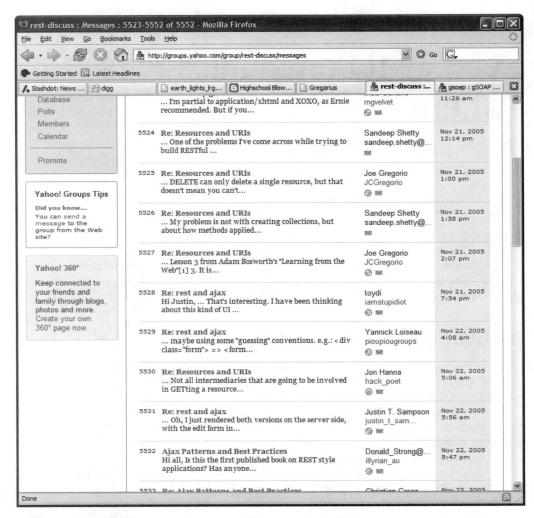

Figure 8-1. *Yahoo! message board that displays messages and the availability of the message creator*

The different services generate very different types of data. When a message is posted, it is read-only. Messages are typically not changed, but they may be deleted. In contrast, the status of the user will change, and more important, a reader does not know when the status will change. Generating content for these two dissimilar streams is complicated because when a message is generated and displayed in an HTML page, it will not change. Yet the status of the user icon can change while the reader is inspecting the postings.

A possible strategy when generating the content is to consider the status of the user as single-shot display-only status. The single-shot display strategy will generate a status as the content is generated, and after that the status is not updated. Most likely, a reader will glance over the messages and decide within a minute or so whether to contact the message poster. If the message poster was available as the content was generated, chances are pretty high that the message poster will be around for a minute or so. The problem with the strategy is that if the

HTML page is loaded and the reader does not read the message until 10 minutes later due to a coffee break, the status will be out-of-date.

Another strategy is to poll the server on the status of the message author. When the page is generated, an initial status is defined. Then, after a minute or whatever period decided by the generated script, the status is updated. The problem with polling is that the status is current only when the poll request has been made. Between polls, the state is considered stale and not representative. So to keep a poll representative, you poll more often, but what is a good polling frequency? Let's say that you poll every second; well, then the waiting time is not significant from a reader perspective. However, for a real-time system that is an eternity. The point is that the poll time needs to be adjusted to the nature of the data and that there is no single best universal poll frequency.

Yet another strategy is for the server to contact the client and inform the client of a change in status. That strategy seems to be the best but is not possible because of the Internet infrastructure. (I will explain the details later, in the "Architecture" section.)

Regardless of the strategy implemented, there is a need for the server to update the client with new information for one reason or another.

Applicability

The main argument for using the Persistent Communications pattern is for the web browser (client) to be able to receive information updates from the server. The server has the ability to communicate to the client, without the server having to wait for the client to ask for an information update.

The pattern has three main implementation types that are direct solutions to the problem that they solve:

- *Status updates:* A status update is a piece of global information that a client is interested in and that is stored on a server. Multiple clients see the same representation of the data. An example is a ticker tape of current stock prices, like the ticker tape on a financial television program. The information is not intended for a specific user, as all users see the same information. To view the information, users do not need to identify themselves. It does not mean that the data is free for all. In other words, a group of authorized people can access the resource, but the resource is not dependent on those accessing the resource.

- *Presence detection:* Presence detection occurs when multiple clients are interested in the same global resource. The global resource has the same representation for all clients, except that the state of the resource is dependent on the clients viewing the resource. Figure 8-1, which shows the status of the message creator, is an example of presence detection. The resource might be updated by an external process but can also be updated by the individual users.

- *Server push:* Server push occurs when multiple clients register with a global resource but are allocated a unique resource. It is the server's discretion on how the identified user is cross-referenced to the unique resource. An example is a user-defined view of a ticker tape. The stock prices are identical for all users, but which stock prices are shown is unique to each user. The server has to manage which information is pushed to which user. The clients indicate only what they are interested in.

The last scenario is explicitly called a server push; however, in theory all three implementation types could be considered a server push because all three involve the server sending data to the client. There are two attributes that separate the various implementation types: what the representation of the resource is, and whether a user has to be identified when accessing a resource.

Associated Patterns

The Persistent Communications pattern has some overlap with the Decoupled Navigation pattern. Specifically, for the Decoupled Navigation pattern it is possible to trigger an event that would call the same server-side resource as the Persistent Communications pattern. The Persistent Communications pattern differs in that its purpose is focused on the server sending data to the client. The purpose of the Decoupled Navigation pattern is not to push data from the server to the client, but to provide a mechanism for separating navigational functionality.

The Persistent Communications pattern does not implement the Content Chunking pattern, or at least is not required to implement the Content Chunking pattern. More likely, the Persistent Communications pattern will send data that implements the Infinite Data pattern. The Persistent Communications pattern is a very specific pattern for a very specific situation, as outlined in the preceding "Applicability" section. Using it in any other situation complicates the solution. In those cases, it would make more sense to make the Decoupled Navigation pattern behave like the Persistent Communications pattern.

Architecture

Explaining the architecture of the Persistent Communications pattern is relatively simple. The problem, though, is that the explanation might have you scratching your head on why such a solution was created in the first place. The solution might seem inefficient and overly complex, and you might think it could have been solved in another way. It is not possible to solve the server-to-client communications in any other way because of how the Internet architecture is implemented.

Even if there were no implementation problems from the perspective of the Internet, defining and implementing the Persistent Communications pattern would still be necessary because the HTTP protocol was not intended for such functionality. The design of the HTTP protocol allows for only stateless interaction that starts with the client, is processed by the server, and ends with the client. The challenge here is that HTTP is being asked to do what it was never designed to do, and this pattern is presenting some solutions.

Before you learn about the architecture of the Persistent Communications pattern, first you need to understand the problem of the "broken" Internet.

Why the Internet Is "Broken"

It is a bold statement to say that the Internet is "broken." I don't mean that it is unfixable or bad, but that the Internet has transformed into an architecture that is not optimal. The "not optimal" part relates to Internet Protocol (IP) addresses. To understand the transformation, let's go back in time and look at how the Internet worked in the late eighties, as illustrated in Figure 8-2.

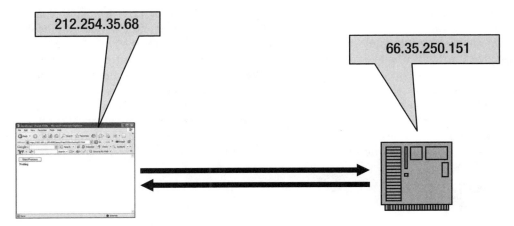

Figure 8-2. *Internet architecture in the late eighties*

In the late eighties (please ignore for the sake of this argument that the browser was invented in the early nineties), had somebody accessed a web server by using a browser, each computer would have had a unique address (for example, 212.254.35.68). This address would have been unique on the entire Internet—only one computer would have had that address. That would have made it possible for the client to talk to the server, and vice versa. Figure 8-2 is a simple view of how a network is constructed. Figure 8-3 is more realistic because it includes routers and computers.

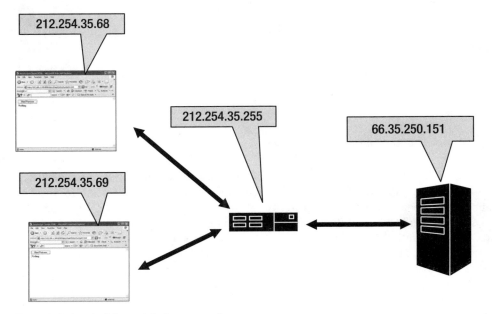

Figure 8-3. *Typical late-eighties network*

The typical network of the late eighties had unique addresses for all devices, so that all devices were uniquely identifiable and information could be routed to the device without any resolution problems. But then something bad happened, and that was the Web. The Internet existed before the Web and was used by a few people,[1] and those who used it generally respected the unwritten rules. I am not trying to knock the Web—the Web created the Internet economy, which is no small feat. Along the way of transitioning from the traditional Internet to the Internet economy, the structure of the Internet changed radically. The transition has made writing applications that use the Internet more complicated. In the transition, the server side of the Internet has remained the same, but everything with respect to the client has changed. The changed structure of the Internet is illustrated in Figure 8-4.

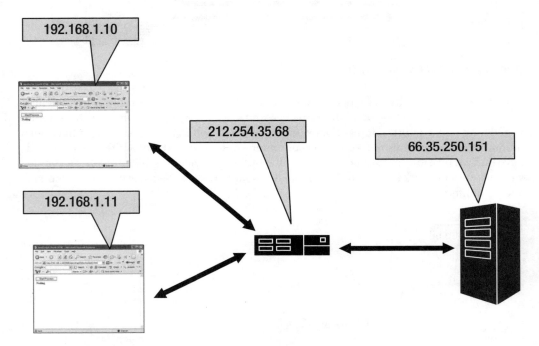

Figure 8-4. *Structure of the Internet after the Web*

Looking at Figures 8-3 and 8-4, your first reaction might be, "So, yeah, some radical change—two new unique addresses." The changed unique addresses make an entire world of difference with respect to Internet structure. The IP addresses 192.168.1.10 and 192.168.1.11 are so-called reserved addresses that cannot be used to uniquely identify computers on the Internet because multiple local area networks will use the same IP addresses. This means that the server 66.35.250.151 does not see the computers 192.168.1.10 or 192.168.1.11, and sees only the router 212.254.35.68. Adding on to the complexity, the router address 212.254.35.68 changes often and cannot be used to uniquely identify a calling network of computers.

---

1. If you know (without searching Google) about Archie, Whois, WAIS, Veronica, Jughead, or Gopher+, then you are showing your age with respect to the Internet!

The result is that the server 66.35.250.151 cannot send information updates to the clients (192.168.1.10 or 192.168.1.11) because the server has no idea how to address the client. The transition did not cause a collapse of the Internet because the router has become more intelligent and created something called Network Address Translation (NAT). NAT is like an early 1900s telephone operator who received a call and then transferred the call to another operator or to the destination. The client making the call and server receiving the call do not contact each other. The router is in contact with both. When the client makes a call to the server, NAT works extremely well and transparently. However, in the other direction, the router cannot decide which client to contact. The solution has been to assign ports on the router that redirect the call from the router to the internal computer. Even with that solution, the router can dedicate only a single computer to a specific port. The NAT solution is not a general networking solution as in the 1980s.

This change in the Internet architecture occurred for multiple reasons: money, IPv4 addressing problems, security, and maintenance. Why these are the reasons does not matter and changes nothing. Focusing on how to deal with the change is more important. From the perspective of an Ajax developer, it is not possible for the server to arbitrarily send messages to a particular client. However, looking at peer-to-peer solutions such as BitTorrent, it would seem the problem is solved. No, the problem is not solved,[2] but delegated as an implementation issue that the user needs to address before running BitTorrent. With respect to the Ajax developer, that is not a solution. The only solution that is both robust and viable is to poll for data.[3]

Implementing a Polling Solution

Having identified that a poll is required for making a reliable and robust server-to-client communication, the challenge is implementing a poll that is effective and that wastes as little resources as possible. For the example that spans the scope of this chapter, the client is a web browser, and the server is the HTTP server. As per the HTTP protocol, the client initiates the request, and the server responds to the request.

Polling involves the querying of a server at specific intervals, like the polling of a Post Office Protocol (POP3) e-mail server. Typically, e-mail is retrieved by polling a POP server for available messages every x minutes. The problem with polling is that it can be inefficient and can miss important events. Imagine polling a server for available messages. The server could say, "No messages," and the client would then wait x minutes. If a message arrives right after a poll is made, the client will know about the message only after waiting x minutes. If the polling frequency period were two hours, a message that arrived after a poll and that was valid for only one hour would be stale by the next poll. If the polling frequency period were 10 seconds, the message would be retrieved fairly quickly and would not be stale.

The downside to a higher polling frequency is that the network and server suffer. The network suffers from excessive network bandwidth usage, and the server suffers from having to constantly respond to a request and respond with a "No message available" answer. In a nutshell, polling when done too slowly will cause messages to not arrive in time, and polling when done

---

2. http://www.bittorrent.com/FAQ.html#firewall. The solution involves opening the router or firewall and redirecting the Internet traffic to the appropriate computer.

3. Some companies will sell components promising to send data asynchronously so that you don't have to poll. The fact is that the poll is hidden within the code of the component. There is no easy technical solution around the NAT addressing problem when writing server-to-client communications.

too quickly will waste network and server resources.[4] This is a sort of damned-if-you-do and damned-if-you-don't situation.

The solution is to create two streams used by the client and server to communicate with one another. The first stream is used to receive messages, and the second stream is used to send messages. To receive messages, the client polls the server with a request for messages. If there are no messages, the server does not respond with an answer immediately. The server puts the poll request on hold for a specific amount of time or until a message is generated by the server. Putting the poll on hold puts the client on hold while waiting for a message. A traditional poll will query the server, get an answer, and then wait until the next poll. The waiting period until the next poll is dead time during which neither the client nor the server can communicate with each other. By converting the dead time into a wait created by the server, the client is waiting for the potential of a message being generated.

Two streams are necessary because while the client is waiting for a response from the server, the client might want to send a message to the server. If one stream is waiting for a response, it is not possible to send content by using the waiting stream. The solution is to create another stream for sending content to the server or for writing purposes. From the perspective of the server, the other stream is a request that sends data.

In terms of HTTP, the reading stream that is put on hold waiting for content is an HTTP GET, and the writing stream that sends content is an HTTP POST or PUT. In technical implementation terms, for the reading stream the HTTP server puts the socket and thread that are processing the request on hold. Putting the thread on hold is not a problem for HTTP servers. What is a problem is that thousands of threads could be waiting for messages that may or may not be generated. One solution is to get a big enough computer with enough RAM. Another solution is to specifically find an HTTP server that can deal with this problem elegantly.[5]

Another potential problem on the HTTP server is that the two streams might conflict. The reading stream executes on one thread, and the writing stream executes on another thread. Both threads might be accessing the same piece of data, and hence synchronization is required.

From an architectural perspective, the two-stream communication mechanism appears similar to Figure 8-5.

In Figure 8-5, the browser interacts with a type called ClientCommunicator. The purpose of ClientCommunicator is to create the two-stream communication mechanism and process messages that are sent and received from the server. In the implementation of ClientCommunicator, two separate instances of XMLHttpRequest are used. One instance of XMLHttpRequest represents the reading stream and calls the resource /resource/receive. The second instance of XMLHttpRequest represents the writing stream and calls the resource /resource/send. On the server side is something called ServerCommunicator, which is responsible for combining the two streams.

The resources /resource/receive and /resource/send were used to illustrate the nature of the data direction; they do not refer to actual URLs. As mentioned earlier, writing involves using HTTP POST or PUT, and reading involves using HTTP GET. Because these two HTTP verbs are distinct from each other, the same URLs can be used for both streams.

---

4. It is possible to use HTTP persistent connections, and doing so reduces network bandwidth and is a good thing in general. However, HTTP persistent connections do not solve the server-to-client communication problem.

5. http://jetty.mortbay.org/jetty/ is a URL to the Jetty HTTP server. For version 6.0, Jetty has solved the waiting thread and resource problem and is a recommended solution for Java programmers implementing the Persistent Communications pattern.

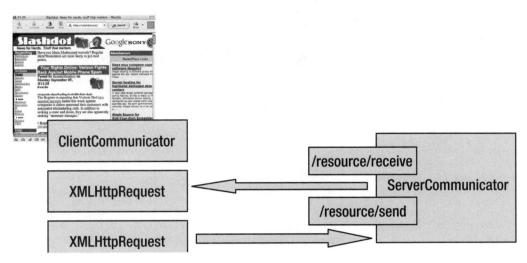

Figure 8-5. *Architecture of Persistent Communications pattern*

Implementation

For the rest of this chapter, the two-stream communication mechanism is going to be implemented in the context of the three scenarios: status updates, presence detection, and server push. The explanations start with the simplest scenario and finish with the most complex. The client code will be developed first because it is identical for all scenarios. The server code is what changes from simple to complex.

Example: A Global Status Resource

Status updates are by their nature global. *Global status updates* does not mean global data. What it means is that the data referenced by the status update is accessible by all, and in terms of the Permutations pattern is a single resource that can have multiple representations. In a nutshell, what you have is shared data that has a single state and does not care about the client. The client considers the data as read-mostly. *Read-mostly data* is updated very little by the client, but may be updated constantly by some external influence. From the perspective of the two-stream communication mechanism, the reading stream will be used most of the time to retrieve the latest status updates. The writing stream (which would be used to update the state) is not used, or at least is used very rarely. However, this is not to say that the writing stream is never used; whether it is used depends entirely on the context.

Implementing the HTML Page

An HTML page that contains the ClientCommunicator and implements the reading and writing streams is presented to the user. The responsibilities of the HTML page are to define a URL, provide a callback function, and begin querying the server using the reading stream. For the example, the HTML page that realizes the responsibilities will have buttons to start and stop the reading stream. In your production application, the triggers to start and stop the reading stream might be an event or a default action started by a script. Figure 8-6 shows the HTML page.

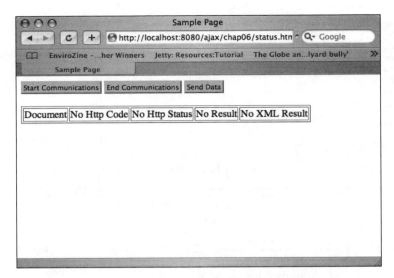

Figure 8-6. *HTML page that interacts with a global status*

The Start Communications button is used to start receiving updates of the global status from the reading stream. The End Communications button is used to stop receiving updates. And the Send Data is used to send text by using the writing stream and to update the global status. The received updates of the global status are stored in the table below the row of buttons. As the HTML page illustrates, any client that accesses the global status resource will receive similar representations of the resource.

The HTML page's code is as follows:

```html
<html>
<head>
<title>Global Status Page</title>
</head>
<script language="JavaScript" src="../lib/factory.js"></script>
<script language="JavaScript" src="../lib/asynchronous.js"></script>
<script language="JavaScript" src="../lib/clientcommunicator.js"></script>
<script language="JavaScript" type="text/javascript">
var client = new ClientCommunicator();
client.baseURL = "/ajax/chap06/status";
client.listen = function(status, statusText, responseText, responseXML) {
    document.getElementById('httpcode').innerHTML = status;
    document.getElementById('httpstatus').innerHTML = statusText;
    document.getElementById('result').innerHTML = responseText;
    document.getElementById('xmlresult').innerHTML = responseXML;
}
function StartCommunications() {
    client.start();
}
```

```
function EndCommunications() {
    client.end();
}
function SendData() {
    var buffer = "hello world";
    client.send("application/text", buffer.length, buffer);
}
</script>
</head>
<body>
<button onclick="StartCommunications()">Start Communications</button>
<button onclick="EndCommunications()">End Communications</button>
<button onclick="SendData()">Send Data</button>
<p><table border="1">
    <tr><td>Document</td>
        <td><span id="httpcode">No Http Code</span></td>
        <td><span id="httpstatus">No Http Status</span></td>
        <td><span id="result">No Result</span></td>
        <td><span id="xmlresult">No XML Result</span></td></tr>
</table></p>
</body>
</html>
```

The HTML page has multiple script tags where the src attribute is defined. Each of the src attribute values represents a JavaScript file that contains reusable generic Ajax code used by the client. The reusable code is from other patterns presented in this book. The code related to the client side of the Persistent Communications pattern is located in the file clientcommunicator.js and will be explained shortly.

At the point in the HTML where the script tag does not have a src attribute, some JavaScript code is defined. The JavaScript code is the code used by the HTML page to make the Persistent Communications pattern code do something useful. After the closing script tag, the remaining HTML code is responsible for creating the HTML page illustrated in Figure 8-6.

Getting back to the JavaScript code that makes the Persistent Communications pattern code do something, the first line of code instantiates the type ClientCommunicator and assigns the instance to the variable client. The type ClientCommunicator is an implementation of the ClientCommunicator, as defined in Figure 8-5. The common URL used by the reading and writing streams is represented by the property client.baseURL. The property client.listen is assigned a function and is called by ClientCommunicator whenever the server sends an update on the reading stream.

Quickly going through the rest of the JavaScript code, you can see that the method client.start() starts the update process of reading content from the reading stream. The method client.end() ends the updates. The method client.send(...) sends updates to the server by using the writing stream and has three parameters. The first parameter ("application/text") represents the MIME type of the sent content, the second parameter (buffer.length) is the content length, and the last parameter (buffer) is the data that is sent to the server.

Without explaining the details of the ClientCommunicator and ServerCommunicator, Figure 8-7 illustrates running the HTML code and how the Persistent Communications pattern functions so that you get an idea of what plumbing code needs to be implemented.

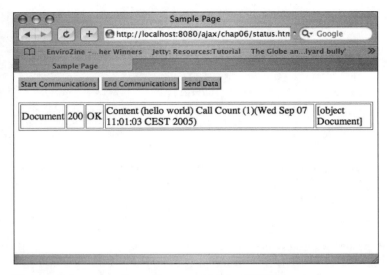

Figure 8-7. *Status updates illustrated in the HTML page*

In Figure 8-7, the table contents have been replaced with some information sent by the server. The data replaced in the table is the result of a round-trip that starts with clicking the Send Data button. Clicking this button generates some content that is written to the writing stream. The server receiving the content on the writing stream stores the data as a global status resource. Then, when the Start Communications button is clicked, the reading stream queries the global status resource. The server will respond by sending the updated global status resource. The client receives the updated information on the reading stream and updates the table. What has occurred in this example is an illustration of how a global status is written and read.

Implementing the ClientCommunicator

With the HTML page illustrated and the behavior of the HTML page explained, it is necessary to begin the implementation of the pattern's plumbing. In the HTML code example, the property `client.baseURL` defines the base URL, and the example base URL is `/ajax/chap06/status`. The URL definition is provided by some human and applied in the JavaScript.

The `ClientCommunicator` code is a larger piece of code; therefore, instead of presenting all of the code at once, I will present and explain smaller pieces. The following code starts the explanation by showing the constructor-related code of `ClientCommunicator`:

```
function CounterHack() {
    this.counter = 0;
}
function ClientCommunicator() {
    this.server2Client = new Asynchronous();
    this.baseURL = null;
    this.username = null;
    this.password = null;
```

```
        this.listen = null;
        this.doLoop = false;
        this.callDelay = 500;
        this.preferredTypes = "text/xml";
        this.index = this.instanceCount.counter;
        this.instances[ this.index] = this;
        this.instanceCount.counter ++;
}
ClientCommunicator.prototype.start = ClientCommunicator_start;
ClientCommunicator.prototype.end = ClientCommunicator_end;
ClientCommunicator.prototype.send = ClientCommunicator_send;
ClientCommunicator.prototype.instances = new Array();
ClientCommunicator.prototype.instanceCount = new CounterHack();
```

The function `ClientCommunicator` is defined to be a constructor because the script of the HTML page in Figure 8-6 instantiates the type `ClientCommunicator`. When `ClientCommunicator` is instantiated, many properties are defined and explained as follows. The property `server2client` is an instance of `Asynchronous` that encapsulates `XMLHttpRequest`. The property `server2client` is responsible for implementing the reading stream. The property `baseURL` has already been discussed. The properties `username` and `password` are used to identify the user, which in the case of the global status resource is not important. Of course, just because the authorization information is not relevant for this specific example, it does not mean that authorization to the global status resource is not needed. The property `listen` has already been discussed. The property `doLoop` is a flag that indicates whether the periodic reading stream checks should be continued. The property `preferredTypes` indicates the preferred MIME types that result in the preferred representation to receive as per the Permutations pattern.

The properties `callDelay`, `index`, `instances`, and `instanceCount` are all related and warrant a more detailed explanation to the problem they solve. The problem relates to how a repeating loop is implemented in JavaScript. In the "Architecture" section, you saw that to implement the reading stream, the client polls the data—meaning a repeating loop is created. Using a JavaScript-defined loop cannot solve the repetitious nature of a poll. A JavaScript loop takes control of the user interface and would lock the client from accepting further input or processing data. Additionally, because asynchronous requests are made, the loop would result in an infinite number of requests to be issued. The real problem here is that JavaScript does not implement true multithreading. Had JavaScript implemented true multithreading, creating a never-ending JavaScript loop would not be a problem.

Even though JavaScript does not have true multithreading capabilities, it is possible to make it appear that it does. An example of pseudo-multithreading was illustrated in Chapter 2 and required the use of a timer. The solution to the problem of a locked browser when using loops is to create the impression of a loop by using a timer that goes off right away and calls a function. The sequence of events that makes a timer look like a loop is defined as follows:

1. When the function is executed, an asynchronous `XMLHttpRequest` request is made, resulting in a calling of the reading stream.

2. The function exits immediately as an asynchronous request is made, and no timer is called. The web browser can continue accepting input and processing data.

3. In the background, the HTTP server has put the asynchronous request that is waiting for a message on the reading stream on hold.

4. When the asynchronous request returns with a response, the response is processed and then a timer is started to call the function that executes another asynchronous request.

What is important about the sequence of events is to call the timer only when the asynchronous request has returned. Calling the timer earlier would result in an infinite number of requests being made immediately, causing the web browser to lock and the server to suffer a denial of service attack.

Using the timer, we are confronted with another problem: the window.setTimeout method requires a reference to a text-based script. The reference cannot be an object reference, because JavaScript when converting an object reference will reference either an undefined reference or a value that does not exist. The problem is clearly illustrated in the following source code:

```
function runIt(value) {
    window.setTimeout("Loop(value)", 1000);
}
```

The function runIt has a parameter, value, which is an object reference and is used in the script expression of the method setTimeout. The problem is that the script expression is a piece of text, and the timer can execute only a piece of text, not a reference to the variable value. A solution is not to reference the variable, but to copy the value of the variable to the text script, as the following source code illustrates:

```
function runIt(value) {
    window.setTimeout("Loop(" + value + ")", 1000);
}
```

In the modified source code, the function Loop will be called properly with the value of the variable value.

Knowing that a variable has to be converted to a value is a step closer to the solution, but is not the entire solution. The main problem is that the variable value will reference an object instance, and serializing an object instance is a bad practice because it results in multiple object instances with similar states. Having multiple versions of the same object results in object state consistency problems. The solution is to pass a value that represents an index of an array. The resulting implementation uses the array property this.instances and associated properties (callDelay, index, instances, and instanceCount) to store and manage references of the reading streams shown in abbreviated detail as follows:

```
this.index = this.instanceCount.counter;
this.instances[ this.index] = this;
this.instanceCount.counter ++;

ClientCommunicator.prototype.instances = new Array();
ClientCommunicator.prototype.instanceCount = new CounterHack();
```

The property instances is assigned an Array instance, but notice that the property instances is associated with the prototype property. This means that whenever ClientCommunicator is instantiated, all instances will share the same Array instances. The result is that whatever the ClientCommunicator instance references, the property prototype. instances will manipulate the same array. Of course, the property instances could have been a global variable, but using the prototype property is object oriented.

The other property, instanceCount, is an example of where the global variable concept does not work. I am going to backtrack a bit on my assertion that the property prototype is object oriented. Let me restate the assertion and say that *the effect* is object oriented. When defining a property associated with prototype, the values of the properties are copied from the property prototype to the property of the ClientCommunicator instance. When the property is a value type such as an integer or a double value, each ClientCommunicator instance will have its own value. If the property is a reference, the reference value is copied. Hence the property instanceCount must refer to a JavaScript reference type. The property index is the index reference for each ClientCommunicator instance.

Following is the source code for the ClientCommunicator.start implementation, which is used to start the polling of the reading stream:

```
function ClientCommunicator_start() {
    if(this.baseURL != null) {
        this.doLoop = true;
        window.setTimeout("PrivateLoop(" + this.index + ")", this.callDelay);
    }
    else {
        throw new Error("Must specify baseURL before starting communications");
    }
}
```

The method ClientCommunicator_start will start the polling only if the property baseURL is assigned. If the property is assigned, a polling operation is started by calling the method setTimeout with the index (this.index) of the ClientCommunicator instance. If the property is not assigned, an Error exception is generated.

When the setTimeout method expires, the function PrivateLoop is called and used to perform physical reading from the reading stream. The implementation of PrivateLoop is as follows:

```
function PrivateLoop(index) {
    var tempReference = ClientCommunicator.prototype.instances[ index];
    tempReference.server2Client.openCallback = function(xmlhttp) {
        xmlhttp.setRequestHeader("Accept", tempReference.preferredTypes);
    }
    tempReference.server2Client.complete = function(status, statusText,
        responseText, responseXML) {
        if(status == 200) {
            if(tempReference.listen != null) {
                tempReference.listen(status, statusText,
responseText, responseXML);
            }
        }
```

```
        if(tempReference.doLoop) {
            window.setTimeout("PrivateLoop(" + tempReference.index +
                ")", tempReference.callDelay);
        }
    }
    tempReference.server2Client.username = tempReference.username;
    tempReference.server2Client.password = tempReference.password;
    tempReference.server2Client.get(tempReference.baseURL);
}
```

In the implementation of PrivateLoop, the parameter index is the index of the
ClientCommunicator instance stored in the array property instances that represents an active
reading stream. The variable tempReference is assigned the currently active instance of
ClientCommunicator. Having a valid instance of ClientCommunicator, an HTTP call can be made.
The next step is to assign the property openCallback with a function implementation that
assigns the Accept HTTP header used to implement the Permutations pattern on the client side.

Then the property complete is assigned a function implementation that is responsible for
processing any messages sent by the server. Notice that only messages that have an HTTP
status code 200 are processed, and the others are ignored. The assumption is that if there is a
message that the server wants to send to the client, the body of the request will contain content,
and hence an HTTP status code 200 is sent. This was done for simplicity purposes, but in your
application you might want to process the error messages and other HTTP status codes. After
the HTTP status code and potential message have been processed, and if the property doLoop
is true, the method window.setTimeout is called again. The delay is not necessary but is specified by the property tempReference.callDelay. And finally, before making the asynchronous
call, the function PrivateLoop assigns the username and password properties for a potential
required authorization. The last action of PrivateLoop is to call the get method to retrieve any
messages that need to be processed by the client.

To end the polling of the reading stream, the previously illustrated ClientCommunicator.
end method is implemented as follows:

```
function ClientCommunicator_end() {
    this.doLoop = false;
}
```

The implementation to end polling the reading stream is simple, but the cessation of
querying does not happen right away. If a query is still executing, it is completed, but a new
query is not started.

The last piece of functionality that needs to be implemented is the ClientCommunicator.
send method that writes content to the writing stream and is implemented as follows:

```
function ClientCommunicator_send(mimetype, contentLength, content) {
    var client2Server = new Asynchronous
    client2Server.username = this.username;
    client2Server.password = this.password;
    client2Server.complete = function(status, statusText,
```

```
responseText, responseXML) {
        if(status != 200) {
            throw new Error("Post resulted in error (" + status + ") error text ("
                + statusText + ")");
        }
    }
    client2Server.post(this.baseURL, mimetype, contentLength, content);
}
```

In the implementation of `ClientCommunicator_send`, the data is sent to the server and the response is forgotten. The response is not necessary because the writing stream does not process any received data, as that is the purpose of the reading stream. This enables the `ClientCommunicator_send` implementation to instantiate an instance of Asynchronous, assign the parameters, call `post`, and forget about the result that is generated. The property `complete` is still assigned to test whether the response code is actually HTTP 200. If the response code is not 200, something has occurred and the client needs to be informed. The best way to inform the client is to throw an exception with the details of the problem.

Wrapping all of this together, the `ClientCommunicator` type is a self-contained type that has separate writing and reading streams used to send and receive information updates. It must be stressed that the implementation of the `ClientCommunicator` does not discriminate or try to process the data that is sent and received. If the data sent from the server is a blob, the receiving client must process a blob. If the data is an incremental update, the client must process the incremental update.

Implementing the ServerCommunicator

For the scope of this section, the `ServerCommunicator` will be implemented by using a Java servlet. However, an ASP.NET handler that implements the `IHttpHandler` interface could have been used. What is important is the association of a resource and its children with a piece of functionality. So, for example, if the URL /resource is associated with a Java servlet, the URL /resource/sub/resource is also processed by the same Java servlet. The idea is that a single handler responds to processing a server-side resource.

The following is an implementation of the Java servlet that processes the resource /ajax/chap06/status, representing the base URL used by the client:

```
import javax.servlet.http.*;
import javax.servlet.*;
import java.io.*;
import java.util.*;
import devspace.book.*;
import devspace.book.definitions.*;

public class GlobalStatus extends HttpServlet implements SingleThreadModel {
    static String _buffer;
    static long _callCount;
```

```
    public void init(javax.servlet.ServletConfig config)
        throws javax.servlet.ServletException {
        _buffer = "";
        _callCount = 0;
    }

    protected void doPost(HttpServletRequest request,
        HttpServletResponse response)
        throws javax.servlet.ServletException, java.io.IOException  {
        ServletInputStream input = request.getInputStream();
        byte[] bytearray = new byte[ request.getContentLength()];
        input.read(bytearray);
        _buffer += new String(bytearray).toString();
        _callCount ++;
    }
    protected void doGet(HttpServletRequest request,
        HttpServletResponse response)
        throws ServletException, IOException {
        PrintWriter out = response.getWriter();
        out.println("Content (" + _buffer + ") Call Count (" +
                    _callCount + ")(" + Calendar.getInstance().getTime()
    + ")");
    }
}
```

Compared to the ClientCommunicator code, the ServerCommunicator is relatively simple, but that is due only to the nature of the global status resource implementation and the example in particular. The server-side implementation of the ServerCommunicator is a minimal solution. As you can see in Figure 8-7, to implement the round trip, the servlet saves state in a data member (_buffer) and records the number of times the state has been modified (_callCount). The method init is called by the HTTP server and initializes the data members.

The method doPost processes the HTTP POST request and is responsible for the writing stream implementation. From the perspective of the two-communication stream mechanism, the method doPost is called by the ClientCommunicator.send method. The data buffer that is sent to the server is read by using the method request.getInputStream. It is important to read the buffer as a stream of bytes because anything could be sent. The method doGet processes the HTTP GET request and is responsible for the reading stream implementation. The method doGet retrieves the state of the data members _buffer and _callCount that are concatenated to form a message sent to the client. From the perspective of the two-communication stream, the method doGet is called by the PrivateLoop function.

Many readers will look at the code and be sticklers with respect to the implementation of doPost and doGet, and how the Java servlet is used. The implementations of doPost and doGet are not checking the MIME types and are violating the Permutations pattern. And the Java servlet is keeping state, although some readers might say that is kludgy coding. Fair enough, the critiques are noted and mentioned, but solving those critiques as a fully complete solution would add complexity to explaining the Persistent Communications pattern. To put it plainly, look at what the implementation is aiming to do, and write better code. Additionally, if you are using Jetty 6.*x*, the code will be slightly different and more resource efficient. For more details of the Jetty code, please see the Jetty documentation.

However, to satisfy those readers who would like to see a correct implementation, the following abbreviated source code is provided. Note that before reading this source code, it is important to fully understand the Permutations pattern because the code has specific references to the implementation of the pattern:

```
class ServerCommunicator extends HttpServlet {
    Class _rewriter;
    Class _router;

    public void init(ServletConfig config) throws ServletException {
        try {
            _rewriter = (IRewriter)ServerCommunicator.class.getClassLoader(
).loadClass(
                config.getInitParameter("rewriter")).newInstance();
            _router = (IRewriter)ServerCommunicator.class.getClassLoader(
).loadClass(
                config.getInitParameter("router")).newInstance();
        }
        catch (Exception e) {
            throw new ServletException(
                "Could not instantiate types", e);
        }
    }
    protected void doPost(HttpServletRequest request, HttpServletResponse response)
        throws javax.servlet.ServletException, java.io.IOException  {
        IRewriter rewriter = _rewriter.newInstance();
        IRouter router = _router.newInstance();
        if (router.IsResource(request)) {
            router.ProcessPost(response);
        }
    }

    protected void doGet(HttpServletRequest request, HttpServletResponse response)
        throws ServletException, IOException {
        IRewriter rewriter = _rewriter.newInstance();
        IRouter router = _router.newInstance();
        if (router.IsResource(request)) {
            router.ProcessGet(response);
        }
    }
}
```

In the implementation of ServerCommunicator, the application logic is missing, as illustrated by the GlobalStatus class. It is not that the application logic completely disappeared, but that the application logic is delegated logic called by ServerCommunicator. As per the Permutations pattern, there are two interface instances: IRewriter and IRouter. The purpose of the IRewriter interface is to read the requested URL, test it for validity, and reorganize the MIME types to their appropriate priorities.

The real work lies in the IRouter interface instance router. It is responsible for sending content that the IRewriter instance wants to send. In the implementation of the modified IRouter interface, the missing application logic would be embedded.

In the Permutations pattern, the IRewriter interface instance was illustrated to rewrite a URL to the most appropriate content. Rewriting the URL usually means sending a new link to the client to download. And in the examples illustrated by the Permutations pattern, that meant having a servlet rewrite the URL so that an ASP.NET or JSP page can process the actual request. In the case of the Persistent Communications pattern, a rewrite is necessary only for the sake of the client because whatever the URL is rewritten to, the servlet will still process the request. Therefore, it is more fitting that the servlet process the request without sending the redirect to the client. Be careful, though, because the redirection that is being discussed is the redirection outlined in the Permutations pattern that matches the resource to the most desired request. If the redirection were to reference another resource, the redirection would have to be sent to the client, as will be illustrated in the "Example: Server Push" section. To manage this additional work, the IRouter interface has two additional methods used to process the HTTP POST (ProcessPost) or GET (ProcessGet).

Calling the ServerCommunicator Intelligently

Both the client-side and server-side implementation are complete. When the Send Data button is clicked and then the Start Communications button is clicked, a round-trip of content will occur. There is a problem in the implementation of ClientCommunicator and GlobalStatus. The problem is that the reading stream will ask whether there is any data available, and the server will respond with a yes and send it. What the reading stream is not asking is whether there is any *new* data available and to send only the new data. As the implementation stands, there is no piece of information sent in the reading that indicates what content has already been sent.

The solution requires changing the way that the resource is called, and specifically adding a custom HTTP header. Remember in the definition of GlobalStatus, there was the data member _callCount. The data member was not added for triviality, but has a specific purpose and is a version number for the latest state. Whenever an HTTP POST is executed, the call counter is incremented, meaning that the state has been updated. Using the call counter as a reference, a server can indicate whether new content is available.

The server cannot know when to send a message to the client without getting a helping hand from the client, because the server does not know which state the client has already received. The client needs to implement a change, whereby the client notes the version number and stores the value somewhere on the client temporarily. Then when the next request is made, the value is sent to the server and that value helps the server decide whether the client should wait for new data or be immediately sent the latest data. The sending and retrieving of the value could be implemented as an HTTP cookie. Using an HTTP cookie is simple because the client has to do nothing other than accept the HTTP cookie. Then every time the client makes a call, the cookie is sent automatically and the server can read which version the client has downloaded.

However, for this example, a custom HTTP header will be written because some people are wary of HTTP cookies. The cookie example will be illustrated in the "Example: Presence Detection" section. On the client side, ClientCommunicator is modified as follows (with the changes in bold):

```
function ClientCommunicator() {
    this.server2Client = new Asynchronous();
    this.baseURL = null;
    this._delegated = null;
    this.username = null;
    this.password = null;
    this.listen = null;
    this.doLoop = false;
    this.callDelay = 500;
    this.preferredTypes = "text/xml";
    this.index = this.instanceCount.counter;
    this.instances[ this.index] = this;
    this.instanceCount.counter ++;
    this.versionTracker = 0;
}

function PrivateLoop(index) {
    var tempReference = ClientCommunicator.prototype.instances[ index];
    tempReference.server2Client.openCallback = function(xmlhttp) {
        xmlhttp.setRequestHeader("Accept", tempReference.preferredTypes);
        xmlhttp.setRequestHeader("X-Version-ID", tempReference.versionTracker);
    }
    tempReference.server2Client.complete = function(status, statusText,
        responseText, responseXML) {
        if(status == 200) {
            tempReference.versionTracker =
                tempReference.server2Client.getResponseHeader("X-Version-ID");
            if(tempReference.listen != null) {
                tempReference.listen(status, statusText,
responseText, responseXML);
            }
        }
        if(tempReference.doLoop) {
            window.setTimeout("PrivateLoop(" + tempReference.index + ")",
                tempReference.callDelay);
        }
    }
    tempReference.server2Client.username = tempReference.username;
    tempReference.server2Client.password = tempReference.password;
    tempReference.server2Client.get(tempReference.baseURL);
}
```

The bolded code introduces the property versionTracker, which contains the value stored in the HTTP header X-Version-ID and is the version number of the server-side state. Whenever a request is made to the server, the HTTP header X-Version-ID is added to the request and extracted from the response. On the server side, the modified GlobalStatus.doGet implementation would be as follows:

```java
    protected void doGet(HttpServletRequest request, HttpServletResponse response)
        throws ServletException, IOException {
        int lastCount = new Integer(request.getHeader(
"X-Version-ID")).intValue();
            int waitCount = 0;
            while(waitCount < 100) {
                if(lastCount < _callCount) {
                    PrintWriter out = response.getWriter();
                    out.println("Content (" + _buffer +
                        ") Call Count (" + _callCount +
                        ")(" + Calendar.getInstance().getTime() +
                        ")");
                    response.setHeader("X-Version-ID",
                        new Integer(_callCount).toString());
                    return;
                }
                try {
                    Thread.currentThread().sleep(1000);
                }
                catch (InterruptedException e) { }
                waitCount ++;
            }
            response.setStatus(408, "No change");
    }
```

When the doGet method is called, the first thing that happens is the extracting of the X-Version-ID header value, which is assigned to lastCount. The next step is to enter a while loop that will count for 100 times, testing for updated data. Within the loop, a test is performed to check whether the sent counter (lastCount) is less than the global counter (_callCount). If the test returns a true value, the output is generated, resulting in the latest changes being sent to the client. Generated in the output is the HTTP header X-Version-ID with the latest version identifier. If there is nothing to send, the current thread is put to sleep by using the method Thread.currentThread().sleep(1000) for a short period of time before beginning a new iteration that tests whether there is new data. If after 100 iterations there are no changes, the HTTP 408 return code is generated, indicating a time-out.

Looking at the HTTP header implementation, the cynical reader would think that the alternate solution looks strikingly similar to an HTTP cookie. In fact, the cynical reader is absolutely correct, but the solution was illustrated to show that HTTP cookies are very useful when used properly. The advantage of using HTTP cookies in contrast to the proposed solution is that there are no necessary changes to make to the client-side code. Only on the server side are changes necessary, and they are very similar to the proposed solution.

Before we move to the next topic, one last item has to be covered. In the original declaration of GlobalStatus, the class implemented the SingleThreadModel interface. This is a unique feature of Java, which says that only one client can call the servlet. I don't advise using the SingleThreadModel for your applications, but it was done for simplicity and ease of illustration. When writing two-stream communication mechanisms, most likely files, object instances, and so on will be shared, which means the data must be synchronized.

Implementing the Server-Side Monitoring Process

One of the major pitfalls of an HTTP server is that it is a reactional server. A *reactional server*, when confronted with a request, will react and generate a response. After having generated the response, the HTTP server sits idly waiting until another request arrives. The problem with this approach is that the standard HTTP server does not process data when there is no request.

Let's consider our two-stream communication mechanism and the status example. As the HTML client is coded, the user is responsible for sending an update. When managing server-side status updates, this is usually not what happens. Instead, some external action occurs that causes an update. The web application needs to be informed of the update, and that is where the problems occur. As illustrated in the version-tracking example, the client waits for the _callCount to increment. Real-life applications are not going to be as simple as waiting for a variable to be incremented. Real-life applications need a signal mechanism.

I will not cover how to implement a signal mechanism because it is beyond the scope of this book. However, the way that many projects solve the problem is by creating an HTTP client application that will act like a web browser and submit data to the server. From an architectural perspective, it appears similar to Figure 8-8.

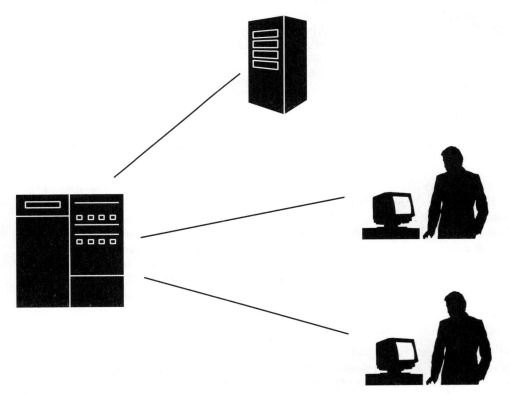

Figure 8-8. *Active server service using the HTTP server*

In Figure 8-8, the HTTP server is hosted on the main server and accessed by multiple clients. Two of the clients are humans using web browsers. The other client is another computer. The client that is a computer is running an application that listens for changing information. If the information changes, it writes data to the writing stream, resulting in an HTTP PUT or POST causing a change in the other two listening clients. Separating the processes makes it possible to change how the service listens and updates the data on the HTTP server.

Example: Presence Detection

Presence detection in code terms is an incremental update of the global status application. The incremental update is the requirement of the global status resource to know who is accessing the resource. The identity of the user is used to enhance the content of the global status resource.

Authenticating the User

The basis code of Presence Detection is the global status code just presented. The client code remains as is, because it already has the facilities to retrieve a username and password. The ServerCommunicator needs to be updated to include functionality used to identify the user. The mechanism used to identify the user could be HTTP authentication or a cookie, but HTTP authentication is used in this example. Because a user might want to implement different forms of authentication, an interface is defined. Following are the interface definitions:

```
public interface UserIdentification {
    public String getIdentifier();
    public Boolean isIdentified();
}
public interface UserIdentificationResolver {
    UserIdentification identifyUser(HttpServletRequest request);
}
```

The interface UserIdentificationResolver identifies a user based on the servlet request interface HttpServletRequest. The interface UserIdentification represents an identified user if the property isIdentified returns true. Looking at the interface definitions, you will probably get a sense of déjà vu, and that would be correct. In the Permutations pattern, identifying the user used the same interface declarations, but the interfaces were declared as IUserIdentificationResolver and IUserIdentification because the code was written in .NET.

If you want to know more about the implementation of user identification interfaces, be sure to read the section "An Example Shopping Cart Application" in Chapter 5.

Updating the ServerCommunicator

The ServerCommunicator functionality for the presence detection will be implemented by using the class WhoisOnline. In implementation terms, WhoisOnline is an increment to the previously defined GlobalStatus. Following is the partial implementation of WhoisOnline:

```
public class WhoisOnline extends HttpServlet implements SingleThreadModel {
    private String _user;
    private UserIdentificationResolver _userIdentification;
    private ArrayList _users = new ArrayList();
    private int _version;

    public void init(javax.servlet.ServletConfig config)
        throws javax.servlet.ServletException {
        _version = 0;
        try {
            _userIdentification =
(UserIdentificationResolver)WhoisOnline.class.
                getClassLoader().loadClass(
                config.getInitParameter("user-identification")).newInstance();
        }
        catch (Exception e) {
            throw new ServletException(
 "Could not instantiate _userIdentification", e);
        }
    }
    protected void service(
        javax.servlet.http.HttpServletRequest request,
        javax.servlet.http.HttpServletResponse response)
        throws javax.servlet.ServletException,
        java.io.IOException {
    }

    protected void doPost(HttpServletRequest request,
        HttpServletResponse response)
        throws javax.servlet.ServletException,
        java.io.IOException  {
    }
    protected void doGet(HttpServletRequest request,
        HttpServletResponse response)
        throws ServletException, IOException {
    }
}
```

The global resource state for WhoisOnline is the data member _users, which is an array list instance of users who are online. The data member _user represents a transient state used to identify the user currently accessing the resource. The value of _user for the present implementation coincides with the identity of the authenticated user, but as will be illustrated in the following "Example: Server Push" section, it is not the rule. The data member _userIdentification represents an instance of the user authentication implementation based on the interfaces defined before this code segment. And the last data member, _version, represents the version number of the state data member _users used to determine whether the reading stream should generate some content.

I have already explained the purpose of the method init, but to quickly summarize, it is used to initialize the Java servlet. In the case of WhoisOnline, the version number (_version) is reset to zero, and the user authentication implementation (_userIdentification) is instantiated. The technique used to instantiate the user authentication implementation relies on using the dynamic loading capabilities of Java.

What is completely new is the method service that is implemented as follows:

```
protected void service(
    javax.servlet.http.HttpServletRequest request,
    javax.servlet.http.HttpServletResponse response)
    throws javax.servlet.ServletException, java.io.IOException {
    UserIdentification userid =
        _userIdentification.identifyUser(request);
        if(userid.isIdentified()) {
            _user = userid.getIdentifier();
            super.service(request, response);
        }
        else {
            response.setStatus(500,
                "User could not be identified");
        }
    }
```

The methods doPost and doGet process HTTP POST and GET actions, respectively. But these methods are not called directly by the HTTP server. Instead, the HTTP server casts the servlet implementation for the Servlet interface. Having retrieved the interface, the method service is called, that in the default implementation will call the appropriate HTTP action method (for example, doPost and doGet). When the user-defined class WhoisOnline implements the method service, WhoisOnline is responsible for processing the individual HTTP action methods.

In the case of WhoisOnline, the purpose of the service method is not to override the default functionality, but to provide a single place where the global action extracting the user identification is placed. In the implementation, the method identifyUser is called and an instance of UserIdentification is retrieved. The instance of UserIdentification will contain the information about the user currently accessing the resource. If the user is identified (userid.isIdentified), the data member _user is assigned the user ID. With an identified user, the implementation can process an HTTP POST or GET. Calling the default service implementation by using the method super.service calls the default functionality that in turn calls doGet and doPost. If the user cannot be identified, the service method implementation will generate an HTTP 500 error code, thus not calling doGet or doPost because only authenticated users can use the presence detection global resource.

The implementation of doPost is as follows:

```
protected void doPost(HttpServletRequest request,
    HttpServletResponse response)
    throws javax.servlet.ServletException, java.io.IOException  {
    Iterator iter = _users.iterator();
    boolean didFind = false;
    while(iter.hasNext()) {
        String user = (String)iter.next();
        if(user.compareTo(_user) == 0) {
            didFind = true;
            break;
        }
    }
    if(!didFind) {
        _users.add(_user);
        _version ++;
    }
    response.setStatus(200, "All ok");
}
```

In the implementation of doPost, the sent data of the HTTP POST is not processed because our presence-detection example needs only to detect the user identity. In the implementation of doPost, what is processed is the user identity. If the user identification (_user) already exists in the list of present users (_users), nothing happens. If the user does not exist, the user is added to the users list, and the version (_version) number is incremented to indicate a change of state. Regardless of whether a user is added, the HTTP 200 code is returned, indicating a successful operation. It could be argued that if the user already exists in the users list, an error should be returned. However, that is not entirely appropriate; if a user is already added to the list, that does not indicate an error condition, but a condition of doing something repeatedly. And doing something repeatedly may be inefficient, but it is not wrong.

Following is the implementation of the doGet and getSentVersion methods:

```
private int getSentVersion(HttpServletRequest request) {
    Cookie[] cookies = request.getCookies();
    if(cookies != null) {
        for(int c1 = 0; c1 < cookies.length; c1 ++) {
            if(cookies[ c1].getName().compareTo("VersionId")
                == 0) {
                return new Integer(
                    cookies[ c1].getValue()).intValue();
            }
        }
    }
    return 0;
}
```

```
protected void doGet(HttpServletRequest request,
    HttpServletResponse response)
    throws ServletException, IOException {
    int sentVersion = getSentVersion(request);
    int waitCount = 0;
    while(waitCount < 100) {
        if(sentVersion < _version) {
            PrintWriter out = response.getWriter();
            Iterator iter = _users.iterator();
            while(iter.hasNext()) {
                String user = (String)iter.next();
                out.println("User (" + user + ")");
            }
            response.addCookie(new Cookie("VersionId",
                    new Integer(_version).toString()));
            return;
        }
        try {
            Thread.currentThread().sleep(1000);
        }
        catch (InterruptedException e) { }
        waitCount ++;
    }
    response.setStatus(408, "No change");
}
```

The doGet method implementation is similar to the doGet method implementation illustrated earlier, in the "Calling the ServerCommunicator Intelligently" section. The difference is
that HTTP cookies are used to track the version number that the client has. The method
getSentVersion extracts the version number from the client-sent cookies. If the version number
does not exist, a value of 0 is returned. Then the server goes through the looping process of
checking for a version number difference. If a version number difference is present, the output
is generated, and the cookie VersionId is sent with the version number of generated content.

Example: Server Push

For each example, the level of complexity has increased, and the only remaining scenario to
explain is the server push. What makes a server push unique is that each client accessing the
global resource (for example, http://mydomain.com/global/resource) has a unique child URL
(for example, http://mydomain.com/global/resource/unique-child). In previous examples,
the URL used was a global resource that was shared among individual users. This time the URL
must be unique because when the server pushes content, it is individualized.

As a side note, when referencing the unique URLs for the scope of this example, the unique
identifier will always be a username or user identifier. That does not need to be the case; it
could be a feed identifier, message queue, and so on. The unique identifier represents some
type of unique resource that distinguishes itself from the other resources. It also does not mean
that a single user is allocated a single resource. It could be that multiple users share the same
unique resource.

Some Thoughts on Specifying URLs

Before continuing with the server push implementation, a bit more thought to specifying the URL has to be given. For the Permutations pattern, I illustrated how to generate and retrieve URLs. You saw techniques for associating a representation with a resource based on the needs of the client. When using the server push, the URL must be unique, and this can be a problem because we don't know what the URL is in the first place. The question is how to figure out that the URL `http://mydomain.com/global/resource/unique-child` is unique based on the global resource `http://mydomain.com/global/resource`.

Using a Hard-Coded URL

A *hard-coded URL* is a URL that is written directly into the HTML, as illustrated by the following example:

```
<html>
<head>
<title>Hard Code Reference</title>
<script language="JavaScript" src="../lib/factory.js"></script>
<script language="JavaScript" src="../lib/asynchronous.js"></script>
<script language="JavaScript" type="text/javascript">

var asynchronous = new Asynchronous();

</script>
</head>
<body>
<button onclick="asynchronous.call('../chap04/chunked.ashx')">
Get Image</button>
<table>
    <tr><td id="counter"></td></tr>
</table>
</body>
</html>
```

In the example HTML code, the button calls the method `asynchronous.call`, and the called URL is `../chap04/chunked.ashx`. In a traditional development, this would be called a hard-coded URL reference. Programmers tend not to like hard-coded URLs because they make it difficult to update a website if the URL changes. In the example, the hard-coded URL may not be optimum. The preferred URL would be `../chap04/chunked` as the preferred URL implements the separation of resource from representation. The point, though, is to reference the design practices of the Permutations pattern.

Specifying a URL by Using User Identification

Another approach to specifying a URL is to use the server-side framework to generate the URL dynamically. In the following example, some ASP.NET code is used to generate the URL dynamically:

```
<%@ Page Language="C#" %>
<script runat="server">
    class DynamicURL {
        public static string GetAsync() {
            return "/url";
        }
    }
</script>
<html>
<head>
<title>Hard Code Reference</title>
<script language="JavaScript" src="../lib/factory.js"></script>
<script language="JavaScript" src="../lib/asynchronous.js"></script>
<script language="JavaScript" type="text/javascript">

var asynchronous = new Asynchronous();

</script>
</head>
<body>
<button
    onclick="asynchronous.call('<%=DynamicURL.GetAsync() %>')">
    Get Image
</button>
<table>
    <tr><td id="counter"></td></tr>
</table>
</body>
</html>
```

In this modified example of the HTML code, there is code that is executed on the server side, and code that is executed on the client side. For those who code in PHP, JSP, or other similar technologies, you will know that what is executed on the server side is surrounded by escape tags. For ASP.NET, the escape tags usually are the <% and %> characters. Another way to run server-side code using ASP.NET is to use the script tag, where the runat attribute has a value of server.

What is of interest is the text DynamicURL.GetAsync, which is a method call issued on the server to generate a URL. In the implementation of the GetAsync method, a hard-coded /url is returned, but the implementation really represents a piece of dynamically generated code.

Generating the URL dynamically is not a real advantage because that is the purpose of the Permutations pattern. Where generating the URL does make sense is if the Content Chunking and Decoupled Navigation patterns are used. In those cases, there are scenarios where functionality is referenced that is orthogonal to the functionality of the HTML page contained in the URL. The orthogonal URL might be a dependency of some web application plug-in, and hence generating the URL gives some extra flexibility. In the case of the server push, the dynamically generated URL can be used to identify the specific URL.

Specifying a URL by Using HTTP Redirection

Looking at the preceding example, you can see that the class DynamicURL, when called, generates a single URL. As I have outlined, one use of the dynamically generated URL is to identify the unique server push URL. The URL is generated by using the early definition approach (the counterpart late definition approach will be illustrated shortly). The approach is called *early definition* because the unique URL is identified after the HTML content has been generated. Using such an approach is not always possible nor useful.

Imagine the scenario where e-mails are sent to ask users to update details. Generating the unique URLs at the time of creating the URLs would be a security risk. A better approach is to let the user log in and then be redirected to the specific URL. The same can be said for the Persistent Communications pattern. The solution is to use HTTP redirection that generates the unique URL at the last possible moment. HTTP redirection uses a late-definition approach.

Following is an example HTTP conversation that performs an HTTP redirection. As usual, a client makes an HTTP request:

```
GET /resource/ HTTP/1.1
Accept: */*
Accept-Language: en
Accept-Encoding: gzip, deflate
User-Agent: Mozilla/5.0 (Macintosh; U; PPC Mac OS X; en)
AppleWebKit/412.6.2 (KHTML, like Gecko) Safari/412.2.2
Connection: keep-alive
Host: 192.168.1.242:8100
```

The URL /resource is recognized by the HTTP server as a generic URL that when called will redirect to a specific URL. The HTTP server responds with an HTTP 302 to indicate a redirection, as illustrated by the following HTTP response:

```
HTTP/1.1 302 Found
Date: Mon, 05 Sep 2005 16:29:04 GMT
Server: Apache/2.0.53 (Ubuntu) PHP/4.3.10-10ubuntu4
Location: /resource/joesmith
Content-Length: 346
Keep-Alive: timeout=15, max=100
Connection: Keep-Alive
Content-Type: text/html; charset=iso-8859-1
```

In the example, the specific URL is defined as /resource/joesmith that is sent to the client. When either a web browser or XMLHttpRequest object receives a redirect, the client will recognize the redirect and attempt to retrieve the contents of the redirected URL, as illustrated by the following final request:

```
GET /resource/joesmith HTTP/1.1
Accept: */*
Accept-Language: en
Accept-Encoding: gzip, deflate
User-Agent: Mozilla/5.0 (Macintosh; U; PPC Mac OS X; en)
AppleWebKit/412.6.2 (KHTML, like Gecko) Safari/412.2.2
Connection: keep-alive
Host: 192.168.1.242:8100
```

An HTTP redirection, whether executed by the web browser or XMLHttpRequest, can be executed only if the redirection follows the same origin policy. If a redirection to another domain is attempted with XMLHttpRequest, the results vary. For example, Microsoft Internet Explorer returns a status code of zero and no further data, Mozilla-based browsers return the status code 302 and the redirected URL, and finally Apple Safari crashes. Note that at the time of this writing, the Safari bug has been filed.

Completing the ServerCommunicator

For the server push implementation, the conversion of the general URL to the specific URL will be implemented by using HTTP redirection. The server push implementation is a wrapping together of all the concepts that the Persistent Communications pattern offers. There is a shared resource, a specific resource, user authentication, and version number tracking. The actions that the ServerCommunicator implements to make a server push happen are as follows:

1. The client accesses the root resource URL (for example, /ajax/chap06/serverpush).

2. The server reads the URL and checks whether there is a user identifier indicating a specific URL.

3. If no user identifier exists, a generic URL has been called that needs to be converted into a specific URL. The conversion involves the reading of the client authentication information that is used to execute a redirection to a specific URL (for example, /ajax/chap06/serverpush/username).

4. If there is a user identifier, the URL is not redirected but processed.

5. If having reached this step the URL is specific and therefore contains a user identifier, the user identifier is extracted from the URL and cross-referenced with a user state.

6. If a user state is not found, an HTTP 500 error is generated.

7. If a user state is found, the cookie associated with the user is retrieved and the version number is extracted.

8. Based on the user state and version number, the server either generates new data or waits for new data to be generated.

In the list of actions are some new actions and some already discussed actions. What is new is the direct reference of the user URL or specific URL. There is an important item to note, in that a redirection is not automatic and will happen only if a user references the root URL. This is done on purpose because it allows a client to access a URL that might not be related to its authentication information. So, for example, if an administrator authenticates herself, then by explicitly referencing a user, the administrator can administer the details of a user. It goes without saying that by implementing the Permutations pattern, an administrator could send a MIME type to the root resource that stops a redirection and instead returns a directory listing of all users. The idea is to allow a certain amount of flexibility by the HTTP server when performing an HTTP redirection based on the user identity and sent HTTP.

For each of the specific URLs, there is an associated user state. The user state could be some data in a database, file, or anywhere else. The user state is a depiction of the data that the client is interested in. In the case of our example, the user state is defined as follows:

```
class UserState {
    private String _userIdentifier;
    private Object _state;
    private int _version;

    public UserState(String userIdentifier, Object state) {
        _userIdentifier = userIdentifier;
        _state = state;
    }
    public String getUserIdentifier() {
        return _userIdentifier;
    }
    public Object getState() {
        return _state;
    }
    public void setState(Object state) {
        _state = state;
        _version ++;
    }
    public int getVersion() {
        return _version;
    }
}
```

The UserState class has three properties: _userIdentifier, which uniquely identifies the user; _state, which references some object instance representing the state of the user; and _version, which represents the version number of the state. The properties _userIdentifier and _version are read-only because you do not want a consumer class to manipulate either of the properties. The property _userIdentified when assigned never changes, whereas _version is incremented every time setState method is called.

The class ServerPush is responsible for the server push ServerCommunicator implementation. The abbreviated implementation of ServerPush that builds on the presence detection implementation is as follows; the new pieces of functionality are bolded for easy reference:

```
public class ServerPush extends HttpServlet implements SingleThreadModel {
    private ArrayList _users = new ArrayList();
    private String _user;
    private String _baseDirectory;
    private UserIdentificationResolver _userIdentification;
```

```
    public void init(javax.servlet.ServletConfig config)
        throws javax.servlet.ServletException {
        _baseDirectory = config.getInitParameter("base-url");
        try {
            _userIdentification = (UserIdentificationResolver)ServerPush.class.
                getClassLoader().loadClass(
                config.getInitParameter("user-identification")).newInstance();
        }
        catch (Exception e) {
            throw new ServletException(
                "Could not instantiate _userIdentification", e);
        }
    }
    protected void service(
        javax.servlet.http.HttpServletRequest request,
        javax.servlet.http.HttpServletResponse response)
        throws javax.servlet.ServletException,
        java.io.IOException {
    }

    protected void doPost(HttpServletRequest req,
        HttpServletResponse resp)
        throws javax.servlet.ServletException,
        java.io.IOException  {
        // Do something with the URL
    }
    protected void doGet(HttpServletRequest request,
        HttpServletResponse response)
        throws ServletException, IOException {
    }
}
```

Looking at the code, you can see that scattered throughout are pieces of bolded new functionality. With respect to data members, the array list _users is newly added. The array list specifies
the state of each individual user. In a real-life application, this is not what you would probably
do because there could be literally thousands of users. In real-life, though, you would associate
the user identifier with a key. The user identifier is the trailing end of the resource URL, and
need not be a username but could be an alphanumeric number or sequence of characters.

The other new data member is _baseDirectory, which represents the root resource URL.
A root resource definition URL is needed because the servlet has to be able to distinguish between
a generic URL (/ajax/chap06/serverpush) and a specific URL (/ajax/chap06/serverpush/
username). The data member _baseDirectory is assigned in the init method implementation
and represents a reference point for all URLs that will be processed by ServerPush.

The modified service method is implemented as follows:

```
protected void service(
    javax.servlet.http.HttpServletRequest request,
    javax.servlet.http.HttpServletResponse response)
    throws javax.servlet.ServletException,
    java.io.IOException {
    String user = request.getRequestURI().substring(
        _baseDirectory.length());

    if(user.length() == 0) {
        UserIdentification userid =
            _userIdentification.identifyUser(request);
        if(userid.isIdentified()) {
            response.sendRedirect(request.getRequestURI()
                + "/"
                + userid.getIdentifier());
            return;
        }
        else {
            response.setStatus(500,
                "User could not be identified");
            return;
        }
    }
    super.service(request, response);
}
```

The new bolded code in the `service` method illustrates the extraction of the user identifier from the called URL that is assigned the `user` variable. If the `user` variable has no length, the root resource URL has been called and therefore a redirect is appropriate. In Java servletspeak, a redirection is performed by using the method `sendRedirect`, which results in an HTTP 302 code being generated. If no redirection is made, a specific URL is being requested and hence processing can continue as usual.

The modified implementation of the method `doPost` is as follows:

```
protected void doPost(HttpServletRequest req,
    HttpServletResponse resp)
    throws javax.servlet.ServletException, java.io.IOException  {
    // Do something with the URL
}
```

What is new in the implementation of the method `doPost` is that there is no implementation. This is because the implementation of `doPost` is completely specific to the application. In the case of the server push, it means receiving data on the writing stream that is used to update a specific resource. In the case of the example, that means processing the sent data and assigning it to the `UserState` object instance.

As a side note, remember that the HTTP server handles authentication. Therefore, if the methods doGet, doPost, and so on are reached, the programmer can be assured that the user has been authenticated and allowed access to that URL. Most web servers, such as Apache and Tomcat, allow a great deal of fine-tuning of the authentication. If that is not enough, or your HTTP server does not support such fine-tuning, you will need to write an authentication filter. The authentication code should under no circumstances be added to the ServerCommunicator.

The modified implementation of doGet is as follows:

```
private int getSentVersion(HttpServletRequest request,
    String user) {
    Cookie[] cookies = request.getCookies();
    String cookieIdentifier = "VersionId" + user;
    if(cookies != null) {
        for(int c1 = 0; c1 < cookies.length; c1 ++) {
            if(cookies[ c1].getName().compareTo(
                cookieIdentifier) == 0) {
                return Integer.parseInt(cookies[cl].getValue())
            }
        }
    }
    return 0;
}
private UserState getUser(String user) {
    Iterator iter = _users.iterator();
    while(iter.hasNext()) {
        UserState userstate = (UserState)iter.next();
        if(userstate.getUserIdentifier().compareTo(user) == 0) {
            return userstate;
        }
    }
    return null;
}
protected void doGet(HttpServletRequest request,
    HttpServletResponse response)
    throws ServletException, IOException {
    UserState userstate = getUser(
            request.getRequestURI().substring(
            _baseDirectory.length()));
    if(userstate != null) {
        int sentVersion = getSentVersion(
                request, userstate.getUserIdentifier());
        int waitCount = 0;
        while(waitCount < 10) {
            if(sentVersion < userstate.getVersion()) {
                PrintWriter out = response.getWriter();
                out.println("User (" + userstate.toString() +
                    ")");
```

```
                    String cookieIdentifier = "VersionId" +
                        userstate.getUserIdentifier();
                    response.addCookie(
                        new Cookie(cookieIdentifier,
                        new Integer(
                            userstate.getVersion()).toString()));
                        return;
                }
                try {
                    Thread.sleep(1000);
                }
                catch (InterruptedException e) { }
                    waitCount ++;
                }
            }
            response.setStatus(408, "No change");
        }
        else {
            response.setStatus(500, "Could not find user state");
        }
    }
}
```

In the doGet method implementation, there are several new aspects. Because any request that reaches doGet or doPost has a user identifier associated with it, extracting the user identifier from the URL is necessary. The user identifier cannot be associated with the user authentication information at the doGet or doPost stage because the user identifier represents a unique identifier. The user authentication at the doGet or doPost stage might be same as is the case if an administrator is verifying some specific URLs. After having extracted the user information from the URL, the method getUser is called to retrieve the state of the user. In the example, that means iterating the _users array list. However, in your application that might mean loading the user state from a database or a file. The key point to notice is that there is a separate function to handle loading the user state.

Going back to the implementation of doGet, after the user state has been retrieved, the cookie is retrieved from the URL. It is important to realize that there is not a single cookie, but a cookie for each user. This is important because if you are an administrator watching multiple users, those users need multiple version numbers. The simplest way to do this is to create a cookie identifier for each user. Or more generally, create a cookie version identifier for each specific URL. Another approach is to create an encoded cookie that identifies the version of each specific URL, but the exact specifics are an implementation detail. The important bit is that it is not possible to use a single version number to track all specific URLs. Having retrieved the user state and version number, and identified that the client does not have the latest version of the state, a response can be generated.

Take a moment to look at this example and consider the individual pieces because it represents a full implementation of the Persistent Communications pattern. Notice how little we edited the ClientCommunicator piece. This is because the ClientCommunicator needs a full implementation from the first example. The ClientCommunicator is not aware of whether the accessed resource is global anonymous, global authenticated, or unique. The client knows only that there is some information it is interested in.

Version Numbers and Updates

The version number is not a common programming concept. Generally speaking, we don't track whether data changes. Yet we should because it is a great way to manage changes. For example, Subversion, which is a great version control system, uses version numbers. Many software programs use build numbers that represent changes in the software. It really begs the question, why not state?

Ajax applications are based on data that has a specific state, and therefore it is a good idea to associate version numbers. Imagine the extended abilities of web applications. For example, say that while you are booking a flight, you try out various permutations and get various results. After seven permutations, your brain begins to fry. It would be fantastic to be able to go back to a state of the web application that represents an earlier request. Current web applications are simply not cut out for that job.

Version numbers in the context of Ajax applications could be defined as their own pattern. But it was decided to not create a specific pattern because the Persistent Communications pattern requires version numbers. Therefore, it was decided that version numbers are an implementation detail, albeit a pretty darn crucial implementation detail.

Performance Considerations

I am not going to pretend that this pattern is not resource intensive. It can be resource intensive if used extensively. The resource drain on the server side is the holding of resources by the reading stream. As was indicated, Jetty has figured out how to deal with the problem as effectively as possible. But if there are thousands of users accessing various global and unique resources, resources will be held in the memory of the server. One rule of thumb to manage resources more effectively is to limit an HTML page to a single Persistent Communications pattern. There is nothing blocking multiple instances, but that could result in a resource explosion on both the client and server. Using the rule of thumb, it effectively means that if there are 100 clients, there will be 100 active connections doing nothing but waiting. Therefore, when implementing this pattern, do a prototype to see how the system will react.

Pattern Highlights

The purpose of the Persistent Communications pattern is to provide a mechanism for the client and server to communicate with each other, whereby data can be sent from the server to the client, without "asking" for it. The pattern illustrates three key scenarios: status updates, presence detection, and server push.

The following points are the important highlights of the Persistent Communications pattern:

- A two-stream mechanism is used to send the data from the server to the client, and from the client to the server.

- The server is responsible for delaying the request if there is no new data for the client to process.

- The data that is sent between the client and server is not processed or managed by the Persistent Communications pattern implementation (ClientCommunicator or ServerCommunicator).

- Implementing the Persistent Communications pattern means implementing the Permutations pattern. It may be that only one set of data is sent to the client, but the `ServerCommunicator` should check what types of data the client is interested in.

- Version numbers are necessary so that state can be tracked and the server knows when to send data to the client.

- It is possible to generate version numbers by using HTTP headers, but HTTP cookies are preferred.

- Although synchronization was only briefly discussed, for your implementations synchronization is very important because the Persistent Communications pattern has a tendency to use shared data.

- Today's HTTP servers are not capable of providing a persistent running thread that will update the global or specific resource when necessary. A solution is to write an HTTP client that posts the updates to the HTTP server using HTTP `POST` or `PUT`.

CHAPTER 9

State Navigation Pattern

Intent

The State Navigation pattern provides an infrastructure in which HTML content can be navigated, and the state is preserved when navigating from one piece of content to another.

Motivation

Web applications have major state and consistency problems, and some Ajax applications amplify those problems. To illustrate, let's go through the process of buying a plane ticket and note the problems.

I fly regularly for business and as such am always looking for the best price. Because of my ticket-searching capabilities, I have become the travel agent for my wife and a few other people. I search many travel sites and use the permutations and combinations strategy to find the cheapest or most convenient ticket. If I find a ticket, I then try to find a better ticket by moving the dates forward or back, switching to a different airport, or even switching travel sites. Trying to find the best ticket by using a web browser has its challenges because of the way many travel websites "remember" the ticket information. The main problem is that travel websites may not remember my original flying times when I click the Back button, or may not remember old flight information when I open a second browser. And worse yet, some sites perform redirections to other sites not asked for, or require you to fly from certain airports. All travel sites at the time of this writing have one problem or another.

Consider Figure 9-1, which is a snapshot from one travel site. I have blanked out the travel site details because the figure is used to illustrate a problem. Figure 9-1 is the result of selecting the starting and ending points of the initial leg of a flight and being offered a set of times and conditions to choose from.

Figure 9-1 shows found flight details, and the user needs to choose one flight before continuing. To continue and to select the return leg of the flight, the user clicks Rueckflug. To go back and start again, the user clicks Zurueck. For interest sake, let's click Zurueck and see what happens. Figure 9-2 shows the resulting HTML page.

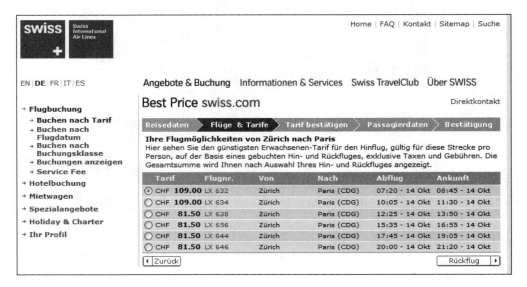

Figure 9-1. *Found flight details*

Figure 9-2. *Initial search page*

Figure 9-2 shows that by going back to start a search, you reset all of your search parameters and have to start from scratch again. This is irritating. The process becomes even more confusing if the user decides to use the navigation buttons and clicks the Back button of the web browser. Figure 9-3 illustrates what happens if the Back and Forward web browser buttons or a combination of those is pressed.

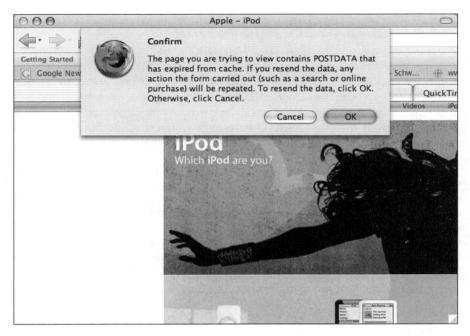

Figure 9-3. *Error that results from pressing the wrong web browser buttons*

Figure 9-3 illustrates how clicking the web browser Back button when pages have been posted using the HTTP POST method can cause the browser to generate errors and dialog boxes asking for further help. In these situations, depending on your actions, either the web application works or you bought a second plane ticket. The user experience is inconsistent and problematic.

To solve these experience inconsistencies, web browsers "remember" what the user entered. The web browser solution involves remembering the state contained within the form elements of the HTML page. This remembering of state causes the web browser to automatically fill in logins or form details without requiring the user to type everything in yet again. Yet the web browser solution does not always work because the state is not always consistently remembered. We can't blame the web browsers for not remembering a correct state because it is not the fault of the web browser. The web browser is just trying to make the best of a bad situation that many web application developers and web application frameworks have forced upon us.

Where heck broke out was when software vendors decided to fix the inherent statelessness of the HTTP protocol. These fixes very often conflict with the functionality of the web browser and introduce their own navigation paradigm. One of the reasons we deviated from the original intention of the Web and the HTTP protocol is our desire to improve and mold things to our liking. Put all of these factors to work and you have the reasons why page navigation is broken.

Applicability

The State Navigation pattern applies in all of those contexts where editable state is associated with an HTML page(s). In most cases, that means workflow or business process operations. It does not mean that only HTML forms that create a workflow are applicable. The state must not be editable in the HTML representation form, because the Representation Morphing pattern can be applied to convert a static representation into an editable representation.

Not all states are created equally. There is binding state and nonbinding state. *Binding state* is the focus in this pattern. *Nonbinding state* is used to represent the binding state. For example, the nonbinding state associated with a mailbox could indicate how to sort the e-mails that are displayed in the mailbox. The resource that represents the e-mails is a listing and is considered a binding state. Nonbinding state can be lost without ramifications to the binding state. If the sorting order were to be lost, the resulting e-mails would have another ordering but no information would be lost. At the worst, the end user is inconvenienced.

Associated Patterns

The State Navigation pattern uses the materials presented in Chapter 2 that define the Asynchronous type. When the State Navigation pattern is implemented, it is assumed that the Permutations pattern is used. The State Navigation pattern does assume the state is defined as a chunk, as defined by the Content Chunking pattern, and that the state of the HTML page uses the Representation Morphing pattern. Where the State Navigation and Content Chunking pattern deviate is that a State Navigation implementation is a single chunk only.

Architecture

When implementing the State Navigation pattern, the primary focus is to manage the state associated with an HTML page. The State Navigation pattern infrastructure is responsible only for serving and receiving the state content. The HTML page is responsible for processing and generating the state. The HTML page is in control of calling the State Navigation pattern infrastructure. If the HTML page does not implement any calls to the State Navigation pattern infrastructure, there is no state managed. The State Navigation pattern infrastructure is defined on a per-HTML page basis. This makes it possible for a web application to have mixed state, where some pages are associated with a state, and other pages are not.

Moving Toward an Ideal Solution from the User's Perspective

It would be simple to say, "This is the way that the State Navigation pattern is designed regardless of how the HTTP or HTML infrastructure functions." However, that is not possible because the HTTP and HTML infrastructure has its own rules. Therefore, the State Navigation pattern solution is entirely dependent on what works best with HTML and HTTP.

Before I illustrate a solution at the technical level, I am going to show you the desired solution from a user's perspective that involves manipulating and navigating HTML pages in a simplistic and fictitious workflow application. Figure 9-4 shows the first HTML page of the workflow application.

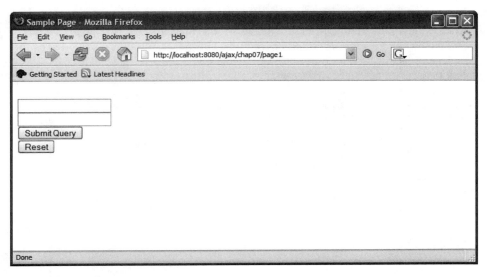

Figure 9-4. *Initial HTML page*

In Figure 9-4, the HTML page has two text boxes and two buttons and is called an *HTML form.* Implementing the Permutations pattern by using an HTML form is a challenge from a resource definition perspective. Contrast the HTML form to a traditional HTML page. When Mary Jane (for example) reads an e-mail entry, the Permutations pattern is applied on the contents of the e-mail entry. The resource is the URL `http://mydomain.com/mailbox/maryjane/entry1234`, and the representation is a transformation of the e-mail entry to content that the client wants. The resource and representation of the e-mail entry cannot be edited or modified.

When the Permutations pattern is applied to an HTML form, the HTML form without any content is the representation of a resource. The URL `http://mydomain.com/resource/step1` is an example resource that maps to the HTML form `http://mydomain.com/resource/step1.html`. The end user fills in the form, and a state is created. If the end user were to press the Back button and then the Forward button on the web browser, the created state would be lost (to avoid losing the state, most browsers "remember" the HTML form element contents). The problem is that the resource URL is for an empty HTML form representation. To remember the state, another URL (for example, `http://mydomain.com/resource/step1/state/1234`) needs to be defined. Defining a new URL is not a problem, and this topic is covered shortly. What needs to be noted is that editable HTML pages have multiple resource URLs that are dependent on the state.

So the problem in Figure 9-4 is how to associate a state with the resource (the example illustrated uses a URL). The association cannot be embedded in an HTTP header or HTML text field or cookie because that would violate the intent of the State Navigation pattern and the general design of URLs. But even simpler, when a URL is copied and pasted into another browser, there is no chance of copying and pasting a cookie, HTTP header, or HTML text field. Therefore, the state or reference to the state must be in the URL.

The solution of associating a state with a resource is to use a special URL, but one that is specialized by using a state identifier. Figure 9-5 illustrates an example HTML page that has been specialized by using a state identifier. For reference purposes, the state was loaded by the XMLHttpRequest object using the Content Chunking pattern.

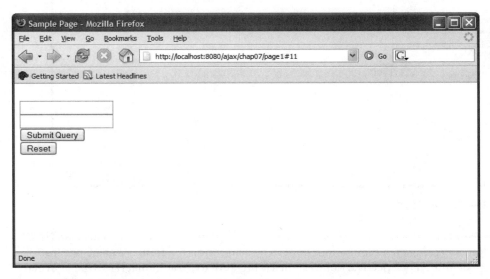

Figure 9-5. *Initial HTML page with session state loaded*

In Figure 9-5, the HTML page has loaded the associated session state. Comparing Figure 9-4 and Figure 9-5, you would not be able to tell because almost nothing has changed. The one change is the appending of the text #11, which is used to indicate the state identifier.

When a URL is associated with a hash character, the browser considers the new URL as unique but does not force a refresh of the browser. For example, if the URL were http://mydomain.com/ajax/chap07/page1/state/11, the HTML page would have been reloaded and the server would have been responsible for associating the HTML form state with the HTML page. The problem with changing the URL to associate a state is that it forces a reload for each and every state. A redirection occurs, and the web application is complicated and potentially prone to fail or load the wrong content. Using the # character does not require a reloading of the HTML page. The # character is ideally suited to be used in the context of the Content Chunking pattern because a script can parse the URL and extract the state identifier. The script then uses the XMLHttpRequest type to retrieve the state from the server and saves it in the HTML page. From the perspective of the server, there exists only the HTML form with no content, and the state. The client-side script associates the state with the HTML form. Do remember that state does not have to be associated with an HTML form, but could be associated with an HTML page that is transformed by using the Representation Morphing pattern.

Going back to Figure 9-5, if the user were to enter some data in the text boxes and then click the Submit Query button, the HTML page in Figure 9-6 would result.

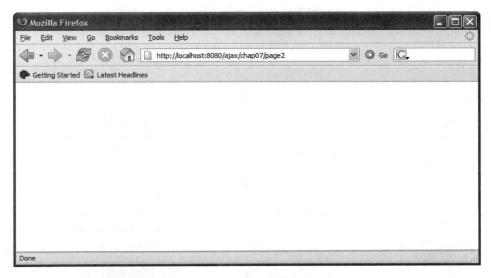

Figure 9-6. *Second page resulting from processed page*

Figure 9-6 is plain vanilla because there is nothing to display. This figure illustrates the process of saving state and loading another HTML page that does not have any state. What happened is that the script saved the state of the previous page and posted the state to the server. After the state was successfully posted, the next HTML page was retrieved by using standard navigation techniques. Separating the posting of the state and retrieving of the next appropriate content solves many problems, with one being the unnecessary dialog box illustrated in Figure 9-3. When the user clicks the Back button, the state in Figure 9-7 is displayed, illustrating the State Navigation pattern.

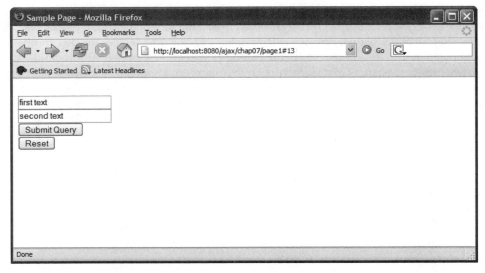

Figure 9-7. *Original page1 is reloaded with last known state*

Looking closer at Figure 9-7, you can see several changes, namely the text boxes are filled with some text, which is the state, and the state identifier has changed to 13, from 11. At this point, you could click the Forward and Back buttons as many times as you wanted; the state would be constantly reloaded, while the state identifier would update itself.

Extending the Solution for a Web Application

The presented solution illustrates how the hash character can be used to load and save the state of an individual HTML page. The individual HTML page or resource saves state on the server side that can be combined into a series of HTML pages that are related to each other. When stringing together multiple HTML pages that are related, problems can occur with a web browser, and two problems are pronounced. The first problem relates to multiple browsers attempting to access the same content that has a state. When this situation occurs, the state associated with the content is dependent on the timing of what content is submitted by one of the browsers. The second problem relates to navigating content by using the Forward and Back buttons, as that can wreak havoc on content that has an associated state.

To illustrate the problem of multiple browsers displaying the same content, let's go through an example. The example will navigate through the resources /resource, /resource2, and /resource3. If users navigated the resources individually, or in an ad-hoc fashion, the web application would have no idea how to manage the state because there is no order to the navigation. To provide order, the resources are strung together by using cookies that manage which resources are called and the state of the called resources. But the HTTP cookies give a false sense of security. The problem is that HTTP cookies do not distinguish between different web browser instances. It does not mean that cookies cannot be used, but they cannot be the reference point used by the server to manage the state of the resources. However, a solution using cookies will not be illustrated because the focus is on the page transitions and managing of the state.

Getting back to the problem of being unable to distinguish between a browser window instance, that problem is best illustrated in Figure 9-8.

In Figure 9-8, the initial browser loaded the URL /resource, and some content was generated. After the user fills in the HTML form and clicks Submit Query, the state of the URL /resource is saved, and /resource2 is loaded. Having loaded /resource2, the user decides to open another browser and copies the URL /resource2 to the second browser that is loaded. At this moment, there are two browser instances that loaded the same content, and both browsers reference the same cookie identifier. Where the server becomes confused is when the user switches back to the first browser, fills in the data, and clicks the Submit Query button, causing /resource3 to be loaded.

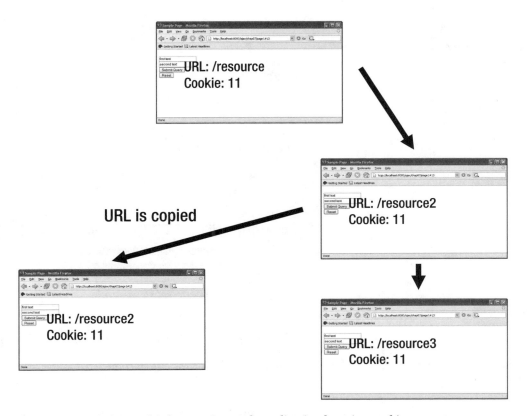

Figure 9-8. *Processing multiple pages in a web application by using cookies*

The confusion with an HTTP cookie occurs when the first web browser loads the represen-tation associated with the resource /resource3, while the second web browser loads the resource /resource2. If the second browser attempts to navigate to the resource /resource3, the server will become confused as to what stage the web browser is really at. The server cannot distinguish between browser instances, and therefore overwrites new data over old, or old data over new, causing consistency problems. The behavior of the cookie is correct, as the cookie specification explicitly says that a cookie is associated with a domain and not a browser instance.

Using a state identifier to manage the state and resources creates a solution in which the state is accumulated. Accumulation of state makes it possible to fork the state if multiple browsers are accessing multiple versions of the state. To understand the logic, consider Figure 9-9, which indicates how unique state identifiers are created.

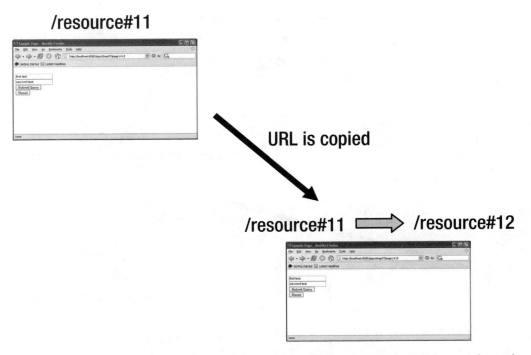

Figure 9-9. *An example of the state identifier being updated after the URL is copied to another web browser instance*

In the upper-left corner of Figure 9-9 is a web browser that has downloaded some content with the URL /resource#11. The loaded content is the resource /resource with the state identifier 11. Imagine the user opening a second browser and copying the link /resource#11. The State Navigation pattern will load the resource /resource and the state associated with the identifier 11. In the second browser, the state identifier is updated to reference 12. If the second browser has the same state identifier as the first, that binds both browsers to the same state and creates concurrency problems. Imagine that the client modifies the state in the first browser; then the second browser would see the same state. This is not desirable, and therefore the state identifier 11 is copied to a new state identifier 12. Then the first and second browser instances for the time being have the same state values, but different references.

The solution in Figure 9-9 needs one additional twist to make it work properly. If the browser were to request the URLs /resource#11 and /resource#12, the resource /resource would be issued twice. This relates back to the purpose of the hash character, which is a reference to a link on an HTML page. This is a good thing, because the State Navigation pattern has separated the resource from the state of the resource. So when the resource /resource#11 is called, the URLs /resource (for example, HTML page) and /resource/state (for example, HTML page state) are called.

By using the XMLHttpRequest object, it is easy to separate the two URL requests, and there are multiple ways to implement the two URLs. But using two URLs is not enough. You also need to use HTTP headers to uniquely identify the request. Figure 9-10 illustrates how Figure 9-8 is fixed by using HTTP headers.

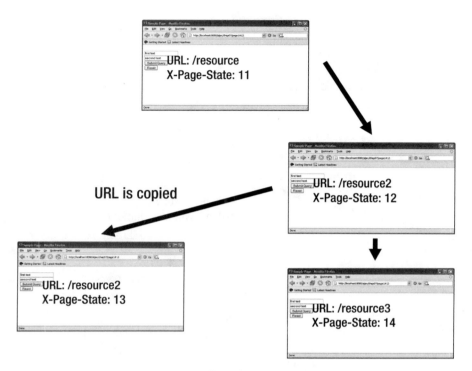

Figure 9-10. *Rearchitecting multiple resources to use a state identifier*

In Figure 9-10, each of the web browser instances is a URL, with a hash code–identified state identifier that is converted into an X-Page-State HTTP header. Each instance of the web browser has an HTTP header that is unique. This is a good thing because now, even though there are two browsers, the resource /resource2 has two separate instances of the associated state.

Having the unique state identifiers works, except it exposes another problem: there is no stringing together of the individual HTML pages to build a web application. What we don't know is how the states relate to each other. Visually, we know that the states 11, 12, and 14 are a single chain. And visually we know that 11 and 13 are another chain. But the server does not know that because the server does not know that state 13 is the result of opening a second browser.

To finish the solution, the history of the URLs is needed. The web browser has that information because it is required for navigating the Forward and Back buttons. The simple solution would be to access the browser-exposed history object and pass those URLs to the HTTP POST. The problem with the simple solution is that it is not generally viable. Accessing the history object by using a script is a security issue, and unless the client has allowed access, will generate an exception.

A more feasible solution is to add an additional HTTP header that uniquely identifies the window used to chain together the HTML pages. Specifically, the property window.name can be assigned and is ideally suited to uniquely identify the individual HTML windows. Figure 9-11 illustrates the final solution.

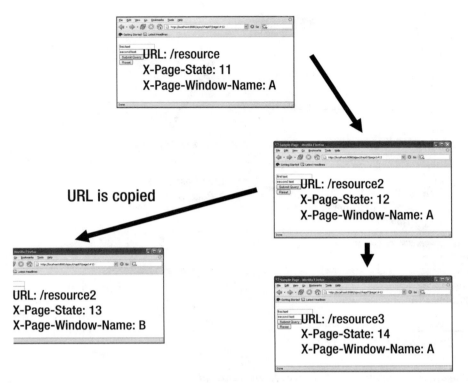

Figure 9-11. *Final solution used to uniquely identify the HTML windows, URL, and associated state*

In Figure 9-11, each browser window instance is unique and can be identified. For example, if the user requests /resource, the window identifier is A, and the state identifier is 11. If the user processes the data, /resource2 is retrieved with a new state identifier 12 and window instance A. If the user were to copy the URL to a new browser instance, the URL /resource2#12 would be copied. The state identifier 12 would be loaded, but the window browser instance is B, and therefore the server knows a new window instance has been created, and a new history is being generated. The server will then associate the state 11 with the newly created state identifier 13. Now both browser instances, A and B, both share the state identifier 11 in their history. Then if the user clicks the Submit Query button of either window, A or B, two unique results will occur that do not conflict with each other. If the example were a plane ticket application, two tickets that start at the same location but end in different locations could be purchased.

A new state identifier is created when the page is refreshed. Considering that we can identify the browser instance by using the window name, the state identifier is not necessary. Using a window name as a state identifier creates a state that is accumulated and organized by resource. When a new browser instance and old URL are copied (for example, state identifier 13), the server is responsible for copying the old state into a new state. The downside of using an accumulated state is that it is not as fine-grained as a state identified by unique identifiers.

Managing State at the Protocol Level

Moving down one level on the technological scale, this section illustrates the HTTP communications between the client and server. The communications are started by having a web browser ask for the resource http://mydomain.com/ajax/chap07/page1, which is illustrated by the following request. Note that the illustrated requests and responses are abbreviated and show only the HTTP information that is relevant for the discussion:

```
GET /ajax/chap07/page1 HTTP/1.1
Accept: text/xml,application/xml,application/xhtml+xml,text/html;q=0.9,
text/plain;q=0.8,image/png,*/*;q=0.5
Accept-Language: en-us,en;q=0.5
Accept-Encoding: gzip,deflate
Accept-Charset: ISO-8859-1,utf-8;q=0.7,*;q=0.7
```

The server accepts the request and responds with the following:

```
HTTP/1.1 200 OK
ETag: W/"1017-1126885576349"
Last-Modified: Fri, 16 Sep 2005 15:46:16 GMT
Content-Type: text/html
Content-Length: 1017
Server: Apache-Coyote/1.1
```

In the response, there is an ETag indicating that the content could be cached by the web browser. If the ETag were sent in response to an XMLHttpRequest request, the Cache Controller pattern could have been used. The server-generated response uses the Permutations pattern and contains information that can be represented by a web browser. The generated response represents the empty or generic representation that does not contain a state. When the generated content has been converted into a processed HTML page, the HTML body onload event is triggered. Triggering the onload event generates a request for the state associated with the resource. Following is the XMLHttpRequest-generated request:

```
GET /ajax/chap07/page1/state HTTP/1.1
Accept: application/xml
Accept-Language: en-us,en;q=0.5
Accept-Encoding: gzip,deflate
Accept-Charset: ISO-8859-1,utf-8;q=0.7,*;q=0.7
X-Page-Window-Name: window-2005-10-03-10-10-10-1245
X-Page-State: none
```

What is unique in the request for the state from the XMLHttpRequest object is that the URL is similar in structure to the resource URL, except that the state keyword is appended to the URL. The state keyword is necessary so that all proxies and browsers can uniquely identify the resource and the state associated with the resource. Using the same URL would cause problems. In the HTTP request, the additional HTTP headers X-Page-State and X-Page-Window-Name are used. The header X-Page-State defines the state identifier, and the header X-Page-Window-Name identifies the name of the window asking for the state. What triggers the server-side State Navigation pattern implementation is either the appended state identifier or the X-Page-State HTTP header. More about the trigger will be discussed in the server-side code implementation.

And last, notice how the Accept HTTP header accepts only the type application/xml. This is on purpose even though a MIME type such as application/ajax-state would have been more appropriate. It is critical to use application/xml because then the XMLHttpRequest and web browser will recognize the returned data as XML. Using another MIME type causes the XMLHttpRequest type to not parse the generated XML and returns the content only as a text stream. As an architectural side note, a format such as JSON could be used to define the state.

When asked for a state for the first time, the server will not have an associated state and will need to create an empty state. The empty state response is illustrated as follows:

```
HTTP/1.1 200 success
X-Page-State: 11
Date: Sun, 18 Sep 2005 11:19:30 GMT
Server: Apache-Coyote/1.1
```

In the response, the server issues an HTTP 200 command to indicate that the request was a success. The body may be empty, but in the case of the example would be the XML <state></state> to indicate an empty state. An empty state is generated so that the requesting client can go through the hoops of asking for a state, but nothing will be modified. The HTTP header X-Page-State is returned to the client to indicate what the state identifier is, and in this case the state identifier 11 is returned.

When associating a state with a URL, that state could be accessible from every browser regardless of location and therefore be considered a security risk. However, in this example, the state is not accessible everywhere because the URL, window name identifier, and state identifier are tied together. A hacker would have to know all three before being able to access the state. Additionally, for extra security, HTTPS or some form of authentication can be used. Depending on the nature of the state, the solution could involve using requesting IP addresses, authentication information, or even cookies.

It is important to realize that if cookies are used to authenticate a user, the usefulness of the State Navigation pattern is extremely limited. Cookies can cross web browser instances, but not different web browser types or computer locations. The better solution would be to use HTTP authentication because the web browser can ask for HTTP authentication regardless of browser or computer location.

When the HTML page and state requests have been processed, the client can fill out the form with some data. Having added all the data into the form, the user can click the Submit Query button. Clicking the button causes the onsubmit event to be triggered, which results in the State Navigation pattern implementation on the client side to call the server by using the XMLHttpRequest object. The call generates a request that is illustrated as follows:

```
POST /ajax/chap07/linkToPage2.xml HTTP/1.1
Accept: application/xml
Accept-Language: en-ca
Accept-Encoding: gzip, deflate
Content-Type: application/xml
Content-Length: 364
Connection: Keep-Alive
Cache-Control: no-cache
X-Page-Original-Url: /ajax/chap07/page1
X-Page-Window-Name: window-2005-10-03-10-10-10-1245
X-Page-State: 11
```

In the example, the request is an HTTP POST that posts to the static file linkToPage2.xml. What is odd is that an HTTP POST has been made to a document that cannot process the post because the file is obviously not a script. This is the uniqueness of the State Navigation pattern in that when data is posted, the result does not have to be another page that is viewed by the web browser.

Normally, when executing an HTTP POST, a server-side script will process the request and generate some output. Unlike an HTTP GET, where data is retrieved, the HTTP POST expects data to be sent before it is retrieved. When creating a workflow application, HTML pages are tied to each other. For example, if the resource /ajax/chap07/page1 contains a POST to /ajax/chap07/page2, only page1 can call page2, because page2 expects data arriving from page1. Of course, the developer could write within the script of page2 a decision block to test how the script is being called and what it should do. Nevertheless, this makes for messy coding.

What is different with the State Navigation pattern is that the sending of the data and retrieving of the next content are separated. The State Navigation posts to a URL that may or may not process the posted content. The State Navigation would capture the request, store the state, and pass the request to another processor on the HTTP server. Another processor would intercept the request, process the state, and let the HTTP server send the data to the client. The state that is sent to the server can be stored or processed and is the discretion of the web server application. The advantage of this approach is that by using the State Navigation pattern, a URL can cumulatively process the state and generate a single transaction.

The solution provided by the State Navigation pattern is to use the POST as a mechanism to record and process data. The workflow is created by documents that contain a link to the next resource. This makes it possible to separate the dependency of page2 to page1. The result is that the web application allows a reorganization of the HTML content flow, allowing decisions to be made on the fly.

Continuing the communications, the server would respond to the HTTP POST with the following answer:

```
HTTP/1.1 200 OK
X-Page-State: 11
ETag: W/"137-1126885576359"
Last-Modified: Fri, 16 Sep 2005 15:46:16 GMT
Content-Type: application/xml
Content-Length: 137
Server: Apache-Coyote/1.1
```

When the client has loaded the returned data, the script searches for a link that indicates the URL to be loaded by the client. The script then redirects the browser by reassigning location.href, causing the following request to be made by the browser:

```
GET /ajax/chap07/page2 HTTP/1.1
Accept: image/gif, image/x-xbitmap, image/jpeg,
image/pjpeg, application/x-shockwave-flash,
application/vnd.ms-excel, application/vnd.ms-powerpoint,
application/msword, */*
Accept-Language: en-ca
Accept-Encoding: gzip, deflate
```

The server will respond with an HTML page that contains no state information. If the loaded HTML page has implemented the State Navigation pattern, the implementation will start from the beginning. The state identifier loaded in the previous page (page1) is lost. The identifier is lost to the script, but in the history of the web browser the state identifier has been recorded. When the user clicks the Back button, the browser will make the request for the URL /ajax/chap07/page1, and the HTML page state with the identifier 11 will be loaded from the history. This again causes the State Navigation pattern to start from the beginning, except this time there is a state identifier requiring a state to be loaded. When the page from the resource has been loaded again, the onload function is called, causing the XMLHttpRequest object to search for the state with the identifier 11, and resulting in the following request:

```
GET /ajax/chap07/page1/state HTTP/1.1
Accept: application/xml
X-Page-Window-Name: window-2005-10-03-10-10-10-1245
X-Page-State: 11
Accept-Language: en-ca
Accept-Encoding: gzip, deflate
```

The server processes the request and generates the following response:

```
HTTP/1.1 200 success
X-Page-State: 12
Content-Type: application/xml;charset=ISO-8859-1
Content-Length: 364
Date: Sun, 18 Sep 2005 11:15:16 GMT
Server: Apache-Coyote/1.1
```

In the response, the state identifier 12 is returned along with some data that the XMLHttpRequest object can process. Illustrating the State Navigation pattern visually and at the protocol level explains how this pattern functions. The remaining step is to explain how the client and server code make everything happen.

Implementation

For the State Navigation pattern to function properly, several other patterns need to be combined. Combining the patterns results in an overall architecture that is used to process requests. The question, though, is how to combine the various patterns.

One solution would be to use the Decorator pattern. That would be a good solution, but is implemented by using the already-existing Decorator pattern facilities of the HTTP server. On the HTTP server side, the Decorator pattern is implemented using HTTP filters. An HTTP filter is used to modify or decorate the request and response, without actually changing the intention of the request. For example, to encrypt or decrypt the contents of the response or request, respectively, an HTTP filter would be used. On the client side, the Decorator pattern is not implemented as an HTTP filter, but as a series of encapsulations. Each encapsulation implements an added value functionality.

Figure 9-12 is a graphical representation of the architecture in terms of layers.

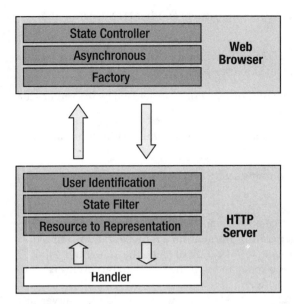

Figure 9-12. *Layered architecture of the State Navigation pattern*

In Figure 9-12, the client side has three layers: Factory, Asynchronous, and State Navigation. The layers Asynchronous and Factory were outlined and implemented in Chapter 2. The layer State Navigation is an implementation of the State Navigation pattern on the client side. The server side has multiple layers, and the User Identification and Resource to Representation layers are modularized implementations of the Permutations pattern. The State Filter layer is an implementation of the State Navigation pattern on the server side. Throughout the rest of this chapter, I will discuss the State Navigation and State Filter layers.

Processing the Requests on the Client

Starting with the client side, the purpose of the State Navigation layer is to send and retrieve the state. As illustrated by the protocol communication, the sequence of events for downloading a resource and its associated state is as follows:

1. Download a URL's representation in the browser.

2. When the download has completed, the HTML body event onload is executed.

3. In the onload event, the XMLHttpRequest object requests the state associated with the resource.

4. The state is downloaded and used to manipulate the HTML document to fill data in an HTML form or to manipulate elements in the HTML document.

If the HTML page contains a Submit button or another HTML element that can be used to send data to the server, the State Navigation layer must be used. Not using the State Navigation layer bypasses the pattern and could corrupt the state. Generally, the sequence of events used to implement the State Navigation pattern is as follows:

1. Clicking, checking, or some other HTML action triggers another HTML action that causes an HTML event.

2. The HTML event, which could be an HTML POST or button onclick, builds a state that is used by the client State Navigation layer to create a request.

3. The request is sent to the server, which may or may not be processed by the server-side State Filter layer, and is passed on to the handler.

4. If the State Filter layer filters the request, it does so transparently without modifying the contents.

5. The handler generates content that contains a link used by the State Navigation pattern to load the next resource.

In this client-side sequence of events, the State Navigation pattern has three responsibilities: populating the representation with state, generating a state from a representation, and redirecting the page when necessary. The client-side ramification of using the State Navigation pattern is that a representation must possess a state, and that the state can be submitted and retrieved only by using the State Navigation pattern.

The state and reference information that is passed between the client side and server side uses XML, but could include other formats such as JSON. For the scope of this pattern, XML is the default data format. The choice of whether to use another format is left up to you.

Using the State Navigation from an HTML Page

On the client side, the implemented HTML page needs to carry only two major tasks: loading and saving the state, and initiating the state loading and saving process. From an architectural perspective, the HTML page initiates a call to the State Navigation layer, which will call back into the page to carry out the application-specific persistence method calls.

Following is an example implementation of the State Navigation pattern that contains an HTML form as illustrated in Figures 9-4 to 9-7:

```
<html>
<head>
<title>Sample Page</title>
</head>
<script language="JavaScript" src="../lib/factory.js"></script>
<script language="JavaScript" src="../lib/asynchronous.js"></script>
<script language="JavaScript" src="../lib/xmlhelpers.js"></script>
<script language="JavaScript" src="../lib/statecontroller.js"></script>
<script language="JavaScript" type="text/javascript">
StateController.onSaveState = function() {
    return this.saveForm( document.getElementById( "BasicForm"));
}

StateController.onLoadState = function( status, xmlstate) {
    this.loadForm( xmlstate);
}
```

```
</script>
<body onload="StateController.loadState()">
<div id="replace">Nothing</div>
<form id="BasicForm" name="BasicForm"
      onsubmit=" return StateController.saveState()"
      action="/ajax/chap07/link.xml" method="POST" >
    <input name="param1" type="text" /><br />
    <input name="param2" type="text" /><br />
    <input type="submit"/><br />
    <input type="reset"/>
</form>
</body>
</html>
```

To explain the HTML page, the code will be cross-referenced to the events that are used to load or save the state.

When an HTML page has finished loading, an event is triggered to indicate that the document is complete and can be manipulated. The event onload is attached to the HTML body tag and assigned to calling the method StateController.loadState(). The variable StateController is a global instance that implements the client-side State Navigation layer. This variable is a global instance because an HTML page cannot contain two states, and hence making the variable a type would be pointless. The StateController.loadState() method is called when the HTML document has finished loading and is used to retrieve the state of the HTML page from the server side. In the implementation of the loadState method, the XMLHttpRequest object is called and asks the server for the state of the page. The server eventually responds, and StateController will automatically call the StateController.onLoadState method defined in the HTML page. The onLoadState method is called after the server has responded with the associated state of the page. The client is responsible for picking apart what the state is and updating the HTML page with the information. In the example HTML page, the method loadForm is called and delegates the state restoration to a StateController-implemented standard function that deserializes the incoming state.

Saving the state is a bit more complicated because it requires that the HTML page interject the HTML form-posting process. To interject, the onsubmit event is implemented and calls the method StateController.saveState(). Calling the saveState method will trigger a State Navigation–defined process that calls the StateController.onSaveState method defined in the HTML page. Within the onSaveState method, the HTML page will generate a user-defined state that is saved. In the case of the HTML page, the method saveForm is called, which will serialize a particular HTML form. In most cases, the Representation Morphing pattern is implemented.

From the perspective of the HTML page, saving and loading the page state requires making the right calls at the right moment. What is important is that the user has the ability to define when and how the state associated with the HTML page is managed. This means that a page state could be saved as the result of a specific hyperlink that is clicked, and that the page state is reloaded as the result of some button that is clicked. Or the developer could choose to ignore saving the state by adding a Cancel or Ignore button. It is the choice of the developer.

As a matter of simplicity and illustration of the Representation Morphing pattern, I chose to define the state of the HTML page as an HTML form, but I could just as easily have defined it as being some text in an HTML div section. It is the responsibility of the HTML methods onSaveState and onLoadState to load and save the data.

In the HTML page implementation, the methods onSaveState and onLoadState could be construed as black magic in that they generate and process data without explaining what the data is. What happens is that the data generated and processed by the HTML page is a blob that is sent and received from the server. Only the client needs to know what the data is, and not the State Navigation implementation. In the example, the variable StateController uses XML persistence as a default persistence format. As a result, when the client uses the standard method calls saveForm and loadForm, the generated data is XML based and would be identical to the following:

```
<state>
    <html-page>
        <form id="BasicForm" >
            <element id='param1' type='text'>Value 1</element>
            <element id='param2' type='text'>Value 2</element>
        </form>
    </html-page>
</state>
```

The root node is data, and contained within it is the HTML state that includes reference information about the state, and the state information associated with the HTML page. Specifically, the individual XML tags are identified as follows:

- html-page: Is a parent XML element used to contain the state details associated with an HTML page.

- form: Is a parent XML element used to contain the values for all HTML form elements.

- element: Identifies a state that is associated with an HTML form element. In the example, all HTML form elements are associated with the XML tag element. But it is also possible to use the id attribute as an XML element identifier. This results in the transformation <param1 ... /> for the XML element with the attribute value param1. Which approach you use depends on your preference; either approach is acceptable.

For consistency, the state that is sent is identical to the state that is received.

The Details of the State Navigation

StateController is a variable instance and a custom single kind of a type. StateController could have been defined as a type that is instantiated, but that would be adding unnecessary complexity. As I am explaining the technical details of StateController, I won't explain all of the code at once. What I will explain is the source code in three pieces: the first piece contains the data members, the second piece contains the logic used to load the state, and the last piece contains the logic to save the state.

Following is the code piece that defines the data members of the StateController variable:

```
var StateController = {
    username: null,
    password: null,
    postURL: null,

    constPageStateHeader : "X-Page-State",
    constPageWindowName  : "X-Page-Window-Name",
    constPageOriginalURL : "X-Page-Original-URL",
    constPageWindowNamePrefix : "StateController",
    constResourceStateContentType : "application/xml",
    constURLStateIdentifier : "/state",

    constStateTag : "state",
    constHtmlPageStateTag : "html-page",
```

StateController has nine data members, which all relate to sending and receiving data to
and from the server. The data members username and password are the authentication identifiers used when accessing protected resources. The data member postURL indicates the URL
used to post the data to the server. In a traditional HTML form, postURL would be the action
attribute identifier. As an optimization, if an HTML form is serialized, the data member postURL
is assigned the HTML form action attribute value. The remaining data members are used to
dissect the communications between the client and server, and to generate and parse the
XML data.

Loading the State

When the HTML page is loaded, the event onload is triggered and causes the HTML state to be
retrieved and added to the HTML page. The onload event is the usual place to put the state-
loading functionality, but any other event could be used. Regardless of where the state-loading
functionality is added, three functions are related to state loading: client implementation,
default form loading, and overall controlling functionality.

Following is the default client implementation:

```
onLoadState : function( status, responseXML) { },
```

The method onLoadState, when it is not implemented by the HTML page, is an empty
implementation that does nothing. In the example HTML page, the onLoadState method
called the method loadForm, which is used as a prepackaged function to load the state of an
HTML form. The method loadForm is implemented as follows:

```
extractFormData : function( element, objData) {
    if( element.nodeType == 1) {
        if( element.nodeName == "form") {
            objData.formId = element.attributes.getNamedItem( "id").nodeValue;
            objData.formNode = document.forms[ objData.formId];
        }
```

```
        else if( element.nodeName == "element") {
            if( objData.formNode != null) {
                var elementIdentifier =
element.attributes.getNamedItem( "id").nodeValue;
                if( element.childNodes[ 0] != null) {
                    var elementValue = element.childNodes[ 0].nodeValue;
                    objData.formNode.elements[
elementIdentifier].value = elementValue;
                }
            }
        }
    }
},
loadForm : function( xmlState) {
    this.verify = this.extractFormData;
    var objData = new Object();
    XMLIterateElements( this, objData, xmlState);
},
```

The implementation of the method loadForm is relatively Spartan, and is used to prepare the iteration of the XML file by using the standard function XMLIterateElements and the user-defined function extractFormData. The assignment of the this.verify method is used to determine whether an iterated XML element is of interest to the user. The creation of the objData variable is required for the function XMLIterateElements and will contain the found data. The combination of objData and the this.verify method deserialize XML content into JavaScript data members. The function XMLIterateElements is used to process an XML file and is implemented as follows:

```
function XMLIterateElements( objVerify, objData, element) {
    objVerify.verify( element, objData);
    for( var i = 0; i < element.childNodes.length; i ++) {
        XMLIterateElements( objVerify, objData, element.childNodes[ i]);
    }
}
```

The function XMLIterateElements has three parameters. The parameter objVerify is an object instance that is called to process an XML element. The parameter objData is a data object that is manipulated by the objVerify.verify method. An object instance is used so that a verify implementation can access the data members of a current object instance. The parameter element represents an XML node. After having called the objVerify.verify method, the child nodes of the element XML node are iterated, and for every iteration the function XMLIterateElements is called recursively. The result is that for each and every element, the method objVerify.verify is called. The purpose of objData is to allow the method objVerify.verify to assign some data members that can be referenced at some later point, during and after the iteration of all the XML elements.

Let's look back at the implementation of loadForm. Notice that it is calling the function XMLIterateElements and that the objVerify.verify method refers to the method extractFormData. Looking at the implementation of extractFormData, you can see that a number of XML DOM methods (for example, `element.[example method]`) are called. What happens in the `extractFormData` method is that the XML elements `form` and `element` are searched for. If a `form` XML element is found, it is a reference to an HTML form that is retrieved from the current HTML page by using the method `document.forms[objData.formId]`. The HTML form reference is needed to assign individual HTML form elements. If an `element` XML element is found, the value is assigned by retrieving the identifier from the XML attribute (`element.attributes.getNamedItem("id").nodeValue`) and the child value (`element.childNodes[0].nodeValue`). The form element is assigned the value by using the reference `objData.formNode.elements[elementIdentifier].value = elementValue`. In the example, there is no attempt made to test whether the HTML element is a check box or list box. This was done on purpose to keep the explanation simple, and in the complete implementation of `extractFormData` those additional attributes would be tested.

The method `loadState` is used to begin the HTML page-loading process and is defined as follows:

```
loadState : function() {
    if( location.hash != null) {
        var asynch = new Asynchronous();
        var thisReference = this;
        asynch.openCallback = function( xmlhttp) {
            if( location.hash.length == 0) {
                xmlhttp.setRequestHeader(
                    thisReference.constPageStateHeader, "none");
            }
            else {
                xmlhttp.setRequestHeader( thisReference.constPageStateHeader,
                    location.hash.slice(1));
            }
            xmlhttp.setRequestHeader( "Accept",
                thisReference.constResourceStateContentType);
            thisReference.verifyWindowName();
            xmlhttp.setRequestHeader( thisReference.constPageWindowName,
                window.name);
        }
        var xmlhttp = asynch._xmlhttp;
        asynch.complete = function( status, statusText, responseText, responseXML) {
            thisReference.verify = thisReference.extractUserData;
            var objData = new Object();
            XMLIterateElements( thisReference, objData, responseXML);
            if( objData.foundElement) {
                thisReference.onLoadState( status, objData.foundElement);
            }
            location.replace( location.pathname + "#" +
                xmlhttp.getResponseHeader( thisReference.constPageStateHeader));
        }
```

```
            asynch.username = this.username;
            asynch.password = this.password;
            var splitLocation = location.href.split( "#");
            asynch.get( splitLocation[ 0] + this.constURLStateIdentifier);
        }
    },
```

In the implementation of loadState, the Asynchronous class that was explained in Chapter 2 is used. The implementation is relatively straightforward in that an HTTP GET is executed, as illustrated by the method call asynch.get. To let the server know that the request is a state request, the HTTP headers identifying the state (X-Page-State, X-Page-Window-Name) are sent by using the method xmlhttp.setRequestHeader. If the HTTP headers were not present, the server side would consider the request as a generic HTTP GET. The HTTP headers are used, as they are easy to verify for existence. Another approach would have been to search for the state keyword in the URL, but that would require parsing the URL. The method thisReference.verifyWindowName is used to generate a State Navigation pattern–compliant window name if there is no window name. Additionally, to identify the request as a state request, the /state is appended to the URL when the asynch.get method is called. Not adding the /state would result in confusing the proxy and potentially having two different representations with a single URL, and as per the Permutations pattern, doing so would be incorrect.

In the implementation of the asynch.complete inlined function, the returned XML document is processed. The XMLIterateElements function is used to find the XML node that contains the HTML page state. If the XML node (objData.foundElement) is found, the loading of the state is passed to the HTML page–implemented function onLoadState. Because a state is retrieved and the server has the power to determine the state identifier, the State Navigation layer must replace the current state identifier. The state identifier is replaced by using the location.replace method so that the old page will be replaced in the history log. Not using the location.replace method would result in the addition of an HTML page to the history, and that would confuse the user from a Forward and Back button navigation perspective. For example, if the history contained /other/url, /resource, /resource2, not using the replace method would generate a history /other/url, /resource, /resource#11, /resource2, instead of /other/url, /resource#11, /resource2.

Saving the State

The implementation of saving the state requires three methods: onSaveState implemented by the client to save the state, the helper method saveForm to convert an HTML form into a state, and saveState to initiate the state persistence.

The method onSaveState needs to be implemented by the HTML page, but the default is that the StateController provides an empty implementation that does nothing. If StateController did not provide a default implementation, a JavaScript error would result. Following is the default empty implementation of the method onSaveState:

```
onSaveState : function() {
    return "";
},
```

The default implementation of onSaveState illustrates the most important thing that any implementation must do: return a buffer that contains the persisted state. It is expected that the buffer that is returned is formatted in XML and that the returned data is XML compliant. The onSaveState-generated XML is inserted as a child of the html-child XML element.

In the HTML client, the implemented method onSaveState calls the method saveForm, which is used to convert the HTML form into an XML data structure. Following is the implementation of the method saveForm:

```
saveForm : function( form) {
    this.postURL = form.action;
    var buffer = "";
    buffer += "<form id=\"" + form.name + "\" >\n";
    for( var i = 0; i < form.elements.length; i++) {
            if( form.elements[ i].type != "submit" &&
                form.elements[ i].type != "reset") {
                buffer += "<element id='" + form.elements[i].name + "' type='" +
                            form.elements[ i].type + "'>" +
                            form.elements[ i].value + "</element>\n";
            }
    }
    buffer += "</form>\n";
    return buffer;
},
```

In the implementation of saveForm, the parameter |form represents the HTML form to persist. The first step of the implementation is to assign to the local instance the form post URL (this.postURL) from the form.action value. Next, the root form XML element is created and assigned to the name of the form. Then the individual HTML form elements are added to the state by iterating the collection form.elements. All HTML form elements are added to the XML data structure so long as the elements are not of type submit or reset. In the saveForm method implementation, only text box elements can be persisted. Normally, though, all HTML form elements could be persisted, but for this explanation the implementation was kept simple.

Calling the method saveState, which is implemented as follows, starts the saving of the state:

```
saveState : function() {
    var buffer = "<" + this.constStateTag + ">";
    buffer += "<" + this.constHtmlPageStateTag + ">\n";
    buffer += this.onSaveState()
    buffer += "</" + this.constHtmlPageStateTag + ">\n";
    buffer += "</" + this.constStateTag + ">";
    var request = new Asynchronous();
    var thisReference = this;
    var oldPath = location.pathname;
    request.openCallback = function( xmlhttp) {
        if( location.hash.length == 0) {
            xmlhttp.setRequestHeader( thisReference.constPageStateHeader, "none");
        }
        else {
            xmlhttp.setRequestHeader( thisReference.constPageStateHeader,
                location.hash.slice(1));
        }
```

```
            thisReference.verifyWindowName();
            xmlhttp.setRequestHeader( thisReference.constPageWindowName, window.name);
            var splitLocation = location.href.split( "#");
            xmlhttp.setRequestHeader(
    thisReference.constPageOriginalURL, splitLocation[ 0]);
        }
        var xmlhttp = request._xmlhttp;
        request.complete = function( status, statusText, responseText, responseXML) {
            if(status == 200 && responseXML != null) {
                thisReference.verify = thisReference.extractLink;
                var objData = new Object();
                XMLIterateElements( thisReference, objData, responseXML);
                location.replace( oldPath + "#" + xmlhttp.getResponseHeader(
                    thisReference.constPageStateHeader));
                location.href = objData.redirectURL;
            }
        }
        request.username = this.username;
        request.password = this.password;
        request.post( this.postURL, this.constResourceStateContentType,
            buffer.length, buffer);
        return false;
}
```

The implementation of the method saveState is more complicated and is responsible for generating the XML state and for sending the state to the server by using an HTTP POST. The variable buffer, and those lines at the beginning of saveState that reference buffer, are used to build the XML state. In the building of the state, the method this.onSaveState is called, letting the HTML page generate the custom parts of the persistence. After the XML state is constructed, it needs to be posted to the server.

As in previous pattern implementations, an HTTP POST is created by using the Asynchronous class type outlined in Chapter 2. What is unique in this posting is the assignment of the custom HTTP headers (X-Page-State, X-Page-Window-Name, and X-Page-Original-URL) and the processing of the response. In the inlined function implementation of request.openCallback, the state reference identifier is extracted from the local URL as stored in the variable location. hash. If the location.hash value does not exist, a none is sent as the page state header to indicate that a state identifier should be created. Otherwise, the location.hash value is sent, minus the prefixed # character. What is new for this request is the assignment of the original URL (X-Page-Original-URL or constPageOriginalURL). This assignment is necessary so the server can cross-reference the state with the resource. Moving to the end of the saveState method implementation, you can see that the method request.post is used to post the data to the server.

When the HTTP POST returns, the inlined method implementation request.complete is called to process the returned XML. The returned XML looks similar to the following:

```
<data>
    <link id="redirect" href="/ajax/chap07/page2" />
</data>
```

The returned XML content is processed by the inlined method `request.complete`. In the inlined method `request.complete`, the returned XML content is parsed by using the function `XMLIterateElements`. The function `XMLIterateElements` is a helper function used to process the returned XML content. Specifically, the function `XMLIterateElements` extracts the destination link from the returned XML content, which in the example happens to be the URL `/ajax/chap07/page2`. In the inlined method, the extracted URL is assigned to the variable `objData.redirectURL` by the function `XMLIterateElements`. But before the extracted URL is reassigned, the state hash code is updated by calling the `location.replace` method. Then after the script replaces the URL, the script can navigate to the extracted URL by using the method `location.href`.

A little side note needs to be added about the purpose of the returned XML. Figure 9-3 shows the problems when HTTP `POST` is used to navigate from HTML page to HTML page. As the State Navigation pattern navigates using the returned XML, the posting of the same content multiple times does not occur. Navigation occurs when using a script that uses HTTP `GET` techniques that are called after a successful posting. And the posting of the state twice is impossible because the state identifier is incremented for each posting. So if a resource is responsible for charging a credit card, posting the same content multiple times can be caught by the server and curtailed.

Processing the Requests on the Server

After the HTML page has been implemented and the state has been loaded and saved on the client side, the remaining responsibility lies with the server. The server will receive the state and store it somewhere, and send the state when it is asked for. However, the general pattern implementation on the server does not attempt to interpret the state, because doing so would add processing that is not necessary. The exception occurs when the processing of the state is application related. The state is processed on the server side by using HTTP handlers.

Knowing When and How to Trigger HTTP Filters

When implementing an HTTP filter, the idea is not to process the request, but to modify and redirect the request. With respect to the HTTP protocol, there are two ways to trigger an HTTP filter: URL and HTTP header. It is possible to trigger an HTTP filter based on some piece of data sent to or generated by the server in the HTTP body. For example, in the state sent to the server, there could be a keyword indicating further actions for the HTTP filter. But using a piece of data in the HTTP body itself is a bad idea because it requires extra processing by the server. The data in the HTTP body is specific to the HTTP handler and should be considered as a single entity. This does not mean that an HTTP filter, after it has been triggered, cannot inspect and manipulate the payload. What this means is that for trigger purposes only, the URL or HTTP header is inspected.

Let's go through the differences of URL vs. HTTP header by using the State Navigation pattern as an example. In the section "Managing State at the Protocol Level," an HTTP header is used to request a state that is associated with a URL, as illustrated by the following HTTP request part:

```
GET /ajax/chap07/page1/state HTTP/1.1
Accept: application/ajax-state
Accept-Language: en-us,en;q=0.5
Accept-Encoding: gzip,deflate
Accept-Charset: ISO-8859-1,utf-8;q=0.7,*;q=0.7
X-Page-Window-Name: window-2005-10-03-10-10-10-1245
X-Page-State: none
```

The request has two pieces of information that could trigger a filter: URL ([url]/state) and HTTP header (X-Page-State). To trigger a filter via a URL, the URL must be processed. Processing a URL is a relatively expensive step and potentially buggy. The bugginess results when a URL has the same text as a trigger. The header is necessary only when the state is retrieved, and that occurs only when the XMLHttpRequest object is used. Thus adding an HTTP header is not complicated or inconvenient. Which solution you use depends on your URLs and what you are comfortable with.

The rule of thumb is that an HTTP header can be used when both the client and the server are capable of processing the custom header, and a URL should be used whenever the server knows what kind of client will process the data.

When implementing an HTTP filter, a basis class that executes the trigger and runs the filter action is illustrated by using the following Java filter code. On other platforms and programming languages, the code will be similar because other platforms also have the concept of an HTTP filter.

```java
public abstract class TriggerFilter implements Filter {
    public abstract Object initializeRequest();
    public abstract void destroyRequest( Object objData);
    public abstract boolean isTrigger( Object objData,
        HttpServletRequest httprequest, HttpServletResponse httpresponse);
    public abstract void runFilter( Object objData,
        HttpServletRequest httprequest, HttpServletResponse httpresponse,
        FilterChain chain) throws IOException, ServletException;
    public void doFilter(ServletRequest request, ServletResponse response,
        FilterChain chain) throws IOException, ServletException {
        HttpServletRequest httprequest = (HttpServletRequest)request;
        HttpServletResponse httpresponse = (HttpServletResponse)response;
        Object data = initializeRequest();
        if( isTrigger( data, httprequest, httpresponse)) {
            runFilter( data, httprequest, httpresponse, chain);
        }
        else {
            chain.doFilter( request, response);
        }
        destroyRequest( data);
    }
}
```

When implementing a Java filter, the class implements the Filter interface. Two methods are not illustrated: init and destroy, which are used to initialize and destroy, respectively, the filter instance. They are not illustrated for simplicity purposes. The class TriggerFilter is implemented as an abstract class because TriggerFilter on its own is not very useful and provides a basic functionality that would otherwise be constantly implemented. TriggerFilter implements the Template pattern, and therefore to have anything happen, some class has to subclass TriggerFilter.

The method doFilter is part of the interface Filter and is called whenever an HTTP request is made. When the method doFilter is called depends on the order of the filter in the configuration file. The order in the configuration file is a Java feature, and other platforms may have other ways to define the order indicating when a filter is called.

When the method doFilter is called, the parameters request and response are converted into the types HttpServletRequest and HttpServletResponse, respectively. This is necessary because the Http types offer methods and properties that help process an HTTP request.

The methods isTrigger and runFilter are declared abstract, which means any class that extends TriggerFilter will need to implement the abstract methods. The method isTrigger is called to check whether the request should be processed by the implemented subclass. The method runFilter is executed to process the HTTP request. If isTrigger returns a value of false, the HTTP request processing continues as usual, and in the case of the example the method chain.doFilter is called.

The State Navigation pattern is implemented by using the TriggerFilter class, but before the architecture of the State Navigation pattern is detailed, the Permutations Pattern is rewritten to use the TriggerFilter class.

Rewriting the Permutations Pattern Implementation

The purpose of rewriting the Permutations pattern is to illustrate how the pattern can be implemented as a filter instead of a handler. The difference between a handler and filter is not huge, but there are some structural changes. Following is the implementation of the Permutations pattern using Java:

```java
public class ResourceEngineFilter extends TriggerFilter {
    private FilterConfig _filterConfig;

    private Router _router;
    private String _clsRewriter;

    public void init(FilterConfig filterConfig) throws ServletException {
        _filterConfig = filterConfig;
        try {
            _router = (Router)ResourceEngineFilter.class.getClassLoader().loadClass(
                filterConfig.getInitParameter("router")).newInstance();
            _router.setProperty( "base-directory", baseDirectory);
            _clsRewriter = filterConfig.getInitParameter("rewriter");
        }
        catch (Exception e) {
            throw new ServletException( "Could not instantiate classes ", e);
        }

    }
```

```
    public Object initializeRequest() {
        return null;
    }
    public void destroyRequest( Object objData) {

    }
    public boolean isTrigger(Object objData, HttpServletRequest request,
        HttpServletResponse response) {
        if (_router.IsResource( request)) {
            return true;
        }
        return false;
    }
    public void runFilter(Object objData, HttpServletRequest request,
        HttpServletResponse response, FilterChain chain)
        throws IOException, ServletException {
        Rewriter rewriter;
        try {
            rewriter = (Rewriter)ResourceEngineFilter.class.getClassLoader().
                loadClass(_clsRewriter).newInstance();
        }
        catch( Exception ex) {
            return;
        }
        _router.WriteRedirection( rewriter, request);
    }
}
```

In the example class ResourceEngineFilter, the methods isTrigger and runFilter are implemented, as required by TriggerFilter. The method init is used to initialize the filter and retrieve the filter configuration information, and specifically the base-directory that is used by the class FilterRouter or the Router interface instance.

In the implementation of init, the default Router instance _router is instantiated by using the configuration declaration item router. In contrast, in the Permutations pattern implementation, the instantiation of Router was hard-coded. Regardless of how the Router interface instance is instantiated, in the example of ResourceEngineFilter, the Router interface instance must be stateless with respect to the HTTP request. The statelessness is required because the Router instance is associated with the ResourceEngineFilter, which is also stateless. What is not stateless, but is instantiated with every triggered filter request, is the Rewriter interface instance. This is because the implementations of the Rewriter will require multiple calls, and the calls will reference some state generated by the HTTP request.

The statelessness results in a modified version of the Router interface that is defined as follows:

```
public interface Router {
    public void setConfiguration( String key, String value);
    public boolean IsResource(HttpServletRequest request);
    public void WriteRedirection( Rewriter rewriter, HttpServletRequest request);
}
```

The modification of the interface involves the addition of the setConfiguration method, which assigns the configuration information. The configuration information is used by the Router interface implementation when figuring out whether a request is a resource or a specific representation. The method WriteRedirection has been modified to include the parameter rewriter. As the configuration information is passed to the Router interface instance, having the parameter rewriter may not seem necessary. It is necessary because otherwise a hidden dependency in the implementation of the interfaces is created, complicating the development of modular code.

The implementations of the Rewriter and Router interfaces remain as illustrated in the Permutations pattern. The resulting implementation is a prototype example for the server side that can be used to filter implementations. When implementing the Decorator pattern, the filters should be stacked by using the HTTP filter mechanism. What is important is the ordering of the filters, because some HTTP filter implementations have an ordering dependency.

Implementing the State Layer

In Figure 9-12, the Resource to Representation filter appears after the State filter, which is important so that not all requests need to be processed. For example, when retrieving the associated state of a resource, it is not necessary to execute a handler. The State layer captures the associated state request and processes it directly.

Managing the State Calls

As per the previous discussion, the filter needs to implement two functionalities: storing the state and retrieving the state. The State layer will extend the TriggerFilter class, and the implementation will be outlined in four pieces.

The first piece is the filter initialization:

```
public class StateFilter extends TriggerFilter {
    private FilterConfig _filterConfig;
    private StateManager _stateManager;
    private String _resourceStateContentType;
    private String _XPageState;
    private String _XPageWindowName;
    private String _URLStateIdentifier;
    private int _URLStateIdentifierLength;
    private String _XPageOriginalURL;
```

```
public void init(FilterConfig filterConfig) throws ServletException {
    _filterConfig = filterConfig;
    _resourceStateContentType = filterConfig.getInitParameter(
        "resource-state-content-type");
    _XPageState = filterConfig.getInitParameter( "page-state-header");
    _XPageWindowName = filterConfig.getInitParameter( "page-window-name");
    _URLStateIdentifier = filterConfig.getInitParameter(
        "url-state-identifier");
    _URLStateIdentifierLength = _URLStateIdentifier.length();
    _XPageOriginalURL = filterConfig.getInitParameter( "page-original-url");
    try {
        String strClass =
            filterConfig.getInitParameter("state-manager");
        _stateManager = (StateManager)
            StateFilter.class.getClassLoader().loadClass(
                filterConfig.getInitParameter(
                "state-manager")).newInstance();
    }
    catch (Exception e) {
        throw new ServletException( "Could not instantiate _stateManager", e);
    }
}
```

In the implementation of StateFilter, the data member assignments are dynamic and can be specified in the HTTP server configuration file. Not all data members will be explained because that would be too lengthy and redundant. The data members _resourceStateContentType and _XPageState are the counterparts to the client-side-defined StateController. constResourceStateContentType and StateController.constPageStateHeader data members, respectively. The data member _stateManager is the state manager implementation. The idea is that the filter manages the state retrieval and storage calls, whereas _stateManager is the implementation of the retrieval and storage of the state. By separating the actual doing from the calling functionality, the doing can determine which persistence medium is used. For the scope of this book, the persistence medium is the memory, but could also be implemented to use a database or hard disk.

The second piece of code relates to the object used to manage state and resource reference information that is created on a per request instance and is passed to the isTrigger and runFilter routines. The implementations for initializeRequest and destroyRequest are as follows:

```
private class Data {
    public String _method;
    public String _stateHeader;
    public String _windowName;
    public int _operation;
    public String _path;
    public void reset() {
        _method = null;
        _stateHeader = null;
        _operation = OP_NONE;
```

```
            _path = null;
            _windowName = null;
        }
    }
    public Object initializeRequest() {
        return new Data();
    }
    public void destroyRequest( Object objData) {
    }
```

The class Data is declared as a private class and is used only in the scope of the StateFilter class. Five publicly declared data members reference the HTTP method, HTTP state header, window name, path representing the URL, and locally defined operation type. In the implementation of initializeRequest, a new instance of Data is returned. There is no implementation for destroyRequest because it is not necessary to do anything when the object is destroyed.

The third piece of the State filter is the code to test whether the request or post is related to manage the server-side state:

```
private static final int OP_NONE = 0;
private static final int OP_RETRIEVE = 1;
private static final int OP_POST = 2;

public boolean isTrigger( Object inpdata, HttpServletRequest httprequest,
    HttpServletResponse httpresponse) {
    String tail = httprequest.getRequestURI().substring(
        httprequest.getRequestURI().length() - _URLStateIdentifierLength);
    String stateHeader = httprequest.getHeader( _XPageState);
    Data data = (Data)inpdata;

    if( tail.compareTo( _URLStateIdentifier) == 0) {
        data._path = httprequest.getRequestURI().substring( 0,
            httprequest.getRequestURI().length() - _URLStateIdentifierLength);
    }
    else {
        if( stateHeader == null) {
            return false;
        }
        data._path = httprequest.getRequestURI();
    }

    data._method = httprequest.getMethod();
    data._stateHeader = stateHeader;
    data._operation = OP_NONE;
    data._windowName = httprequest.getHeader( _XPageWindowName);
    if( data._method.compareTo( "GET") == 0) {
        data._operation = OP_RETRIEVE;
        return true;
    }
```

```
        else if( data._method.compareTo( "PUT") == 0 ||
            data._method.compareTo( "POST") == 0) {
            if( _resourceStateContentType.compareTo(
                httprequest.getContentType()) == 0) {
                data._path = httprequest.getHeader( _XPageOriginalURL);
                data._operation = OP_POST;
                return true;
            }
        }
        data.reset();
        return false;
    }
```

The method isTrigger is used to determine whether the method runFilter should execute, and if so, isTrigger populates the Data type instance. That way, if runFilter executes, runFilter will not need to organize the details of the state or resource call. For the method isTrigger, the first parameter inpdata is the object instantiated by the method initializeRequest. Hence the first step of isTrigger is to typecast the parameter to the type Data and assign the instance to the variable data.

The variable tail is the end of the URL and is used to test whether the state identifier /state is present. If the identifier does exist as per the decision (if(tail.compareTo(_URLStateIdentifier...), the URL assigned to data._path must not contain the state keyword. If the URL does not contain the state keyword, a test is made to see whether the state header (stateHeader) exists. If the state header does not exist, the request is not a State Navigation request. If the state header does exist, the URL assigned to data._path is the same as the input URL. The example illustrates testing for two conditions, but it is possible to test for only a single condition and make a decision. The example of two conditions was shown to illustrate the code for each condition.

If the code after the initial decision block is reached, we are assured the request is a State Navigation request and the standard variables can be assigned. The variables data._method, data._stateHeader, and data._windowName are assigned to the HTTP method, HTTP header, and window name, respectively, so that they may be used by the runFilter method.

The last decision block in the implementation of isTrigger tests which State filter operation is being executed. The operation can be one of two values: HTTP GET or HTTP POST. Support is added for the HTTP PUT, which is classified as an HTTP POST. If either decision block returns a true value, the data member data_operation is assigned to OP_RETRIEVE or OP_POST.

Having isTrigger return a true value will cause the runFilter method to be executed, which is implemented as follows:

```
public void runFilter(Object inpdata, HttpServletRequest httprequest,
    HttpServletResponse httpresponse, FilterChain chain)
        throws IOException, ServletException {
    Data data = (Data)inpdata;
    if( data._operation == OP_RETRIEVE) {
        State state;
        if( data._stateHeader.compareTo( "none") == 0) {
            state = _stateManager.getEmptyState( data._path, data._windowName);
        }
```

```
        else {
            state = _stateManager.copyState( data._stateHeader, data._path,
                data._windowName);
        }
        httpresponse.setContentType( _resourceStateContentType);
        httpresponse.setHeader( _XPageState, state.getStateIdentifier());
        httpresponse.setStatus( 200, "success");
        PrintWriter out = httpresponse.getWriter();
        out.print( state.getBuffer());
        return;
    }
    else if( data._operation == OP_POST) {
        ServletInputStream input = httprequest.getInputStream();
        byte[] bytearray = new byte[ httprequest.getContentLength()];
        input.read( bytearray);
        State state = _stateManager.copyState( data._stateHeader, data._path,
            data._windowName);
        state.setBuffer( new String( bytearray).toString());
        httpresponse.addHeader( _XPageState, state.getStateIdentifier());
        chain.doFilter( httprequest, httpresponse);
        return;
    }
}
```

In the implementation of runFilter, the first parameter is the object instance allocated by the method initializeRequest. And as with isTrigger, a typecast is made to convert the type and assign it to the variable data. From there, the decision blocks are based on the data members of the variable data that were assigned in isTrigger.

There are two state operations: retrieve state and post state. The first decision block (== OP_RETRIEVE) tests whether the operation is a state retrieval, and the second decision block (== OP_POST) tests whether the operation is a post. If the operation is a state retrieval and the asked-for state is none (indicating that the client has not associated a state with an HTML page), an empty state is created. A new empty state is created by using the method getEmptyStateHashcode(), and the method getHashcode() retrieves the hash code of a state. By default, when creating an empty state, a hash code will automatically be created. Using the method copyState copies the old state to a new state, and is explained shortly. After calling the copyState method, various methods on the httpresponse variable are called to generate the response.

If the operation is a posting, the posted stream is retrieved from the request by using the method input.read. The read buffer is stored in the variable bytearray, which happens to be an array of bytes. As when a state is retrieved, the state is copied by using the method copyState, and then assigned by using the method state.setBuffer. The state is copied from the original reference, and the new data overwrites the old. By copying a state, the state manager can create a trail of dependencies and associations that could be used by the state manager for optimization purposes. In the response, the newly generated state header is added by using the method addHeader.

The last and very important step is to call the method chain.doFilter because that allows the posting to be processed by a handler. This raises the question, "If the state is stored, why process it?" Let's say that I buy a ticket and fill out the form. When I click the Submit button, I want to buy the ticket; but when I click Back, I want to know the form details used to buy the ticket. Knowing the details, I can click Forward, and a ticket will not be bought twice—which would have happened if I had to click Submit. Therefore, to buy the ticket, some handler has to process the posted data, thus requiring the State filter to store the data and to let the handler process the data.

An Example State Manager Handler

In the `StateFilter` implementation, the variable `_stateManager` references the type `StateManager`. The type `StateManager` is an interface and manages the state that is posted and retrieved. Using interfaces makes it possible to separate intention from implementation as per the Bridge pattern.

The `State` interface is defined as follows:

```
public interface State {
    public String getURL();
    public void setURL( String URL);
    public String getWindowName();
    public void setWindowName( String windowname);
    public String getBuffer();
    public void setBuffer( String buffer);
    public String getStateIdentifier();
    public void setStateIdentifier( String hashcode);
}
```

The interface is based on four properties (`URL`, `WindowName`, `Buffer`, and `StateIdentifier`) that are implemented as getters and setters. The property `Buffer` is used to assign and retrieve the state sent by the client. The property `StateIdentifier` is used to assign and retrieve the state identifier of an HTML page. The property `URL` is the URL of the state, and finally `WindowName` is the associated window name. A minimal implementation of the `State` interface would define four private data members of the type `String`, `String`, `String`, and `String`.

What is more complicated is the implementation of the `StateManager` interface. An advanced implementation is beyond the scope of this book and depends on the context of the problem. The `StateManager` interface is important in the overall architecture because it is meant to be shared by servlets and external processes. A servlet could be used to manage and accumulate the state, whereas a J2EE server could be used to execute the transaction on the accumulated state. The idea is to implement the State filter and let the architecture manage the state. The `StateManager` interface is defined as follows:

```
public interface StateManager {
    public State getEmptyState( String url, String windowName);
    public State copyState( String stateIdentifier, String url, String windowName);
    public State[] getStateWindowName( String windowName);
}
```

The method `getStateWindowName` is used to retrieve an array `State` interface instance based on the name of a window. In the `StateFilter` class implementation, the method is not used because the method is intended to be used by some other processor carrying out some application logic. The method `getEmptyState` returns an empty `State` instance based on the URL and window name. The method `copyState` is used to transfer the state of one state instance to another. The method `copyState` might do a physical copy from one `State` instance to another `State` instance. Or the method `copyState` might do an in-place copy. It depends on the implementation of `StateManager` and is kept flexible for diversity purposes.

Pattern Highlights

The State Navigation pattern is used to solve the web application usability problem associated with HTTP `POST` and with the inconsistencies of running a web application using multiple web browsers. Using the State Navigation pattern, you can separate the state of an HTML page from the HTML page. With a separation, it is simpler to manage and accumulate state that can be used by a process to execute a single transaction. The State Navigation pattern requires active participation by the programmer to make everything work and as such could be prone to problems.

The following are the important highlights of the State Navigation pattern:

- The pattern is used to associate a state with an HTML page.

- The associated state is in most cases nonbinding, and therefore, if lost, will not cause an application malfunction. In the worst case, a lost state results in the user having to reenter the data.

- HTML frames, when used extensively, may pose a problem for the pattern because the way that the browser manages navigation is modified and typically frames are given a name. Normally frames are not problematic, but if HTML frames are used, you should build a prototype so that there are no surprises.

- The pattern makes it possible to build applications that are transaction friendly because the state is cumulated by a state manager and can later be referenced as single action.

- The pattern provides a consistent user interface because posting the data is a separate step that is not part of the web browser's history. This solves the problem of posting data again when navigating HTML pages based on the history.

- The window name is a physical window name but could be used as an application grouping. For example, if a window is popped up, a window name could be reused, creating a relation between two separate HTML windows without sacrificing the ability to try out permutations of a form.

CHAPTER 10

■ ■ ■

Infinite Data Pattern

Intent

The purpose of the Infinite Data pattern is to manage and display data that is seemingly infinite, in a timely manner.

Motivation

Databases have become very large and are growing by the day. For example, Google (the corporation) has databases so large that managing them literally requires thousands of computers. In the late nineties, the prevailing idea was to buy a very large computer with a dozen or so CPUs that would manage thousands of transactions. The question in the nineties was how to keep one or two or even four of those computers running. In the new millennium, the question has become how to manage the databases that have been building over the decades.

Many companies today have databases that cannot be managed by one or four large computers. Many companies—for instance, Google— have databases that are terabytes and potentially petabytes large. Just to provide context to the situation, today it is possible to buy a terabyte of storage for the price of a low-end computer. Think hard about that and consider the ramifications. Unless they happen to have one large movie, most people will have personal videos, holiday pictures, e-mails, documents, and other information that will fill the terabyte. Now imagine every person decides to publish 100 megabytes on the Internet. The fact that Google can organize such a gargantuan amount of data is amazing. You could do some mildly fun math showing that to iterate petabytes of information would seem virtually impossible. Yet we do sift through the Google data and we even think that Google is extremely fast.

The giganticness of the data poses some very interesting problems in that when a user queries for some data, which data is found? Imagine that you are a farmer who has 5,000 acres of farm land. Three months into the growing season you need to consider whether your land needs water or pesticides. What criteria do you use to decide how much water and pesticides are required? Having your 5,000 acres of land is not like having a garden on 1 acre. If you had a smaller piece of land, you could walk the land and look at the conditions of the entire property and make a quick decision. It is not possible to walk 5,000 acres and then decide what to do. You need to develop a strategy, or a plan of action.

When writing your own applications that execute long calculations, long transactions, or long queries, you cannot ask the user to wait for the answer to appear. You cannot justify the wait to the user by saying, "Please wait; we need to build a complete result set." The problem is that with a large and incomplete database, what constitutes a complete result set? To generate the result set, you need to redesign your strategy by implementing an asynchronous task that generates the results piecemeal. This is the essence of the Infinite Data pattern.

The pattern is called "Infinite Data" because the results that it generates are on a piece-meal basis. Each individual result when viewed independently is a piece of information. Put three results together, and you start to get an idea of the context. Put twenty results together, and the context of the data is clearer than when there were three results. Add more results, and the picture becomes less clear because of the variation of the data. Then to get a clear idea, you gather more results, and more results, and the results never stop because the data stream is infinite. As more data is retrieved, the context of the data is lost and you are just gathering data for the sake of data because it seems that there is an infinite data stream. The ramification of an infinite (seemingly) data stream is that you are literally finding a needle in the haystack.

Applicability

It would seem that the Infinite Data pattern works only in those scenarios where the data set being operating on is incomplete and large. However, the Infinite Data pattern is applicable to many scenarios, which are listed as follows:

- Querying and manipulating of very large data sets when the operation takes longer than what the user deems acceptable. For example, if an operation takes longer than the four-second rule, the Infinite Data pattern is applicable.

- Server-side operations that query other remote services that generate an incomplete result set. Examples include using Google, eBay, or Amazon.com web service application programming interfaces (APIs).

- Operations that take a long time to carry out and can be divided into smaller operations that can be considered intelligent guesses. The subdivided operation is an intelligent guess because the data that is generated is correct; however, the search is incomplete and therefore could miss important data. Missing important data is unavoidable because the problem of infinite data is too much data. The generated data can be displayed to indicate progress or allow further computations. Examples include the calculation of prime numbers and mechanical stress calculations.

- Any operation that could be converted into an asynchronous operation, allowing the application to generate results as the data arrives. Examples include asynchronous database queries or messaging applications.

In a nutshell, the Infinite Data pattern is used to present timely data from a seemingly infinite data set. The idea is to generate results incrementally so that an HTML page is built incrementally, and not as a single operation that can cause dramatic effects in the HTML client.

Associated Patterns

The Infinite Data pattern is used to send tasks to be executed and receive results from executed tasks. The basis of the Infinite Data pattern is the Persistent Communications pattern. The

Persistent Communications pattern is used because it is able to receive data asynchronously, which is a fundamental aspect of the Infinite Data pattern.

The Infinite Data pattern is not related to any operations that define the basis of an HTML page. The Infinite Data pattern is not intended to be used as a replacement for the Content Chunking pattern, because the HTML content retrieved by the Content Chunking pattern is not processed. It is inserted into the HTML page. The results retrieved from the Infinite Data pattern are processed and transformed into content that is added to an HTML page.

Architecture

The nutshell description of the Infinite Data pattern is the building of a result set incrementally. Therefore, when implementing the Infinite Data pattern, the task executed must be able to generate results as the further results are being generated. When generating a result set, don't think of having to generate an individual result that is sent to the client immediately. It is acceptable to generate a set of results that are sent in batches to the client. Think of how search engines function. You create a query and are presented with an HTML page that probably contains a dozen results. To get the next dozen, another HTML page is loaded. The results are sent to you in batches.

Some readers may say that with a database query it is not possible to generate a subset of results. A query generates a result set that is iterated. The argument is that the query that might take a long time cannot be subdivided into smaller queries. This is not entirely correct, as recently many databases and programming platforms such as .NET and Java have introduced APIs to execute asynchronous requests on a database. The asynchronous APIs will not be discussed because they are beyond the scope of this book. This chapter, though, does provide enough information on how the asynchronous APIs could be used.

The aim of the Infinite Data pattern from the perspective of the client side is to send a task to the server, return control to the client, and then wait for the results to arrive from the server. From the server perspective, the Infinite Data pattern needs to implement the details of the Persistent Communications pattern. This means the server side has to implement concurrent programming techniques because requests and results are asynchronous of each other. The details of the Persistent Communications pattern require the implementation of threads, processes, or even an additional application server (for example, Java J2EE application server, COM+, or Zope).

From an architectural perspective, an Infinite Data pattern implementation requires the execution of the following actions, which are not in sequential order:

- The client and server use the Persistent Communications pattern, which is responsible for sending and receiving data.

- The client creates a structure that contains the actions to be executed on the server.

- The server parses the actions and creates a task that is executed.

- The executed tasks process the information and if necessary generate a result(s).

- The client queries the server for a result. If a result is retrieved, it is processed on the client side.

The actions, converted into a UML activity diagram, are illustrated in Figure 10-1.

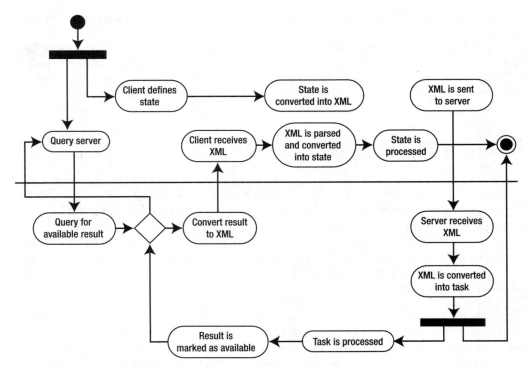

Figure 10-1. *UML activity diagram for the Infinite Data pattern*

In Figure 10-1, a line splits the activity diagram into two pieces. The upper section is the client, or web browser. The lower section is the server side, or the HTTP server. For those not acquainted with UML activity diagrams, the starting point is the black dot in the upper-left corner, and the ending point is the black dot with a white circle around it on the right side.

The first action after the starting point is a black bar indicating parallel actions. The client follows two routes because of the way that the Persistent Communications pattern is implemented using two communication streams. The route that starts with the action item Client defines state is used to generate the structure that is sent to the server for further processing. The route that starts with the action box Query server is used to retrieve the results from the server that are then processed by the client.

Let's focus our attention on the route that generates the structure that is sent to the server for further processing. The route starts with the action Client defines state that is used to transform the information on the client side into a structure. As an example, the information could be the values in an HTML form. The idea is to identify some information that when assembled as a single self-contained package represents a structure that a task on the server side operates on. The task is executed asynchronously and potentially generates some results.

The next action items, State is converted into XML and XML is sent to server, represent conversion of the structure into an XML document that is sent to the server. The structure does not need to be formatted as an XML document, even though it is the preferred format. The information could be formatted by using some other text format such as XML-embedded Java-Script or JSON (http://www.json.org). As a side note, this pattern is conducive to using a format such as JSON because structured data, and not document-based data, is manipulated.

In the action boxes `Server receives XML` and `XML is converted into task`, the client-side structure is converted into data that is associated with a task. When the data is associated with the task, multiple tasks may process a single piece of data. More about multiple tasks and the data will be covered shortly. After the conversion action box is another black bar that indicates an execution of parallel task paths, where one path causes a thread to be spun off to start a task. The other patch represents the original thread, which is finished, as there are no further actions. The main reason for the execution of tasks is to start the thread(s) used to process the task(s).

When the spun-off task executes, a result could be generated that is added to the result database, as indicated by the actions `Task is processed` and `Result is marked as available`. The diamond shape on the left side of Figure 10-1 represents a decision and the joining of server-side with client-side actions. What happens is that the client-side route is querying the server as defined by the action items `Query server` and `Query for available result`. If there is a result available, the server converts the result into an XML content chunk that is sent to the client for processing. The action items `Client receives XML`, `XML is parsed and converted into state`, and `State is processed` represent the receiving and processing of the XML content chunk to generate some result.

The action items of Figure 10-1 form a big-picture perspective showing a client-generated structure that is converted into data that is associated with a task that generates another result structure that is processed by the client. There is a disjoint in that the client has two parallel tasks running, and this means the logic used to send the structure is not the logic used to receive the result structure. In a nutshell, the left hand has no idea what the right hand is doing. The problem relates to two queries running on behalf of a single client. When the client receives a result, how does the client know which query the result belongs to?

Putting this practically, imagine an HTML page with two text boxes. Each text box represents an instance of the same task, but different task data. Each text box starts the same task, resulting in two task instances executing with different data. The problems begin when the client retrieves a result. The receiving algorithm does not know which text box a result belongs to.

The solution for the identification problem is to use a transaction identifier. In the activity diagram, the concept of the transaction identifier is not illustrated. It is not illustrated because the transaction identifier is a piece of information in the generated structure. The transaction identifier is generated by the client, sent to the server, sent to the executing task, and sent to any generated result. Then when the client receives a result, the client can associate the sent transaction identifier with a received transaction identifier. Thus the client can decipher which text box a result is destined for. From the perspective of the server, the transaction identifier is a black box and not processed.

Combining the actions, activity diagram, and other details, the implementation of the Infinite Data pattern involves three major pieces: HTML client, task manager, and task implementation. The *HTML client* is used to send and receive the structures. The *task manager* is responsible for creating the task data, managing the tasks, and managing the results. The *task implementation* is the application logic, which in the case of this chapter is the prime number calculation and is responsible for the task data association and results generation.

Implementation

The Infinite Data pattern implementation in this chapter will be a simple example of calculating all prime numbers up to a specified value. So if the specified value were 9, all the prime numbers up to the number 9 would be 2, 3, 5, and 7. This simple algorithm is useful because it allows us to focus on the architecture and mechanics of the Infinite Data pattern. For those wondering, the prime number calculation routine is a brute force technique that tests whether a number is prime. What is desired with the implementation is the ability to display seemingly infinite data in a timely manner, hence the prime number algorithm is a secondary concern. Calculating the prime number of a large enough maximum value will require some time and allow the testing of multiple concurrently running tasks.

The pattern implementation uses the Persistent Communications pattern. In the definition of the Persistent Communications pattern, there are three variations that can be implemented. The Infinite Data pattern uses the server push variation without implementing user identification.

A *server push* is when the client sends a request to a generic URL, and the server responds with a specific URL used to process requests. In the case of the prime number calculation, the generic URL could be /ajax/chap08/PrimeNumberHandler, and the specific URL would be /ajax/chap08/PrimeNumberHandler/1_101. It sounds ideal and would work if it were not for ASP.NET. One of the problems implementing the Infinite Data pattern is that infrastructures such as ASP.NET are not always implementation friendly. The problem is that the Infinite Data pattern uses URLs in a way that is not friendly with the default ASP.NET infrastructure. ASP.NET, unlike Java Servlet, does not understand the notion of generic URLs. When using ASP.NET, using a specific URL such as /ajax/chap08/PrimeNumberHandler.ashx would be necessary.

Some readers will remember that when the Permutations pattern was implemented, ASP.NET was used. The reason why the Permutations pattern worked is because ASP.NET HTTP modules were used. In Javaspeak, a *module* is a filter, and the module redirected to a specific URL. The difference is that one handler will process multiple requests associated with a URL and its descendent URLs. The Permutations pattern redirected to a URL used to process a single request.

So one solution could be to have the generic URL redirect to something specific such as /ajax/chap08/PrimeNumberHandler/1_101.aspx. Again, the problem is that that does not work in ASP.NET. There has to be a file 1_101.aspx in the directory PrimeNumberHandler. The HTTP module could copy a file to satisfy the reference of the specific file. The solution, though technically possible, is not practically viable. The URL used in the server push is generated dynamically, and there could be hundreds of thousands of URLs. Managing hundreds of thousands of files is not an option.

Another solution would be to attach a CGI parameter to the URL as follows: /ajax/chap08/PrimeNumberHandler.ashx?task=1234. Attaching the CGI parameter would work, but it is not a best practice. Doing so is a so-called necessary practice as the infrastructure does not allow anything else. The problem of using CGI parameters in this context is that it conflicts with caching on the Internet.

Another clever approach would be not to use the task identifier, but the URL /ajax/chap08/PrimeNumberCalculatorTask.ashx?number=20. The new URL is saying, "Please calculate the prime numbers up to the number 20." Using the URL in that manner is not bad idea, because then the answer for the prime numbers up to 20 could be cached. In fact, an optimization would be to cache the prime numbers calculated. Then as a larger number is referenced, only the difference between the previously largest value and new large number needs to be calculated. But we won't use that approach in this chapter because we would be diverting from using a classic implementation of the Infinite Data pattern. The optimizations illustrated for calculating the prime number are optimizations that could be used in the implementation of the prime number task. The overall infrastructure would remain identical, and focusing on the optimization would take attention away from implementing the Infinite Data pattern.

As already indicated, using the CGI parameter as a task identifier is an example of a necessity practice. Regardless of the client calling the server and using the same task identifier, the same results would be generated. The problem with using a task identifier of 20 is that the task identifier has to be determined by the server, and not the client, adding a wrinkle to the solution.

The implementation of the pattern is a server push, without user authentication. Looking back at the Persistent Communications pattern implementation, the server push used authentication, and that would seem to be a conflict in this implementation. The Infinite Data pattern uses a shopping cart approach, where the identification of the user will use an HTTP cookie. Using cookies or authentication is not a necessity, but a nice-to-have feature. Otherwise, anybody can access a specific task. For example, if the URL is `/ajax/chap08/PrimeNumberHandler.ashx?task=1234`, not using an HTTP cookie as an authorization mechanism would allow everybody to retrieve the results for task 1234.

Implementing the HTML Client

For the scope of the prime number application, the HTML client is used to define and process the prime number. The HTML client presents an HTML form consisting of a text box and button. The text box is used to define the maximum number for which all prime numbers are calculated. The button is used to submit the maximum number to the server. The results area displays the generated numbers.

Figure 10-2 is the HTML page used to process two prime numbers.

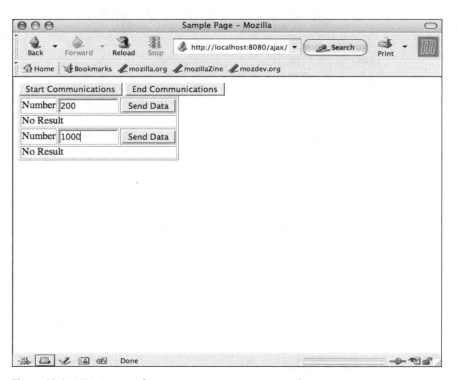

Figure 10-2. *HTML page that processes two prime numbers*

Figure 10-2 shows two text boxes; one text box has the value of 200, and the other has the value of 1000. Each text box represents the maximum number to find all primes. The result area is where the text No Result is displayed. The Send Data buttons are used to send the maximum number value to the server. The Start Communications and End Communications buttons are used to start and stop the Persistent Communications pattern. These two buttons are not necessary and can be automatically controlled by the Send Data buttons. They were kept in the HTML page to illustrate how the Persistent Communications and Infinite Data patterns work seamlessly together.

Overall Implementation Details of the HTML Page

The implementation of the HTML page will be presented as a series of code segments. The first code segment is the overall HTML page, with most of the implementation missing for clarity purposes. Then as needed each missing code segment will be illustrated and explained.

The overall structure of the HTML page illustrated in Figure 10-2 is as follows:

```html
<html>
<head>
<title>Infinite Data</title>
<script language="JavaScript" src="../lib/factory.js"></script>
<script language="JavaScript" src="../lib/asynchronous.js"></script>
<script language="JavaScript" src="../lib/xmlhelpers.js"></script>
<script language="JavaScript" src="../lib/clientcommunicator.js"></script>
<script language="JavaScript" type="text/javascript">

var client = new ClientCommunicator();
client.baseURL = "/ajax/chap08/PrimeNumberHandler.ashx";

</script>
</head>
<body>
<button onclick="StartCommunications()">Start Communications</button>
<button onclick="EndCommunications()">End Communications</button>
<table border="1">
    <tr>
        <td>Number</td>
        <td><input type="text" size="10" id="number1" /></td>
        <td><button onclick="SendData1()">Send Data</button></td>
    </tr>
    <tr>
        <td colspan="4"><span id="result1">No Result</span></td>
    </tr>
    <tr>
        <td>Number</td>
        <td><input type="text" size="10" id="number2" /></td>
        <td><button onclick="SendData2()">Send Data</button></td>
    </tr>
```

```
<tr>
    <td colspan="4"><span id="result2">No Result</span></td>
</tr>
</table>
</body>
</html>
```

The HTML page implementation, like previous pattern implementations, includes a number of JavaScript files referenced by using the script HTML tag. Unlike previous patterns, on the client side the Infinite Data pattern does not reference any script files that implement a generic Infinite Data infrastructure. There is no Infinite Data infrastructure; the activity diagram illustrated in Figure 10-1 shows that all of the logic is application specific.

The Infinite Data pattern does instantiate the ClientCommunicator type that is an implementation of the Persistent Communications pattern. The instantiated Persistent Communications pattern is assigned to the variable client, and the property baseURL is assigned to the file /ajax/ chap08/PrimeNumberHandler.aspx. The file /ajax/chap08/PrimeNumberHandler.aspx represents the server-side implementation of the Infinite Data pattern.

The HTML page contains the HTML element table that contains four rows used to send and receive the Infinite Data state. When the buttons that have the onclick event handlers defined as SendData1 or SendData2 are clicked, the structure is assembled and sent for processing to the server. The sent structure is stored in the input elements with the identifiers number1 and number2. When the result structures are received, they are processed and inserted into the span elements with the identifiers result1 and result2.

Defining the Sending and Receiving Contract

Before further illustrating the code on the client and server sides, the contract between the two sides needs to be defined. The *contract* in an Ajax application is the data that is sent between the client and the server. In the Infinite Data pattern implementation, there are two contracts: what the client sends as a structure to be processed by the server, and the result structures sent by the server and processed by the client.

The state for the structure is stored in the HTML form input fields, which happen to be text fields, number1 and number2. When the appropriate button is clicked, the function SendData1 or SendData2 is called. What you should notice is that all of the identifiers are appended with a number to indicate whether the button represents the first task or the second task (or more appropriately called the first or second transaction identifier).

When the results are generated using the transaction identifier, we know which span element, result1 or result2, the result structures are destined for. Let's say that the text field with the identifier number1 contains 20, and the button associated with the function SendData1 is clicked. The generated structure that is sent to the server is represented using the following XML:

```
<Action>
    <TransactionIdentifier>1</TransactionIdentifier>
    <Number>20</Number>
</Action>
```

In the XML, the element `TransactionIdentifier` has an associated value of 1, and the XML element `Number` has an associated value of 20. When a result structure is generated, the XML will appear similar to the following:

```
<PrimeNumber>
    <Result>success</Result>
    <TransactionIdentifier>1</TransactionIdentifier>
    <Number>9</Number>
</PrimeNumber>
```

The main difference between the XML to be sent and received is the additional XML element `Result` to indicate a success. The `Result` element is necessary so that the client knows what to do with the XML content. For example, imagine sending a state that has incorrect data. The error condition is not generated on the sending of the data, but on the receiving of the data. This is due to the requirement of the Persistent Communications pattern and asynchronous communications. To indicate that an error has occurred, a result has to be sent with the error. Another reason for using the `Result` element is to indicate a finished operation, indicating that all results have been found and that the client will not receive any more results.

There is one weakness with using simple transaction identifiers 1 and 2: if a user sends an `Action` XML document with transaction identifier 1, and then shortly thereafter sends another `Action` XML document with the same transaction identifier, the results will be corrupted. The results are corrupted because two tasks would generate data using the same transaction identifier even though the state for each transaction identifier may be different.

The solution is to create a unique transaction identifier for each and every sending of structured data that generates results. The following modified `Action` XML document references the corrected transaction identifier:

```
<Action>
    <TransactionIdentifier>1_1</TransactionIdentifier>
    <Number>20</Number>
</Action>
```

In the modified XML, the transaction identifier has encoding so that the first digit represents the first or second result field, and the second digit is the transaction identifier counter. The encoding of the transaction identifier seems arbitrary, and is arbitrary from the perspective of the server because only the client knows how to decipher the identifier. The server, when presented with the transaction identifier, does not attempt to decipher what the identifier means. The server is responsible only for cross-referencing the transaction identifier with the received and result data.

Generating the Content for the Contract

Having defined the contract between the client and server, the next step is to generate the content for the contract. The JavaScript code used to generate the state will be illustrated first, and then the code used to process the received results. For this explanation, it is assumed that the server sends and receives the data without any errors or problems.

The data sent from the client to the server is created in either the function `SendData1` or `SendData2`. For explanation purposes, the implementation of `SendData1` is outlined. It is not necessary to explain `SendData2` because it is nearly identical to `SendData1`. The main difference between SendData1 and SendData2 is that one function uses the identifier 1, and the other uses the identifier 2. For those readers who are cringing because of using the hard-coded numeric identifiers 1 and 2, well, you are right. There is a better way of writing the code, but it will not be illustrated here because that would make the explanation of the pattern more difficult. Here is the implementation of SendData1:

```
function SendData1() {
    transactionIdentifier1Counter ++;
    document.getElementById( "result1").innerHTML = "No Result";
    var buffer = GenerateActionData( "1_" + transactionIdentifier1Counter,
        document.getElementById( 'Number1').value);
    client.send( "application/xml", buffer.length, buffer);
}
```

Calling SendData1 means creating a new task on the server, thus invalidating the results of the old tasks that may be executing. The implementation of SendData1 begins with the incrementing of the first task transaction identifier (transactionIdentifier1Counter). Using a static random transaction identifier would result in the scenario where multiple requests would be sending results with the same transaction identifier, thus corrupting the results. As a new task is being created, the content of the result span element (result1) is cleared. The XML buffer that is sent is created by using the function GenerateActionData. The function GenerateActionData has two parameters; the first parameter is the transaction identifier, and the second parameter is the maximum number to calculate all primes for. The generated XML buffer is sent to the server by using the method client.send.

Following is the implementation of GenerateActionData that generates the XML buffer:

```
function GenerateActionData( transactionIdentifier, number) {
    return
        "<Action>" +
        "<TransactionIdentifier>" + transactionIdentifier +
        "</TransactionIdentifier>" +
        "<Number>" + number + "</Number>" +
        "</Action>";
}
```

The implementation of GenerateActionData is a straightforward string concatenation.

When the buffer is sent by using the client.send method, the server is responsible for translating the XML buffer into a task. The client.send method does not wait for a response and returns immediately without a response. The caller of client.send does not know if the task has been started or is working. The caller assumes everything went okay and will expect some results in the receiving part of the HTML page.

Deciphering the Protocol

The receiving of the results is started when the method client.start() is called as per the explanation in the Persistent Communications pattern. When a result is retrieved, the method reference of client.listen is called, which is implemented as follows:

```
client.listen = function( status, statusText, responseText, responseXML) {
    if( status == 200 && responseXML != null) {
        var objData = new Object();
        objData.didFind = false;
        objData.verify = IterateResults;
        XMLIterateElements( objData, objData, responseXML);
        if( objData.didFind == true &&
            IsActiveTransactionIdentifier( objData.transactionIdentifier) == true) {
            var spanElement = document.getElementById(
                GetResultField( objData.transactionIdentifier));
            spanElement.innerHTML += "(" + objData.number + ")";
        }
    }
}
```

The implementation of client.listen is a bit more complicated because the function has to process the received XML and ensure that the results are not stale. A *stale* result is a result that does not belong to the currently executing transaction identifier. The first step in the implementation of the client.listen method is to ensure that results have been successfully retrieved, where the HTTP response code is 200, and that the responseXML parameter is not null. As the contract relies on XML if the responseXML parameter is null, most likely the response was not encoded using XML and thus is not applicable in the context of the pattern.

If the responseXML field can be processed, the XML data needs to be iterated by using the function XMLIterateElements. The results of the iteration are written to data members of the variable objData. Specifically, the data members transactionIdentifier, didFind, and number are manipulated. The data member transactionIdentifier represents the received transaction identifier, and number represents the prime number found. The purpose of the data member didFind is to indicate whether the data members transactionIdentifier and number are valid.

If the data member didFind is assigned a value of true, a result was found. But to process and display the result, the function IsActiveTransactionIdentifier first verifies that the result is not stale and belongs to an active transaction identifier. The implementation of the function IsActiveTransactionIdentifier will be covered shortly. If the retrieved result can be processed, the data member's objData.number value is added to the destination span element. To know which span element to update (results1 or results2), the function GetResultField is called to extract the span element identifier from the received transaction identifier. The found span element instance is assigned to the variable spanElement, and the value of the spanElement.innerHTML property is appended with the found prime number (objData.number).

The function IsActiveTransactionIdentifier is used to determine whether the retrieved result is active and is implemented as follows:

```
function IsActiveTransactionIdentifier( transactionIdentifier) {
    var reference = transactionIdentifier.charAt( 0);
    var valIdentifier = parseInt( transactionIdentifier.substring( 2));
    if( reference == "1" && valIdentifier == transactionIdentifier1Counter) {
        return true;
    }
```

```
    else if( reference == "2" && valIdentifier == transactionIdentifier2Counter) {
        return true;
    }
    else {
        return false;
    }
}
```

In the implementation of `IsActiveTransactionIdentifier`, the parameter `transactionIdentifier` is from the result, where an example would be 1_101. The transaction identifier parameter is encoded and needs to be separated into two pieces; the first piece is the destination span element, and the second piece is the transaction identifier (`transactionIdentifier1Counter` or `transactionIdentifier2Counter`). The two pieces are verified, and if the destination span element references an active transaction identifier, a `true` is returned; otherwise, a `false` is returned. Returning `true` allows a result to be processed.

If the result is processed, the destination of the result needs to be extracted by using the function `GetResultField`, which is implemented as follows:

```
function GetResultField( transactionIdentifier) {
    var reference = transactionIdentifier.charAt( 0);
    if( reference == "1") {
        return "result1";
    }
    else if( reference == "2") {
        return "result2";
    }
    throw new Error("Invalid transaction identifier value");
}
```

In the implementation of `GetResultField`, the code used to extract the field reference is identical to the code used in the function `IsActiveTransactionIdentifier`, and this is done for illustration purposes only. The decision block tests to see if the variable reference has the value 1 or 2, and if so returns the appropriate HTML identifier. If the variable reference is neither 1 or 2, an exception is thrown to indicate an incorrectly formatted `transactionIdentifier` parameter.

Earlier it was mentioned that on the client side there is no reusable code because the implementation of the pattern is specific to the problem being solved. This is not entirely correct, because some pieces of the HTML client code could have been combined into a small library. The small library could be have been used in this context, but probably could not be reused in another context. An example would have been the functions `IsActiveTransactionIdentifier` and `GetResultField`.

Be wary of adding small libraries of reusable code. Often there is no real advantage to using the functions because doing so does not save you much coding time or logic. It does not mean that all client-side Infinite Data implementations will be hard-coded as in the example prime number application. Some things could be abstracted, but it very much depends on the specifics of the applications that you are creating. What could be useful is the creation of helper routines. *Helper routines* are encapsulated pieces of code that make it quicker to implement certain functionalities. Going back to the illustrative example of functions, they could be abstracted to a set of helper functions used to create and decipher the transaction identifier. The helper functions should be implemented only after you have determined what a standard transaction identifier is.

Implementing the Task Manager

On the server side, two pieces of functionality are implemented: the task manager and the implementation of the task. In the case of the prime number algorithm, that means implementing a task to find all prime numbers. Interfaces are used so that there are no dependencies between the task manager, results, and tasks. The task manager, prime number task, and prime number result algorithms each implement one of the interfaces. The role of the task manager is to wire all of the interfaces together and provide a working solution to the Infinite Data pattern on the server side.

Defining the Task Manager Interfaces

There are three main interfaces for the Task Manager: ITask, ITaskManager, and IResult. The three interfaces are defined as follows:

```
public interface ITask {
    long TransactionIdentifier { get; set;}
    void Execute( ITaskManager taskManager);
}
public interface IResult {
    string Result {
        get;
    }
    long TransactionIdentifier {
        get;
    }
}
public interface ITaskManager {
    void AddResult( IResult result);
}
```

The interface ITask is implemented by the individual tasks, with an example being the prime number algorithm. The ITask interface has one property and one method. The property TransactionIdentifier contains the value of the client-provided transaction identifier (for example, 1_101). The method Execute is called by the task manager to run the task. The parameter taskManager is a callback interface used by the task to save the generated results.

The interface IResult is composed entirely of properties that represent the status of the result (Result) and the transaction identifier (TransactionIdentifier). The IResult interface's definition is incomplete, allowing a developer to subclass IResult by adding properties specific to the task. The idea of the IResult interface is to provide a common interface and a placeholder that can be referenced by other parts of the Infinite Data implementation without having to know the type of the result. The consumer of the IResult interface would know the different result implementations and if necessary be able to perform a type cast.

The interface ITaskManager is implemented by the task manager and has a single method, AddResult. The AddResult method is used by an ITask interface instance to pass an IResult instance to the task manager. When the task manager receives an `IResult` instance, it is saved and passed to the calling client when asked for.

Before describing the implementation of the task manager interfaces, I will illustrate the code that uses the interfaces. Understanding how the interfaces are used makes it simpler to understand the implementations. The following code is going to implement an ASP.NET handler, which translated into Java would be a Java servlet. The handler or servlet would be responsible for interacting with the defined interfaces. Additionally, the handler or servlet needs to fulfill the server-side requirements of the Persistent Communications pattern. This means that the handler or servlet must process the HTTP `GET` to send results to the client, and HTTP `PUT` or `POST` to process client-sent structure instances.

Packaging the Implementations

When implementing the server-side part of the Infinite Data pattern using an ASP.NET handler or a Java servlet, it is possible to put everything into one distribution unit that is a jar or assembly. Another approach would be to split the logic so that some is in the handler or servlet and the rest is in another distribution unit. Creating multiple distribution units makes it simpler to update each unit independently. For example, the general task handler infrastructure would not be updated as often as the task implementations. Figure 10-3 illustrates an example distribution unit structure.

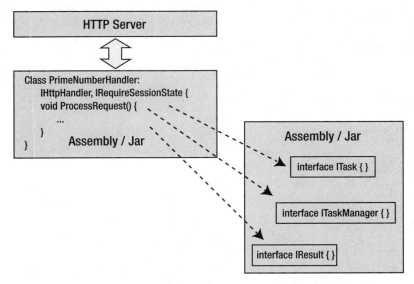

Figure 10-3. *Packaging structure of handler and interface implementations*

In Figure 10-3, the HTTP server calls the handler `PrimeNumberHandler.ProcessRequest`. That call in turn generates a series of calls to the interfaces `ITask`, `ITaskManager`, and `IResult`. Even though the diagram references the interfaces, types that implement the interfaces process the calls. What is being illustrated is how one distribution unit references another distribution unit. The interfaces in the one distribution unit provide the common reference points for the two distribution units. The separation of the two distribution units makes it possible for the task implementations to be called directly from unit tests or other application servers.

Figure 10-4 illustrates how the distribution unit can be called by the NUnit testing framework.

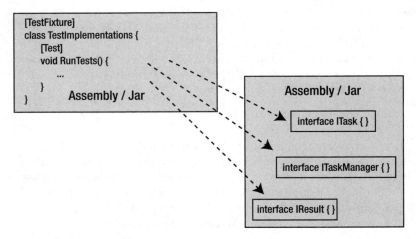

Figure 10-4. *Testing package structure of the interfaces*

Calling the Interface Implementations

Having resolved how to separate the code, the class `PrimeNumberHandler` is an HTTP handler that calls the distribution unit and implements the task interfaces. `PrimeNumberHandler` is implemented as follows (with code pieces removed for clarity):

```
<%@ WebHandler Language="C#" Class="PrimeNumberHandler" %>
using System;
using System.Web;
using System.Web.SessionState;
using System.Threading;
using PrimeNumberCalculator;
using TaskManager;

public class PrimeNumberHandler : IHttpHandler, IRequiresSessionState {

    public void ProcessRequest (HttpContext context) {
        TaskManagerImpl taskManager = GetTaskManager( context);

        if (context.Request.HttpMethod.CompareTo("GET") == 0) {
            // Abbreviated for clarity
        }
        else if (context.Request.HttpMethod.CompareTo("PUT") == 0 ||
            context.Request.HttpMethod.CompareTo("POST") == 0) {
            // Abbreviated for clarity
        }
    }
```

```
    public bool IsReusable {
        get {
            return true;
        }
    }
}
```

The class `PrimeNumberHandler` implements both the `IHttpHandler` and `IRequireSessionState` interfaces. The interface `IRequireSessionState` does not define any methods or properties, but is required if an ASP.NET handler wants to manipulate the ASP.NET sessions. The method `ProcessRequest` is defined by the interface `IHttpHandler`, and its purpose is to process an incoming HTTP request. The method `IsReusable` is defined by the interface `IHttpHandler` and is used to indicate whether two requests share the same instance. This level of control is not available using Java servlets. As in the Java Servlet implementation of the State Navigation pattern, the problem was how to share state across method calls. Java servlets by default are single instances and are reused. The problem of sharing data across methods is not a problem with ASP.NET.

The knowledge of whether handlers are single instances and are reused is important for the Infinite Data pattern implementation. The class `PrimeNumberHandler` has no data members that are assigned or instantiated in the context of a request. Thus the class `PrimeNumberHandler` can be instantiated as a single instance and reused by the server. Had `PrimeNumberHandler` assigned data members during a request, a handler would have to be instantiated per request; otherwise, data would be corrupted.

In the implementation of `ProcessRequest`, the first action is to call the method `GetTaskManager`. The method is used to retrieve the task manager instance associated with the user. HTTP cookies are used to authorize and associate a client with the tasks that are executed. However, realize that `GetTaskManager` was explicitly separated from the main code so that the implementation of associating the request to the task manager could vary. Another implementation that analyzes the URL and cross-references pieces of the URL to a task is possible without changing the calling code.

Following is the implementation of `GetTaskManager`:

```
private TaskManagerImpl GetTaskManager(HttpContext context) {
    HttpSessionState session = context.Session;
    if (session != null) {
        object obj = session["taskmanager"];
        TaskManagerImpl taskManager = null;

        if (obj != null) {
            taskManager = (TaskManagerImpl)obj;
        }
        else {
            taskManager = new TaskManagerImpl();
            session["taskmanager"] = taskManager;
        }
        return taskManager;
    }
    return null;
}
```

In the implementation of GetTaskManager, the association of a client to a cookie to a task manager is very simple because ASP.NET has the session object HttpSessionState. The session object instance is retrieved by using the property context.Session, and it is necessary to test whether the session object instance exists. If the session object instance does not exist, a null value is returned. Attempting to reference a session with a null value will result in an exception. To retrieve the task manager instance, the session object indexer session["taskmanager"] is used. For those readers who do not code in .NET, an indexer behaves like an array reference, but is implemented as an operator by the type.

The task manager can be associated to the session, meaning that there is an association to the cookie. The tasks executed and managed by the task manager, though, should be managed by the application state in ASP.NET. The task manager associated with the session can also reference the task, but it is important that the application state be included as a reference. Not doing so would result in tasks that are accessible only by the cookie associated with a user.

When the session indexer returns a task manager instance, it is explicitly assigned to the variable obi, which is of the type object. When the task manager instance is referenced from the session object for the first time, the variable obj will be a null value. The reason is obvious: it is impossible to reference an instance if the instance has not been allocated. If a typecast were performed on a null object instance, an exception would be generated. A way to get around the typecast problem in .NET is to use the as operator, although that was not used in this example. An explicit test for a null object instance was used in this example. If the obj instance is not a null value, it can be typecast to the variable taskManager. If the object instance is a null value, a new task manager instance (new TaskManagerImpl()) needs to be instantiated and associated with the session object instance. The last action of GetTaskManager is to return a task manager instance.

Getting back to the PrimeNumberHandler.ProcessRequest method, after the task manager instance has been retrieved, a decision block is executed. The decision block is used to test whether the HTTP request is sending or retrieving data. The if statement is a decision to retrieve data, and the HTTP method GET is tested by using the property HttpMethod. The else if statement is a decision for sending, and the property HttpMethod is tested for the HTTP method POST or PUT.

Sending Tasks

If the data is being sent to the server, that means an XML document with the Action tag is being sent. The server would need to convert the XML document into a .NET class instance populated with the content from the XML document. With a valid class instance, the server can start a task. The implementation of the HTTP POST or PUT part of the decision block from PrimeNumberHandler is as follows:

```
else if (context.Request.HttpMethod.CompareTo("PUT") == 0 ||
    context.Request.HttpMethod.CompareTo("POST") == 0) {

    ActionData data = Serializer.Parse( context.Request.InputStream);
taskManager.AddTask(
        new Calculator( data.Number, data.TransactionIdentifier));
    taskManager.RunThreadedTasks();
}
```

In the implementation, the XML document is converted to a .NET instance by using the method `Serializer.Parse`. This custom method implementation converts the XML document contained in the HTML stream (`context.Request.InputStream`) into a .NET class instance. The deserialization details are beyond the scope of this book and will be kept as an abstract action. The deserialization instantiates the type `ActionData`, which is the data used by the task `Calculator`. The task `Calculator` is added to the list of tasks to be executed by using the method `taskManager.AddTask`. To run the task, the method `taskManager.RunThreadedTasks` is called.

When the method `RunThreadedTasks` is executed, a background thread is started that will execute any task that has been added via the method `AddTask`. The background thread is started by the HTTP request but does not belong to the request. After the method `RunThreadedTasks` has been called, the client returns immediately without sending any data as a response, as is expected. What is not explicitly outlined but must be possible is the running of background tasks or threads on the HTTP server that is not associated with a request. Additionally, if the thread is run in the background, the server should not keep an HTTP connection open. Otherwise, unnecessary resources will be wasted. If the HTTP server were to freeze or force the exit of the background thread, the Persistent Communications pattern could not be implemented. When it is not possible to run a background thread, the solution would be to use an interprocess calling mechanism that calls a server waiting for requests. The downside to the interprocess calling mechanism is that a server process has to be created that waits for requests to be made.

Retrieving Results

If the client makes a request, an HTTP GET is executed, and the client expects to retrieve a generated result. In the contract section, the client expects to receive an XML document. The XML document can contain a single node, or if a result is returned, the `PrimeNumber` tag is expected.

The implementation of retrieving a result is illustrated as follows:

```
if (context.Request.HttpMethod.CompareTo("GET") == 0) {
    IResult result = taskManager.GetResultWait(10);
    context.Response.ContentType = "text/xml";
    if (result != null) {
        context.Response.Output.Write(
            Serializer.Generate((PrimeNumberData)result));
    }
    else {
        context.Response.Output.Write("<result>none</result>");
    }
}
```

The act of retrieving a result is straightforward. The method `taskManager.GetResultWait` is called with a parameter value of 10. The value 10 indicates to wait 10 seconds if there is no available result. The wait is part of the Persistent Communications pattern in that the server uses a signal to wait for an answer. The result that is returned is assigned to the variable `result`. If `result` is not null (indicating a retrieved result), an XML document is generated by using the method call `Serializer.Generate`. If the result is null, an empty document `<result>...</result>` is generated.

Being Aware of Multiple Types

The example implementation of sending and retrieving .NET object instances and converting them to XML documents is simple and logical. The deficiency of the example is that the task manager can process only a single task type. It is not possible to process multiple task types. The reality is different because there will be multiple task types to execute.

To avoid processing multiple task types with a single instance of the Persistent Communications pattern, you can instantiate multiple `ClientCommunicator` instances. The result of multiple `ClientCommunicator` instances is multiple streams. And multiple streams waste resources, as defined in the explanation of the Persistent Communications pattern. The solution must be a single stream, where the server has to be able to distinguish between different XML document types. The problem of recognizing multiple XML document types is figuring out how to transform XML into a class instance.

The problem of converting an XML document into a class instance and vice versa is a well-understood problem in .NET and Java. The solution is to use a metadata description language that a mapping tool can use. In XMLspeak, this means using XML schemas. In a nutshell, *XML schemas* are XML files used to describe the XML elements of a document. XML schemas are beyond the scope of this book, but they are extremely useful when writing Ajax applications that exchange XML data.

Let's revisit the XML document sent by the client to the server and go through an example of defining a transformation using XML schemas:

```
<Action>
    <TransactionIdentifier>1_101</TransactionIdentifier>
    <Number>20</Number>
</Action>
```

The XML document has the root element `Action` and two child elements: `Number` and `TransactionIdentifier`. The XML document converted into an XML schema is illustrated as follows:

```
<?xml version="1.0" encoding="UTF-8" ?>
<xs:schema xmlns:xs="http://www.w3.org/2001/XMLSchema">
  <xs:element name="Action">
    <xs:complexType>
      <xs:sequence>
        <xs:element ref="TransactionIdentifier"/>
        <xs:element ref="Number"/>
      </xs:sequence>
    </xs:complexType>
  </xs:element>
  <xs:element name="Number" type="xs:string"/>
  <xs:element name="TransactionIdentifier" type="xs:string"/>
</xs:schema>
```

The XML schema is another XML document, and the elements are used, and their structure is targeted, but their meaning is relevant only to an XML schema parser. Looking at the XML schema, the identifier `element` is used as a cross-reference with an XML element in a document. There are three first-level child elements, which directly correspond to the XML elements in the document. Each of the first-level child elements has an attribute name, used to identify the name of the XML element in an XML document. The attribute type is used to define the type of an XML element in an XML document. If an XML element contains child elements of type complexType, an XML structure is being defined. Otherwise, the referenced XML elements are simple types, where the type can be defined using the XML schema specification (for example, the type xs:int for the Number schema definition).

The XML schema is then used as a script for a tool to generate source code that manages the serializing and deserializing of XML documents. For .NET, the xsd.exe command-line utility is used, and for Java, Java Architecture for XML Binding (JAXB) is used. To convert the example XML schema into a set of .NET classes, the command xsd.exe ActionData.xsd /classes is executed and generates the following source code:

```
using System.Xml.Serialization;
[System.SerializableAttribute()]
[System.Xml.Serialization.XmlTypeAttribute(AnonymousType=true)]
[System.Xml.Serialization.XmlRootAttribute(Namespace="", IsNullable=false)]
public partial class Action {
    private string transactionIdentifierField;
    private string numberField;
    /// <remarks/>
    public string TransactionIdentifier {
        get {
            return this.transactionIdentifierField;
        }
        set {
            this.transactionIdentifierField = value;
        }
    }
    /// <remarks/>
    public string Number {
        get {
            return this.numberField;
        }
        set {
            this.numberField = value;
        }
    }
}
```

In the generated source code, the class name and properties directly correlate to the XML elements in the XML document. The class name is Action because the root XML element is Action. Associated with the class are a number of .NET attributes that are used for XML serialization. The generated types are used by the serialization methods that were defined as an abstracted method in the "Sending Tasks" and "Retrieving Results" sections (Serialization. Generate, Serialization.Parse).

The infrastructure used to perform the serialization of the XML documents is implemented very differently on Java and .NET. And if there are multiple types to serialize and deserialize, the process of serialization becomes more complicated. In general, to be able to parse multiple

XML document types, a registry of document types has to be registered. JAXB is helpful in that JAXB manages registries of XML document types that can be processed by using Java namespaces of generated classes. To get the same effect when using .NET, multiple XMLSerializer instances need to be created. Then to check whether an XML document can be processed, the CanDeserialize method is called. It is important to keep the Serialization.Generate and Serialization.Parse methods abstract so that the serialization of multiple types is managed by the abstract method.

On the client side, managing multiple types is more complicated because of automatic serialization techniques. For the focus of this book, serializing XML documents by using JavaScript means being able to iterate the JavaScript XML Document Object Model, and that means extending the XMLIterateElements function. This is why in this instance a format such as JSON can simplify the process of serialization.

Being able to serialize and deserialize XML documents is solving one problem, but the next problem is being able to associate an object instance with a task. The solution is to let the object instance take care of itself. That would mean introducing one more interface that each object instance implements and that is defined as follows:

```
public interface IData {
    ITask InstantiateTask();
}
```

The interface IData has one method, InstantiateTask, that is used to instantiate the task associated with the object instance. In patternspeak, the method InstantiateTask implements the Factory pattern. The generated Action class would then be extended as follows:

```
public partial class Action : IData {
    public ITask InstantiateTask() {
        return new Calculator(numberField);
    }
}
```

The class Action implements the IData interface, and in the implementation of IData instantiates the task Calculator. The .NET implementation of Action uses a .NET 2.0 feature not available in Java. The keyword partial makes it possible to define two "classes" that are merged when the compiler generates the .NET bytecode. Partial classes make it possible to separate the generated code from the handwritten code. To achieve the same effect in Java, the following source code would have to be written:

```
public partial class ActionImpl extends Action implements IData {
    public ITask InstantiateTask() {
        return new Calculator(numberField, transactionIdentifier);
    }
}
```

Going back to the "Sending Tasks" section, the source code used to instantiate a task would be rewritten to the following:

```
else if (context.Request.HttpMethod.CompareTo("PUT") == 0 ||
    context.Request.HttpMethod.CompareTo("POST") == 0) {
    ITaskData taskdata = Serializer.Parse(
        context.Request.InputStream);
    taskManager.AddTask( taskdata.InstantiateTask());
    taskManager.RunThreadedTasks();
}
```

The rewritten code is simpler in that the source code does not have to deal with the specific types ActionData and Calculator. The source code needs to manipulate only standard interfaces, thus allowing the implementation of Serializer and ITaskData to determine what the specific types are. This is *encapsulation,* and the Serializer implementation should implement the Template pattern or Chain of Responsibility pattern for more flexible and dynamic logic of processing types and XML documents.

Understanding the Details of the Task Manager

The task manager implements the ITaskManager interface, and the interface has a single method, making the task manager an easy implementation, albeit lacking in functionality. As described in the beginning of this chapter, the task manager on the server has been responsible for managing the tasks to be executed and their results. Executing the tasks and managing their results requires that the task manager be able to juggle multiple threads and to manage collections of objects.

I will explain the task manager not as one code segment, but multiple smaller segments: overall class structure, task management, and results management. The overall class structure is similar to the following class declaration:

```
public class TaskManagerImpl : ITaskManager {
        private Queue<ITask> _tasks = new Queue< ITask>();
        private Queue<ITask> _completedTasks = new Queue< ITask>();
        private Queue<IResult> _results = new Queue< IResult>();
        private Thread _thread = null;

        public TaskManagerImpl( ) {
        }
}
```

The class TaskManagerImpl implements the ITaskManager interface, where the method to be implemented will be discussed shortly. In the overall class structure, the important pieces are the data members. There are four data members: _tasks, _completedTasks, _results, and _thread. Other than the _thread data member, the other data members are Queue<> typed lists. The Queue<> list is being used because a producer-consumer threading architecture is implemented.

In a *producer-consumer architecture,* there is a producer of data and a consumer of data. The producer-consumer architecture strictly requires that only one thread can produce data, and another thread consumes data. The dedication of functionality makes it simpler and more efficient to manage objects between multiple threads. The data member _tasks contains the list of tasks to be executed. The data member _completedTasks contains the list of tasks that have been completed. The idea of these two data members is to retrieve a task from the _task queue, execute the task, and after the execution add the task to the _completedTasks queue. The data member _results is a queue of generated results from the various executed tasks.

When a client calls the method AddTask, the client adds a task to the queue _tasks. Just adding a task to the queue does not start the task. The client that adds the task is the producer. Another thread that pulls the task from the queue is the consumer. The implementation of AddTask is as follows:

```
public void AddTask( ITask task) {
    AddToApplication( task);
    lock( _tasks) {
        _tasks.Enqueue( task);
    }
}
```

The AddTask method does two things: adds a task to the task queue, and adds the task to the global application task list. The method AddToApplication is used for reference purposes so that potentially another user can reference a task. The method used to add a task to a queue is Enqueue. Because threads are being used, synchronization is required, and in the case of .NET the keyword lock is used. The lock keyword expects an object instance that defines a specific lock reference.

After a task is added, the next step is to execute threads by using the method RunThreadedTasks, which processes the tasks in the queue. The threads started by RunThreadedTasks are the consumer part of the producer-consumer architecture in that the threads retrieve tasks from the task queue. Following is the implementation of RunThreadedTasks and its associated dependencies:

```
private ITask GetTask() {
    ITask task = null;
    lock( _tasks) {
        if( _tasks.Count > 0) {
            task = _tasks.Dequeue();
        }
    }
    return task;
}
public void ProcessTasks() {
    ITask task = null;
    while( true) {
        task = GetTask();
        if( task != null) {
            task.Execute( this);
            lock( _completedTasks) {
                _completedTasks.Enqueue( task);
            }
        }
```

```
            else {
                lock( this) {
                    task = GetTask();
                    if( task == null) {
                        _thread = null;
                        break;
                    }
                }
            }
        }
    }
    public void RunThreadedTasks() {
        lock( this) {
            if( _thread == null) {
                _thread = new Thread(
                    new ThreadStart( this.ProcessTasks));
                _thread.Start();
            }
        }
    }
}
```

Let's start with the bottom method, RunThreadedTasks. In the implementation of RunThreadedTasks, there is another synchronization, but this time the object instance is the this object. A decision is made to see whether the data member _thread is null or not null. The idea is that with RunThreadedTasks, each client has only one associated thread-processing task. This would stop a scenario of the server coming to a standstill because some client(s) is issuing too many requests for calculating a series of prime numbers.

The thread calls the method ProcessTasks, which contains a never-ending loop (while(true)). For each iteration of the loop, the method GetTask is called. The method GetTask is used to retrieve a task from the queue. In the implementation of GetTask, there is a test to see whether any tasks are queued. Not having the test would result in an exception being generated if Dequeue were called on an empty queue. When GetTask returns control to ProcessTasks, the variable task will either be null or will reference an object instance. If the variable task references an object instance, the method task.Execute is called to let the task do its work. When the method task.Execute has completed, the finished task is added to the executed list of tasks queue (_completedTasks).

When GetTask returns control to ProcessTasks and the task variable is null, there are no more tasks to execute and the thread will exit. If the thread exits, the data member _thread needs to be assigned a null value to indicate that there is no running thread. Assigning _thread a null value creates a place of contention between the producer and consumer threads. The producer when there is no thread running will start a thread, and the consumer when it has finished its work exits the thread. The data member _thread needs to be protected by using a synchronization lock. To protect the data member, the lock keyword is used in the context of GetTask.

The logic of the problem is that there is a small amount of time that exists between the producer checking whether a thread has been started, and the consumer exiting the thread. If in that small period of time the consumer exits the thread, and the producer doesn't start a new thread, a task will be sitting in the queue waiting to be executed. The simplest solution is to never let the consumer exit and to put the thread to sleep when the consumer has nothing to do. Another solution is to create a situation that when the consumer thread exits, the consumer thread creates a lock where the producer is put on hold while the data member _thread is reset.

The complete implementation of the logic is in the consumer and the method ProcessTasks, which is illustrated again as follows:

```
public void ProcessTasks() {
    ITask task = null;
    while( true) {
        task = GetTask();
        if( task != null) {
            task.Execute( this);
            lock( _completedTasks) {
                _completedTasks.Enqueue( task);
            }
        }
        else {
            lock( this) {
                task = GetTask();
                if( task == null) {
                    _thread = null;
                    break;
                }
            }
        }
    }
}
```

The problem of having a waiting task in the queue is caused by the _thread data member not being assigned and checked at the right moment. Look at the last lock with the object reference this. If the consumer thread reached the last lock, a condition for exiting the thread was encountered. The first step in the exit strategy is to lock the current instance. With the current instance locked, the producer cannot add a task and therefore has to wait before adding a task and has to wait before checking on whether a consumer thread needs to be started. The next step in the exit strategy is to check whether there are waiting tasks (GetTask). What could have happened is that while the exit strategy was attempting to acquire a lock, the producer was adding a task to the queue. If there is no waiting task, then the consumer thread can exit and safely assign the data member _thread to null.

Some .NET readers would point out that ThreadPool should be used to solve this problem. ThreadPool is a good idea, but the fact is that you cannot control the behavior of the default thread pool, and there is a maximum number of threads that could cause your server to become needlessly unresponsive. At the URL http://www.codeproject.com/csharp/SmartThreadPool.asp is a .NET implementation of a flexible thread pool. For Java developers the same can be said, and Apache Jakarta Commons (http://Jakarta.apache.org) has a useful thread pool implementation.

Regardless of whether you use a thread pool or manage the threads yourself or use some application server, there will be a fair amount of concurrency. Therefore, when implementing the Infinite Data pattern or the Persistent Connections pattern, you will need to know about concurrency and synchronization. Not knowing about these concepts could cause your code to deadlock at the worst times. Of course, a deadlock could be debugged, and then magically as the debugger is started the deadlock disappears. At that point, your choice is to distribute the application while running the debugger or write code that is logically correct.[1]

The last part of the task manager are the methods used to manage the results. These methods use synchronization techniques that do not involve the lock keyword. The synchronization mechanism is a Monitor. A Monitor and lock act similarly, but a Monitor has one ability that lock does not: monitors can be signaled. *Signaling* is the ability of a thread to put itself to sleep while waiting for some action to happen. After the action happens, another thread sends a signal. If there are any threads asleep, they will be awoken and given the chance to process the data of the action.

The implementation of the results management functions is illustrated as follows:

```
public void AddResult(IResult result) {
    Monitor.Enter( _results);
    _results.Enqueue( result);
    Monitor.Pulse( _results);
    Monitor.Exit( _results);
}
private IResult GetSingleResult() {
    IResult result = null;
    if( _results.Count > 0) {
        result = _results.Dequeue();
    }
    return result;
}
public IResult GetResult() {
    Monitor.Enter( _results);
    IResult result = GetSingleResult();
    Monitor.Exit( _results);
    return result;
}
public IResult GetResultWait( int timeout) {
    IResult result = null;
    Monitor.Enter( _results);
    result = GetSingleResult();
    if( result == null) {
        Monitor.Wait( _results, timeout * 1000);
        result = GetSingleResult();
    }
    Monitor.Exit( _results);
    return result;
}
```

---

1. For multithreaded programming for Java, I recommend reading Doug Lea's *Concurrent Programming in Java* (Addison-Wesley Professional, 1999). For .NET, the book *.NET Multithreading* by Alan Dennis (Manning Publications, 2002) is available.

There are three public methods: AddResult, used to add a result to the results queue (_results); GetResult, used to return a single result; and GetResultWait, used to return a single result where the method will wait for a result. In detail, GetResultWait checks whether any results are available; if not, the method puts itself to sleep and waits until there are results available. The data member _results is not illustrated, but is defined as a collection. For each of the public methods, the first action is to call the method Monitor.Enter, which acquires a lock based on the object instance _results. At the end of each of the public methods, the method Monitor.Exit is called to release the lock based on the object instance _results. The code between the Monitor.Enter and Monitor.Exit method calls is synchronized code in which only one thread may perform actions.

Synchronization and how to use it is easy to follow for all methods. What is more complicated is the signaling of the waiting thread. When the method GetResultWait executes a Monitor.Wait, the method has control of the lock. No other method may add or remove results from the collection. If the method GetResultWait realizes that there are no results in the collection, the method Monitor.Wait is called, putting the thread executing GetResultWait to sleep. In the method implementation Monitor.Wait, there is a time-out, which means that the sleep of the thread will not be infinite. A time-out causes an automatic reawakening of the thread even if no signal has been sent. When the thread reawakens, it needs to check whether the reawakening was due to a signal or time-out, and in the case of the method implementation, the collection is tested for available elements.

A signal to reawaken a sleeping thread is executed by calling the method Monitor.Pulse, but from a thread that is not sleeping. In the example, it is the method AddResult.

What is not obvious from the code is what happens to the lock when a thread is put to sleep and then awakened. If a thread goes to sleep while keeping a lock, no other threads could execute because the other threads would be waiting for the thread to awaken. The solution of a monitor is to give up the lock when a thread goes to sleep. When a pulse is sent, the reawakened thread does not execute immediately. The reawakened thread puts in a request for the lock before continuing execution. Thus, when a signal is pulsed, the reawakened thread will execute only after the lock has been acquired.

Using monitors as a synchronization mechanism is imperative because you want to implement the requirements of the Persistent Communications pattern without having to waste resources. While a monitor is waiting for a result, it is using the least amount of resources possible. You may be wondering whether monitors could also have been used to implement the background thread. And the answer is yes. Though, ideally, for the background thread, a thread pool would be a better solution. A thread pool makes it simpler to implement a producer-consumer architecture.

Implementing the Task

The last piece of code that needs to be explained is the task itself. In the example, that means explaining the class Calculator, which is illustrated as follows. Some parts of the class have been deleted for clarity:

```
public class Calculator : TaskManager.ITask {
    private long _transactionIdentifier;
    private long _number;

    public long TransactionIdentifier {
```

```
            get {
                return _transactionIdentifier;
            }
            set {
                _transactionIdentifier = value;
            }
        }
        public void Execute( TaskManager.ITaskManager mgr) {
            mgr.AddResult( new PrimeNumberData( 1, _transactionIdentifier));
            for( int c1 = 2; c1 <= _number; c1 ++) {
                if( IsPrime( c1)) {
                    mgr.AddResult(
                        new PrimeNumberData( c1,
                        _transactionIdentifier));
                }
            }
        }

        public Calculator( long number, long transactionIdentifier) {
            if( number < 1) {
                throw new IndexOutOfRangeException(
                    "Number must be greater than 0");
            }
            _number = number;
            _transactionIdentifier = transactionIdentifier;
        }
    }
}
```

The constructor of Calculator accepts two parameters: the number to be calculated and the transaction identifier. In the example of Calculator, the runtime data is copied via the constructor parameters, but it does not need to be. The runtime data could be assigned via a property or method. The task manager does not assign the runtime data, and that needs be assigned in some other fashion. The most logical is in the implementation of the ITaskData. InstantiateTask method. In the example, the constructor referenced the task data explicitly, but the constructor could have been written as follows:

```
public Calculator( ActionData data) { ... }
```

The class Calculator implements the ITask interface, which means the property TransactionIdentifier and method Execute are implemented. The property Transaction➥ Identifier is a simple property that assigns the data member _transactionIdentifier. In the implementation of Execute, results are added by using the mgr.AddResult method. The first thing that the Execute implementation does is add the prime number 1 to the result list. Then a loop is started, where each number up to the maximum prime number is iterated and tested to see whether it is a prime number. The method IsPrime is not illustrated; it is a simple calculation to test whether a number is a prime number. If a number is prime, it is added to the results by using the method mgr.AddResult.

The implementation of the task is the last piece of the Infinite Data pattern. At this point, it is possible to execute the application and start generating prime number sequences.

Pattern Highlights

The implementation of the Infinite Data pattern is largely dependent on the server implementation because the server is responsible for generating the data. The client has the responsibility of creating the correct task data and associating the results with the submitted task data.

The following points are the important highlights of the Infinite Data pattern:

- The pattern is used to generate data on a piecemeal basis.

- The pattern is useful in those situations where the executing task can generate data as it does its work. For example, when using a relational database that supports piecemeal results, it is necessary to use asynchronous callbacks.

- Synchronization and background threads or processes need to be used. It is important to understand concurrency issues so that deadlocks do not occur.

- Sending and receiving XML messages, and associating data types and tasks, requires a certain amount of automation. XML schemas are very helpful.

- Even though the preferred format is XML, a format such as JSON would be useful when implementing this pattern because quite a bit of serialization and marshaling is involved.

- The basis of the Infinite Data pattern is the Persistent Communications pattern.

■ ■ ■

CHAPTER 11

REST-Based Model View Controller Pattern

Intent

The REST-Based Model View Controller pattern is used to access content that is external to the web application and used to transform the content so that it appears as if the web application generated it.

Motivation

Every application, whether it be on the Web or in a traditional form, has a purpose and solves either a single or multiple problems. Features of an application tend to be specific to that application and do not relate to other domains. A word processor is a word processor, and an e-mail program is an e-mail program. Each application is responsible for its own data and user interface. The question then arises: why can you not take the contents of a document and press a button to convert it into an e-mail, or vice versa? Why must one application be separate from another application? The typical solution for converting an e-mail into a document is to use Copy and Paste to transfer the contents from one application to another, which works quite effectively but requires an extra step.

Now imagine that an application had the capability to integrate content or functionality from another application and make it part of the original application. Such a solution would look like Figure 11-1.

The application in Figure 11-1 is called Lilina, which is a blog news aggregator. Lilina can be used to read multiple blogs and present them as web pages. What makes Lilina unique is its ability to search for blog entries by using the Google search engine and to present those results as part of a blog entry. If you think about it, Lilina is a unique next-generation application in that it has the ability to combine multiple streams of information (blogs and Google search) into a single stream. In a nutshell, Lilina is an example of the REST-Based Model View Controller pattern.

With the existence of the XMLHttpRequest object, using the REST-Based Model View Controller pattern might seem unnecessary. After all, the XMLHttpRequest object could be used to integrate content from various sources. However, the truth is that it is not possible at a technical level to easily integrate content from various sources, because of the same origin policy.

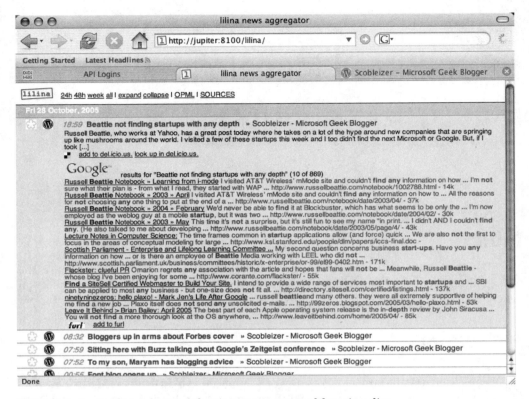

Figure 11-1. *Example application that integrates external functionality*

The same origin policy was described in Chapter 2. Essentially the main idea behind this policy is to not allow a JavaScript script to make a cross-domain script call (XSS).[1] The same origin policy exists to enhance security and should not be thought of as a programmatic inconvenience. History has shown that hackers can and will hijack websites and cause grief to users if they are able to.

Another two reasons for using the REST-Based Model View Controller pattern are to create a consistent user experience and to not overload the web browser with unnecessary business logic. In Figure 11-1, the HTML content looks and feels like a single application, even though multiple data streams are integrated into a single HTML stream. The server does this by extracting the important pieces from an individual data stream and then using the important pieces as the basis of the new HTML content.

In theory, everything that the server does, the browser can do, and that includes the extraction and transformation of information. Although a web browser is a useful piece of software capable of running sophisticated scripts, that does not mean that a 2-megabyte JavaScript file should be downloaded and executed. A web browser should be considered an intelligent thin client. Also, as you will see in the "Architecture" section of this chapter, the purpose of the REST-Based Model View Controller pattern is to offload processing tasks from the client to the server.

---

1. http://en.wikipedia.org/wiki/XSS

Applicability

Thinking of a scenario of when to use the REST-Based Model View Controller pattern is not difficult. You need to use it when you want to access content that is not available in the currently referenced web application because of the same origin policy. Therefore, this pattern might seem like a hack used to get around something that gets in your way when developing applications. However, that is an incorrect assumption; the purpose of the REST-Based Model View Controller is to make it possible to combine single or multiple streams and expose them as a single stream that fits into the architecture of the user-defined web application.

You use the REST-Based Model View Controller pattern in the following contexts:

- To access a data stream that cannot be accessed by the client because of same origin policy restrictions.

- Defined in simple terms, as a way to convert the format of one data set into the architecture-defined data set. An example is the integration of a data stream generated by a version of the web application prior to the version being constructed. Using the REST-Based Model View Controller pattern in this fashion makes it possible to run multiple versions of the same web application concurrently without conflicts.

- As a way to integrate dissimilar technologies. For example, Google exposes its search engine by using the web service technology Simple Object Access Protocol (SOAP). SOAP can be used with HTTP, but a web browser does not understand SOAP, and hence the REST-Based Model View Controller pattern is used to convert a SOAP request into an Ajax HTTP request.

Associated Patterns

The REST-Based Model View Controller pattern is similar to an *n*-tier architecture and a Model View Controller (MVC) architecture. The pattern is similar to an MVC in that the *model* is considered other servers (for example, web sources, data sources), the *controller* is the controller that is managing the content from the other servers, and the *view* is the REST client reading the data. The REST client can be a browser, XMLHttpRequest object, or even a command-line utility. The pattern does deviate from the classical MVC with respect to being event driven. Unlike the classical MVC, this pattern does not implement an event model.

The REST-Based Model View Controller pattern can be used in two forms: synchronous and asynchronous. In *synchronous* form, a request is made and the client waits for the external network calls to return, aggregates the results, and presents them to the client. In *asynchronous* mode, a request is made and the client does not wait for the results. Instead, the results are sent to the client asynchronously.

If the REST-Based Model View Controller pattern is used in a synchronous style, the generated data will resemble the data generated by the Content Chunking pattern. If the REST-Based Model View Controller pattern is used in an asynchronous style, the generated data will resemble the data generated by the Infinite Data pattern. In addition, when using the asynchronous style, the client implements the Persistent Communications pattern.

Regardless of whether synchronous or asynchronous style is used, the Permutations pattern will need to be applied. The idea is to convert the data from one format into another format desired by the client, which is the aim of the Permutations pattern. The data that is generated is not stable and will constantly change because it is based on information from the external network, and hence the Cache Controller pattern cannot be applied. One exception exists—if the external request generates information that the Cache Controller pattern can use. However, don't count on it, and expect for the most part to not be able to use the Cache Controller pattern.

Architecture

The REST-Based Model View Controller pattern implements several patterns and the Model View Controller architecture. In its simplest form, the pattern is a wrapper to access external content. In its most complex form, it is an application in its own right.

The Big Picture

Dissect the Model View Controller aspect of the pattern and you'll see that the *model* is the external content generated by the various HTTP servers. The *controller* performs operations on the model and generates a view, but only the view required by the client. The *view* is an implementation of the Permutations pattern and defines a resource and representation. Figure 11-2 illustrates an example architecture that implements the REST-Based Model View Controller pattern.

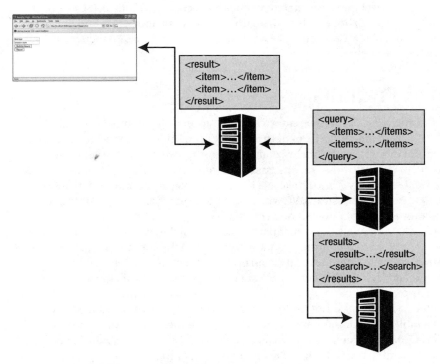

Figure 11-2. *Architectural implementation of REST-based Model View Controller pattern*

In Figure 11-2, the web browser (which will be called the *view* throughout this chapter) makes a request to the local server (called the *controller* throughout this chapter). The controller makes a request to the external servers (called the *model* throughout this chapter) by using a local client. The controller might make a single local client call or multiple local client calls, and it depends entirely on the application. The local client is responsible for receiving the results and converting the received results into a structure that the controller expects. The controller gathers the results, performs some business operations, converts them into a view the client expects, and then finally sends the view to the client.

The outcome of this quick overview of the architecture is that the client can call the controller and expect a specific view. The local clients adapt the remote results into local results, creating stability and robustness of the data. The controller can perform optimizations, and if necessary could integrate other sources to enhance the results. The controller could implement the Permutations pattern and the Persistent Communications pattern. The idea is that the controller can act as an aggregator that slices and dices the information retrieved. Architecturally, the various terms are assembled as in Figure 11-3.

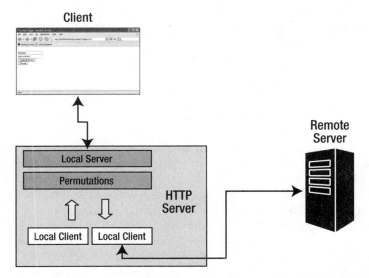

Figure 11-3. *Terms assembled into an architecture for REST-Based Model View Controller pattern*

In Figure 11-3, the client calls the local server, or controller, which calls the Permutations layer, which calls the local client, which calls the remote server. The controller can embed business logic, and more importantly can act as a locally installed application. Think of it this way. A traditional client is installed on the local computer. Thus far, all Ajax applications have been thought of as executing on two separate computers. However, with the REST-Based Model View Controller, the notion of a traditional application can be implemented in that the HTTP server executing the controller is on the same computer as the web browser. The effect is a server application that communicates with other server applications, building a matrix of applications that can seamlessly interact and interchange data. Right now, to have a traditional application communicate with another traditional application is not easy and requires extra steps such as

Copy and Paste. However, with the REST-Based Model View Controller, a document processor could read an e-mail and directly process the data into a document, and vice versa.

The concept of location when used with the REST-Based Model View Controller becomes irrelevant because users can access their data from home, from the office, or from anywhere else. Location is irrelevant because it is replaced with a resource. Of course, you might say, "But if the resource is located at the URL `http://myserver.mydomain.com/resource`, the resource is locked to the server `myserver.mydomain.com`." What you would be missing is that `myserver.mydomain.com` is a server name, and a resource that is translated by a Domain Name System (DNS)[2] into an IP address. It can be pointed out that a DNS server does implement a form of the Permutations pattern. By combining a DNS server with the HTTP server-based Permutations pattern implementation, you can make a URL an abstract resource.

Defining an Appropriate Resource

Important to the implementation of the REST-Based Model View Controller pattern is the resource used to access a view of the controller. It is tempting to simplify the pattern and generate a URL that is similar to, if not identical to, the URL used to access a model. The controller would be a mirror of the remote server, thus acting as a way to get around the same origin policy restriction. Illustrating the mirror technically, to call the Alexa search engine, you can make a REST request using the URL `http://awis.amazonaws.com/onca/xml`. The mirrored controller URL would be `http://amazon.mydomain.com/onca/xml` and would be a delegation of functionality from the controller to the model. Implementing a delegation does not implement the pattern and is an implementation of the Proxy pattern.

A Proxy pattern implementation occurs when the interface exposed by the controller is identical to the interface exposed by the remote server. Note that when the word *interface* is mentioned, it is referenced in a code sense, and not in a user interface sense. A Proxy pattern, when implemented properly, is transparent to the client, which would suggest that the client thinks it is connected directly to the remote server.

Implementing the Proxy pattern would result in an architecture identical to Figure 11-4.

Figure 11-4 shows a client making a request to perform a search on the Google and Amazon.com search engines. The client communicates to the local server, which communicates to the remote servers Amazon.com and Google. If the local server acted like a proxy, the URL, request data, and response data would have to be unique for each search engine. The client would have to do the heavy lifting of figuring out what to send and how to process the response. This is wrong because the client should not need to do that. If a client were to do the heavy lifting, the JavaScript script would become large, complicated, and hard to maintain.

The solution is not to let the client do the heavy lifting, but to let the controller and local clients do it. Specifically, the controller has the following responsibilities:

- Defining the views available to the client

- Defining the resources used by the client

- Executing and managing the local clients used to call the remote servers

2. `http://en.wikipedia.org/wiki/DNS`

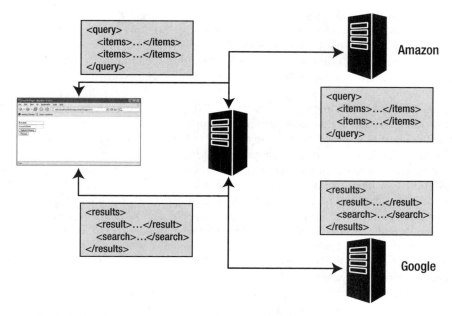

Figure 11-4. *Architecture of a server acting like a proxy*

All is well and good, but the main question still persists: what URL does the client use when wanting to make a query? The answer is that it depends entirely on the nature of the application. The "Associated Patterns" section outlined that the synchronous interface generates data similar to that of the Content Chunking pattern. And the asynchronous interface generates data like that of the Persistent Communications pattern. This means that the URL must resemble what the Content Chunking or Persistent Communications patterns recommend.

For the search example, the proposed URL would be `http://mydomain.com/search`. The choice of the `/search` identifier is arbitrary and is representative of the task being accomplished. Previous patterns such as Content Chunking and others have outlined various ways of defining a URL identifier. The `/search` identifier is used by the controller to execute the local clients for both Amazon.com and Google. If the client wanted to execute a search only on Amazon.com, the Amazon.com-specific search URL would be `http://mydomain.com/search/impl/amazon`. The identifier `impl` indicates implementation, and the identifier `amazon` indicates the Amazon.com search engine.

If `http://mydomain.com/search` searches both Amazon.com and Google, and `http://mydomain.com/search/impl/amazon` searches Amazon.com, how do I even know that `amazon` is a valid identifier to append? If I decided to append `yahoo` and created the URL `http://mydomain.com/search/impl/yahoo`, the question is, would I get an answer? The real simple answer is, if somebody says that Yahoo! exists, the URL exists. What is wrong with this approach is that a user has to rely on human intervention. The available implementations and listing of available implementations is a task that a controller should take care of. That way, if the client were to query the URL `http://mydomain.com/search/impl`, the links `http://mydomain.com/search/impl/amazon` and `http://mydomain.com/search/impl/google` would be returned.

Now that the URL is defined, the next piece of information to define is the query text that is sent to the controller and delegated to the individual local clients. The simple strategy would be to encode the variable and make it part of the URL, like the following: `http://mydomain.com/search?query=Ajax+Applications`. The URL is encoded by using Common Gateway Interface (CGI) encoding. The text after the question mark is the CGI query string, but to avoid confusion, it will be called the *query string*. Contained within the query string are a number of variables and their associated values. For this chapter, let's call the individual variables *URL request variables* for lack of a better term.

The URL request variables are encoded by using the CGI interface. Another approach is to do what many other patterns of this book have been doing and that is to send and receive data using XML. Yet another approach to rewrite the URL would be to reference the URL without a query string, as illustrated by the following: `http://mydomain.com/search/query/Ajax+Applications`. This approach would be better and would be more compliant to what other patterns in this book have discussed and even harped on.

The supposedly correct URL would work, but it is unsettling because the data referenced by the URL is not a constant per se. For example, imagine switching around the query text to `Applications+Ajax`. Would that not result in the same result set? Yet they are two different URLs. What about `Apps+Ajax`? The combinations and permutations are large and would require too many unique URLs. It is not that the supposedly correct URL is unusable in general; it is unusable for the search example. For example, in the case of Map.search.ch, the URL to my previous home was `http://map.search.ch/8143-Stallikon/3-Muelistrasse`. In that case, it was good to convert the query string into a resource because it is a steady resource that is not likely to change too quickly (barring some natural disaster, but then you would have bigger problems than figuring out whether your URL is well designed).

The rule of thumb for knowing when to use a query string and when to use a complete URL depends on the nature of the data referenced by the resource. If the resource represents a mailbox(es), invoice(s), address(es), model part(s), or something that can be described by a noun, it is a completely defined resource. If the represented data is an action on the noun, you should use a query string. This means you could search for addresses or could filter invoices.

The difference between a query string and a complete URL is minimal in some cases, and some individuals prefer a query string to a URL. One big reason to use URLs and not query strings has to do with Internet infrastructure. Consider the URL `http://mydomain.com/8143-Stallikon/3-Muelistrasse` and its equivalent as a query string, `http://mydomain.com/?zip=8143&city=Stallikon&street=3+Muelistrasse`. In the case of the query string, the URL without the query string is `http://mydomain.com`. Because the same URL is called, the Internet infrastructure cannot use HTTP validation because the variation of the URL is the query string. If a large amount of data is downloaded, potentially a resource drain will have been created. The better option would have been to use a unique URL that can be validated or cached.

Having written all that, some servers will cache data based on the query string. However, doing that can be very dangerous from a caching perspective. The reason has to do with the fact that a query string is intended for HTML forms, or is considered a processing directive. If you are unsure and want to be correct, use a unique URL.

Defining the Calling Interface

So now we've defined the resource, or URL, and the query string used by the client to call the controller. What has not been defined are which HTTP verbs are used and how to call those HTTP verbs. In terms of patterns in this book, the HTTP verbs can be called by using either the Content Chunking pattern (synchronous) or the Persistent Communications pattern (asynchronous).

When calling the resource by using the Content Chunking pattern, the web browser uses the XMLHttpRequest object. A sample HTTP communication scenario is illustrated in Figure 11-5.

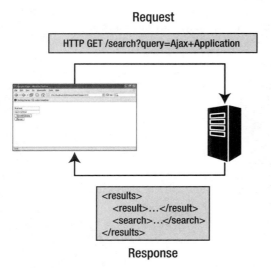

Figure 11-5. *HTTP communication for a synchronous interface*

For a synchronous request, there is a single HTTP GET request. The request is made to the controller, and the client waits for the results. When the server sends the results, they are sent as a single content block, which in the case of Figure 11-5 happens to be XML. The content block sent is the result of applying the Permutations pattern and need not be XML (but could be HTML).

In previous implementations of the Permutations pattern, an HTTP filter was used. The HTTP filter reacts to all HTTP requests and performs filtering operations on the request—but does not process the request. Implementing the REST-Based Model View Controller pattern with the Permutations pattern requires a different approach because for the context the HTTP filter approach is long-winded.

In the previous implementations of the Permutations pattern, the redirection was from an HTTP filter to another processing framework such as an HTTP handler. It was assumed that the Permutations pattern would redirect to another piece of logic. In the case of the REST-based MVC, the handler that manages the global resource URL also manages the redirected URL. For example, if the original URL were http://mydomain.com/search, and a client wanted HTML content, the redirected URL would be http://mydomain.com/search/html. When the same handler manages both URLs, adding an HTTP filter to redirect from one URL to another URL is adding unnecessary work. The reason why the REST-Based Model View Controller pattern manages the redirection, and not the Permutations Pattern–implemented filter, is because the logic of the redirection is specific to the REST-Based Model View Controller. The better approach is to let the HTTP handler manage everything and not use an HTTP filter.

If an HTTP handler implements a synchronous request that is using the Content Chunking pattern, the HTTP verbs GET and POST are used in a certain context. When using the Persistent

Communications pattern to implement the asynchronous request, you might be tempted to use the same HTTP verb implementations. This is not possible because in the context of the Persistent Communications pattern, the HTTP verbs GET and POST fulfill different roles. For the asynchronous request, the HTTP GET retrieves results, and the HTTP POST or PUT sends data to the server. Regardless of whether the HTTP GET or POST/PUT is used, the data sent to start the execution of the local clients is still encoded as a query string. Figure 11-6 illustrates the communications between the server and the client for the asynchronous interface.

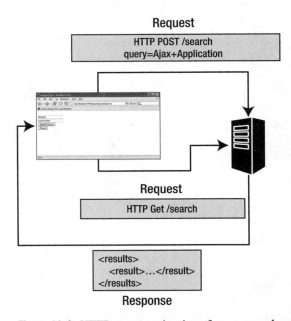

Figure 11-6. *HTTP communications for an asynchronous interface*

As per the Persistent Communications pattern, there are two communication streams. Data is sent by using an HTTP POST/PUT, and results are retrieved by using HTTP GET. Figure 11-6 doesn't show how the HTTP GET knows which search to retrieve the results for. The solution is to use a unique identifier that is associated with a user's cookie or, if possible, a user's authentication information. The solution was illustrated in the Infinite Data pattern. For the synchronous request, the Permutations pattern can be implemented.

Because the synchronous and asynchronous requests use the HTTP verbs differently, this raises the question of whether both request interfaces can share a common URL. As you can see in Figures 11-5 and 11-6, the HTTP GET operations have different functionalities and thus are in conflict with each other. The simplest solution is to reference the two HTTP GET verb implementations by using two separate URLs. However, you could use a common URL. The server, as will be illustrated, can distinguish between synchronous and asynchronous requests. However, what does not change is that the client must implement either the Permutations pattern for asynchronous queries, or Content Chunking for synchronous queries.

A synchronous client makes a request and waits for the answer. An asynchronous client is capable of making multiple requests and processing multiple responses. The asynchronous client needs to track the requests and cross-reference the query identifier with a posted query. In essence, what differentiates a synchronous request from an asynchronous request is the use of a query identifier. Combining the asynchronous and synchronous interface would result in the HTTP request definitions illustrated in Figure 11-7.

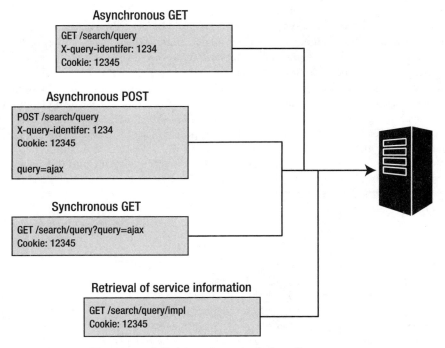

Figure 11-7. *HTTP request definitions for a single interface*

In Figure 11-7, the same URL (/search/query) is used for three requests. Two are for the asynchronous interface, and one for the synchronous interface. What distinguishes the asynchronous and synchronous HTTP GET is the use of the HTTP header X-query-identifier, which is the query identifier. Another difference is that the asynchronous HTTP GET does not use a query string. The X-query-identifier identifier could have been made part of the HTTP query string, and in fact that is something that an implementation would decide. If the X-query-identifier were made part of the query string, a plain-vanilla web browser using refresh tags could download and display asynchronous query results. No matter where the X-query-identifier identifier is defined, it is what makes the difference between a synchronous and asynchronous request.

Defining the Data Format Foundation and the Extras

The last piece of our architecture is to define the format of the data sent between the client and controller that are using either the synchronous or asynchronous interface. To keep everything simple, the two interfaces will send and receive the same data formats. Doing otherwise would unnecessarily complicate the application.

The data that is sent and received must be identical when the same representation is sent, regardless of the interface type. If a synchronous interface generates a result for the type text/ xml, then if another identical request is made to an asynchronous interface and the text/xml type is returned, the generated results must be identical. The commonality factor is important so that when different client types are used, they will get the same data regardless of how the interface is called.

The data that is sent between the server and the client could be described as the lowest common denominator, but that is not entirely correct. The format of the data is best described as the least amount of data uniquely required to describe a request and result. In contrast, the lowest common denominator means to look at the results of all local clients, and from that, figure out a common format. The real problem when defining a format is to determine the data that the client needs, and then have all of the local clients generate the necessary data. Applying this thinking to the context of a search, the necessary data for a request includes sending the search engine query string, and the necessary data for a response includes receiving the title, the URL of the found link, and a short description. Both Amazon.com and Google fulfill the requirements for the necessary data; even though both generate extra data, it is not needed.

The necessary data for the request has already been outlined in the form of a query string. What has not yet been defined is the data format necessary for the response. The following is an example:

```
<results>
    <result>
        <URL>http://forum.goteamspeak.com/showthread.php?t=6885</URL>
        <Title>TeamSpeak - How do I set the Max-Users to
            <b>another</b> <b>value</b> than 16?</Title>
        <Snippet><![CDATA[Go Back, TeamSpeak &gt; General &gt;
            FAQ &middot; Reload this Page How do I set the Max-Users
            <br>  to <b>another</b> <b>value</b> than 16? User Name,
            Remember Me? Password <b>...</b>]]></Snippet>
    </result>
</results>
```

The example XML contains data necessary to define a result. There is the URL, Title, and Snippet (a short description of the URL). Notice in the declaration of the snippet content that a CDATA tag is used. This is important because otherwise the data contained by the Snippet tag might be interpreted as XML content. Worse yet, the snippet might be ill-formed XML or HTML and cause XML parsing errors.

There is not much more to tell about the result. What the client and local client may want to do, though, is add extra information in the result. The extra information may be specific to a particular search engine, but the client knows this and wants it anyway. One approach to adding the extra information is to extend the request and response structures to include the extra information. If the extra data existed for Amazon.com, but not Google, it would mean in the request or response structure there would be a valid value, and a default value in the response structure. Adding the extra information for all instances of the request works, but is a program-matic solution.

There is an XML solution to this dilemma: you can use namespaces to inject information that belongs to the result but is considered separate from the rest of the information. Consider the following XML content that includes generated information from the Google search engine:

```
<results>
    <result>
        <google:cachesize xmlns:google="http://google.search.devspace.com">
           100
        </google:cachesize>
        <URL>http://forum.goteamspeak.com/showthread.php?t=6885</URL>
        <Title>TeamSpeak - How do I set the Max-Users to
            <b>another</b> <b>value</b> than 16?</Title>
       <Snippet><![CDATA[Go Back, TeamSpeak &gt; General &gt;
            FAQ &middot; Reload this Page How do I set the Max-Users
            <br>  to <b>another</b> <b>value</b> than 16? User Name,
            Remember Me? Password <b>...</b>]]></Snippet>
    </result>
</results>
```

Added to the generated XML is the XML element cachesize, which is prefixed with the identifier google. The identifier google and attribute xmlns:google is the notation used to define an XML namespace that relates to google. The addition of a namespace-tagged XML element says that the information is useful for those wanting to parse the information, but it does not belong to the main results. By using XML namespaces, you can add information that will not conflict with the XML elements of the default namespace. This is useful when using tools that automate XML.

Another potential piece of extra data that could be added to the response is the identifier indicating which implementation generated the response. This information could be provided so that the client could drill down to get more data using a particular implementation. The solution for this problem would again use namespaces, as illustrated in the following XML:

```
<results>
    <result>
        <google:cachesize xmlns:google="http://google.search.devspace.com">
           100
        </google:cachesize>
        <implementation:link
            href="/search/impl/google"
            xmlns:implementation="http://search.devspace.com" />
        <URL>http://forum.goteamspeak.com/showthread.php?t=6885</URL>
        <Title>TeamSpeak - How do I set the Max-Users to
            <b>another</b> <b>value</b> than 16?</Title>
       <Snippet><![CDATA[Go Back, TeamSpeak &gt; General &gt;
            FAQ &middot; Reload this Page How do I set the Max-Users
            <br>  to <b>another</b> <b>value</b> than 16? User Name,
            Remember Me? Password <b>...</b>]]></Snippet>
    </result>
</results>
```

The generated XML contains the additional `link` element, which has an attribute `href`. The value of the attribute `href` is a link to the implementation that generated the result. Notice how the `link` element is encapsulated in another namespace. Now, the XML content has two elements that define extra information and do not conflict with the core result. As a sideline issue, SOAP in its latest specification was adamant that namespaces be used exactly for the reasons just described.

This wraps up the architecture and allows you to implement the pattern by using your own technology. In the following section, the search example from this section will be implemented. The example will use Java servlets.

Implementation

Implementing the search engine example will be unique because this is the only pattern for which no client code will be illustrated. The code on the client could be whatever, or wherever, and from the perspective of the server it does not matter. The soul of the REST-Based Model View Controller pattern is the server side only—specifically, the controller, local client, and remote server are of interest. The implementation will explain the remote servers first, then the local clients, then the controller; finally, everything will be put together into a solution. When reading the code for the implementation, it is important to realize that the implementation is only a prototype. Your implementation may have the same structure, but probably will have entirely different pieces.

Implementing a Search

Implementing the local clients means implementing a search client, which is called by both the synchronous and asynchronous interfaces. The Amazon.com and Google search engines were chosen as examples because each one uses a different web service technology. For the Amazon.com search engine, the local client will use client-side REST technologies. For the Google search engine, the local client will use client-side SOAP technologies. For each of the local client implementations, the implementation must be thread-safe and scalable. Of course, most of the client technologies in .NET and Java are thread-safe and scalable.

Using Amazon.com to Search for Something

To make a REST request, two technologies are needed: an XML processor and an HTTP client library. In the explanation of the Infinite Data pattern, I illustrated the concept of using XML schema to generate stubs that are used to read and write XML. The same XML strategy is used here, and the details are beyond the scope of this chapter. If you want to see the details, please refer to the "Being Aware of Multiple Types" section in the chapter about the Infinite Data pattern, which explains how to read and write XML.

The Details of the REST Request

Executing a query by using the Amazon.com REST interface is identical to calling another Ajax-type web service. The Amazon.com REST request is an HTTP request that is illustrated as follows and is executed on the server `awis.amazonawis.com`:

```
GET /onca/xml?Service=AlexaWebInfoService&
    Operation=WebSearch&
    AWSAccessKeyId=[REPLACED]&
    Signature=FQTh4DvvIwVB1QrVcUrgSqFXgNo%3D&
    Timestamp=2005-10-31T19%3A44%3A24.516Z&
    ResponseGroup=Results&
    Query=Applications HTTP/1.1
Content-Type: text/html; charset=UTF-8
User-Agent: Jakarta Commons-HttpClient/3.0-rc3
Host: awis.amazonaws.com:80
```

The indented code in the preceding example is part of a single line but has been separated for better clarity. The text [REPLACED] is pseudo-text for the Amazon.com access key, which you need to perform a search. For a search, there are multiple variables: Service, Operation, AWSAccessKeyId, Signature, Timestamp, ResponseGroup, and Query. The purpose of the variables is beyond the scope of this chapter and is best explained by the Amazon.com documentation. What this does is highlight that to perform a search by using the Amazon.com search engine, there are a number of variables to define that are not available in the necessary data passed to the local client from the client. When the client calls either the synchronous or asynchronous interface, the only information passed is the query string, which relates to the Amazon.com variable Query. The remaining variables are constants and need to be configuration items, or dynamically generated, or require the client to provide the variables.

When using the Amazon.com search engine, the client does not have to provide the additional information because the variables are constants that can be defined elsewhere. However, not all applications are that straightforward, and the complication can be illustrated using the Amazon.com access key identifier. The purpose of the access key identifier (AWSAccessKeyId) is to identify which registered developer is making the request. Most web service providers such as Amazon.com have restrictions on the number of times a request can be made per day, week, or month. In the case of the current local client implementation, each and every request will use the same Amazon.com access key. This might be unacceptable because the owner of the controller and the local clients might have too many requests and have to pay for those extra requests. An option is to require each user to have their own access key that must be passed to the local client. The necessary data would have to be expanded to include the access key identifier, and the URL would then need to be updated to the following:

```
http://mydomain.com/search?query=Applications&Amazon=[REPLACED]
```

The extra variable is Amazon, and the access identifier is associated with that variable. How the client gets this value from the user of the HTML page depends on how the HTML page is implemented. Suppose a client does not have an Amazon.com access key. Then there would be no Amazon variable. In that case, the server would not be able to execute a query and therefore would ignore the Amazon.com search request.

If the client does have an Amazon.com access identifier, it could be made persistent on the client side by using client-side cookies. Or the controller could implement client authorization and store the Amazon.com access identifier when the client authenticates himself. Either way, the Amazon.com access identifier has to come from somewhere, and when planning local clients, the problem of defining and adding extra necessary information will occur.

Using an HTTP Client Library to Execute a Query

An HTTP request is not complicated to create, but there are some things that need to be accounted for. For example, when making a request by using the query Newest Applications, the query has to be URL-encoded to Newest+Applications. If you do not URL-encode the query string, problems will occur because the server will most likely be unable to process the request. Therefore, when making HTTP requests, use a client library that manages URL encodings, HTTP cookies, and anything associated with the technical details of using the HTTP protocol.

The examples in this book use Java and the library HttpClient, which is an Apache Jakarta Commons library (http://jakarta.apache.org). Following is the Java source code used to prepare the request:

```
HttpClient client = new HttpClient();
HttpMethod method = new GetMethod( _endpoint);
String timeStamp = Signature.generateTimestamp();
String signature;
String operation = "WebSearch";
try {
    signature = Signature.generateSignature(operation, timeStamp, _secretAccessKey);
}
catch (SignatureException e)
{ return; }
```

The variable client is the top-level variable used to make an HTTP request. The variable method defines the parameters of the HTTP request. The Amazon.com search request requires an HTTP GET, which is possible by instantiating the GetMethod class. The signature and operation variables contain the values used to define the associated URL variables. The variable _endpoint contains a value from the configuration file that is the HTTP URL used to call the Amazon.com web service. The method Signature.generateSignature converts the configuration-defined Amazon.com secret access key (_secretAccessKey) into a hash-encoded value.

To call the Amazon.com REST web service, the variables are assembled and form an HTTP request:

```
NameValuePair[] items = new NameValuePair[] {
        new NameValuePair( "Service", "AlexaWebInfoService"),
        new NameValuePair( "Operation", operation),
        new NameValuePair( "AWSAccessKeyId", _accessKey),
        new NameValuePair( "Signature", signature),
        new NameValuePair( "Timestamp", timeStamp),
        new NameValuePair( "ResponseGroup", "Results"),
        new NameValuePair( "Query", _request.getQueryString())
};
method.setQueryString( items);
try {
    client.executeMethod(method);
    if( method.getStatusCode() == 200) {
        processResults( _request.getQueryIdentifier(),
            method.getResponseBodyAsStream());
    }
```

```
}
catch (IOException e) {
    System.out.println( "oop error (" + e.getMessage() + ")");
}
```

The type NameValuePair defines an array of key value pairs that are assembled and URL-encoded into a query string. The method setQueryString converts the array into a query string. To execute the HTTP request, the method executeMethod is called. If the return code is 200, the request was successful. Because the HTTP request was successful does not mean that the response will contain any data. To know if there are any results, a parser will need to inspect the response. The undefined method processResults converts the response from an XML stream into a result that is added to the controller (further details of this method are beyond the scope of this chapter). The method getQueryIdentifier is used to identify which query identifier the result is associated with. The query identifier is part of the Persistent Communications pattern and is used to identify which query a result belongs to.

Using Google to Search for Something

Google allows outside developers to access their search engine technologies by using the SOAP web service API. In the example, the Java-based Axis 1.*x* engine was used to convert a Web Services Description Language (WSDL) file into a client stub. The client stub performs an automatic serialization of the XML data. In essence, a WSDL file does the same thing as an XML schema file used to generate a serialization stub. The serialization stub contains a number of types that are used to serialize and deserialize XML. For reference purposes, a WSDL file does contain an XML schema file.

The following source code illustrates how to call the Google search engine web service:

```
String queryIdentifier = _parent.getQueryIdentifier();
GoogleSearch searchRequest = new GoogleSearch();
if( _endPoint.length() > 0) {
    searchRequest.setSoapServiceURL( _endPoint);
}
searchRequest.setKey( _key);
searchRequest.setQueryString( _request.getQueryString());
try {
    GoogleSearchResult searchResult = searchRequest.doSearch();
    if( searchResult != null) {
        GoogleSearchResultElement[] results =
            searchResult.getResultElements();
        for( int c1 = 0; c1 < results.length; c1 ++) {
            _parent.addResult( new SearchResult(
                                results[ c1].getURL(),
                                results[ c1].getTitle(),
                                results[ c1].getSnippet(),
                                transactionIdentifier));
        }
    }
}
catch (GoogleSearchFault e)
{ return; }
```

The Google search implementation is simpler than Amazon.com's because it uses the generated client stub. All of the classes that are prefixed with the Google identifier are the generated classes. The variables _endpoint and _key are values from a configuration file. The variable _endpoint is used to define the server called to execute a search. The variable _key is the Google access identifier that serves the exact same purpose of identification as the Amazon.com access identifier key. The variable queryIdentifier is the client-provided query identifier if an asynchronous request is made. If a synchronous request is made, the query identifier length is zero. In the implementation, though, the method addResult is always called with a query identifier. This is okay, because the servlet or handler that converts the results into XML (or HTML, or other content returned to the client) will know whether or not to process the query identifier.

When the executed search responds, the found entries are added to a result set by converting the results to the type SearchResult. The found types are not converted into XML because that would couple the results to a specific data format. This would be problematic for the Permutations pattern, which generates the format that the client wants to see and thus prefers to manipulate objects and not have to parse an XML file again.

Creating a Search Engine Client Infrastructure

I have very quickly described the implementations that execute a search on Amazon.com and Google. My objective is not to explain how the Amazon.com and Google search engine APIs function. My objective is to illustrate the following requirements used to finish implementing a controller:

- The request information provided by the client will in most cases not be enough to perform a request to the remote servers. A client can provide the extra information, but that should be avoided whenever possible because a dependency to a specific implementation is created.

- Extra request information would be stored as configuration items that are loaded by the controller and passed to the local client. Hard-coding any of the parameters is not advised.

- The local clients should not couple themselves to specific data formats or types. This means the local clients should not assume XML, and should not assume being called from a specific controller technology such as a Java servlet or ASP.NET handler.

These requirements dictate that the controller implementation should be kept as general as possible. Individual model details are managed by the local clients that convert the specifics into a general model used by the controller. However, the reality is that there are specifics. For example, the Amazon access identifier requires extra information stored in a configuration file or sent by the client to the controller that is then sent to the local client. Programmatically, being generic and specific at the same time is impossible or at least it can seem impossible. The solution to this dilemma is to use the Extension pattern.

The purpose of the Extension pattern is to be both a general and a specific solution. The best way to understand this is to consider the following source code:

```
interface General { }

interface Specialization {
    public void Method();
}

class Implementation implements General, Specialization {
    public Implementation( String extraInfo) { }
    public void Method() { }
}

class Factory {
    public static General CreateInstance( String extraInfo) {
        return new Implementation( extraInfo);
    }
}
```

The interface General is a minimal interface, a sort of placeholder. In the example, the General interface has no methods, but there could have been methods. The aim is to keep methods and property declarations to a minimum. The other interface, Specialization, has a single method, but is an interface used to specialize or provide a specific functionality not offered by the General interface.

Where the Extension pattern comes into play is when the class Implementation implements both General and Specialization. A user of Implementation would see the General interface, but could carry out a typecast that converts General into Specialization, as illustrated by the following source code:

```
Specialization specialized = (Specialization)genericInstance;
```

Notice that a typecast was made from one interface to another interface, and not to the implementation type Implementation. This is the essence of the Extension pattern, where interface instances are typecast to the required interface, assuming that the interface instance implements all of the required interfaces. By using the Extension pattern, a framework can deal with objects generically, and then by using typecasting can ask for specialized functionality. You might ask, "Why not just pass around the type Object, because Object is very generic—and after all, you are typecasting, and typecasting an Object is easy." Passing around Object is not suitable because Object is too generic. Even though the Generic interface had no methods, it is still a type that indicates whoever implements Generic does realize that there are other interfaces that could be implemented as well. Using Object says that any object can be stored, even an object that has absolutely nothing to do with the problem being solved.

Although I've said that you do not typecast to Implementation, but to an interface, there are occasions when typecasting to Implementation would be acceptable. For example, sometimes it would be silly to implement an interface for the sake of implementing an interface, because the derived type would be used only in a single solution domain space. What's more, that scenario will be illustrated by the types SearchResult and SearchRequest.

With the advent of Java 1.5 and .NET 2.0, another programming technique called generics is available. Generics, in conjunction with constraints, could very well be used to implement the Extension pattern, but it is beyond the scope of this chapter. Those interested in further details should seek a book on that topic. For the .NET developers, I recommend my book, *Foundations of Object-Oriented Programming Using .NET 2.0 Patterns* (Apress, 2005) as it goes into detail regarding the use of .NET generics.

Defining the Abstracted REST-Based Model View Controller Pattern

Finishing the controller implementation means applying the Extension pattern for two levels of abstraction. The first level is the general case of implementing the REST-Based Model View Controller pattern. The second level is the case of implementing a search engine based on the REST-Based Model View Controller pattern. This section focuses on the first level of abstraction.

The controller manages the local clients. In the context of the REST-Based Model View Controller pattern, the controller fulfills the abstract role of executing the local clients, managing the local clients, managing the request, and managing the results that will be returned to the client. The controller exposes itself to the local client by using an interface called Parent that is defined as follows:

```
public interface Parent {
    public void addResult( Result result);
    public Request getRequest();
    public void addCommand( Command cmd);
    public Iterator getCommands();
    public void processRequest( Request request);
    public void processRequest( String type, Request request);
    public String getTransactionIdentifier();
}
```

The methods of Parent use general types such as Result, Command, and Request. Result defines a result generated by a local client. Request defines the HTTP request parameters such as the query string. And the local clients implement Command. There are two variations of the method processRequest. The processRequest with a single parameter will execute a search on all local clients. The processRequest with two parameters has as a first parameter the identifier of the local client that will process the request and generate the results (for example, amazon).

The Request and Result interfaces are defined as follows:

```
public interface Result {
}
public interface Request {
}
```

The interfaces have no method implementations and therefore represent pure general types, as illustrated by the Extension pattern example. The local clients implement the Command interface, which is defined as follows:

```
public interface Command {
    public void setRequest( Request request);
    public void assignParent( Parent parent);
    public String getIdentifier();
}
```

The method `assignParent` is used to assign the parent controller with the local client. The association is needed when the local client generates a result and wants to pass the result to the controller, which then passes it to the client. The method `getIdentifier` is used by the implementation of the method `Parent.processRequest( String type, Request request)` to identify which `Command` instance is executed.

Implementing the Search Abstractions

The search engine local clients (Amazon.com and Google) implement two interfaces: `Command` and `Runnable`. The search engine local clients are managed by `Parent` using the `Command` interface, but `Parent` executes the local client by using the `Runnable` interface. The reason is that the controller executes each local client on its own thread. The reason for an individual thread will be discussed shortly. An example implementation of the Amazon.com search engine local client would be as follows (note that some details have been removed for clarity):

```
public class AmazonSearchCommand implements Command, Runnable {
    private String _endpoint;
    private String _accessKey;
    private String _secretAccessKey;
    private Parent _parent;

    public void assignParent( Parent parent) {
        _parent = parent;
    }
    public AmazonSearchCommand( String endpoint,
        String accessKey, String secretAccessKey) {
        _endpoint = endpoint;
        _accessKey = accessKey;
        _secretAccessKey = secretAccessKey;
    }
    public String getIdentifier() {
        return "amazon";
    }
}
```

The `run` method implementation has been removed and was already shown in the section "Using Amazon.com to Search for Something." What has been kept are the details relating to the instantiating and configuring of the Amazon.com local client. The method `getIdentifier` is a hard-coded string that returns the identifier `amazon`. Normally, hard-coded strings are a bad idea, but because the Amazon.com local client is being referenced, the identifier is not going to change. Let's put it this way: you are not going to reference the Amazon.com local client as Google or Barnes & Noble. The identifier `amazon` is identical to the URL `/search/impl/amazon`. The same value is not a coincidence because when the `/search/impl` is retrieved, the generated links are generated by the controller that iterates the local clients, which in turn are queried by using the method `getIdentifier`.

In the section "Using Amazon.com to Search for Something," there were references to configuration items such as the access key. The configuration items are passed to the client using the constructor. The constructor was chosen so that under no circumstances can the

Amazon.com local client be instantiated without having a valid configuration. The use of passing configuration items by using the constructor would apply to the Google search engine client and any other local client.

To wire the local clients to the controller, another method that implements the Builder pattern is used. An example of implementing the Builder pattern for the local clients is as follows:

```
public class SearchBuilder {
    private static String _amazonEndPoint;
    private static String _googleEndPoint;
    private static String _amazonAccessKey;
    private static String _amazonSecretKey;
    private static String _googleAccessKey;
    private static boolean _didAssign = false;

    public static void assignConfiguration( String amazon,
        String amazonAccessKey, String amazonSecretKey,
        String google, String googleAccessKey) {
        _amazonEndPoint = amazon;
        _amazonAccessKey = amazonAccessKey;
        _amazonSecretKey = amazonSecretKey;
        _googleEndPoint = google;
        _googleAccessKey = googleAccessKey;
        if( _amazonEndPoint == null || _amazonEndPoint.length() == 0 ||
            _googleEndPoint == null || _googleEndPoint.length() == 0 ||
            _amazonAccessKey == null || _amazonAccessKey.length() == 0 ||
            _amazonSecretKey == null || _amazonAccessKey.length() == 0 ||
            _googleAccessKey == null || _googleAccessKey.length() == 0) {
            throw new IllegalStateException( "configuration data invalid");
        }
        _didAssign = true;
    }
    public static void buildCommands( Parent parent) {
        if( ! _didAssign) {
            throw new IllegalStateException( "configuration data not assigned");
        }
        parent.clearAllCommands();
        parent.addCommand( new AmazonSearchCommand(
                            _amazonEndPoint, _amazonAccessKey, _amazonSecretKey));
        parent.addCommand( new GoogleSearchCommand(
                            _googleEndPoint, _googleAccessKey));
    }
}
```

The class SearchBuilder has two static methods: assignConfiguration and buildCommands. The method assignConfiguration assigns the default configuration to the Amazon.com or Google local clients when the local clients are instantiated. In the example, the configuration values are referenced as simple strings, but those strings could have been converted into types, and the method assignConfiguration could have referenced those types. Converting the strings would probably have been a good idea because five parameters can become a bit tedious to maintain. Shown only with a basic amount of code is the validation of the data in the assignConfiguration method. Validating the data is good practice so that whenever local clients are instantiated, they are instantiated with valid values.

The other method, buildCommands, adds local client-instantiated objects to the controller that can be executed whenever a request for execution happens. In the implementation of buildCommands, the method clearAllCommands removes all of the past instantiated Command instances. The old local client instances are cleared so that multiple threads do not use the same local client instances. The method addCommand is called to add the Amazon.com local client and Google local client instances to the controller. When the method buildCommands returns, the Parent interface instance contains a collection of Command implementations that can be called to perform some action and generate results.

One last detail is to explain the implementations of the Result and Request interfaces, which are illustrated as follows:

```
public class SearchRequest implements Request {
    private String _query;

    public SearchRequest( String query) {
        _query = query;
    }
    public String getQueryString() {
        return _query;
    }
}
public class SearchResult implements Result {
    String _url;
    String _title;
    String _snippet;
    String _transactionIdentifier;

    public SearchResult( String url, String title, String snippet, String transId) {
        _url = url;
        _title = title;
        _snippet = snippet;
        _transactionIdentifier = transId;
    }
    public String getTransactionIdentifier() {
        return _transactionIdentifier;
    }
    public String getURL() {
        return _url;
    }
    public String getTitle() {
        return _title;
    }
    public String getSnippet() {
        return _snippet;
    }
}
```

While I was explaining the Extension pattern, I recommended that you use interfaces to perform typecasts, but in this case there are only the base Request and Result interfaces. There are no SearchResult and SearchRequest interfaces because the classes SearchResult and SearchRequest are specific to the domain of searching. The likelihood that the classes SearchResult and SearchRequest would be used in a different context is fairly unlikely. Though we still want to implement the Extension pattern, we don't need to use an interface, but can use an interface and a class declaration.

The other item to note is that both SearchResult and SearchRequest are immutable types. An *immutable type* is a type that once assigned cannot be modified. In the case of SearchResult and SearchRequest, the data members are assigned in the constructor. The only methods exposed allow the retrieval of the data members, but not modification or assignment.

Putting All of the Pieces Together

The final step after defining the architecture and implementing the individual pieces is to put everything together into a working solution that can be called a REST-Based Model View Controller pattern. From an architectural perspective, a Java servlet or ASP.NET handler will interact with a Parent implementation. The Parent implementation is what pulls everything together and defines the model, view, and controller. Putting it all together, the architecture would appear similar to Figure 11-8.

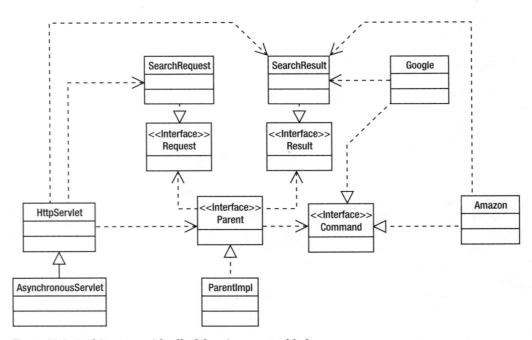

Figure 11-8. *Architecture with all of the pieces assembled*

The UML diagram in Figure 11-8 looks complicated, but it can be separated into two blocks of functionality. There is an inner circle of interfaces and an outer circle of implementations. The inner circle has the types Request, Result, Parent, and Command. The outer circle has the types Amazon, Google, SearchResult, SearchRequest, ParentImpl, HttpServlet, and AsynchronousServlet.

Parent is the core of the entire system and is the bridge that binds all the pieces together. However, to keep it simple for Parent, Parent knows about only the inner circle of types. In the diagram, Google, Amazon, and HttpServlet know about the outer circle of types (SearchRequest, SearchResult) that are passed across the bridge.

Implementing a Parent

Implementing the Parent interface is a two-step process because the Parent interface plays the central role of processing the data. Let's consider the context. The Parent interface instance is responsible for executing the Command implementations, gathering the results, and making the request information available. Through all of these responsibilities, the Parent interface cannot use specific types but must use the general defined types. Additionally, the Parent interface implementation has to function whether the request is asynchronous or synchronous.

The first step when implementing Parent is to define a base class that provides a certain amount of common functionality. The second step is then to create either an asynchronous or synchronous implementation. You need to separate an asynchronous implementation from a synchronous one because of how the results and threads are managed.

Implementing the Base Class

Before the synchronous and asynchronous Parent implementations are outlined, the first step is to outline the base type. The class ParentBase implements Parent, and a subset of the implemented functionality is outlined as follows (the remaining pieces will be explained in a moment):

```
public abstract class ParentBase implements Parent {
    private List _commands = new LinkedList();

    public void addCommand( Command cmd) {
        _commands.add( cmd);
    }
    public Iterator getCommands() {
        return _commands.iterator();
    }
    public void clearAllCommands() {
        _commands.clear();
    }
```

The code excerpt shows that the individual local client instances (Command) are managed in a LinkedList. To add a local client, the method addCommand is used. To remove all local client instances, the method clearAllCommands is used. Because we are coding in a managed code environment, removing the Command instances does not equate to deleting them. They will be deleted when there are no references to the local client instances. This is important because when the local client instances are cleared, the threads referencing the local client instances will still be executing. It would be very inappropriate to have to wait until all of the old local client instances have finished executing, or to stop the execution in midstream.

The remaining functionality implemented by ParentBase relates to executing the local clients through the Command interface. The execution of the local clients is on a per thread basis. Each local client is allocated a thread so that the individual executions can occur concurrently. Some readers may comment that spinning off an individual thread in a heavily multithreaded environment is inefficient. Granted, the statement is true, but consider the context, where the greater cost is the waiting time of the network communications. Therefore, to be robust, it is best if each local client waits individually and indicates to the controller when they have completed. While an individual thread is waiting, it is not consuming resources, and therefore having multiple waiting threads is not a problem for the server. Following is the implementation of the command execution:

```
protected List _runningThreads = new LinkedList();
public abstract void addResult(Result result);

public void processRequest( Request request) {
    Iterator iter = _commands.iterator();
    _runningThreads.clear();
    while( iter.hasNext()) {
        Command cmd = (Command)iter.next();
        cmd.setRequest( request);
        cmd.assignParent( this);
        Thread thrd = new Thread((Runnable)cmd);
        _runningThreads.add( thrd);
        thrd.start();
    }
}
public void processRequest( String impl, Request request) {
    Iterator iter = _commands.iterator();
    _runningThreads.clear();
    while( iter.hasNext()) {
        Command cmd = (Command)iter.next();
        if( cmd.getIdentifier().compareTo( impl) == 0) {
            cmd.setRequest( request);
            cmd.assignParent( this);
            Thread thrd = new Thread( (Runnable)cmd);
            _runningThreads.add( thrd);
            thrd.start();
            break;
        }
    }
}
```

The data member _runningThreads is a list of threads that are executing. The list is required by the synchronous or asynchronous controller implementations to know when a thread has completed. The method addResult, which is used to add a result to the controller, is defined as abstract because the synchronous or asynchronous implementations define their own way of managing the results. You will see this difference shortly. The processRequest methods are used to execute the Command interface instances. There are two versions of the processRequest method. The version with a single parameter executes all local clients. The version with two parameters executes a specific local client.

Regardless of whether a single local client or all local clients are executed, they are executed on their own threads. This keeps the architecture simple so you don't have to deal with too many architectural variations.

Implementing an Asynchronous Parent Interface Instance

The big challenge with implementing an asynchronous Parent interface instance is managing the results. With the asynchronous Parent instance, multiple threads will be representing multiple local clients, and each local client will be generating results that need to be handed off to the controller. Synchronization is required when multiple Command instances hand off their results to the Parent instance that is running on a different thread to the local clients. Following is the implementation of the asynchronous class, which inherits from the previously defined ParentBase class:

```
public class AsynchronousParent extends ParentBase {
    private LinkedList _results = new LinkedList();

    public void addResult(Result result) {
        synchronized( _results) {
            _results.addLast( result);
            _results.notify();
        }
    }
    public Object getResult() {
        synchronized( _results) {
            if( _results.size() > 0) {
                return _results.removeFirst();
            }
            else {
                try {
                    _results.wait(15000);
                }
                catch (InterruptedException e) {
                    return null;
                }
                if( _results.size() > 0) {
                    return _results.removeFirst();
                }
                else {
                    return null;
                }
            }
        }
    }
    public AsynchronousParent() { }
}
```

The data member _results represents the list used to manage the results handed to the controller from the executing local clients. The method addResult is used to add a result to the list, and getResult is used to retrieve a result. Both the adding and removing from the list is embedded in a synchronized keyword, where the synchronization object is the list itself. Using the synchronized function in this way ensures that only one thread is adding or removing a result from the list.

An additional item to note is that the wait function with the value 15000 is used. Using the wait function is like using a Monitor in .NET. The wait function will wait to get pulsed, with the maximum wait being 15 seconds. A pulse is sent in the function addResult by using the notify method. The idea is that if there are no results to retrieve, the thread should wait a maximum of 15 seconds to retrieve a result. The strategy of waiting is part of the Persistent Communications pattern, in which the server will wait for a result to become available.

Implementing a Synchronous Parent

Implementing a synchronous Parent interface instance subclasses ParentBase and uses synchronization techniques, but in a different manner from the asynchronous Parent interface instance. The Parent interface instance instantiates the local clients and waits for all the Command interface instances to finish execution. During the execution, the Parent interface instance waits and does not accept further requests. In the synchronous implementation, the place where synchronization is needed is when the individual Command interface instances hand off results to the waiting Command interface instance. When the Command interface instance processes the results, all the Command interface instances have finished executing, and thus there is no concurrency. Following is the synchronous implementation:

```
public class SynchronousParent extends ParentBase {
    private List _results = new LinkedList();

    public synchronized void addResult(Result result) {
        _results.add( result);
    }
    public Iterator getResultsIterator() {
        return _results.iterator();
    }
    public SynchronousParent() {
    }
    public void processRequest(Request request) {
        super.processRequest( request);
        Iterator iter = _runningThreads.iterator();
        while( iter.hasNext()) {
            Thread thrd = (Thread)iter.next();
            try {
                thrd.join();
            }
            catch (InterruptedException e) {}
        }
    }
}
```

The SynchronousParent class has only one data member, _results, which is used to store the results generated by the Command interface instances. The method addResult is synchronized, allowing only a single thread to access the method and allowing only a single thread to add a result to the results list.

Look at the implementation of the method processRequest. The first call is to call the method super.processRequest, which translates to calling the ParentBase.processRequest method. The base class method implementation will start all the threads. Then, when the base class returns, SynchronousParent retrieves the Iterator instance to the currently executing threads. The method processRequest will use the iterator to iterate each thread ID and call the method thrd.join. Calling thrd.join will call the calling thread to wait until the thread referenced by the variable thrd has finished executing. The idea is to call the join method on each of the executing threads, and if all have been called, then no thread will be executing.

Relating this back to the addResult method, what happens is that a caller of SynchronousParent will expect to execute all the Command interface instances. Let's call that the main thread. SynchronousParent then spawns a number of child threads. The main thread then waits until all child threads have executed. During the execution of the child threads, results will be added by using the method addResult. However, no results will be retrieved because the main thread is waiting for all the child threads to finish. After all the child threads have finished executing, the main thread returns control to the caller of SynchronousParent, who then proceeds to iterate the results. When the results are iterated, there will be only one thread accessing the data.

This finishes the basic architecture of the REST-Based Model View Controller pattern. The last remaining piece is to implement the Java servlet. The implementation of the Java servlet will be broken into two pieces; one is used to handle asynchronous requests, and the other to handle synchronous requests. The implementation is broken into two pieces because of the complexity associated with the implementation. Remember from the architecture that the REST-Based Model View Controller pattern needs to implement the Permutations pattern. Combining the Permutations pattern with the asynchronous and synchronous implementations would be too much complexity in one explanation.

Handling an Asynchronous Search

The asynchronous Java servlet search will be discussed first because it will not implement the Permutations pattern. The focus of the asynchronous Java servlet is to configure the REST-Based Model View Controller pattern implementation, illustrate how to make a call, and then process the results.

Posting a Query

Consider the following source code that defines the Java Servlet class AsynchronousServlet and configures the SearchBuilder class:

```
public class AsynchronousServlet extends HttpServlet {
    public void init(javax.servlet.ServletConfig config)
        throws javax.servlet.ServletException {
        SearchBuilder.assignConfiguration(
            config.getInitParameter( "amazon-endpoint"),
            config.getInitParameter( "amazon-access-key"),
            config.getInitParameter( "amazon-secret-key"),
            config.getInitParameter( "google-endpoint"),
            config.getInitParameter( "google-access-key"));
    }
```

The configuration of the SearchBuilder class is relatively simple. The init method is overridden, and the configuration values are retrieved from the configuration file associated with the web application.

In the "Architecture" section of this chapter, the asynchronous interface implements the Persistent Communications pattern, and implements the HTTP GET and HTTP POST, which in Java Servletspeak means to implement the doPost and doGet methods. Following is the implementation of the doPost method:

```
protected void doPost(HttpServletRequest request,
    HttpServletResponse response)
    throws javax.servlet.ServletException, java.io.IOException {
    HttpSession session = request.getSession( true);
    AsynchronousParent parent = null;
    if( session.isNew()) {
        parent = new AsynchronousParent();
        session.setAttribute( "parent", parent);
    }
    else {
        parent = (AsynchronousParent)session.getAttribute( "parent");
    }
    String value = request.getParameter( "query");
    String queryIdentifier = request.getHeader( "X-query-identifier");
    if( value != null && value.length() > 0) {
        synchronized( parent) {
            SearchBuilder.buildCommands( parent);
            parent.processRequest( new SearchRequest(queryIdentifier, value));
        }
        response.setContentType( "text/xml");
        PrintWriter out = response.getWriter();
        out.println( "<result>success</result>");
    }
}
```

At the beginning of doPost, the session is retrieved by using the method getSession and is assigned to the variable session. The session is associated with an HTTP cookie. Using Java servlets, it is possible to query whether a new session has been created by using the method isNew. If isNew returns true, an instance of AsynchronousParent (which is the asynchronous controller) is instantiated and assigned to the session by using the method setAttribute. If isNew does not indicate a new session, the already-existing AsynchronousParent instance is returned by using the method getAttribute.

From that point on, there is a valid AsynchronousParent instance that is responsible for instantiating the Command interface instances and collecting the results. To execute a search, the value for the query string variable query is retrieved by using the method getParameter. The method getParameter can be called even though an HTTP POST is made. The query identifier that is stored as an HTTP header is retrieved by using the method getHeader and is assigned to queryIdentifier.

If the query value is not null and has some value, a synchronized block is entered. The synchronized block is important because no two requests should be executing queries at the same time. Think of it this way: a client creates an application in which a user could very quickly generate search requests. Those two very quickly executed requests could run concurrently but should not.

Do not make the mistaken assumption that the synchronized block cannot run multiple queries at the same time. It can have multiple queries going at the same time. What is not possible is to *start* multiple queries at the same time. The problem of starting multiple queries at the same time is that the AsynchronousParent is a session variable that could be associated with multiple web browsers. Remember from previous examples, an HTTP cookie is associated with a URL, and if multiple windows of a web browser reference the same URL, so will the same HTTP cookie.

Some readers may argue that my code is not efficient enough. True, but my objective was to illustrate that when executing requests asynchronously, there is one AsynchronousParent instance associated with one session, which is one cookie that collects all results and multiple queries running at the same time. When running in an asynchronous manner, there are concurrency issues to consider that must not be taken lightly.

Let's get back to the synchronization block. After the method processRequest is called, the generated output is a simple success. Anything more than a successful result is not required as the Persistent Communications pattern expects results when using the HTTP GET.

Before I continue the discussion, a side step is necessary regarding the query identifier. In the Persistent Communications pattern, the query identifier was called a version number. In the Persistent Communications pattern, the version number was used by the server to know when to return data to the client. The query identifier in the example is used to identify the version number of the query.

Retrieving a Result

To retrieve a result, an HTTP GET is executed, and that means the doGet method needs to be implemented. The implementation of doGet will test the AsynchronousParent instance for available results and is implemented as follows:

```
protected void doGet(HttpServletRequest request,
    HttpServletResponse response)
    throws ServletException, IOException {
    HttpSession session = request.getSession( true);
    Object obj = session.getAttribute( "parent");
    if( obj != null) {
        AsynchronousParent parent = (AsynchronousParent)obj;
        SearchResult result = (SearchResult)parent.getResult();
        if( result != null) {
            response.setHeader( "X-transaction-identifier",
                result.getTransactionIdentifier());
            PrintWriter out = response.getWriter();
            out.println( "<results>");
            out.println( "<result>");
```

```
                    out.println( "<URL>" + result.getURL() + "</URL>");
                    out.println( "<Title>" + result.getTitle() + "</Title>");
                    out.println( "<Snippet><![CDATA[" +
                        result.getSnippet() + "]]></Snippet>");
                    out.println( "</result></results>");
            }
        }
        return;
    }
```

In the implementation of doGet, the first step is to retrieve the session by using getSession, which is then used to retrieve the AsynchronousParent instance by using getAttribute. The return value of getAttribute is assigned to an Object type because if the value of obj is null and a typecast is attempted, an exception will arise. If the value of obj is not null, it is possible to perform a typecast to AsynchronousParent. The cast value is assigned to parent, which retrieves a value by using the method getResult. If there is a result, the retrieved value will be non-null, allowing the appropriate XML content to be generated.

Notice how the query identifier is assigned to an HTTP header, which the client will need to process. Based on the query identifier, the client would know whether the result is stale or to which query the result belongs. If the result is valid, it can be manipulated by the client and transformed to HTML or parsed to fill some HTML.

Handling a Synchronous Search

The other way of calling the REST-Based Model View Controller pattern implementation is to use the synchronous interface. A web browser, HTTP client, or even another REST-Based Model View Controller pattern implementation can call the synchronous interface. As the synchronous interface is a standard HTTP GET, the Permutations pattern is applicable.

Implementing the Servlet-Based Permutations Pattern

In the Permutations pattern, the example illustrated how to implement the pattern by using an HTTP filter or module. The Permutations pattern is implemented in the Java servlet or ASP.NET handler to reduce the number of redirections. However, when a Java servlet or ASP.NET handler implements the Permutations pattern, an object redirection (instead of a URL redirection or rewriting) occurs. The object redirection is illustrated in Figure 11-9.

In Figure 11-9, the Handler class receives an HTTP request. In the implementation of the method doGet, the Permutations pattern is implemented. The URL along with the HTTP headers would be read in the doGet method. Like the original Permutations pattern, the acceptable types would be iterated for which a new URL could be rewritten or redirected to. In this implementation of the Permutations pattern, the acceptable types would be iterated and matched to an object instance that could process the acceptable type. The object instances implement the Representation interface. For Handler, there are two appropriate Representations: XML and HTML. The cross-referencing of the acceptable type and object instance is based on the getType method that returns the MIME type that it can process. The idea of the outlined architecture is to mimic a redirection infrastructure of Java Servlet or ASP.NET handlers.

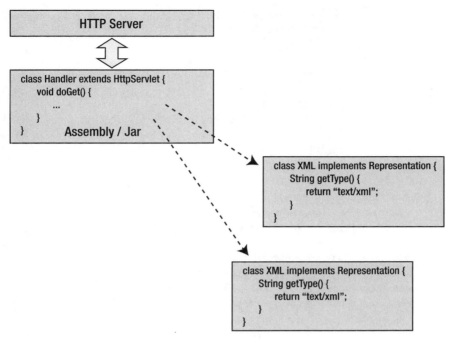

Figure 11-9. *Object redirection architecture*

Implementing the architecture requires a servlet that manages the various representation implementations and reacts appropriately to an HTTP request. Following is the implementation of the class PermutationsServlet, with some parts missing for clarity:

```
public abstract class PermutationsServlet extends HttpServlet {
    List _representations = new LinkedList();

    public PermutationsServlet() {
    }
    protected Representation getRepresentationInternal(
        String mimetype, HttpServletRequest request) {
        Iterator repIter = _representations.iterator();
        while( repIter.hasNext()) {
            Representation representation = (Representation)repIter.next();
            if( representation.canProcess( mimetype, request)) {
                return representation;
            }
        }
        return null;
    }
```

```
    protected Representation getRepresentation(HttpServletRequest request) {
        ArrayList elements = parseHeaders( request.getHeader( "Accept"));
        Iterator iter = elements.iterator();
        while( iter.hasNext()) {
            StringTokenizer tokenizer = new StringTokenizer(
                (String)iter.next(), ";");
            Representation representation =
                getRepresentationInternal( tokenizer.nextToken(), request);
            if( representation != null) {
                return representation;
            }
        }
        return getRepresentationInternal( "*/*", request);
    }
    protected void doGet(HttpServletRequest request,
        HttpServletResponse response)
        throws ServletException, IOException {
        Representation representation = getRepresentation( request);
        if( representation != null) {
            representation.doGet( request, response);
        }
        return;
    }
}
```

The data member _representations represents a list that contains all of the representations. PermutationsServlet implements the method doGet, which will be called whenever an HTTP GET request is received. In the doGet method implementation, getRepresentation is called, and that is the implementation of the Permutations pattern. The method getRepresentation is responsible for cross-referencing the acceptable types sent by the client, with a representation from the list of representations.

In the implementation of getRepresentation, the Accept HTTP header is parsed for the individual MIME types that are acceptable by using the method parseHeaders. For better clarity, the method parseHeaders is not illustrated. To see an actual implementation, please see the Permutations pattern chapter. After the MIME types have been ordered, each value is iterated and attempted to be matched with a representation by using the method getRepresentationInternal. In the implementation of getRepresentationInternal, the method representation.canProcess is called. The canProcess method requires two parameters: the MIME type and HTTP request. It is important to realize that not only the MIME type determines whether a representation can process the request, but also the request parameters. If a match is made, getRepresentation will return immediately and stop iterating. If a match cannot be made, the catch-all MIME type (*/*) is queried for a representation. Getting back to the doGet implementation, if a representation is found, the method representation.doGet is called with the HTTP request and response types.

Processing a Request

The class PermutationsServlet is implemented as an abstract class that requires another class to subclass PermutationsServlet. The goal is to require a class to subclass PermutationsServlet and associate with PermutationsServlet the representations that can process requests. Following is the example implementation for the SynchronousServlet class:

```
public class SynchronousServlet extends PermutationsServlet {
    public void init(javax.servlet.ServletConfig config)
    throws javax.servlet.ServletException {
        SearchBuilder.assignConfiguration(
            config.getInitParameter( "amazon-endpoint"),
            config.getInitParameter( "amazon-access-key"),
            config.getInitParameter( "amazon-secret-key"),
            config.getInitParameter( "google-endpoint"),
            config.getInitParameter( "google-access-key"));
        addRepresentation( new XMLContent());
        addRepresentation( new OtherContent());
    }
}
```

The implementation of the SynchronousServlet class requires the implementation of only the method init. The method init would like AsynchronousServlet to retrieve the configuration information from a web application configuration file. The methods addRepresentation instantiate two types, XMLContent and OtherContent, that are used to generate content as either XML or the default HTML content.

What is interesting is that the implementations of the classes XMLContent and OtherContent are very similar to the AsynchronousServlet implementation. The major difference is that SynchronousParent is used instead of AsynchronousParent.

Because the similarities are so great, an argument could made that the synchronous and asynchronous functionality should have been combined into a single implementation. The fact is that it probably could have been done, but was not done so that I could illustrate the thinking required to implement either a synchronous or asynchronous interface.

Pattern Highlights

In conclusion, the REST-Based Model View Controller pattern is an example pattern for which it is more important to understand the details of the architecture than the example implementation. As much as I would like to say that the example implementation should always be used, it is not possible. The reason why I say that every REST-Based Model View Controller is a custom implementation is due to the nature of remote servers defining the model. Maybe it is necessary to call only a single remote server. Or maybe you first call one remote server and then call another remote server. Those details will change how the local client is implemented, and potentially how the controller interacts with the local client.

The following points are the important highlights of the REST-Based Model View Controller pattern:

- Each and every implementation of the pattern should have a controller, local client, and model. The controller and local client are managed as a package, but are two separate pieces of software. The controller executes the local clients, manages the request information, manages the results, and is responsible for interacting with the client. The local clients manage the models exposed by the remote servers.

- A pattern implementation will expose either an asynchronous or synchronous interface, or potentially both. If a synchronous interface is exposed, it fulfills the Chunked Content pattern. If an asynchronous interface is exposed, it fulfills the Persistent Communications pattern.

- The view interacts with the controller, using well-defined URLs specific to the domain of the problem.

- The data that is exchanged between the client and the server is the least amount required to uniquely describe the information.

Index

forums.apress.com

FOR PROFESSIONALS BY PROFESSIONALS™

JOIN THE APRESS FORUMS AND BE PART OF OUR COMMUNITY. You'll find discussions that cover topics of interest to IT professionals, programmers, and enthusiasts just like you. If you post a query to one of our forums, you can expect that some of the best minds in the business—especially Apress authors, who all write with *The Expert's Voice*™—will chime in to help you. Why not aim to become one of our most valuable participants (MVPs) and win cool stuff? Here's a sampling of what you'll find:

DATABASES
Data drives everything.

Share information, exchange ideas, and discuss any database programming or administration issues.

INTERNET TECHNOLOGIES AND NETWORKING
Try living without plumbing (and eventually IPv6).

Talk about networking topics including protocols, design, administration, wireless, wired, storage, backup, certifications, trends, and new technologies.

JAVA
We've come a long way from the old Oak tree.

Hang out and discuss Java in whatever flavor you choose: J2SE, J2EE, J2ME, Jakarta, and so on.

MAC OS X
All about the Zen of OS X.

OS X is both the present and the future for Mac apps. Make suggestions, offer up ideas, or boast about your new hardware.

OPEN SOURCE
Source code is good; understanding (open) source is better.

Discuss open source technologies and related topics such as PHP, MySQL, Linux, Perl, Apache, Python, and more.

PROGRAMMING/BUSINESS
Unfortunately, it is.

Talk about the Apress line of books that cover software methodology, best practices, and how programmers interact with the "suits."

WEB DEVELOPMENT/DESIGN
Ugly doesn't cut it anymore, and CGI is absurd.

Help is in sight for your site. Find design solutions for your projects and get ideas for building an interactive Web site.

SECURITY
Lots of bad guys out there—the good guys need help.

Discuss computer and network security issues here. Just don't let anyone else know the answers!

TECHNOLOGY IN ACTION
Cool things. Fun things.

It's after hours. It's time to play. Whether you're into LEGO® MINDSTORMS™ or turning an old PC into a DVR, this is where technology turns into fun.

WINDOWS
No defenestration here.

Ask questions about all aspects of Windows programming, get help on Microsoft technologies covered in Apress books, or provide feedback on any Apress Windows book.

HOW TO PARTICIPATE:
Go to the Apress Forums site at **http://forums.apress.com/**.
Click the New User link.

You Need the Companion eBook

Your purchase of this book entitles you to its companion eBook for only $10.

We believe this Apress title will prove so indispensable that you'll want to carry it with you everywhere, which is why we are offering the companion eBook for $10 to customers who purchase this book now. Convenient and fully searchable, the eBook version of any content-rich, page-heavy Apress book makes a valuable addition to your programming library. You can easily find, copy, and apply code—and then perform examples by quickly toggling between instructions and the application. Even simultaneously tackling a donut, diet soda, and complex code becomes simplified with hands-free eBooks!

Once you purchase this book, getting the $10 companion eBook is simple:

❶ Visit **www.apress.com/promo/tendollars/**.

❷ Complete a basic registration form to receive a randomly generated question about this title.

❸ Answer the question correctly in 60 seconds and you will receive a promotional code to redeem for the $10 eBook.

2560 Ninth Street • Suite 219 • Berkeley, CA 94710

Offer valid through 8/13/06.